Tourism in South and Southeast Asia: Issues and Cases

*This book is dedicated to Jody
and to The Wandering Islands*

and to the memory of Martin Oppermann

Tourism in South and Southeast Asia: Issues and Cases

C. Michael Hall and Stephen Page

OXFORD AUCKLAND BOSTON JOHANNESBURG MELBOURNE NEW DELHI

Butterworth-Heinemann
Linacre House, Jordan Hill, Oxford OX2 8DP
225 Wildwood Avenue, Woburn, MA 01801-2041
A division of Reed Educational and Professional Publishing Ltd

 A member of the Reed Elsevier plc group

First published 2000
Reprinted 2000

British Library Cataloguing in Publication Data
Tourism in South and Southeast Asia
  1. Tourist trade – South Asia   2. Tourist trade – Asia,
  Southeastern
  I. Hall, Colin Michael, 1961–   II. Page, Stephen, 1963–
  338.4'791'54

Library of Congress Cataloguing in Publication Data
A catalogue record for this book is available from the Library of Congress

ISBN 0 7506 4128 2

Composition by Scribe Design, Gillingham, Kent
Printed and bound in Great Britain

FOR EVERY VOLUME THAT WE PUBLISH, BUTTERWORTH-HEINEMANN
WILL PAY FOR BTCV TO PLANT AND CARE FOR A TREE.

Contents

Contributors

T.C. Chang – Department of Geography, National University of Singapore, Singapore

Malcolm Cooper – University of Southern Queensland, Harvey Bay, Queensland, Australia

Anne de Bruin – Department of Commerce, Massey University – Albany, Auckland, New Zealand

Ngaire Douglas – Southern Cross University, Lismore, New South Wales, Australia

Norman Douglas – Pacific Profiles, Alstonville, New South Wales, Australia

Ross Dowling – Department of Marketing and Tourism, Edith Cowan University, Joondalup, Western Australia, Australia

C. Michael Hall – Centre for Tourism, University of Otago, Dunedin, New Zealand; New Zealand Natural Heritage Foundation; and School of Food and Leisure Management, Sheffield Hallam University, UK

James Higham – Centre for Tourism, University of Otago, Dunedin, New Zealand

Shankar Koirala – Ministry of Home Affairs, Kathmandu, Nepal

Alan A. Lew – Department of Geography and Public Planning, North Arizona University, Flagstaff, Arizona, USA

Ghazali Musa – Centre for Tourism, University of Otago, Dunedin, New Zealand

V. Nithiyanandam – Department of Commerce, Massey University – Albany, Auckland, New Zealand

Alfred L. Oehlers – Department of Commerce, Massey University – Albany, Auckland, New Zealand

Stephen Page – Centre for Tourism Research, Massey University – Albany, Auckland, New Zealand; and Faculty of Agriculture, Food and Land Use, Seale Hayne Campus, University of Plymouth, UK

Greg Ringer – Centre for Asian Studies, University of Oregon, Eugene, Oregon, USA

David G. Simmons – Department of Human Sciences, Lincoln University, Lincoln, New Zealand

Shalini Singh – Centre for Tourism, Lucknow, India

Tej Vir Singh – Centre for Tourism, Lucknow, India

Russell Arthur Smith – Hospitality and Tourism Management, Nanyang Business School, Nanyang Technological University, Singapore

Trevor H.B. Sofield – Murdoch University, Western Australia, Australia

Peggy Teo – Department of Geography, National University of Singapore, Singapore

Acknowledgements

To attempt to provide an overview of tourism in South and Southeast Asia is an enormous undertaking. Numerous individuals and organizations have greatly assisted with the research undertaken as part of this book. We would like to thank the various national tourism organizations who assisted the editors and the authors in their tasks. We would particularly like to note the generous assistance of the Pakistani agencies which supplied requested information at short notice. We would also like to acknowledge the efforts of the various authors, particularly those who completed chapters and case studies at short notice when other authors either withdrew or failed to deliver.

In undertaking research related to the book Michael would like to thank Fiona Apple, Gavin Bryars, Dick Butler, Dimitrios Buhalis, Sonia Casey, Bruce Cockburn, Angela Elvey, Sandra James, Ed Kuepper, Alan Lew, Richard and Carlene Mitchell, Meiko Muramaya, Vanessa O'Sullivan, Rachel Samways, Brian and Delyse Springett, The Sundays and the staff of the Centre for Tourism, University of Otago and School of Food and Leisure Management, Sheffield Hallam University, UK. Stephen would like to thank Lynne for her unceasing typing and editing as well as the kind assistance from John Monin who supplied photographs of Myanmar. The Massey University Albany staff provided extensive help in locating material. He would also like to thank Jo, Graham and Paul at Seale Hayne, as well as colleagues at Massey University who have assisted in various ways including Mark Orams, Keith Dewar, Rolf Cremer and Jo Cheyne, and Ross Dowling at Edith Cowan University. Finally, we would like to thank our friends and families for their care and support.

We would like to acknowledge permission to use Figures 9.1, 9.2, 9.3 and 9.4, supplied by Charles Higham.

C. Michael Hall
Stephen Page
City Rise
Albany
December 1999

Figures

Tables

Part One

Region and Context

1

Introduction: tourism in South and Southeast Asia – region and context

C. Michael Hall and Stephen Page

Private sector debt is now equivalent to twice the region's annual economic output
(Saludo and Shameen, 1998).

Introduction

The Asian economic crisis of 1997 and 1998 focused the world's attention on the region as never before. Images of dramatic currency and stock market collapse, loss of foreign reserves and political instability have reverberated around the globe, dramatically affecting policy and investment decisions as well as tourist flows.

The changes in the region and their effects on confidence in the global economy reflect the increasing globalization, not only of the economy, but also of communication, information and tourism. In recent years, Asia has become a region of major importance in the world economy and has become increasingly integrated with the economies of Europe and North America. Furthermore, there has been an intensification of intraregional linkages as trade and investment within the region have grown

(Economic and Social Commission for Asia and the Pacific (ESCAP), 1997; Hall, 1997). Nevertheless, with growth came problems. Levels of debt increased dramatically. Loose monetary policy and over-eager borrowers and lenders pouring unprecedented amounts of credit into property, industry and financial assets bankrolled a bubble economy which finally collapsed. When the collapse in property prices in Thailand in 1997 prompted foreign creditors to call in loans to Thai banks and businesses, the resultant need for hard currency and the subsequent devaluation of the baht led to a financial meltdown which reverberated throughout the region, forcing countries such as Indonesia and Thailand to sign up for International Monetary Fund (IMF) loans and programmes (Saludo and Shameen, 1998). Devaluation, debt and the forced deregulation of many parts of national economies have led to the contraction of many economies and the threat of a sustained period of recession marked by greater unemployment, greater political instability, possible food shortages in the case of Indonesia and likely even less attention to the need to prevent environmental degradation.

In this environment tourism – for long one of the mainstays of the region's economy, accounting for 10.3 per cent of Asia's GDP (Bacani, 1998) – has now become an even more important source of economic development and foreign exchange, as well as a mechanism for employment generation. As Hitchcock *et al.* (1993: p. 1) reported

the phenomenal growth in tourism in S. E. Asia, as elsewhere in the developing world, has been associated with a number of factors and processes. One of the more important of these has been an increase in people's ability to afford to travel to the region. This may be attributed to parallel factors: first, rising levels of affluence in the main sources areas, and second, the steadily falling cost, in real terms, of travel to the region.

Until the onset of the Asian financial crisis (World Tourism Organization 1999), the region was also developing as a major source of outbound tourism. Intraregional travel is still significant, though the decline in the region's economies has meant that regionally generated inbound tourism has deflated across the region. Inbound tourism from outside the region has therefore become extremely valuable – and extremely competitive. The decline in the value of the region's currencies in relation to major tourism-generating regions of North America, Europe, and even Australia, Japan and New

Zealand, has meant that, apart from external perceptions of instability in some cases, the region has become an extremely attractive destination in terms of exchange rates.

Table 1.1 illustrates some of the fluctuations in tourism numbers which have occurred in the region in 1997 and the first half of 1998. Within the region only Thailand, which has taken a very aggressive stance in attracting tourists, and China have shown substantive tourist growth. Although, in the case of China it should be noted that growth has occurred because of increased arrivals from Hong Kong, Taiwan and Macau, with arrivals outside these markets actually dropping by 2.2 per cent in the first quarter of 1998.

These dramatic fluctuations, and their wider significance beyond tourism, graphically illustrate the need for a contemporary assessment of tourism in what has been one of the most dynamic regions for the industry over the past two decades. Although, as Qu and Zhang (1997) suggest, it is impossible to take full account of future events as tourism markets within the region are far from mature, unpredictable and, in some cases, unstable (as the discussion of visitor arrivals in different chapters suggest), it is nevertheless vital that students of tourism are aware of the factors and issues which are shaping the region's future, not only in tourism but in its wider political, economic, social and environmental context. This first chapter, and

Table 1.1   *Fluctuations in arrivals for select Asian destinations 1997 and 1998*

Country	1997 arrivals (million)	% change from 1996	1997 tourism earnings (US$billion)	% change from 1996	1998 arrivals (million)	% change from same period in 1997
China	57.6	12.6	12.0	17.6	12.4	(Jan–March) 10.6
Hong Kong	10.4	–11.1	9.3	–14.7	4.5	(Jan–June) –21.0
Thailand	7.3	0.7	7.0	–19.5	3.8	(Jan–June) 4.8
Singapore	7.2	–1.3	6.8	–13.9	3.0	(Jan–June) –13.9
Malaysia	6.2	–13.0	3.7	–16.3	n.a.	n.a.
Indonesia	5.2	3.0	5.3	–15.6	1.5	(Jan–June) –15.6
South Korea	3.9	5.4	5.1	–5.8	2.4	(Jan–July) –5.8
Philippines	2.1	9.5	2.8	4.8	1.1	(Jan–July) –1.9

Note
n.a., not available

Source: various

the following series of overview chapters on tourism in the region, therefore provide the context within which the chapters on national tourism should be seen.

Southeast Asia as a region

For any study of a region such as Southeast Asia, it is important to establish the geographical frame of reference and, in simple terms, what is the regional context. According to Dwyer (1990: p. 1) 'it is something of a paradox that although the concept of South East Asia as a geographical region is relatively recent, in terms of international relationships its significance in the world today is profound'. This somewhat sweeping statement illustrates that Southeast Asia is a region that was created in international and political terms in the post-war period because 'Before world war II South East Asia was scarcely even a geographical expression. For the West, it was little more than an undifferentiated part of Monsoon Asia, the teeming eastern and southern margins of the great Asian continent; for Asians themselves it had no significance at all' (Fryer, 1970: p. 1).

One of the most influential studies of the post-war period was Fisher's (1962) assessment of Southeast Asia as the Balkans of the Orient, in which he depicted the region as an area of transition, geographic variation and potential instability. In the post-war period, Fisher (1962) identified the implications of post-colonial transition, from subjugation under colonial rule to nation status, where many states contained an enormous diversity of population with varied cultures and religions. Fisher highlighted the role of economic development in determining the political future of most states. In his highly influential 831 page seminal study on Southeast Asia, Fisher (1964) depicts the spatial delimitation of Southeast Asia in that

it is only since the second world war that the term South-east Asia has been generally

accepted as a collective name for the series of peninsulas and islands which lie to the east of India and Pakistan and to the south of China. Nor is it altogether surprising that the West should have been slow to recognise the need for some common term for this area, which today comprises Burma [Myanmar], Thailand, Cambodia, Laos, Vietnam, the Federation of Malaysia, Singapore, Brunei, Indonesia and the Philippines (Fisher, 1964: p. 3).

In fact, one of the unifying features which explains the common development histories of many of the countries within the region is their different imperial groupings (with the exception of Thailand), with terms such as Further India, Far Eastern Tropics and Eastern Asia previously used to identify the region.

For the purpose of this book, Fisher's poignant comments of 1964 (p. 5) still hold true in that 'from a geographical point of view South East Asia must be accounted a distinctive region within the larger unity of the Monsoon lands ... and worthy to be ranked as an intelligible field of study on its own'. However, in terms of the geographical context of the region, this book incorporates a number of countries from the margins of the monsoon lands to extend the scope to South and Southeast Asia, with Fisher's (1964) designation extended to include Sri Lanka, Bangladesh and Pakistan (Figure 1.1), because too little research on and knowledge of the region has been disseminated, even though Fisher (1964) rightly debated the logic of Sri Lanka being incorporated under the heading Southeast Asia (Ceylon was the strategic location of the Southeast Asia Command during the Second World War).

Kirk (1990) explored the colonial past of Southeast Asia, building on the excellent historical analysis of the region's development by Fisher (1964), to indicate that a series of core areas developed prior to and during the period of European colonization (1500–1950). These core areas were largely established prior to European rule and accentuated the existing forms of core and periphery so that a series of

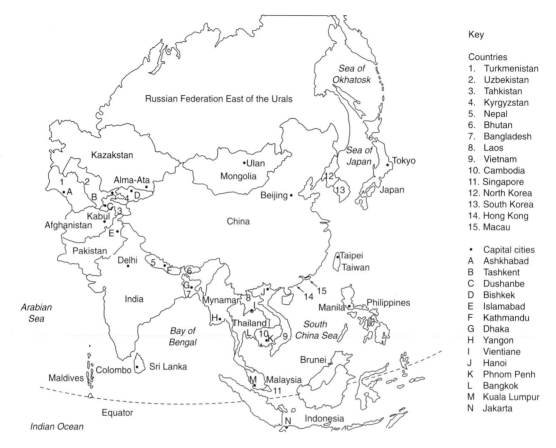

Figure 1.1   *The regional context*

patterns emerged as illustrated in Figure 1.2. Kirk (1990) examined the core areas in Thailand, British Burma, India, the Malayan west coast, Dutch Indonesia and French Indochina. These processes of colonization did little to reduce regional inequalities. In fact, Dixon and Smith (1997: p. 4) argue that

The incorporation of Southeast Asia into the emergent global capitalist system took place under the auspices of colonial economic and, except for Thailand, political control. By the end of the colonial period for much of Southeast Asia an extremely uneven pattern of development had emerged. The post-colonial states were charac-terised by high levels of ethnic diversity, limited national integration, little contact with their *neighbours, unbalanced urban hierarchies and unevenly developed economies, both spatially and by sector. These situations have had a profound impact on both the subsequent development of the region's economies and on economic policies that have followed.*

Thus, the decolonization era saw many of the former colonies become nation states with very little adjustment of political boundaries. Likewise, many of the new states inherited the development problems of the former colonies, not the least of which were related to the divisive social struc-tures fostered by former colonies. In economic terms, Kirk (1990: pp. 44–45) argued that, follow-ing the colonial era, 'over-dependence on a few commodities to earn foreign exchange ... [with] ...

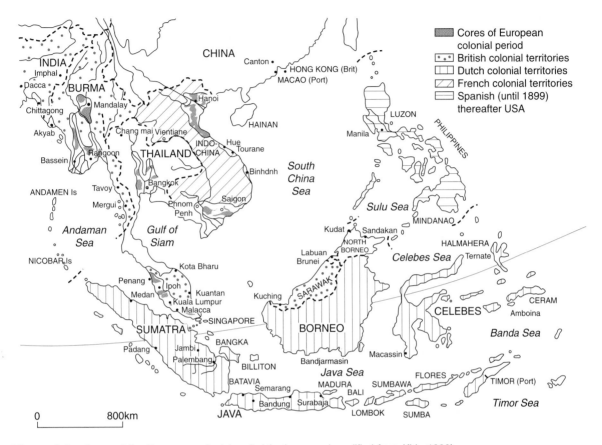

Figure 1.2   *Cores of the European colonial period (redrawn and modified from Kirk, 1990)*

foreign capital still prominent in new forms of dependency'. This virtually encouraged a greater core–periphery pattern of neo-colonial development. In fact, 'the core infrastructures built during the colonial era, have provided the main attraction to new industrial and commercial developments, and central governments, whatever their political policies and ideals' (Kirk, 1990: pp. 45–46). This point is developed by Dixon and Smith (1997: p. 5) who argue that

the emergence and/or intensification of core areas during the colonial era was closely associated with the development of a series of major port cities – Bangkok, Jakarta, Manila, Rangoon, Saigon-Cholon and Singapore. These centres became the major focus for their respective national economies and the principal interface with the international economy. The emergence of these major cities has resulted in the South East Asian region exhibiting high levels of urban primacy and remarkably unbalanced urban hierarchies.

Therefore, in any discussion of the Southeast Asian region two fundamental features of the social, economic and political landscape need to be considered: the population and its distribution and the related theme of urbanization, since each has continued to lead to greater concentrations of economic activity around the core areas. As a result, any discussion of tourism, its development and use of infrastructure and the social and cultural landscape needs to pay attention to the existing patterns of development.

Population, economic development and the space economy in Southeast Asia: megacities, extended metropolitan regions and globalization

The population of any country, comprises the basic human resource for the development of economic activity and, in tourism, is the manpower and labour component. Dixon (1990) provides a detailed analysis of the demographic structure and cultural influences impacting upon the population of Southeast Asia (e.g. the distribution of native people and languages), much of which is drawn from the classic study of the region by Fisher (1964, and subsequent editions). Hull (1997) described the recent population, where variations in mortality and fertility rates occur throughout the region. The cultural geography of the area is also an important backdrop to the discussion of the development of plural societies in the region, particularly during colonization, and the concept of cultural clusters where nations were created with little attention to the cultural distribution of population. Likewise, the policies of colonial powers which actively encouraged the inward migration of Chinese labour to many parts of the region in the nineteenth century, followed by migrants from the Indian sub-continent, created plural societies. This also created a host of political and racial issues for the post-colonial powers, and some of these political and racial tensions attracted world media attention as a result of the economic downturn associated with the Asian crisis.

Devas and Rakodi (1993) highlighted the demographic challenge facing the region, where South and Southeast Asia combined account for one-third of the developing world's urban population. This population increased by 4 per cent per year between 1970 and 1985. Much of the growth is due to in-migration and the natural growth of the existing population, with the attraction of urban lifestyles and improved economic opportunities in both the formal and informal sectors of the economy (e.g. the casual labour market). This has simply reinforced the core patterns of development that were encouraged and enhanced during the colonial era. Although this is a gross simplification of the economic landscape of Southeast Asia, since the debate over globalization versus localization (Gertler, 1997) in terms of the creation of localities and regions where the conditions for economic success were right, the role of the state and supranational bodies in influencing the geography of production has been questioned. Tang and Thant (1994) examine this in relation to the success of growth triangles which sometimes transcend national borders. Tang and Thant also highlight the continued significance of the inflow of foreign direct investment into Southeast Asia and regional economic cooperation, notably the role of trading blocs. Therefore such developments impact upon population distribution, further concentrating the workforce in specific areas of economic potential.

The recent Asian Development Bank (1998a) report (http://asaindevbank.org/megacity/index.htm) highlights the scale of urban and population development in the region. The definition of megacity, as an area of population in excess of 10 million people, has been used by the Asian Development Bank to examine the prospects for the region into the next millennium. The urban population of Asia has increased from 0.4 billion in 1965 to 1.1 billion in 1998, with the level of urbanization increasing from 22 per cent to 33 per cent over the same period (i.e. the population that is now urban-based). Dixon and Smith (1997) point to the increasing concentration of urban economic activity into larger complexes. They refer to the concept of extended metropolitan regions (EMRs), which represent something different from urbanization elsewhere in the world because they are driving both regional and national economic growth. In fact, Douglass (1995) identifies five patterns of restructuring which are occurring in Southeast Asia based on the experience of EMRs like Bangkok. These are:

• National economic development is being polarized into a small number of core regions.

- Mega-urban regions are emerging (or, as the Asian Development Bank call them, megacities), which are linked through technological, economic and social networks (see Rimmer 1997) to enable a pattern of multinuclear development to occur. Both local and global processes are at work, a feature explored in detail by Gertler (1997) and many of the papers in the recent book by Rimmer (1997) characterized by the localization/globalization debate.
- The new EMRs are the focus of the accumulation and circulation of global capital, a feature which has attracted a great deal of attention among economic geographers since the influential work of Dicken (1988) and Olds *et al.* (1999). These EMRs are also part of a global pattern of world cities.
- A number of transborder regions are emerging where urban agglomerations cut across national borders (the growth triangles concept) which is highlighted in Figure 1.3. These regions of economic activity are based upon emerging international networks of 'transportational, communicational and decision-making corridors of international development, designed to integrate the region as a whole into the global system of finance, production, trade and consumption' (Dixon and Smith, 1997: p. 15).

Explaining the factors which have promoted the emergence of EMRs is a function of three processes: globalization; the transactional revolution; and structural change. In terms of globalization, national governments have encouraged export-orientated manufacturing and investment (foreign direct investment – FDI) based on the East Asian experiences. Through increased labour productivity, the use of flexible labour strategies in the post-Fordist era and the provision of improved

existing spaces or by creating new spaces to attract these activities ... states and firms are reshaping the landscape of production within Pacific Asia, with the spatial impact being felt at a variety of *levels from the purely local to the emergence of complex growth corridors* (Dixon and Smith (1997: p. 10).

What Dixon and Smith (1997) highlight is the growing international competition within the region, with Singapore acting as a source of investment financing this pattern of development. In terms of transactional costs, the greater use of technology to facilitate decision making with information and capital flows transmitted electronically, has meant that many EMRs have developed electronic nodes. The spatial outcome of such developments is that transportation is vital in the connection of the multiple nodes (polynodal) that develop in EMRs, such as a tourism region, multiple business centres, retail districts, port zones and industrial areas. New developments often gravitate towards the new infrastructure routes where new tourism regions can be created (see Wongsuphaswat, 1997, on the implications of the extended Bangkok metropolitan region). As McGee and Greenberg (1992) recognized, EMRs not only stem from industrial deconcentration, but FDI and new business start-ups seeking new locations fuel this pattern of growth. The third process, that of structural change, illustrates that development planning has been sectoral rather than spatial in its focus, with the focus on export-based growth, in which tourism has also been incorporated, in the development strategies of many countries. Tourism has been a major beneficiary of the EMR developments, not only for business travel related to economic development and growth, but also owing to the primacy role of many EMRs in the national urban hierarchy, so that they also function as the main gateways to the country. Given this pattern of growth, many of the urban and regional planning problems facing Southeast Asia are likely to be focused on the growth effects of EMRs.

Figure 1.4, based on the United Nation's (1998) report (http://www.undp.org), illustrates the scale of the growth in urban areas in Southeast Asia. Based on the United Nations forecasts of population growth (Asian Development Bank,

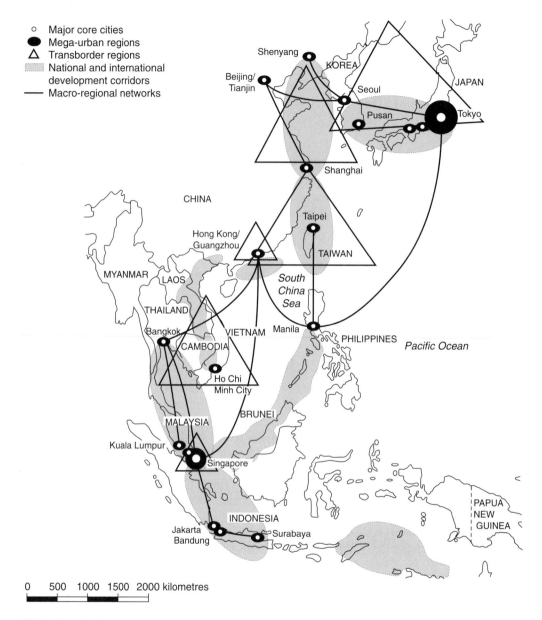

Figure 1.3   *Growth triangles in Asia (after Douglass, 1993; Hall and Samways, 1997)*

1998a), the population residing in Asian mega-cities will rise from 126 million people in 1995 to 382 million in 2025 (see Figure 1.4). Of the twenty megacities forecast for growth in Asia, ten will be in Southeast Asia. The existing cities are Tokyo, Osaka, Seoul, Shanghai, Calcutta, Bombay and Jakarta, and those expected to reach megacity status by 2025 are Bangalore, Karachi, Tienching, Lahore, Rangoon, Bangkok, Shenyang, Manila, Madras, Dhaka and New Delhi (see Forbes 1996 for more detail on urban-ization). These cities are characterized by a series

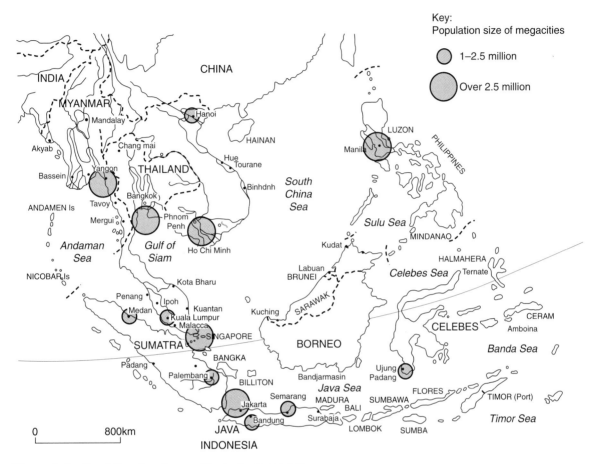

Figure 1.4 *Population size of megacities in Southeast Asia*

of problems including: a declining environmental quality; inadequate housing; social alienation and insecurity with a need for comprehensive urban management strategies (see Devas and Rakodi, 1993), although Dixon and Smith (1997: p. 18) argue that 'Comprehensive planning is virtually impossible within rapidly developing EMRs but the focus will need to recognise the regional dimension of these entities' and urban governance is likely to have to change at the national and regional level to establish policies which can accommodate the geographical bases of the EMRs – a feature which McGee (1995) calls 'metrofitting'. One of the pressing needs for many of the cities is infrastructure provision, a major concern since these cities play a major role

in creating GDP. For example, in 1990, the two Japanese megacities (Tokyo and Osaka) were responsible for 36 per cent of that country's GDP; Bangkok was responsible for 37 per cent of Thailand's GDP and Manila for 24 per cent of the Philippines' GDP. One of the prevailing problems which has important consequences for tourism is the impact of megacities on the quality of life of residents and visitors. For example, McGee (1979: p. 186) indicated that tourism had accompanied urbanization in Southeast Asia since

At the beginning of the 1960s, most of the large cities of the region received fewer than 100,000 tourists a year. By the mid-1970s many were

already receiving more than half a million visitors a year and the influx of tourists on the cities' economies is significant both in terms of job creation and income generation.

Thus, if the quality of life deteriorates, the attraction for visitors will diminish too. This is dealt with in the recent United Nations (1998) report on the Human Development Index which examines a range of social and economic indicators for various countries throughout the world and then rates human development from high levels of development (e.g. Canada with a value of 0.96) through to medium levels of development (e.g. Suriname with a value of 70.9) through to low levels of development (e.g. Sierra Leone with a value of 0.185). Table 1.2 outlines a number of the countries in the various categories and includes all countries in Southeast Asia to illustrate the varying levels of human development which prevail throughout the region. What the table indicates is that, within Southeast Asia, the experiences of human development are extremely varied, from the former growth economies of Singapore, Thailand, Malaysia and Indonesia to the other countries which rated between medium and low on the human development index. While such measures are based on a limited number of indices it highlights the diversity of development states for many countries within the region. In fact, a recent Asian Development Bank (1998b) report, *Emerging Asia: Changes and Challenges* (http://asiandevbank.org/pubguide/emergingasia), highlights the growing divergence in Asian development scenarios, with some countries reaching the development status of industrialized countries while others have large populations living in poverty with a poor quality of life and environment which is also a major issue for the region.

The Asian economic miracle

Rigg (1997) discussed the concept of the East Asian Miracle which was publicized by the World Bank's (1993) report which contends East Asian countries 'do share some economic characteristics that set them apart from most other developing countries' (World Bank 1993: p. 2). This is exemplified by Rigg (1997: p. 9) who compares the features of the miracle from the points of view of the World Bank and Hill (1993). However, Booth (1995) suggested that the experiences of the high-performing Asian economies in Southeast Asia were significantly different from the experiences of the East Asian economies (i.e. South Korea, Japan and Taiwan) in a number of ways: an overdependence upon an export-led economy and over-rapid growth. This is typified by the case of Thailand, which Bell (quoted in Rigg, 1997) claims is characterized by maldevelopment, 'a pattern of development with strongly negative socio-economic consequences in terms of inequality, unevenness, cultural fragmentation and a negative impact on the environment'.

Rigg (1997) summarizes the consequences and essential features of economic development and the social and environmental ramifications in terms of:

- Economic development which is vulnerable and dependent upon footloose businesses and inward investment (see Nestor, 1997, for the situation in Vietnam where FDI for the period 1988–1995 saw tourism as the second largest beneficiary of investment);
- development which has perpetuated poverty (see Booth, 1995, 1997; Asian Development Bank, n.d.) and poor working conditions, especially the impact on female workers which has been described as the feminization of poverty (Bell, 1992). In the case of the Philippines, McIlwane (1997) examines the gender dimension and contribution to inequality while in the case of Singapore, Davidson and Smith (1997) examine this issue;
- development that is destructive of the natural environment and not environmentally sustainable (Bryant and Parnwell, 1996);
- development that undermines local culture and creates an ethic of consumerism which is creating a homogenization of Southeast Asian culture (Escobar, 1995); and

- development that widens inequality between people, rural and urban areas and between regions. As Rigg (1997: p. 71) poignantly concludes, 'a hallmark of many of the critiques of S. E. Asia's economic development is the extent to which the benefits of growth have been unequally distributed', a feature emphasized by Parnwell and Arghiros (1996) that has exacerbated uneven development in space. This has led to a distinct geography of exclusion for the poor in terms of the prevalence of rural poverty despite a general decrease in the extent of poverty owing to rising living standards. However, the unequal distribution of wealth and income in Southeast Asia has certainly led to a greater geographical marginality for the poor in terms of their distribution in traditional rural areas and the expansion within the growing megacities and urbanized areas of the region.

Rigg (1997) is also mindful of the lack of critical debate of Southeast Asian economic development from indigenous researchers, who have often used Western concepts of development and added a Southeast Asian facade. As a result, Alatas (1995: p. 135) called for a greater indigenization which means 'filling these voids by looking at the various non-Western philosophies, cultures and historical experiences as sources of inspiration, insights, concepts and theories for social science'. As a result, Dixon and Smith (1997) summarize the overall impact of economic development and its implications in terms of unevenness which varies within and between countries thus:

It is particularly evident in the distribution of income, the spatial pattern of development, the lack of congruity between the structures of employment, national income and export earnings, access to education, the level of urbanisation, the incidence and intensity of metropolitan dominance, sharp divisions on the basis of gender and ethnicity, and the limited development of civil society and access to power. It is not that any of these features are unique to the South East Asian

countries, indeed they are common features of the Third World as a whole (Dixon and Smith, 1997: pp. 1–2).

Given the concern with ethnicity, it is pertinent to consider the role of ethnicity and tourism, particularly the way that ethnicity has been used in the marketing of Southeast Asian tourism.

Marketing tourism: using ethnicity as a saleable commodity

Within the wider development of tourism in Southeast Asia, the achievements of destinations and countries in expanding their visitor base and positively developing a burgeoning tourism industry since the 1960s (Wood, 1979) is no mean feat, particularly given the vagaries of colonialization and the limited experience of tourism as a form of revenue generation. Against this background, one cannot ignore the role marketing has played in the ability of destinations and regions to harness their tourism potential and to develop a viable tourism business based on the one commodity which provides the 'differentness': ethnic diversity as 'large numbers of tourists may be attracted to the region by its perceived 'differentness', lured by the images of culture and landscape which are vividly portrayed in the promotional literature' (Hitchcock *et al.*, 1993: p. 3). This point is, in part, explained by Wood (1997) in terms of

an increasingly significant market segment has come to be known as ethnic or cultural tourism, characterised by the tourist's interest in being exposed to and experiencing some form of cultural otherness. Tourism entrepreneurs, indigenous groups states, municipalities, multinational corporations, and a variety of other actors have scrambled to promote and market ethnicity and culture to tourists, both domestic and international. Inevitably, this promotion has led to the extension of commodity relationships into new

Table 1.2 Selected indices used to construct a human development index for Asian and non-Asian countries

Rank	Country	Life expectancy at birth (years) for 1995	Adult literacy rate (%) for 1995	Combined first-, second- and third-level gross enrolment ratio (%) for 1995	Real GDP per capita (PPP$) for 1995	Adjusted real GDP per capita (PPP$) for 1995	Life expectancy index	Education index	GDP index	Human development index (HDI) value for 1995
High state of human development		*73.52*	*95.69*	*78.68*	*16 241*	*6193.0*	*0.8087*	*0.9002*	*0.9809*	*0.8966*
1	Canada	79.1	99.0	100.0	21 916	6230.98	0.9008	0.9933	0.1987	0.96
2	France	78.7	99.0	89.0	21 176	6229.37	0.8948	0.9567	0.987	0.946
3	Norway	77.6	99.0	92.0	22 427	6231.96	0.8758	0.9667	0.987	0.943
4	USA	76.4	99.0	96.0	26 977	6259.29	0.8562	0.98	0.992	0.943
5	Iceland	79.2	99.0	83.0	21 064	6229.11	0.9028	0.9367	0.987	0.942
6	Finland	76.4	99.0	97.0	18 547	6218.88	0.8563	0.9833	0.985	0.942
7	Netherlands	77.5	99.0	91.0	19 876	6225.7	0.8747	0.9633	0.986	0.941
8	Japan	79.9	99.0	78.0	21 930	6231	0.9142	0.92	0.987	0.94
9	New Zealand	76.6	99.0	94.0	17 267	6197.05	0.8607	0.9733	0.982	0.939
10	Sweden	78.4	99.0	82.0	19 297	6223.42	0.8895	0.9333	0.986	0.936
25	Hong Kong, China	79.0	92.2	67.0	22 950	6232.88	0.9007	0.8379	0.987	0.909
28	Singapore	77.1	91.1	68.0	22 604	6232.28	0.8687	0.8325	0.987	0.896
30	Korea, Rep. of	71.7	98.0	83.0	11 594	6139.72	0.779	0.9298	0.972	0.894
35	Brunei Darussalam	75.1	88.2	74.0	31 165	6282.54	0.8347	0.8363	0.995	0.889
59	Thailand	69.5	93.8	55.0	7 742	6073.72	0.7423	0.8098	0.962	0.838
60	Malaysia	71.4	83.5	61.0	9 572	6109.7	0.7737	0.7603	0.968	0.834
Medium state of human development		*67.47*	*83.25*	*65.61*	*3 390*	*3390*	*0.7078*	*0.7737*	*0.5297*	*0.6704*
65	Suriname	70.9	93.0	71.0	4 862	4862	0.7657	0.8566	0.767	0.796
66	Lebanon	69.3	92.4	75.0	4 977	4977.44	0.7377	0.8644	0.785	0.796
67	Bulgaria	71.2	98.0	66.0	4 604	4604.04	0.7692	0.8733	0.725	0.789
68	Belarus	69.3	97.9	80.0	4 398	4397.66	0.7387	0.9193	0.692	0.783
69	Turkey	68.5	82.3	60.0	5 516	5516.31	0.7242	0.7504	0.872	0.782
70	Saudi Arabia	70.7	63.0	57.0	8 516	6090.51	0.7608	0.6093	0.964	0.778
71	Oman	70.3	59.0	60.0	9 383	6106.44	0.7543	0.5923	0.967	0.771
72	Russian Federation	65.5	99.0	78.0	4 531	4530.9	0.6745	0.92	0.713	0.769
73	Ecuador	69.5	90.1	71.0	4 602	4602.45	0.7415	0.8359	0.725	0.767
75	Korea, Dem. People's Rep. of	71.6	95.0	75.0	4 058	4058.09	0.7773	0.8833	0.637	0.766
90	Sri Lanka	72.5	90.2	67.0	3 408	3408	0.7915	0.8252	0.533	0.716
95	Maldives	63.3	93.2	71.0	3 540	3540.01	0.6383	0.8578	0.554	0.683
96	Indonesia	64.0	83.8	62.0	3 971	3970.96	0.6492	0.7661	0.623	0.679
98	Philippines	67.4	94.6	80.0	2 762	2762.09	0.7068	0.897	0.429	0.677
101	Mongolia	64.8	82.9	53.0	3 916	3916	0.663	0.7287	0.614	0.669

103	Turkmenistan	64.9	98.0	90.0	2 345	2345	0.6648	0.9533	0.361	0.66
104	Uzbekistan	67.5	99.0	73.0	2 376	2376.31	0.708	0.9033	0.366	0.659
106	China	69.2	81.5	64.0	2 935	2934.93	0.7362	0.757	0.456	0.65
110	Azerbaijan	71.1	96.3	72.0	1 463	1462.95	0.7675	0.882	0.219	0.623
118	Tajikistan	66.9	99.0	69.0	943	942.86	0.6988	0.89	0.136	0.575
122	Vietnam	66.4	93.7	55.0	1 236	1236.45	0.69	0.8083	0.183	0.56
	Low state of human development	56.67	50.85	47.09	1 362	1362	0.5278	0.496	0.2032	0.409
131	Myanmar	58.9	83.1	48.0	1 130	1130.24	0.5645	0.7129	0.166	0.481
132	Cameroon	55.3	63.4	45.0	2 355	2354.93	0.5052	0.5739	0.363	0.481
133	Ghana	57.0	64.5	44.0	2 032	2032.45	0.5333	0.5755	0.311	0.473
134	Lesotho	58.1	71.3	56.0	1 290	1290.46	0.5517	0.6637	0.192	0.469
135	Equatorial Guinea	49.0	78.5	64.0	1 712	1712.01	0.4002	0.7368	0.26	0.465
136	Lao People's Dem. Rep. of	52.2	56.6	50.0	2 571	2570.76	0.454	0.5434	0.398	0.465
137	Kenya	53.8	78.1	52.0	1 438	1437.73	0.4805	0.6928	0.215	0.463
138	Pakistan	62.8	37.8	41.0	2 209	2209.13	0.6295	0.3887	0.34	0.453
139	India	61.6	52.0	55.0	1 422	1421.99	0.6098	0.529	0.213	0.451
140	Cambodia	52.9	65.0	62.0	1 110	1109.63	0.4643	0.6403	0.163	0.422
147	Bangladesh	56.9	38.1	37.0	1 382	1381.9	0.531	0.376	0.206	0.371
152	Nepal	55.9	27.5	56.0	1 145	1144.81	0.515	0.3704	0.168	0.351
155	Bhutan	52.0	42.2	31.0	1 382	1382.24	0.4493	0.3845	0.206	0.347
	All developing countries	62.2	70.44	57.49	3 068	3068	0.62	0.6612	0.4778	0.5864
	Least developed countries	51.16	49.2	36.42	1 008	1008	0.436	0.4494	0.1462	0.3439
	Industrial countries	74.17	98.63	82.81	16 337	6194	0.8195	0.9336	0.9811	0.9114
	World	63.62	77.58	61.59	5 990	5 990	0.6437	0.7225	0.9482	0.7715

Source: modified from United Nations (1998; http://www.undp.org/undp/hdro)

areas of social life along with the intrusion of the tourists themselves (Wood, 1997: pp. 1–2)

which led to critical questions from anthropologists over what is ethnic tourism, what is an authentic ethnic tourism experience and the extent to which it is now a staged and commodified experience for tourists (see Smith, 1989, for a more detailed discussion of tourism and the host–guest relationship from an anthropological perspective). In fact, one of the important findings of Picard and Wood's (1997) scholarly synthesis of tourism and ethnicity is that tourism does not necessarily have to have an ethnic dimension to have consequences for ethnic groups. Furthermore, it is important to recognize that the relationship between tourism, ethnic groups and tourists is a fluid, ever-changing situation and state institutions can have a major bearing on its use for national and regional tourism promotional purposes. In fact, Crystal's (1989) very interesting longitudinal assessment of the impact of tourism on the Toraja people of Sulawesi, Indonesia, is a fascinating reconstruction of the effects on the local culture in a period where

tourism in Tan Toraja has changed from a peripheral phenomenon intriguing to locals and bemusing to provincial officials into a major and probably permanent fact of local economic, social and cultural life ... Now with the recent designation of Tana Toraja as the second most important tourist destination in Indonesia, only active government intervention in concert with the local Toraja community leaders can preserve cultural artefacts, orient visitors, and regulate the imposition of external demands upon local village generosity ... unlike the four million person strong civilization of Bali to the south, the relatively small (population 320,000) religiously heterodox, and intensely fragmented Toraja culture region is singularly unprepared to cope with a major tourist influx (Crystal, 1989: pp. 167–168).

What this example illustrates, is that even where the state may have not intended or delib-

erately promoted a major tourist expansion to a particular region, the unintended consequences may have a far-reaching impact when marketing cultural and ethnic identity as a unique element of a country's tourism product. However, there is a great deal of confusion within the academic literature over the role of marketing in tourism, although any practitioner involved in this field is usually clear about what needs to be done to achieve promotional and market growth objectives. Holloway and Robinson (1995: p. 4) point to the definition of marketing given by the Chartered Institute of Marketing in the UK as

... the management function which organises and directs all those business activities involved in assessing customer needs and converting customer purchasing power into effective demand for a specific product or service, and in moving that product or service to the final consumer or user so as to achieve the profit target or other objective set by the company or other organisation.

This definition is useful in that it highlights how marketing is a management function within individual businesses and organizations associated with tourism. It also highlights the underlying philosophy that permeates an organization: its customer orientation, with tourists being the focus of the business activity. Oppermann and Chon (1997) highlight a key factor associated with the growth of tourism as the aggressive marketing by National Tourism Organizations (NTOs), the ability of the countries to finance tourism infrastructure development and rapid economic growth. Therefore, in this section, attention focuses on the key role of NTOs and the significance of image promotion, product development and building awareness of the region's tourism potential for intraregional and inbound tourism and, more recently, for domestic tourism. Research by Ashworth and Voogd (1990a) highlights the role of place marketing for cities and more recent studies have highlighted the role of geographical marketing (Oppermann, 1997) for regions such as Southeast Asia by regional organizations such as the Association of South East Asian Nations (ASEAN). A common theme which Ashworth and Voogd (1990b) highlight is the way in which a number of different philosophies have been used by the public sector in tourism planning. In fact, Ashworth and Voogd (1990b) reiterate the role of marketing in promoting tourism destinations where they are promoted as products. Whilst there are a number of fundamental differences between a conventional marketable good or service such as a hotel room and a place, Hall (1997) outlines many of the peculiarities associated with regional and place marketing (i.e. the use of geography, place and space) to promote areas for tourism. This is a major component which belies the success of the marketing of the region.

There is a growing literature on the role of NTOs in the development and promotion of tourism in destination areas (World Tourism Organization, 1996) and a recent World Tourism Organization report (World Tourism Organization, 1997) highlighted the budgets which these organizations used for promotional purposes.

The marketing of Southeast and South Asian tourism by National Tourism Organizations

The recent reports by the World Tourism Organization (1996, 1997), marked the first comprehensive synthesis of the marketing of the region and the activities of the NTOs, as well as the revenue expended on different activities. While the World Tourism Organization (1996) is not able to provide detailed data for every destination, owing to the reliance upon NTOs responding to a questionnaire survey, the material analysed does at least provide an indication of how the region fares in a global context and the types of activities which NTOs undertake in each country which responded. On a global scale, the World Tourism Organization regional

breakdown of total budgets expended on marketing tourism show that Europe remains the largest spender with a total of US$1004 million, followed by East Asia Pacific with US$559 million, the Americas with $432 million, Africa with $130 million, South Asia with $56 million and the Middle East with US$25 million. Thus, a total expenditure for those countries responding of US$2206 million existed for tourism marketing and promotion in 1995. The methods of funding the NTOs in Asia are outlined in Table 1.3 which highlights the dominant role of central government in supporting marketing and promotion and the limited role of the private sector (excluding Bangladesh, Hong Kong and China and, to a lesser degree, in the case of the Philippines and Maldives).

Table 1.4 outlines the manner in which the NTOs spend their budgets on tourism marketing and promotional activities in Asia where advertising and promotion consume the majority of the expenditure, usually in excess of 75 per cent of the total funding for each NTO. Table 1.5 shows that, within a global context, a number of the Asian destinations (e.g. Singapore, Thailand, Korea, Hong Kong) are competing aggressively for the international visitor market through the amount of money spent on promotional activities. This is further developed in Table 1.6 where the expenditure in local currencies for the period 1991–1995 shows the significant sums spent by Southeast Asian destinations. It is also interesting to observe which types of target markets the various Asian destinations are seeking to develop (Table 1.7). As Table 1.7 shows, most destinations are seeking the high-spending long-haul and medium-haul outbound markets from the USA and Japan, as well as intraregional travel from within the Asia Pacific (Hall, 1997). Although the prioritization of markets and the precise mix of inbound tourists varies according to destination, there is a clear focus on a core range of source markets which are a function of historical ties, growing outbound markets and the location and attraction of each destination. What is also clear from the analysis of NTOs by the World Tourism Organization (1996) is that the governments of some destinations (e.g. Singapore and Thailand) are now major players in terms of the budgets and promotional activities funded to develop tourism (see Singh and Chon, 1996, for a detailed analysis of the situation in Singapore). This, of course, does not include the marketing and promotion undertaken by other tourism businesses (e.g. airlines) which is complementary to the work of the NTOs and certainly significant in the image formulation and direct contribution to the development of inbound tourism. In the case of Singapore, Ragaraman (1997) discusses the impact of airline development on nation-building, although few studies have examined the cooperative marketing undertaken between NTOs and airlines in pursuit of similar goals – to increase visitor arrivals. Although Oppermann and Chon (1997: p. 131) argue that 'historically, the principal marketing role of NTOs has been seen in the fairly narrow promotional terms of creating and communicating overall appealing destination images and messages to the target market'.

It is evident from the World Tourism Organization (1996) data that this narrow role is also changing with a growing interest in private–public sector partnerships to market the region, reflected in the Tourism Authority of Thailand's collaboration with airlines, hotels and tour operators – 'The World Our Guest' campaign. This sought to invite 11 000 travel intermediaries (e.g. travel agents and tourists) in response to the adverse publicity associated with spread of AIDS, the Gulf War and political unrest in 1992. There have been few critiques of the role of national tourism promotion, although perhaps the most candid and meaningful (which is not laden with post-modern critiques of brochures such as Selwyn, 1993) is that by Leong (1997), focused on Singapore. Leong (1997) examines the historical development of tourism promotion by the Singapore Tourist Promotion Board since 1964 and notes that

Before political independence in 1965, Singapore was like any other Southeast Asian city, an apparent haphazard maze of diverse land uses ... Beginning in *the late 1960s, urban and industrial development progressively bulldozed such landscapes and living traditions ... Two mass campaigns instituted at this time were Keep Singapore Clean and Towards a Green Garden City – self-conscious efforts of the new nation-state to construct and transform a new environment for tourism and urban development* (Leong, 1997: p. 78).

As a result, other less appealing activities to tourists (e.g. hawkers and the informal sector) were progressively abolished and what has resulted is an 'antiseptic and culturally sterile' (Leong, 1997: p. 78) tourist city as described in various tourist guide books. In one sense, social anthropologists and historians argue that these changes removed both the culture and heritage from Singapore, where nation-building effectively removed the past to the extent that Leong (1997; p. 83) argues that 'Geography and landscape are not selling points for tourism in Singapore. Priorities of industrial and urban development have left little picturesque scenery for the mass tourist'.

Even so images promoting tourism in Singapore use the multicultural traditions of the country, ethnic traditions, unique and exotic images associated with festivals, eating and cultural performances. Thus, the multicultural traditions replace the absence of scenic landscape and heritage attractions, as a living form of tourism organized around the theme of ethnicity. By commodifying ethnicity, with the Chinese, Malay, Indian and other ethnic groups, a particular form of food tourism has been developed and promoted in the absence of other conventional products, based upon the historical and indigenous people. It appeals to global consumerism and mass market, with official policies designed to incorporate various ethnic groups into the tourism product and promotion.

Yet one should also not underestimate the role of other tourism promotion agencies and initiatives in the region. For example, in recent years ASEAN nations have undertaken joint promotion, marketing and research activities such as Visit ASEAN Year in 1992 (Hall, 1997). Such

Table 1.3 The funding of National Tourism Organizations in Asia in 1995

Country	Funding of NTOs total budget (% of total budget)					Funding of promotional budget (% of promotional budget derived from)	
	Central government	Local authorities	Taxes	Contribution of private sector	Other	Public funds	Non-public funds
Bangladesh[a]	–	–	15.00	–	85.00	–	–
China	100.00	–	–	–	–	–	50.00
Hong Kong[b]	–	–	90.00	10.00	–	95.00	5.00
India[b]	100.00	–	–	–	–	–	–
Indonesia[b]	100.00	–	–	–	100.00	–	–
Korea, Republic of	100.00	–	–	–	0	100.00	–
Malaysia	100.00	0	0	0	–	100.00	–
Maldives	100.00	–	–	–	–	–	4.76
Myanmar[c]	100.00	–	–	–	–	–	–
Nepal[c]	100.00	–	–	–	–	–	–
Pakistan	100.00	–	–	–	–	–	–
Philippines	–	25.00	1.00	4.00	70.00	99.00	1.00
Singapore[c]	100.00	–	–	–	100.00	100.00	0
Sri Lanka	100.00	–	–	–	–	100.00	–
Taiwan (Prov. of China)[d]	100.00	–	–	–	–	–	–
Thailand[e]	100.00	–	–	–	–	100.00	–

Notes
[a] Provisional
[b] Fiscal year: April 1994–March 1995
[c] Fiscal year: July 1994–June 1995
[d] Fiscal year: October–September
[e] Fiscal year: April–March

Source: World Tourism Organization, 1996.

Table 1.4   *National Tourism Organization budgets in Asia: allocation of funds by activity 1991–1995*

Country	Activity	% of Budget				
		1991	1992	1993	1994	1995
China	Advertising	–	–	23.55	30.41	32.42
	Public relations and press	–	–	7.95	11.41	5.95
	Promotional activities	–	–	24.07	43.49	40.74
	Public information	–	–	–	–	–
	Research activities	–	–	6.26	3.59	20.90
	Other	–	–	38.17	11.11	–
	TOTAL	–	–	100.00	100.00	100.00
Hong Kong[a]	Advertising	60.50	56.05	60.03	60.79	48.18
	Public relations and press	9.63	8.89	8.72	7.11	7.32
	Promotional activities	27.32	30.85	27.13	21.64	32.88
	Public information	–	–	–	–	–
	Research activities	1.23	1.82	1.61	1.23	2.47
	Other	1.32	2.38	2.50	9.22	9.15
	TOTAL	100.00	100.00	100.00	100.00	100.00
Macau	Advertising	48.95	32.98	38.60	29.08	47.35
	Public relations and press	1.50	3.35	3.84	4.03	3.01
	Promotional activities and public information	49.55	63.66	57.56	66.89	48.79
	Research activities	–	–	–	–	0.85
	Other	–	–	–	–	–
	TOTAL	100.00	100.00	100.00	100.00	100.00
South Korea	Advertising	43.82	50.51	54.79	51.07	57.28
	Public relations and press	1.30	2.60	1.77	0.94	1.66
	Promotional activities	52.41	43.01	38.62	42.78	39.30
	Public information	–	–	–	–	–
	Research activities	0.22	0.19	0.13	0.12	0.24
	Other	2.16	3.69	4.68	5.09	1.53
	TOTAL	100.00	100.00	100.00	100.00	100.00
Indonesia[a]	Advertising	22.35	22.24	20.84	20.83	17.58
	Public relations and press	–	–	–	–	–
	Promotional activities	77.65	77.76	79.16	79.17	82.42
	Public information	–	–	–	–	–
	Research activities	–	–	–	–	–
	Other	–	–	–	–	–
	TOTAL	100.00	100.00	100.00	100.00	100.00
Malaysia	Advertising	43.42	37.13	–	–	–
	Public relations and press	12.14	7.68	–	–	–
	Promotional activities	27.98	36.71	–	–	–
	Public information	14.22	15.19	–	–	–
	Research activities	2.25	3.29	–	–	–
	Other	–	–	–	–	–
	TOTAL	100.00	100.00	–	–	–
Philippines	Advertising	32.73	22.20	29.41	30.29	24.74
	Public relations and press	–	–	–	–	–
	Promotional activities	56.24	70.82	63.04	62.50	68.18
	Public information	–	–	–	–	–
	Research activities	–	–	–	–	–
	Other	11.03	6.98	7.55	7.21	7.08
	TOTAL	100.00	100.00	100.00	100.00	100.00
Singapore[b]	Advertising	46.04	44.74	47.33	44.85	–
	Public relations and press	6.72	8.84	8.52	7.44	–
	Promotional activities	46.41	44.97	43.09	46.64	–
	Public information	0.05	0.36	0.28	0.11	–
	Research activities	0.78	1.08	0.78	0.96	–
	Other	–	–	–	–	–
	TOTAL	100.00	100.00	100.00	100.00	–

Table 1.4 *Continued*

Country	Activity	% of Budget				
		1991	1992	1993	1994	1995
Thailand[c]	Advertising	43.76	43.79	46.84	68.92	58.81
	Public relations and press	12.23	13.51	21.66	11.73	12.66
	Promotional activities	35.09	33.74	24.12	15.73	24.53
	Public information	–	–	–	–	–
	Research activities	7.18	6.97	6.34	3.03	3.02
	Other	1.75	1.99	1.04	0.58	0.98
	TOTAL	100.00	100.00	100.00	100.00	100.00
Bangladesh[d]	Advertising, public relations and press	82.72	93.90	92.59	32.89	51.35
	Promotional activities	17.28	6.10	7.41	67.11	48.65
	Public information	–	–	–	–	–
	Research activities	–	–	–	–	–
	Other	–	–	–	–	–
	TOTAL	100.00	100.00	100.00	100.00	100.00
India[e]	Advertising	60.09	60.09	60.66	60.09	60.10
	Public relations and press	–	–	–	–	–
	Promotional activities	29.04	29.05	29.32	29.05	29.09
	Public information	6.58	6.57	6.63	6.56	6.56
	Research activities	0.54	–	–	–	–
	Other	3.74	4.30	3.39	4.29	4.25
	TOTAL	100.00	100.00	100.00	100.00	100.00
Maldives	Advertising	6.34	7.51	8.22	7.51	7.55
	Public relations and press	7.66	6.30	6.99	5.58	5.64
	Promotional activities	68.22	70.11	68.23	71.66	69.11
	Public information	14.67	11.55	13.55	12.61	14.81
	Research activities	3.12	4.53	3.01	2.63	3.52
	Other	–	–	–	–	–
	TOTAL	100.00	100.00	100.00	100.00	100.00
Nepal[f]	Advertising	–	57.86	48.15	29.00	25.36
	Public relations and press	–	1.26	1.59	–	2.61
	Promotional activities	–	30.82	33.86	51.14	18.44
	Public information	–	1.89	–	5.25	–
	Research activities	–	7.55	8.47	7.53	2.70
	Other	–	0.63	7.94	7.08	2.70
						48.20[g]
	TOTAL	–	100.00	100.00	100.00	100.00
Sri Lanka	Advertising	–	–	0.24	1.22	1.14
	Public relations and press	–	–	7.20	4.26	3.31
	Promotional activities	–	–	86.10	85.14	83.35
	Public information	–	–	6.22	7.80	10.03
	Research activities	–	–	0.24	0.49	0.68
	Other	–	–	–	1.10	1.48
	TOTAL	–	–	100.00	100.00	100.00

Notes
[a]Fiscal years: April 1991–March 1992 to April 1995–March 1996.
[b]Fiscal year: April–March.
[c]Fiscal year: October–September.
[d]Fiscal years: July 1990–June 1991 to July 1994–June 1995.
[e]European market only.
[f]Fiscal year: 16 July–15 July.
[g]This amount is allocated to a Tourism Promotional Fund which is spent on specific promotional activities rather than on regular ones.

Source: World Tourism Organization, 1996.

Table 1.5   *Promotional budgets of the top forty National Tourism Organizations in 1994 and 1995*

Rank 1995	Country	US$ (000s)		% change 1994–1995
		1994	1995	
1	Australia[a]	75 811	87 949	16.01
2	United Kingdom[b]	77 885	78 710	1.06
3	Spain	77 457	78 647	1.54
4	France	62 729	72 928	16.26
5	Singapore[c]	49 695	53.595	7.85
6	Thailand[d]	42 907	51 198	19.33
7	Netherlands	43 800	49 700	13.47
8	Austria[e]	45 694	47 254	3.41
9	Ireland	41 830	37 811[f]	–9.61
10	Portugal	34 904	37 271	6.78
11	Israel	25 000	33 300	33.20
12	Switzerland	27 613	32 233	16.73
13	New Zealand[g]	29 718	31 597	6.32
14	Canada[b,h]	11 743	31 504	168.28
15	Puerto Rico	20 117	30 807	53.14
16	Korea, Republic of	30 486	30 308	–0.58
17	Hawaii (USA)[g]	20 861	28 686	37.51
18	Hong Kong[b]	24 940	28 637	14.82
19	Morocco	21 588	24 541	13.68
20	South Africa[c]	27 758	23 809	–14.23
21	Mexico	55 087	22 574	–59.02
22	Egypt	21 000	21 000	0.00
23	Cyprus[i]	18 561	20 790	12.01
24	Turkey	18 804	20 520	9.12
25	Germany	17 375	20 151	15.98
26	India[b]	19 127	18 648	–2.50
27	Finland	18 000	17 777	–1.24
28	Bermuda[b]	16 871	16 565	–1.81
29	Tunisia	15 124	16 423	8.59
30	USA[j]	14 000	15 000	7.14
31	Croatia	13 241	14 498	9.49
32	Italy	9 412	14 198	50.85
33	Aruba	13 455	12 876	–4.30
34	Philippines	9 898	7 080	–28.47
35	Poland	4 641	6 709	44.56
36	French Polynesia	5 853	6 629	13.26
37	Hungary	6 450	6 612	2.51
38	Costa Rica	7 168	6 450	–10.02
39	Curacao	5 913	5 671	–4.09
40	Macau	2 657	5 083	91.31

Notes
[a]Fiscal years: July 1993–June 1994; July 1994–June 1995.
[b]Fiscal years: April 1994–March 1995; April 1995–March 1996.
[c]Fiscal year : April–March.
[d]Fiscal year : October–September.
[e]Including domestic tourism.
[f]Data for 1995 is provisional.
[g]Fiscal year : July–June.
[h]Excludes partnership funding from state/territorial authorities and the private sector for 1994/1995.
[i]Promotional budget does not include fixed costs of the central administration.
[j]Estimation excluding Hawaii.

Source: World Tourism Organization, 1996.

Table 1.6 *Promotional budgets of Asian National Tourism Organizations 1991–1995*

	Unit of currency	1991	1992	1993	1994	1995
Northeast Asia						
China[a]	Yuan renminbi	16 890	24 190	36 800	37 055	42 922
Hong Kong[b]	Dollar (HK$)	129 897	145 867	148 911	194 527	223 372
Korea, Republic of	Won (W)	14 104 736	16 582 326	21 363 191	24 388 974	24 246 468
Macau	(MOP)	13 302	15 269	21 054	21 255	40 666
Taiwan (Prov. of China)[c]	New Taiwan dollar	9 500	20 379	14 027	10 281	9 421
Southeast Asia						
Indonesia[b]	Rupiah (Rp)	5 250 661	6 018 288	6 662 126	8 750 960	9 345 897
Malaysia	Ringgit (M$)	61 078	65 000	–	–	–
Philippines	Peso (P)	58 300	194 910	202 420	256 020	183 130
Singapore[d]	Dollar (S$)	60 788	60 021	67 793	72 604	74 818
Thailand[e]	Baht (B)	410 764	496 066	607 774	1 072 664	1 279 957

Notes
[a]Excluding staff costs.
[b]Fiscal years: April 1991–March 1992 to April 1995–March 1996.
[c]Fiscal years: July 1990–June 1991 to July 1994–June 1995.
[d]Fiscal year: April–March.

Source: World Tourism Organization, 1996.

initiatives have had value not only in promoting the image of the region externally but also in encouraging greater intra-ASEAN travel. In addition to government promotional initiatives, the private sector is also playing an increasingly important role. For example, the private sector Indonesian Tourism Promotion Board launched a five year campaign in 1994 to encourage inbound tourism from Japan, Taiwan, Singapore, Germany and Australia, with an initial budget in 1994 of US$14 million (Wall and Nuriyanti, 1997). However, what has assisted in the rapid development of Indonesia's inbound tourism is the ability of Indonesia's Tourist Development Corporations to provide and develop infrastructure in peripheral locations and in the main tourism destinations (Hall, 1997). This coordinated approach together with the provision of capacity on airlines to facilitate the growth in arrivals has accelerated growth. In contrast, Ragaraman (1998) examines the situation in India, where a key factor associated with the slow growth in international arrivals is the lack of access by air. Although tourism is a central component of the national planning process in India, Ragaraman (1998) highlights the emphasis needed for improving marketing and promotion for overseas tourism: better coordination with operators, improved tourism information services and coordination of the national tourism development with the activities of the various states in India (see Chapters 14 and 15). In 1994–1995, the Department of Tourism allocated 60 per cent of its budget to marketing and publicity (US$20.7 million), of which US$17.2 million was for overseas promotion. Nevertheless, Ragaraman (1998) argues that this is relatively little for a country the size of India when compared with Malaysia and Singapore where the expenditure on promotion is almost double. This also has to be set against a growing competitive market for Southeast Asian tourism. Even so, it is clear from the limited examples given above of the NTOs in South and Southeast Asia that a substantial element of the promotional budget is designated for overseas promotion (which also includes intraregional markets) to build the image of the destination.

Table 1.7 *The top ten target markets for Asian destinations in 1995*

Country	Target markets									
	1	2	3	4	5	6	7	8	9	10
China	USA	Japan	Singapore	UK	France	Germany	Australia	Spain	Israel	
India[a]	Germany	France	Italy	Spain	Netherlands	Switzerland	Sweden and Scandinavia			
Indonesia	Japan	UK	Singapore	USA	Germany	Australia	Taiwan	Malaysia	Netherlands	France
South Korea[b]	Japan	USA	Taiwan	Germany	UK	Australia	Hong Kong (HK)	Canada	Singapore	France
Malaysia	Japan	USA	UK	Australia	Germany	Hong Kong	Taiwan	Singapore	France	Thailand
Philippines	Asia/Pacific	Europe	USA							
Singapore[c]	Japan	USA	UK	Australia/New Zealand	France/Italy/Spain	HK/Taiwan	Germany	Asia[d]	South Korea	Switzerland
Sri Lanka	Germany	France	UK	Japan	Scandinavia Australia/NZ	Benelux	Italy	Switzerland	Austria	Spain
Taiwan	Japan	Europe	North America	Asia[e]						
Thailand	Japan	USA	Taiwan	Germany	UK	Malaysia	Hong Kong	South Korea	Singapore	Australia

Notes
[a]European market.
[b]Data refers to 1993.
[c]Data refers to 1994.
[d]Excluding Japan, Australia, New Zealand, South Korea, Hong Kong and Taiwan.
[e]Excluding Japan.

Source: World Tourism Organization, 1996.

Context and issues

From the discussion so far, it is evident that tourism in South and Southeast Asia has undergone both a dramatic growth and significant change in recent years (see Teo and Chang, 1998, for a recent review). In fact the recent study by Bar-on (1998) indicates that South Asia and Southeast Asia will experience further changes in relation to its tourism economy. Bar-on envisages a growth rate in tourism employment which will be the highest of the world regions, based on the World Tourism Organization forecasts for the period 1998–2010. For South Asia this growth is expected to be 1.5 times the world rate of 3 per cent per year for the world in real annual growth in tourism employment. However, a range of events and crises have beset the wider South and Southeast Asia region which point to a greater degree of caution in interpreting such forecasts. For example, the Asian economic crisis is one further dimension of the continuing rapid change that both the population and economies of the region have experienced in the post-colonial period. In fact, one of the consequences of colonialism was relative economic stability and ongoing economic development, albeit for the benefit of metropolitan powers. The dependence upon primary products in the export economies of many former colonies not only required a very specific economic and physical infrastructure but also determined many of the patterns of development and population prior to 1945. In this respect, the post-war period has seen the entire region undergo rapid and tumultuous change of an unprecedented magnitude. Against this context of rapid economic change, one has to superimpose tourism which is best described as the supposed smokeless industry of the future, based on the region's two essential assets: the environment and its people, both of which are characterized by diversity.

In any one book, it is impossible to realistically separate out the holistic nature of the impact and overall consequences of such rapid change induced by tourism. However, for the purposes of understanding the intricacies, effects and significance of tourism in different regions, countries, places and in different times, one is forced to adopt the classical deductive approach used widely in human geography: that is to look at the existing model of tourism development in a regional and global context and the various facets and systematic dimensions of the 'tourism experiences' and development in the region (Hall and Page, 1999). Only by segmenting this tourism experience into various facets (e.g. historical patterns of development, social and cultural impacts, economics, policy, transportation, politics, environment and planning) can one begin to appreciate how the development patterns of tourism have emerged in the different countries and regions. In this respect, the chapters which follow describe a model of tourism which is then examined in more detail within different spatial, economic, political and environmental contexts to begin to reconstruct the patterns of tourism development that have occurred, to establish what is currently happening and to define some of the prospects for future growth and development in the region. This book is by no means comprehensive, since it is regrettable that countries such as the Philippines and Brunei, and issues such as human resource management, tourism education, health and disaster planning have largely not been covered, primarily owing to the constraints of space. Nevertheless, the following chapters do seek to provoke and challenge their readers and, in some small way, attempt to compensate for the prevailing paucity of critical perspectives on tourism in the region. The breadth of the chapters and the range of subjects and authors are therefore part of this desire to present a range of perspectives and understandings of the processes and forces shaping tourism in this fascinating and dynamic region of global tourism activity.

Note: The report *WTO in Asia and the Pacific*, by the World Tourism Organization is a useful source which provides an overview of tourism in the region and the work of the World Tourism Organization. This report outlines all projects

undertaken in the region including those in policy and planning; tourism development; tourism marketing; human resource development; cultural tourism; environmental projects; technical cooperation projects; regional surveys and technical seminars, and workshops. More details can be obtained from the following web site:
csa-cap@world-tourism.org

References

Alatas, S., 'The theme of relevance in third world human sciences', *Singapore Journal of Tropical Geography* 162, 1995, pp. 123–140.

Ashworth, G. and Voogd, H., *Selling the City*, Belhaven Press, London, 1990a.

Ashworth, G. and Voogd, H., 'Can places be sold for tourism?', in G. Ashworth and B. Goodall (eds), *Marketing Tourism Places*, Routledge, London, 1990b, pp. 1–16.

Asian Development Bank, *The Development and Management of Asian Megacities*, Asian Development Bank, Manila, 1998a.

Asian Development Bank, *Emerging Asia: Changes and Challenges*, Asian Development Bank, Manila, 1998b.

Asian Development Bank, *Escaping the Poverty Trap: Lessons from Asia*, Asian Development Bank, Manila, n.d.

Bacani, C. 'The perfect vacation', *AsiaWeek*, 6 November 1998.

Bar-on, R., 'South Asia and WTO's global forecasts to 2020', *Tourism Economics*, 4(4), 1998, pp. 387–94.

Bell, P., 'Gender and economic development in Thailand', in P. van Esterik and J. van Esterik (eds) *Gender and Development in Southeast Asia*, Canadian Council for Southeast Asian Studies Toronto, 1992, pp. 61–81.

Booth, A., 'Southeast Asian economic growth: Can the momentum be maintained?', *Southeast Asian Affairs 1995*, Institute of Southeast Asian Studies, Singapore, 1995, pp. 28–47.

Booth, A., 'Poverty in South East Asia: Some comparative estimates', in C. Dixon and D. Smith (eds) *Uneven Development in South East Asia*, Ashgate, Aldershot, 1997, pp. 45–74.

Bryant, R. and Parnwell, M., 'Politics, sustainable development and environmental change in South-East Asia', in M. Parnwell and R. Bryant (eds) *Environmental Change in South East Asia: People, Politics and Sustainable Development*, Routledge, London, 1996, pp. 1–20.

Davidson, G. and Smith, D., 'The price of success: Disadvantaged groups in Singapore', in C. Dixon and D. Smith (eds) *Uneven Development in South East Asia*, Ashgate, Aldershot, 1997, pp. 75–99.

Devas, N. and Rakodi, C. (eds), *Managing Fast Growing Cities: New Approaches to Urban Planning and Management in the Developing World*, Longman, Harlow, 1993.

Dicken, P., *Global Shift: Industrial Change in a Turbulent World*, Paul Chapman, London, 1988.

Dixon, C., 'Human resources', in D. Dwyer (ed.) *South East Asian Development*, Longman, Harlow, 1990, pp. 110–139.

Dixon, C. and Smith, D. (eds), *Uneven Development in South East Asia*, Ashgate, Aldershot, 1997.

Douglass, M., 'Global interdependence and urbanization: Planning for the Bangkok mega-urban region', in T. McGee and I. Robinson (eds), *The Mega-Urban Regions of Southeast Asia*, UBC Press, Vancouver, 1995, pp. 45–77.

Dwyer, D. (ed.), *South East Asian Development*, Longman, Harlow, 1990.

Economic and Social Commission for Asia and the Pacific (ESCAP), *Economic and Social Survey of Asia and the Pacific 1997, Asia and the Pacific Into the Twenty-first Century: Opportunities and Challenges for the ESCAP Region*, ESCAP, Bangkok, 1997.

Escobar, A., *Encountering Development: The Making and Unmaking of the Third World*, Princeton University Press, Princeton, NJ, 1995.

Fisher, C., 'South East Asia: The Balkans of the Orient', *Geography* 47, 1962, pp. 347–367.

Fisher, C., *South-East Asia*, Methuen, London, 1964.

Forbes, D., *Asian Metropolis: Urbanisation and the Southeast Asian City*, Oxford University Press, Melbourne, 1996.

Fryer, D., *Emergent South East Asia: A Study in Growth and Stagnation*, Philip, London, 1970.

Gertler, M., 'Globality and locality: The future of geography', in P. Rimmer (ed.) *Pacific Rim Development: Integration and Globalisation in the Asia-Pacific*

Economy, Allen and Unwin, St Leonards, 1997, pp. 12–33.

Hall, C.M., *Tourism in the Pacific Rim*, 2nd edn, Addison Wesley Longman, South Melbourne, 1997.

Hall, C.M. and Page, S.J., *The Geography of Tourism and Recreation: Environment, Place and Space*, Routledge, London, 1999.

Hall, C.M. and Samways, R., 'Tourism and regionalism in the Pacific Rim: An overview', in M. Oppermann (ed.) *Pacific Rim Tourism*, CAB International, Wallingford, 1997, pp. 31–44.

Hill, H., 'Southeast Asian economic development: an analytic survey', Economics Division Working Papers No. 93/4, Research School of Pacific Studies, Australian National University, Canberra, 1993.

Hitchcock, M., King, V. and Parnwell, M. (eds), *Tourism in South East Asia*, Routledge, London, 1993.

Holloway, C. and Robinson, C., *Marketing for Tourism*, Third Edition, Longman, Harlow, 1995.

Hull, T., 'The setting: Demographic mosaic of the Asia Pacific region – issues defining the future', *Asia Pacific Viewpoint* 38 (3), 1997, pp. 193–200.

Kirk, W., 'South East Asia in the colonial period: Cores and peripheries', D. Dwyer (ed.) *South East Asian Development*, Longman, Harlow, 1990, pp. 15–47.

Leong, L., 'Commodifying ethnicity: state and ethnic tourism in Singapore', in M. Picard and R. Wood (eds), *Tourism, Ethnicity and the State in Asian and Pacific Societies*, Hawai'i University Press, Honolulu, 1997, pp. 71–98.

McGee, T., 'The changing cities' in R. Hill (ed.) *South-East Asia: A Systematic Geography*, Oxford University Press, Kuala Lumpur, 1979, pp. 180–191.

McGee, T., 'Metrofitting the emerging mega-regions of ASEAN: An overview', in T. McGee and I. Robinson (eds) *The Mega-Urban Regions of Southeast Asia*, UBC Press, Vancouver, 1995, pp. 3–26.

McGee, T. and Greenberg, C., 'The emergence of metropolitan regions in ASEAN', *ASEAN Economic Bulletin* 9(1), 1992, pp. 5–12.

McIlwane , C., 'Fringes or frontiers? Gender and export-oriented development in the Philippines', in C. Dixon and D. Smith (eds), *Uneven Development in South East Asia*, Ashgate, Aldershot, 1997, pp. 100–123.

Nestor, C., 'Foreign investment and the spatial pattern of growth in Vietnam', in C. Dixon and D. Smith (eds), *Uneven Development in South East Asia*, Ashgate, Aldershot, 1997, pp. 166–195.

Olds, K., Dicken, P., Kelly, P., Wong, L. and Yeung, H. (eds), *Globalization and the Asia-Pacific*, Routledge, London, 1999.

Oppermann, M., (ed.), *Geography and Tourism Marketing*, Haworth Press, New York, 1997.

Oppermann, M. and Chon, K., *Tourism in Developing Countries*, International Thomson Business Publishing, London, 1997.

Parnwell, M. and Arghiros, D., 'Uneven development in Thailand', in M. Parnwell (ed.), Avebury, Aldershot, 1996, 1–27.

Picard, M. and Wood, R. (eds), *Tourism, Ethnicity and the State in Asian and Pacific Societies*, Hawai'i University Press, Honolulu, 1997, pp.1–34.

Qu, H. and Zhang, H., 'The projected inbound market trends of 12 tourist destinations in S.E. Asia and the Pacific 1997–2001', *Journal of Vacation Marketing* 3(3), 1997, pp. 247–263.

Rigg, J., *Southeast Asia: The Human Landscape of Modernization and Development*, Routledge, London, 1997.

Rimmer, P. (ed.), *Pacific Rim Development: Integration and Globalisation in the Asia-Pacific Economy*, Allen and Unwin, St Leonards, 1997.

Raguraman, K., 'Airlines as instruments for nation building and national identity: case study of Malaysia and Singapore', *Journal of Transport Geography*, 5(4), 1997, pp. 239–56.

Raguraman, K., 'Troubled passage to India', *Tourism Management*, 19(6), 1998, pp. 533–44.

Saludo, R. and Shameen, A., 'How much longer?', *AsiaWeek* 17 July 1998.

Selwyn, T., 'Peter Pan in South East Asia: views from the brochures', in M. Hitchcock, V. King and M. Parnwell (eds), *Tourism in South-East Asia*, Routledge, London, 1993, pp. 117–137.

Singh, A. and Chon, K., 'Marketing Singapore as an international destination', *Journal of Vacation Marketing* 2(3), 1996, pp. 239–257.

Smith, V., (ed.), *Hosts and Guests: The Anthropology of Tourism*, Second Edition, University of Pennsylvania Press, Philadelphia, 1989.

Tang, M. and Thant, M., *Growth Triangles: Conceptual*

Issues and Problems, Economics Staff Paper Number 54, Asian Development Bank, Manila, 1994.

Teo, P. and Chang, T.C. (eds) Special issue of *Singapore Journal of Tropical Geography*, **19**(2), 1998.

United Nations, *Human Development Report*, United Nations, New York, 1998.

Wall, G. and Nuriyanti, W., 'Marketing challenges and opportunities facing Indonesian tourism, *Journal of Travel and Tourism Marketing*, **6**(1), 1997, pp. 69–84.

Wood, R., 'Tourism and underdevelopment in Southeast Asia', *Journal of Contemporary Asia*, **9**(3), 1979, pp. 274–87.

Wood, R., 'Tourism and the state: ethnic options and constructions of otherness', in M. Picard and R. Wood (eds), *Tourism, Ethnicity and the State in Asian and Pacific Societies*, Hawai'i University Press, Honolulu, 1997, pp. 1–34.

Wongsuphaswat, L., 'The Extended Bangkok Metropolitan region and uneven development in Thailand', in C. Dixon and D. Smith (eds), *Uneven Development in South East Asia*, Ashgate, Aldershot, 1997, pp. 196–220.

World Bank, *The East Asian Miracle: Economic Growth and Public Policy*, Oxford University Press, Oxford, 1993.

World Tourism Organization, *Budgets of National Tourism Administrations: A Special Report*, World Tourism Organization, Madrid, 1996.

World Tourism Organization, *Budgets and Marketing Plans of National Tourism Administrations*, World Tourism Organization, Madrid, 1997.

World Tourism Organization, *WTO in Asia and the Pacific*, World Tourism Organization, Madrid, 1998.

World Tourism Organization, *Impacts of the Financial Crisis in Asia's Tourism Sector*, World Tourism Organization, Madrid, 1999.

2

Tourism in South and Southeast Asia: historical dimensions

Ngaire Douglas and
Norman Douglas

Suddenly a puff of wind, a puff faint and tepid and laden with strange odours of blossoms, of aromatic wood, comes out of the still night – the first sigh of the East on my face. That I can never forget. It was impalpable and enslaving, like a charm, like a whispered promise of mysterious delight.

Joseph Conrad, *Youth.*

Those who have never been in the East have missed the better part of the earth.

Robert Payne,
The White Rajahs of Sarawak.

Introduction

East is a geographical direction, one of the cardinal points of the compass. But *the East* was much more, a complex European construct that embodied a set of assumptions and a mystique. As a synonym for *Asia* it was even less precise, but more suggestive. It was a less pretentious alternative to *the Orient*, a term which in any case became appropriated over time by scholars and extended into Orientalism with its implications of serious learning. But 'the very power

and scope of Orientalism produced not only a fair amount of exact positive knowledge about the Orient but also a kind of second order knowledge – lurking in such places as the 'Oriental' tale, the mythology of the mysterious East, notions of Asian inscrutability – with a life of its own, what V.G. Kiernan has aptly called 'Europe's collective day-dream of the Orient' (Said, 1995: p. 52). The day-dream may have begun as close to Europe as Venice, which for centuries hovered uncertainly between East and West, but for many the true East was from India onward (Figure 2.1).

The spiritual father of European travellers to the East was the Venetian, Marco Polo; and perhaps also of travel writers since, as one of his modern translators notes, he had a keen eye for the exotic but a 'rather less assured' grasp of history. Moreover, Polo's *Travels*, first published in the late thirteenth century, can be enjoyed by the modern reader 'as a vivid description of a fantastic world so remote from his own experience that it scarcely matters whether he thinks of it as fact or fiction' (Latham, 1958: p. 7), an observation that says not only a good deal about travel writing but also about the process of travel itself. A more recent – but hardly less

SMART CINGALESE. "These is genuine Ceylon elephant, an' I know you will say, 'Made in Birmingham,' but it is not so; they was made in Japan."

Figure 2.1   *The mystic East demystified in a* Punch *cartoon of the 1930s (from Hammerton, J. (ed.),* Mr Punch on his Travels, *c. 1935)*

but the striking visuals are designed to resemble the jackets of pulp novel adventure-romances, and bear such titles as *The Leopard Sang in Sarawak, The Lost Idols of Sarawak* and so on (Sarawak Tourism Board, 1998).

Whatever the literary legacy of Polo's journey, its purpose was essentially the development of trade which, with religion, supplied the main motive for travel in those times. Travel for mere curiosity's sake lay some distance in the future, travel for recreational purposes further still. Following the voyages of Columbus – himself an admirer of Polo – in the late fifteenth century, travel for trade became an even more vigorous contest and led inevitably to territorial acquisition and expansion. Only a few years after Columbus's first voyage in 1492, the Portuguese had established bases in India, later in Ceylon and Southeast Asia. The (British) East India Company was established by royal charter in 1600 and given a monopoly over trade with the Far East, from India to China. Two years later the Dutch responded in kind by creating a similar organization to monopolize trade in the East Indies (later Indonesia). The French, as eager for trade with the East but slower to institutionalize it, did not form a company with similar ambitions until 1664.

None of these bodies proved permanent: the Indian Mutiny of 1857 helped to bring about the demise of the British Company, while the Dutch organization had been disbanded by the Netherlands government even earlier, in 1798, by which time many of the arrangements put in place by the French had been swept away by the events of the French revolution. Their spheres of activity, at least those of the British and Dutch, were taken over by their respective governments. In each case, however, the companies had provided forms of government and had created the more or less stable conditions for their trade activities to prosper; the very sorts of conditions which would begin to encourage travellers whose purpose was mainly to look, even such unlikely ones as unescorted women.

well-known – traveller has claimed that 'the nearest thing to writing a novel is travelling in a strange country' (Theroux, 1986: p. 140). It was the indistinct boundary between fact and fiction – often wilfully blurred by Europeans – which accounted for much of the fascination of Westerners for the East. To a very great extent it still does. Anyone who doubts this might consider a recent campaign by the Sarawak Tourism Board to promote the attractions of that Malaysian state. Not only does the verbal text incorporate and mimic many of the scarcely credible observations of early visitors to Borneo,

Perceptions of the East: two nineteenth century travellers

'From my earliest childhood', wrote the Austrian, Ida Pfeiffer, in 1851, 'I had always the greatest longing to see the world. When I met a travelling carriage I used to stand still and gaze after it with tears in my eyes ... till it vanished from sight' (Pfeiffer, 1988: introduction). Those seeking evidence of continuity in the travel impulse may find it more than 100 years later in Paul Theroux's opening sentence of the *Great Railway Bazaar*: 'Ever since childhood ... I have seldom heard a train go by and not wished I was on it' (Theroux, 1975: p. 2). Pfeiffer was by no means the nineteenth century's first European traveller, but her voyage in 1846–1848, which took in China, Singapore, Ceylon and India, in addition to many parts of the 'Middle East', is significant for a number of reasons. She was an unaccompanied woman; she was perhaps the first European woman to see certain places; she had no official 'purpose', that is she was not travelling for the sake of scientific enquiries or to propagate religion or to visit friends or family, and she was in India in 1847, a decade before the Mutiny and a time when such unstructured travelling was quite rare. She financed her travels by the sale of her books, a practice that numerous other travel writers have since adopted. She would have agreed with Robert Louis Stevenson that travel should be for travel's sake, 'the great affair is to move'.

Exceptional as a traveller, she was probably typical as a European, with many of the biases of her age. 'A baser, falser, crueller people than the Chinese I never met with', she wrote; 'and one proof of this is, that their greatest diversion consists in tormenting animals' (Pfeiffer, 1988: p. 53). 'In the arts of trickery and deceit of all kinds ... the Europeans certainly cannot come near them' (*ibid*: p. 51). Her attitude towards non-Westerners, however, was by no means consistent. She was more sympathetic towards Indians and travelled quite extensively in India, displaying astonishment at the opulence with which the British inhabitants of Calcutta surrounded themselves.

The American author, Mark Twain, free of most of the prejudices which often accompanied European travellers as part of their luggage, delighted in almost everything he saw, from the cities – Calcutta 'a city huge and fine' (Twain, 1971: p. 517) – to the colour of the inhabitants. 'Nearly all black and brown skins are beautiful', wrote this son of the American South, 'but a beautiful white skin is rare' (*ibid*: p. 381), an observation that few British travellers of the time would have made, or at least would have made public. In recognizing that tourist attractions owe their appeal as much to their received reputations as to any intrinsic merit, Twain anticipated the theorizing of tourism analysts such as MacCannell and Urry by many decades. 'I find that as a rule, when a thing is a wonder to us it is not because of what we see in it, but because of what others have seen in it. We get almost all our wonders at second hand ... just the deep privilege of gazing upon an object which has stirred the enthusiasm ... is a thing which we value' (*ibid*: p. 507).

Steamships and other ways to the East

Pfeiffer and Twain arrived in the East by travelling west; she from Europe around Cape Horn at the stormy tip of South America and across the Pacific. But for most nineteenth-century travellers this was a needlessly difficult route. Advances in marine technology and design in Europe from the mid-nineteenth century resulted in larger and faster ocean-going vessels. A long-held ambition to join the waters of the Mediterranean and the Red Sea led to the eventual construction of the Suez Canal in 1869. With the demise in 1858 of its formidable rival, the East India Company, which had maintained a monopoly on the steamship route to Bombay, and the opening of the Canal, the Peninsular and Oriental Steam Navigation Company consolidated and extended a relationship with India and other countries of the East, making its

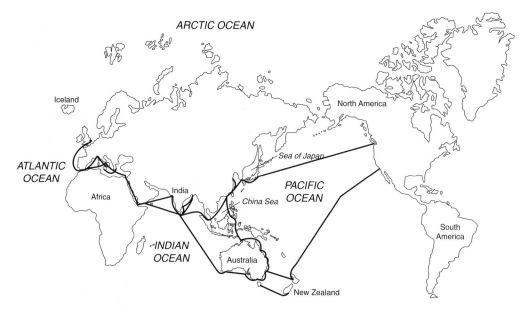

Figure 2.2   *P&O steamer routes circa. 1890*

official abbreviation, P&O, all but synonymous with travel to the region for more than a century (see Figure 2.2). The association was further strengthened by giving many vessels on the India run names which would evoke various facets of the 'Jewel in the Crown'; *Hindostan*, *Himalaya*, *Lahore*, *Viceroy of India*. From the opening of its first mail routes until the independence of India in 1947 and the disintegration of the colonial empires, the influence of P&O on travel to the East for both official and recreational purposes can hardly be overestimated. 'In England, India began at Victoria Station or Charing Cross, where the P&O special trains steamed out twice a week for the south. In India if anyone glimpsed the P&O house flag on a ship in port, they recognized the romantic link with home' (Howarth and Howarth, 1994: p. 69).

There were, of course, other shipping companies, representing other national interests. In 1879 a traveller described the traffic in the harbour of Hong Kong, a British possession since 1841. 'Besides the P and O, the Messageries Maritimes, the Pacific Mail Company, the Eastern and Australian Mail Company, the

Japanese 'Mitsu Bichi' [sic] Mail Company etc., all regular mail lines, it has a number of lines of steamers trading to England, America and Germany, with local lines both Chinese and English ...'(Bird, 1992: p. 39). But P&O's securing of key mail routes meant that well before the end of the nineteenth century its network covered India and much of East and Southeast Asia, up to Japan and down to Australia and New Zealand. The result was not only a regularization of the mails but a considerable increase in passenger traffic, including temporary visitors, since 'most people who had come before had come in the expectation of staying there all their lives, but now there were transient visitors who came one month and might be gone the next' (Howarth and Howarth, 1994: p. 78).

P&O's association with travel organization Thomas Cook and Son ensured that the greater number of visitors to India, Malaya and often beyond were in the hands of British travel entrepreneurs. Cook and Son, having by the early 1870s rendered most of Europe safe for British travellers, undertook their first world tour in 1872–1873 (200 days at £1 per day), not surprisingly using P&O

Figure 2.3   *A poster for Cook's first round the world tour featured Eastern transport with Western passengers (Thomas Cook Archives)*

ships for the main sea travel (Figure 2.3). The tour took in India, Southeast and East Asia, and helped to give the company a permanent presence in the region. By 1886 Cook and P&O were organizing trips from Bombay to Jeddah for Moslem pilgrims, an activity for which the shipping company later built a special vessel, and in 1890 the first edition of Cook's *Oriental Traveller's Gazette* for India and Southeast Asia appeared (Cook, n.d. c. 1995–1996: p. 11). In 1923 a separate edition for Malaya was created (Cook, 1923–1932), by which time there was also one for China.

John Murray's first *Handbook for India* appeared in 1859, a mere two years after the Mutiny, although then it had a cautionary tone: 'Bombay is at present weak against invasion' (quoted in Tindall, 1992: p. 167). Other editions appeared at various times during the nineteenth century. By the early twentieth century the visitor traffic was regular enough for Murray, a

publisher of guide books and imperial histories, to produce *The Imperial Guide to India* (Anonymous, 1904, with special thanks for their assistance to Messrs Thomas Cook and Son) and address it immediately to the tourist. Its first entry is headed 'Tourist Season'.

Since the opening of the Suez Canal India has become more and more known to the Western world. She is no longer the land of mystery she once was – the land of the lotus eater and the pagoda-tree. Year by year more and more tourists – chiefly English and American – find their way to the East (Anonymous, 1904: p. 2).

By contriving to make India appear less exotic Murray undoubtedly hoped to make it more popular, but the implication that increased numbers of visitors had assisted in the demystification of the East is not borne out by other evidence, of the period or later. Mark Twain found 'Bombay! A bewitching place ... the Arabian nights come again' (Twain, 1971: p. 345). 'Nothing has been left undone, either by man or Nature, to make India the most extraordinary country that the sun visits on his round' (*ibid*: p. 544). Until the eve of the Second World War travel posters by both Thomas Cook and P&O Cruises invariably displayed the fabled, mystic India, with caparisoned elephants or snake charmers prominently featured. At the end of the twentieth century this sort of defining imagery of India – now a country with nuclear capability and highly developed electronic industries – is still paramount (see San Michele Travel, 1998).

Why did Europeans, by no means all of them British, go to India? To act as voluntary extras in the great pageant of colonialism? Perhaps. 'Much hospitality', said Murray, 'is shown to tourists in India, and they should therefore be prepared, particularly if they have letters of introduction, for dinner-parties and dances' (Anonymous, 1904: p. 5). The hill station, Simla, for instance, 'is a very fashionable and expensive place during the season ... and those who have money and friends can spend a most enjoyable time' (*ibid*: p. 180) while Darjeeling 'is very gay socially during the hot weather' (*ibid*: p. 91). Thomas Cook and Son, reflecting later on these times, felt that 'South East Asia became a popular holiday area due to the large numbers of Europeans who worked in this part of the Imperial world' (Postcard caption, Cook's *Time Traveller and Archives*, n.d. c. 1995).

Was there anything else? Murray was generally enthusiastic about India's historic sites and provided detailed descriptions of many, but thought that 'European architecture in India is, on the whole, of no great interest', presumably not being sufficiently ancient (Anonymous, 1904: p. 19). Calcutta, for example, the 'City of Palaces' and 'chief city of the Empire', had 'little to boast of. Its buildings are modern and mostly of bad design' (*ibid*: p. 80). In Simla 'the scenery is very fine ... but there is nothing in ancient buildings or antiquities to attract a stranger'

(*ibid*: p. 180). The assumption that the visitor would be 'attracted' primarily if not solely by 'ancient buildings or antiquities' was understandable enough, since Murray – and his German contemporary and rival, Karl Baedeker – had already defined in numerous guidebooks those sights of Europe (almost invariably antiquities) which were essential for tourist consumption. In the *Imperial Guide* Murray wrote enthusiastically about Indian antiquities, 'should be seen', 'must not be missed', providing fairly extensive descriptions of many, and dismissing towns and cities which lacked these as 'of little [or no] interest to the tourist'. Landscape, however, receives summary treatment in Murray. The scenery from hill stations is 'magnificent' or 'very fine', and we pass on quickly to the 'season'. The 'estheticizing' of landscape, the extended description of it as though it were a painting (Pratt, 1992: p. 204) is not really attempted, although rhapsodizing over landscape was a very significant feature of Victorian travel writing. This may be one of the features that distinguished the 'travel guide' from the 'travel book' (see below).

The recreational slaughter of animals was widely regarded as an essential tourist pastime. The section of the *Imperial Guide* headed 'Sport' begins: 'There is no licence to shoot required by the European in India' (Anonymous, 1904: p. 10). No other form of sport is mentioned, not even under the heading 'games', although British team games such as cricket, football and hockey were well established, as were more individualistic activities such as golf and tennis. However, Murray cautioned against shooting birds and animals which were 'objects of veneration' or shooting in the vicinity of temples, and suggested that when sportsmen hunted the Indian antelope 'care should be taken not to shoot villagers working in the fields or tending cattle' (*ibid*: p. 10). There were echoes elsewhere. Writing on *Bangkok, Its Life and Sport*, Lieut-Col. C.H. Forty ('late Royal Siamese Gendarmerie') devotes a chapter to 'Guns and Appurtenances' followed by descriptions of the kingdom's 'coastal and island game areas' (Forty, 1929:

p. 81). In his guide to Malaya in 1923, Cuthbert Woodville Harrison includes a chapter on big game shooting: 'There is a certain fascination about the expression 'Big Game Shooting' which appeals to most Britishers' (Harrison, 1985: p. 230). The association that some writers (e.g. Buzard, 1993: pp. 315–330) have made between tourism and imperialism/militarism finds more than adequate illustration here.

There is not much indication that women visitors engaged in shooting or would have been expected to, although their presence occasionally enlivened a pigsticking. Indeed, there is strong evidence that unmarried females often journeyed to India – perhaps more than other parts of the British colonial world – to hunt a different sort of game entirely. 'The Fishing Fleet', as an annual visitation of young women was known, consisted of the 'eligible, beautiful daughters of wealthy people living in India', who came out 'to meet eligible young men and marry' (Allen, 1978: p. 42). In Malaya, however, 'if an unaccompanied English girl came out on the mail boat the CID sent her back on the next one', evidently fearing she would join the ranks of the European prostitutes who could be found at some of the larger hotels (Allen, 1983: p. 52).

Well before the end of the nineteenth century the relentless advance of the curiosity-seeking traveller had become noticeable. Isabella Bird could write that 'Canton and Saigon ... are on one of the best beaten tracks of travellers' (Bird, 1992: p. 1). Parts of French Indo-China, including Cambodia, appear to have been more accessible to the traveller in the late nineteenth and early twentieth century than they became in later decades. Except for the indefatigables, who regarded a measure of discomfort and inconvenience as an essential part of their experience, the extension and the success of pleasure travel depended in great measure on the stability and the improvements in transport and communications provided by the consolidation of colonial rule. Although Murray could claim in 1904 that 'Burma has, up to the present time, been comparatively little visited by the tourist' (Anonymous, 1904: p. 192), by the late

nineteenth century very few locations, no matter how seemingly bizarre, were visitor free. In Borneo the White Rajahs of Sarawak were themselves a visitor attraction; travellers expressed disappointment if they failed to gain an audience with the rajah during their stay (Douglas and Douglas, 1999).

Exceptions to the trend were short-lived. 'The Dutch do not welcome tourists, nor encourage one to visit their paradise of the Indies', wrote Eliza Scidmore in 1899. 'Too many travellers have come, seen, and gone away to tell disagreeable truths about Dutch methods and rule ... The tourist pure and simple, the sight-seer and pleasure traveller, is not yet quite comprehended ...' (Scidmore, 1907: pp. 22–23). But a short time later a change in administrative policy resulted in the lifting of restrictions on tourist movements and a visitors bureau, funded by the government, was distributing a number of publications aimed at facilitating the visitor experience, though mainly in Java, the seat of colonial government (Cribb, 1995: p. 195). The ultimate paradise of the Indies, Bali (Powell, 1986), had not been completely pacified by the Dutch when visitors began arriving in discernible numbers in Java. But within barely a decade of the full imposition of Dutch rule the island was well on the way to acquiring its reputation as 'the nearest approach to Utopia' (Gorer, 1988: p. 52), because of the attention given it by writers, painters, anthropologists, photographers and film-makers (Vickers, 1989: pp. 91–130).

Verbal and visual representations of the East

The new expansionist era of European colonialism in the second half of the nineteenth century created conditions which were appropriate for travel, and the advance of organizations such as P&O and Thomas Cook helped to popularize the activity. Imperialism, industrialization and the growth of social democracy, the three great forces transforming Europe, were responsible for creating a new social entity, the tourist as everyman, and a new cultural activity, popular tourism. The period was significant also for the development and dissemination of two activities which rapidly became not only inseparable from travel and tourism but essential aspects of their mystique; travel writing and photography.

Travel writing in the widest sense was not a product of the nineteenth century, but aided by greater social mobility – especially ease of movement internationally – advances in publishing and increased literacy and leisure time, the activity expanded considerably, especially during the last few decades. The century did give birth, however, to one of travel's most easily recognizable products, the guide book. For that achievement John Murray and Karl Baedeker were almost completely responsible. Their names in travel publishing survive to this day. Murray's handbooks or guides to India were the original inspiration for almost every other travel guide to Asia. Limitations of space preclude an examination of the historical progress of the travel guide, but something should be said about the travel book; that is, the personalized account of a voyage or journey, not only because the genre itself has remained enormously popular, but also because many of the nineteenth-century accounts are enjoying a revival as reprints and/or being subjected to close scrutiny in the light of late twentieth-century stances on gender and post-colonialism (e.g. Pratt, 1992).

While a number of the better-known travel accounts of the East had a scientific pretext, with naturalists or ethnologists predominant among their authors, including Wallace (1869), Mouhot (1864), Bock (1884), Hornaday (1885) and Beccari (1904) (Saunders, 1993: pp. 280–281). They were nonetheless received and read in the main as works of travel and adventure, their descriptions of the landscape and the dangers experienced along the way accounting for much of their popular appeal. All of them contained passages in which the ostensible scientific purpose of the journey was relieved by experiences of pure

Figure 2.4   *Isabella Bird (from Barr, 1970)*

pleasure (Douglas and Douglas, 1999). Readers were thus able to admire the scientific initiative that lay behind each expedition, and simultaneously envy the protagonist's ability to have a good time in the most exotic or even threatening of contexts.

The above writers were all men; there were no female naturalists or ethnologists in those times. For all that, the second part of the nineteenth century produced a significant number of women travellers and several of the more intrepid of these were attracted to the East. Ida Pfeiffer, by 1855, had twice voyaged around the world. Isabella Bird had travelled in Japan before visiting Malaya in 1879; later she would go to Tibet, China and Korea (Barr, 1970) (Figure 2.4). Pfeiffer and Bird travelled on their own to a great extent, but Anna Forbes accompanied her naturalist husband Henry throughout the

East Indies (now Indonesia), choosing to write her own account of the journey because 'many of my own sex ... may find some interest in reading my simpler account' (Forbes, 1987: preface). This seems unreasonably modest; not only did she visit some of the remotest parts of the archipelago – many of which are still difficult to access – but she did what few other travel writers of that or any other period usually considered doing, by revealing something of the literary construction of her book. A common structural device in travel writing of the era was to present the material in the form of a journal or letters, presumed to have been written either while the events were taking place or shortly after, and thus adding to the immediacy and perhaps the credibility of the account. 'I may confess that I did not write these letters [which make up most of the book] *en route*', writes Anna Forbes. Rather, the work was 'pieced together from letters actually written home, from my journal and from recollections' (*ibid*). While the epistolic style of travel writing appears to have died out with the period, the journal structure endured to form the basis of scores of travel accounts and, in many cases, was given a further gloss of immediacy by the writer's use of the present tense throughout.

Rudyard Kipling, Joseph Conrad and W. Somerset Maugham turned their actual experiences with life in the East into widely read fiction which to this day is used as a measure of the 'authentic' and continues to have a profound influence on travellers to the region. 'Kipling's India' has become a common way of referring to many northern areas of the sub-continent, while Maugham is regularly associated with Singapore and Penang, especially with the historic hotels of these two places. In the late twentieth century few people are likely to quote Ida Pfeiffer's opinions of India, whatever their merits, but Conrad, Maugham and Kipling, writers of fiction, have become almost household names among latter-day travellers and are regularly invoked by those who have never read them and have only the vaguest idea of where in the East they travelled.

Visual representations of the East by Europeans had become common by the mid-nineteenth century. The work of painters Auguste Borget and George Chinnery in China helped to define both the Chinese landscape and the Chinese people for Europeans. 'I am at last in China', wrote Borget in 1838; and, expressing the Imperial impulse, 'I have taken possession of the Celestial Empire!' (Hutcheon, 1979: p. 41). At an even earlier time, Thomas and William Daniell had 'taken possession' of India on behalf of many Britons who had never seen it by producing hundreds of landscapes and other subjects over a ten-year period of travel throughout the sub-continent and Ceylon. William Daniell later applied his skills to Malaya also.

But even these prolific efforts were eclipsed by the introduction of photography and the arrival of photographers in the region. Technological advances in photography coincided with and were encouraged by the extension of empire and the growth of travel (Museum voor Volkenkunde, 1986). Photographers from Europe and the USA established studios in the major cities of the East, Calcutta, Singapore, Canton, Hong Kong, Jakarta, and journeyed extensively in search of marketable images. As early as the 1860s 'the travel photographer in India could follow a well-trodden path made by Anglo-Indian tourists and artists in search of the picturesque' (Ryan, 1997: p. 49). The work of Samuel Bourne in India, John Thomson in China and Southeast Asia, and the firm of G.R. Lambert & Co. in Singapore laid the foundations for decades of travel photography in the region and, arguably, even identified which subjects were most appropriate to photograph. The activity was astonishingly comprehensive. By 1900 the catalogue of Lambert & Co. alone comprised some 3000 subjects 'relating to Siam, Singapore, Borneo, Malaya and China' (cited Falconer, 1987: p. 27). Unlike the one-of-a-kind painting or the limited edition art print, the expense of which restricted its circulation, the photographic print was cheap to produce and cheaper still to duplicate; hundreds of prints could be made from one negative. But the postcard was cheaper still and more versatile and, following its introduction in Austria in 1869, quickly attained universality to become one of tourism's essential icons, being only temporarily set back by the development of simplified 'amateur' photographic equipment at the end of the nineteenth century. The range of subjects depicted by the postcard, however, appears to have been relatively narrow, as one Malaysian historian/collector of the artefact has noted (Ng and Tate, 1989: preface).

Growth of transport and other facilities

Advances in land-based transport, intended generally to increase administrative convenience and aid economic exploitation, also facilitated the movement of non-official residents and visitors. Railways were one of the glories of the British Empire especially, but France and the Netherlands, the other two major colonial powers in the East were only slightly less ambitious, constrained chiefly by the size of their holdings. The remarkable development of rail services in India was one of the wonders of the age, but the British also used their skill and experience in railway building to strike a deal with the government of Siam by which they extended their territory in northern Malay partly in return for assisting the Siamese in the construction of their train lines. Burma had its first railway as early as 1877, French Cochin-China in 1881, British Malaya in 1886. The elderly Malay sultan of Selangor, after experiencing the new technology, is said to have described it as 'the best bullock-cart he ever travelled in' (Barr, 1978: p. 73; Gullick, 1994: p. 16). On Penang, an island, British enthusiasm for railways resulted in two novelties; one a funicular railway up Penang Hill, the other a railway station which never saw a train.

In the fragmented Netherlands East Indies only Java, the centre of administrative power,

Figure 2.5   *A Dutch East Indies railway poster of the 1930s: but there were no trains on Bali (Raffles Collection)*

received a comprehensive rail network (Cribb, 1995: p. 194) (Figure 2.5); in the Philippines, under USA control after 1898, there were trains only on Luzon. But generally the value of the train to both official and recreational travel was quickly realized. Railway handbooks and guides appeared in a number of countries proclaiming the advantages of trains and the appeal of the towns and cities served by rail. 'It is difficult to set down in words, precisely whence comes the elusive fascination of Bangkok', reads the guide published by the Royal State Railways of Siam (Seidenfaden, 1932: p. 1). In Malaya, at least, well-appointed hotels were built adjoining the railway stations to cater for overnight visitors.

Figure 2.6   *Raffles Hotel, Singapore, c. 1910 (Raffles Collection)*

Station hotels were, of course, only one small aspect of the growth of accommodation facilities which accompanied increases in the numbers of Europeans in the East, either as residents or tourists. Some of the region's 'grand' hotels were built as early as the 1860s (Hoyt, 1991: pp. 60–62; Stockwell, 1993: pp. 267–268), though they were less grand then than present-day nostalgia marketing has made them seem. The good fortune of some is to have endured for a century or more. Partly because of its longevity, the much transformed *Raffles* has come to stand for all the hotels of old Singapore (Figure 2.6), if not, as Maugham is supposed to have said, 'for all the fables of the exotic East' (cited Flower, 1984: p. 162). In the 1920s, however, it contended for popularity with at least two others; the *Van Wijk* – 'a place for European women of easy virtue' – and the *Hotel de l'Europe*, the preferred choice of many overseas visitors and week-ending residents from Malaya's country stations (Allen, 1983: p. 52).

The proliferation of Europeans gave rise to two other distinctively colonial forms which could be said to have assisted the development of an early kind of domestic tourism. These were the 'Dak bungalow', or government rest house, and the hill station. The latter, occasionally referred to as 'sanatoria' because of their salubri-ous nature, were, 'specialised highland outposts of colonial settlement ... insular little worlds that symbolised European power and exclusiveness' (Aiken, 1994: p. vii). India was the place of origin of hill stations, where they functioned as annual refuges for the governing class who found condi-tions in India's cities far too debilitating in summer for the normal conduct of their duties. But the refuges quickly took on the qualities of resorts: 'specialised social places the Europeans frequented for fun and relaxation ... or for mere dalliance' (Aiken, 1994: p. 2). Simla, the summer capital of British India, was the quintessential hill station, in both historical significance and social reputation (Kipling, 1987; Kanwar, 1990), but there were others in the sub-continent and also in Ceylon, Malaya, Burma, the Dutch East Indies, French Indo-China and the Philippines. There was none in Thailand or in the Unfederated (Eastern) Malay States; these places were never brought directly under European control (Aiken, 1994: p. 1).

The rest house also had an official purpose, initially being intended, in the absence of other lodgings, to accommodate the touring colonial administrator in the course of his supervisory duties in the remoter districts. Rest houses were especially prolific in the British colonies; in 1923 Harrison listed forty-six in the four Federated Malay States alone (Harrison, 1985: pp. 229–230). Again, the tradition had begun in India, although the increasing expectations of travellers on non-official business made it appropriate to remind tourists that the 'first comer has the right to accommodation and no room can be retained beforehand. After 24 hours the traveller must make way for others if necessary' (Anonymous, 1904: p. 8). Like the hill stations, the rest houses outlived their original function: years after the arrival of political independence many became low cost 'tourist lodges'.

Both the expansion of the road network and the sealing of roads developed rapidly after the introduction of motor vehicles. In Malaya, with 4000 miles of roads ('mostly of bitumen') by the late 1920s, the popularity of cars led to a journal devoted to the needs of the touring motorist and hostile to 'that modern mechanical abortion, the tram' (Automobile Association of Malaya, 1933, 1: p. 1). Cook's *Traveller's Gazette* thought that the 'roads compare favourably with those of England itself' (Cook, August 1932: p. 17).

Figure 2.7   *The Simla rickshaw: the hills made additional pullers necessary (from Kanwar, 1990)*

American influence in the Philippines ensured that Manila was thronged with vehicles of most kinds, including streetcars. But to many people, especially tourists and the manufacturers of postcards, the most 'Asian' of all forms of human transport was the (jin)rickshaw, an invention actually attributed to an American missionary in Japan in the mid-1800s. Within a couple of decades it had spread all over east Asia even as far as India's hill stations (Figure 2.7) (Yule and Burnell, 1990: p. 459), where topography necessitated the services of three or four pullers per vehicle. With the rapid proliferation of other forms of transport in urban areas, however, the long-term future of rickshaws was considered limited. In Siam one observer described them in the 1920s as a 'glorified form of bath chair ... They are now decreasing, and are likely to go on doing so, for they are a menace to other traffic', among which were 'numerous privately owned motor cars, motor cycles and push bikes ... Almost every road has its electric and motor omnibus running' (Forty, 1929: pp. 25–26). The observation would have provided an apt summary of traffic conditions in most large Asian cities. Rickshaws survived where they did for various reasons. In Calcutta mainly out of the desperate need of the rickshaw pullers, and in Vietnam, Indonesia and parts of the Malay peninsula – in their more sophisticated manifestation as bicycle-powered *cyclo*, *becak* or *trishaw* – mainly because of their economy and versatility. Only in Singapore was their survival – indeed, eventual renaissance – a result almost wholly of tourist demand. Aircraft, beginning to appear regularly in the East from the late 1920s, had a negligible impact on recreational travel until well after the Second World War.

sula had been timed to coincide with its invasion of Pearl Harbor, Hawai'i on 7 December 1941. By early the following year the whole of mainland and island Southeast Asia was under Japanese control. Burma, the eastern gateway to India, had been one of the earliest to fall. Ceylon was threatened and India's erstwhile capital, Calcutta, an industrial and transport base of major significance, was bombed by Japanese aircraft in raids originating in Rangoon (now called Yangon).

But neither India nor Ceylon were occupied. Understandably, leisure travellers from Europe no longer came, but residents, both British and indigenous, continued to travel recreationally within both countries even during the war years – quite unlike most other parts of Asia. Reprimanding railway posters with slogans borrowed whole from war-time Britain ('Is your journey really necessary?') ensured that travellers understood the seriousness of the situation and perhaps felt appropriately guilty about using the well-established transport system for their own amusements. Hill stations maintained their resort qualities and appeal, despite the presence in some of numbers of Commonwealth and US troops. Indeed, this feature almost certainly enhanced their desirability for many of India's European and part-European women. The Anglo-Indian female population of Darjeeling is said to have risen considerably between 1942 and 1945, becoming an extended version of the Simla 'season' of earlier times, an event which has been described as an 'annual tribal migration' (Laski, 1987: p. 27). In the larger cities and towns some of the diversions, including dances organized for allied troops by such groups as the Women's Volunteer Service, had more than a little of the festive about them. In more formal imperial precincts garden parties continued (Barr, 1989: p. 151).

The impact of the Second World War

The rapidity of the Japanese occupation of Southeast Asia stunned European colonial powers. Japan's move down the Malay penin-

The new Asia and the new tourism

Occupied or not, the countries of South and Southeast Asia were radically transformed by the war. In the heady and frequently violent atmosphere which accompanied post-war decolonization movements there was very little time to think about recreational pursuits. Advances in transport and communication technology that had been encouraged by the needs of war – the development of faster and larger aircraft, for example – were turned to purposes far more urgent than leisure travel. The independent nations that emerged over several decades gave little immediate consideration to the benefits to be derived from tourism, having more pressing needs in a number of other sectors. It would be the 1970s before tourism was thought about seriously in many parts of the region, and later still in others.

The changed political conditions affected those organizations which had previously prospered from the strong European interest and presence in the East. Without their considerable number of regular passengers to and from the colonies, shipping companies were forced to withdraw or cut down their services considerably. In many cases their fleets had been much reduced by the war: P&O lost eight of its twenty-one passenger vessels; many of the group's subsidiary companies lost far more (Howarth and Howarth, 1994: p. 151). The costs of shipbuilding or maintenance had risen and mail services were increasingly provided by airlines. The airlines would be the victors in the contest with other forms of passenger transportation. Ocean voyaging, once the staple in international travel, was reduced to the status of an occasional diversion. The wide-bodied jet and the resort-based holiday brought about a revolution in tourism, with which cruise ships could cope eventually only by becoming more like resorts themselves. For all the rhetoric of colonial governments and European writers and artists, the East had never been so successfully 'possessed' as it was to be by the package tour wholesalers.

As domestic and regional tourists in the countries of the East begin to considerably outnumber those from the West, it is increasingly evident that tourism is no longer solely the preserve of Western middle and upper classes, but has become an exercise for any with discretionary income and susceptibility to promotional hyberbole. The issue of whether this behaviour is simply imitative or whether it represents the first stages of a developing Asian form of tourism must go unexplored here. The question of how 'the Other' regards itself has been raised recently by Professor Wang Gungwu of Singapore's National University (Wang Gungwu, 1998: p. 38). It is a question with intriguing implications for the future of tourism in the East.

Yet the mystique of the East, once an imperial conceit, remains as a tourism marketing tool: the streets in Singapore's southeastern quarter 'carry jewelled names from the Arabian nights – Baghdad, Muscat, Kandahar', proclaims the Singapore Tourist Promotion Board (STPB, 1987: p. 25). The fantasy is accepted, it appears, as readily by visitors from within the region as from without, since the same promotional material is used. Nostalgia for and evocation of earlier days of travel has become a literary sub-genre, as writers journey *In Search of [Joseph] Conrad* (Young, 1991) or in *The Quest for Alfred [Russell] Wallace* (Severin, 1997). A remarkable number of works of early travel have been reissued, with all their imperial prejudices intact, and some with admiring introductions written by Asian scholars. 'She reminds us what travelling ought to be like' writes one of Isabella Bird (Bird, 1992: p. ix). If the activity of being a tourist has been assimilated by the East, in the thinking of tourism the East remains a construct of the West, perhaps the final lingering expression of 'Europe's collective day-dream'.

References

Anonymous, *The Imperial Guide to India: Including Kashmir, Burma and Ceylon*, John Murray, London, 1904.

Aiken S.R., *Imperial Belvederes: The Hill Stations of Malaya*, Oxford University Press, Singapore, 1994.

Allen, C. (ed.), *Plain Tales of the Raj*, Andre Deutsch/BBC, London, 1978.

Allen, C. (ed.), *Tales From the South China Seas*, Andre Deutsch/BBC, London, 1983.

Automobile Association of Malaya, *The Malayan Motorist*, Malayan Motorist Publishing Co., Kuala Lumpur, 1, 1933, p.1.

Barr, P., *A Curious Life for a Lady: The Story of Isabella Bird*, Macmillan and John Murray, London, 1970.

Barr, P., *Taming the Jungle: The Men who made British Malaya*, Readers Union, London, 1978.

Barr, P., *The Dust in the Balance: British Women in India 1905–1945*, Hamish Hamilton, London, 1989.

Bird, I., *The Golden Chersonese: The Malayan Travels of a Victorian Lady*, Oxford University Press, Singapore, 1992, 1st edn 1883.

Beccari, O., *Wanderings in the Great Forests of Borneo*, Oxford University Press, Singapore, 1989, 1st edn 1904.

Bock, C., *Temples and Elephants*, Oxford University Press, Singapore, 1986, 1st edn 1884.

Buzard, J., *The Beaten Track: European Tourism, Literature and the Ways to 'Culture', 1800–1918*, Clarendon Press, Oxford, 1993.

Cook, Thomas & Son *The Malayan Traveller's Gazette*, Thomas Cook & Son, Singapore, 1923–1932.

Cook, Thomas & Son *The Time Travel Gazette*, Thomas Cook, London, n.d., c. 1995–1996.

Cribb, R., 'International tourism in Java', *South East Asia Research* 3: 2 September 1995, pp. 193–204.

Douglas, N.I. and Douglas N.M., 'Towards a history of tourism in Sarawak', *Asia Pacific Journal of Tourism Research*, **3**(2), 14–23, 1999.

Falconer, J., *A Vision of the Past: The History of Early Photography in Singapore and Malaya*, Times Editions, Singapore, 1987.

Flower, R., *Raffles: The Story of Singapore*, Croom Helm, Singapore, 1984.

Forbes, A., *Unbeaten Tracks in Islands of the Far East*, Oxford University Press, Singapore, 1987, 1st edn 1887.

Forty, C.H., *Bangkok: Its Life and Sport*, H.F. and G. Witherby, London, 1929.

Gorer, G., *Bali and Angkor: A 1930s Pleasure Trip Looking at Life and Death*, Oxford University Press, Singapore, 1988, 1st edn 1936.

Gullick, J., *Old Kuala Lumpur*, Oxford University Press, Singapore, 1994.

Hammerton, J. (ed.), *Mr Punch on his Travels*, The Educational Book Company, London, 1935.

Harrison, C.W. *An Illustrated Guide to the Federated Malay States*, Oxford University Press, Singapore, 1985, 1st edn 1923.

Hornaday, W., *The Experiences of a Hunter and Naturalist in the Malay Peninsula and Borneo*, Oxford University Press, Singapore, 1993, 1st edn 1885.

Howarth, D. and Howarth, S., *The Story of P&O*, Weidenfeld and Nicholson, London, 1994.

Hoyt, S.H., *Old Penang*, Oxford University Press, Singapore, 1991.

Hutcheon, R., *Souvenirs of Auguste Borget*, New Straits Times, Hong Kong, 1979.

Kanwar, P., *Imperial Simla: The Political Culture of the Raj*, Oxford University Press, Delhi, 1990.

Kipling, R. (ed. Rutherford, A.), *Plain Tales from the Hills*, Oxford University Press, Oxford and New York, 1987, 1st edn 1888.

Laski, M., *From Palm to Pine: Rudyard Kipling Abroad and at Home*, Facts on File Publications, New York, 1987.

Latham, R. (ed.), *The Travels of Marco Polo*, Penguin Books, Harmondsworth, 1958.

Mouhot, H., *Travels in Siam, Cambodia and Laos, 1858–1860*, Oxford University Press, Singapore, 1992, 1st edn 1864.

Museum voor Volkenkunde, *Images of the Orient: Photography and Tourism, 1860–1900*, Fragment Uitgeverij, Amsterdam, 1986.

Ng, D. and Tate, D.J., *Malaya Lifestyles 1900–1930*, Penerbit Fajar Bakti, Petaling Jaya, 1989.

Pfeiffer, I., *A Lady's Voyage Round the World*, Century Hutchinson, London, 1988, 1st edn 1851.

Powell, H., *The Last Paradise: An American's Discovery of Bali in the 1920s*, Oxford University Press, Singapore, 1986, 1st edn 1930.

Pratt, M., *Imperial Eyes: Travel Writing and Transculturation*, Routledge, London and New York, 1992.

Ryan, J.R., *Picturing Empire: Photography and the Visualization of the British Empire*, Reaktion Books, London, 1997.

Said, E., *Orientalism*, Penguin Books, Harmondsworth, 1995.

San Michele Travel, *Great Tours of India*, San Michele Travel, Sydney, 1998.

Sarawak Tourism Board, *Sarawak: The Hidden Paradise of Borneo*, Sarawak Tourism Board, Kuching, 1998.

Saunders, G., 'Early travellers in Borneo', in M. Hitchcock, V. King. and M. Parnwell (eds), *Tourism in*

Southeast Asia, Routledge, London, 1993, pp. 271–285.

Scidmore, E., *Java: The Garden of the East*, Century, New York, 1907, 1st edn 1899.

Seindenfaden, E., *Guide to Bangkok: With Notes on Siam*, Royal State Railways of Siam, Bangkok, 1932.

Severin, T., *The Spice Islands Voyage: The Quest for Alfred Wallace*, Little Brown and Company, London, 1997.

Singapore Tourist Promotion Board, *Singapore Official Guide*, Tourist Promotion Board, Singapore, 1987.

Stockwell, A., 'Early tourism in Malaya', in M. Hitchcock, V. King and M. Parnwell (eds), *Tourism in Southeast Asia*, Routledge, London, 1993, pp. 234–257.

Theroux, P., *The Great Railway Bazaar: By Train through Asia*, Imperial Book, Sound & Gift Co., Taipei, 1975.

Theroux, P., *Sunrise with Seamonsters*, Penguin Books, Harmondsworth, 1986.

Tindall, G., *City of Gold: The Biography of Bombay*, Penguin Books, Harmondsworth, 1992.

Twain, M., *Following the Equator*, AMS Press, New York, 1971, 1st edn 1897.

Vickers, A., *Bali: A Paradise Created*, Penguin Books, Ringwood, 1989.

Wallace, A.R., *The Malay Archipelago*, Graham Brash Pte. Ltd., Singapore, 1987, 1st edn 1869.

Wang Gungwu, '"Other" is a view of where you are', *The Australian* 29 July 1998, p. 38.

Young, G., *In Search of Conrad*, Hutchinson, London, 1991.

Yule, H. and Burnell, A.C., *Hobson–Jobson: A Glossary of Colloquial Anglo-Indian Words and Phrases*, Rupa & Co., Calcutta, 1990, 1st edn 1886.

3

Rethinking and reconceptualizing social and cultural issues in Southeast and South Asian tourism development

Trevor H.B. Sofield

Introduction

The rapid growth of tourism in Asia in recent years has generated concern about the socio-cultural, economic and environmental impacts on Asian societies and communities. Until recently, most commentary was from a Western orientation assuming tourism as Caucasian with impacts perceived through Western values. In some Asian destinations, such as Thailand, Malaysia and China, their Asian visitors greatly outnumber Caucasian visitors and domestic tourists greatly outnumber international visitors. In short, tourists are not homogenous yet many analyses are based on Western perceptions of Western tourists impacting upon Asian societies and purport to cover the entire canvass of tourism in Asia, when in fact they will provide only a partial and segmented assessment.

There is a similar misconception about host communities. They tend not to be passive unitary receptacles of tourism; they also are highly differentiated and often pro-active in adapting to different categories of tourists. What once may have been interpreted as adverse impacts caused by the secularism of modern Western values introduced by (Caucasian) tourists may have a multi-faceted basis. The result is a need to re-conceptualize socio-cultural change arising from tourism and to re-examine many of the prevailing stereotypes about tourism's impacts.

It is also imperative to examine tourism in the context of ethnicity, definitions of culture, and the state. There is a natural affinity between tourism and the nation-state in the sense that both have a profound interest in presenting the place as differentiated and unique, with boundaries around both geographical and socio-cultural space (Leong, 1989; Sofield and Li, 1998a). This is particularly true of multi-ethnic states and newly independent states which, in the post-colonial period, may face the problem of trying to create a sense of, and commitment to, national unity where previously such a sentiment did not exist. Ethnicity has become 'more than a neutral social scientific term: it has become part of the way people factually and prescriptively see themselves and others ... historically constructed and re-constructed' (Wood, 1997: p. 7). International tourism plays a major role in this discourse and nation states will utilize the opportunities provided by ethnic tourism to objectify symbols and markers to meet political and policy objectives (see Wood, 1997, for a fuller sociological discussion of symbols and markers in contemporary tourism analysis). This chapter explores some of the implications of tourism development and its socio-cultural impacts in Asian countries. Comments are framed against an outline of the four so-called 'platforms' of writings on tourism in order to provide some insight into the positions adopted by different researchers.

Tourism research

As Jafari (1990: p. 33) noted, 'There is no consensus on what tourism is and what it can do. Where once there were widely accepted notions that travel is broadening, that tourism is educational – as Mark Twain wrote: "Travel is fatal to prejudice, bigotry and narrow-mindedness" – today, tourism as the "largest peacetime movements of people in the history of mankind" (Greenwood, 1972: p. 81) can provoke passionate disagreement about its value, benefits and impacts. It now means different things to different people.' To put the development and growth of tourism in Asia into some perspective it is instructive to re-visit the four 'platforms' or orientation of tourism writings, research and commentary which have developed in the past decades (Jafari, 1990). While there is an evolutionary characteristic to

these four platforms, succeeding platforms have not replaced their predecessor/s and all continue to co-exist.

The first, the *advocacy platform*, was originally occupied by those attracted to the economic prospects of tourism, which in the 1960s was proposed as the panacea to the problems of the Third World (now termed less developed world) such as underdevelopment (e.g. International Bank for Reconstruction and Development, 1966). It was advocated for all developing countries but particularly those which were deficient in natural resources, such as small island countries. Tourism's importance to the economy rested in its capacity to be:

- a generator of foreign exchange;
- a generator of development;
- a generator of employment (because it is labour intensive);
- a generator of supporting services and industries with backward linkages into other sectors such as agriculture and light industry (e.g. furniture) to supply its needs;
- a generator of infrastructure for the economy as a whole (e.g. roads, airports, harbours and power stations); and as
- an active contributor to decentralization (Jafari, 1990).

Such arguments remain but the advocacy platform has been bolstered in the past decade by an increasing number of issues related to non-economic areas. These include arguing the case for tourism in terms of:

- conserving and preserving the natural environment;
- conserving man-made environments (heritage);
- conserving/reviving past traditions;
- promoting cultural heritage, cultural performances and festivals, etc.;
- constituting a relatively benign form of development compared with alternatives such as industrialization (the so-called 'smokeless industry');

- playing an educational role, both specifically (e.g. special interest tourism and archaeological tours) and in general; and
- promoting international understanding and peace.

The *cautionary platform* arose in response to the often uncritical assumptions and self-serving industry voices of the advocates of tourism and the fact that in some countries (e.g. the Caribbean) tourism did not provide instant answers to development. This platform constituted a 'natural' home for concerned social scientists and a few economists who were more rigorous in their examination of the potential benefits of tourism than earlier enthusiasts. For any claim of the advocacy platform there have been counterclaims by the cautionary platform – with a fruitful dialogue between proponents 'the exception rather than the norm' (Jafari, 1990: p. 34). Cautionary writers are critical of the impacts of tourism and their views could be summarized as follows:

- the economic benefits of tourism are overstated. Often overlooked or under-estimated is the leakage factor (i.e. the need to import many items for the tourism industry so that much of the foreign exchange earned must then be expended on foreign goods and services: also repatriation of profits where overseas interests are involved);
- tourism is often seasonal and generates mostly part-time, unskilled jobs for local people, with specialist and management positions occupied by expatriates;
- by far the greater benefits flow to developers and investors (often multi-national companies, hotel chains and international airlines) rather then to local communities;
- they (local communities) are often exploited and their resources taken over by outside interests for tourism;
- tourism destroys natural environments, e.g. through large-scale resorts, golf courses and marinas, and is a major polluter through sewage and other waste discharge;

- tourism destroys/degrades tradition;
- it commoditizes people and culture;
- it produces 'de-agriculturization' (younger people leaving rural farms for paid employment in the tourism industry); and
- tourism disrupts the structure of host societies.

Since the polarized arguments of the advocacy and cautionary platforms have been concerned mainly with the perceived impacts of tourism, a third platform gradually developed in which alternative forms of tourism were suggested. The *adaptancy platform* favoured new forms of tourism responsive to host communities and their natural environments, socio-cultural environments and man-made (heritage) environments (Jafari, 1990: p. 35). Adapted tourism should be community-centred, employ locals, utilize local resources, be relatively easy to manage, be not destructive and benefit host and guest alike. It is characterized as 'sensitive' tourism, is set in opposition to mass tourism and has been given numerous labels such as alternative tourism, green tourism, ecotourism, soft tourism, appropriate tourism, people-to-people tourism and so on. A major international organization has been created to advocate adaptive tourism, the Ecumenical Coalition on Third World Tourism, which is based in Bangkok. However, as Butler (1992) noted, alternative tourism strategies have not been fully developed and economically they can never replace mass tourism. Increasing numbers are attracted to the promise of more rewarding experiential travel which alternative tourism offers but they remain a small fraction of the total. Furthermore, operators involved in mass tourism have appropriated many of the strategies and incorporated them into their present structures so that definitions based on differentiation have become increasingly difficult to sustain. Since the first three platforms represented only partial treatment of tourism, Jafari (1990) argues that the fourth, the *knowledge-based platform*, emerged to counter the general focus of the advocacy and cautionary platforms on impacts of tourism; and the focus of the adaptancy platform on forms of development.

Increasingly, a number of observers of tourism considered that by studying tourism as a whole its underlying functions and structures could be understood and the resulting knowledge would foster the development of a body of theoretical constructs (Jafari, 1990: p. 36). Where much of the work from the other three platforms is subjective, the knowledge-based platform positions itself on a scientific foundation. It is research-based, multi-disciplinary, aimed at objective analysis, designed to maintain bridges with appropriate paradigms and knowledge from the other three platforms, but is more holistic in its treatment of tourism.

Socio-cultural impacts: the emic versus the etic approach

When one examines commonly held perceptions about the impacts of tourism, especially those which are adverse, one finds that much of it is not knowledge-based but located in the 'cautionary platform'. Rhetoric often outweighs research. An example of this approach can be discerned from contents of *Contours*, the journal of the Ecumenical Coalition on Third World Tourism. Now in its eighth year it is a widely read and quoted source about the evils of tourism. Newspaper journalism is a common source of its reporting. In a recent issue, for example, under a heading 'Destroying heritage sites' it asserted that Nepal's temple towns, which are 'architectural and cultural marvels that today attract hundreds of thousands of tourists every year', are under threat (*Contours*, 1996, 7, 7, p. 37). The impression is given that tourism is the responsible agent. However, the article itself notes that 'graceful mud and brick homes with intricately carved wooden doors and windows are giving way to ugly concrete high-rises to accommodate Kathmandu's 1.2 million population which is growing at the astonishing rate of 5.7 percent per year'

(*Contours*, 1996, 7, 7, p.37). There is an acknowledgement that the people themselves want concrete homes and a government official is also quoted as saying that it is much more expensive to build and conserve traditional structures. It is the combination of population pressure, rapid urbanization and increased building costs, not tourism, which is the cause of change. However, there is certainly a role for a platform which advocates a non-official view of tourism and which stimulates debate on tourism issues even if it poses an anti-thesis which then has to be rejected by more systematic research.

Tourism planners in fact are at the forefront in trying to conserve sites and buildings with heritage values and the government has successfully obtained International Union for the Conservation of Nature and Natural Resources (IUCN) accreditation for seven World Heritage Sites in Kathmandu and an eighth site, Lumbini, the birthplace of Buddha, in the south of the country. Further, the United Nations Development Programme has provided more than US$1.5 million for its Nepal Partnership for Quality Tourism Project (1994–1998) which has resurrected two heritage sites amongst other projects (Banskota *et al.*, 1995; Sofield, 1998). Private tourism entrepreneurs are also participating in the effort to preserve Nepal's architectural heritage, such as the owners of Dwarika's Hotel who have spent thirty years collecting the hand carved windows and doors from demolished buildings and have recently completed a new sixty-bed hotel in Kathmandu, incorporating them. The entire hotel is designed around traditional features utilizing original materials (Sofield, 1998).

The projection of outside values onto analysis of a particular situation (termed 'imposed etic' by Berry (1990)) may also result in less than profound understanding. Thus, the use of *becaks* (tricycles) for taking tourists around the sights of Yogyakarta and Surakarta in Central Java has been put forward as evidence of the way in which tourism demeans locals and turns them into 'beasts of burden' for pleasure-seeking tourists. But this is an etic approach which fails to be 'processural, contextual, comparative and emic' (Cohen, 1979: p. 31). Note the comments on *becak* use by R.B. Soemanto from the Engineering Department of the Universitas Sebelas Maret, Surakarta, in a survey of the 5844 registered *becaks* in Surakarta Municipality:

> Becaks *are considered important in preserving cheap local transportation services. Their continued functioning is needed by the whole social strata of the community since all social levels at some time draw on their services. While tourists use the* becaks *for 'generalised sight-seeing', residents use the* becaks *for specific functional purposes. They are used (by them) to transport residents to friends and relatives, to take children to and from school safely, and so forth ... [Tourist use is] very small by comparison (with local use) ... but highly valued because the* becak *drivers received higher charges from foreign tourists than from their local passengers. The drivers considered it an opportunity to get more income* (Soemanto, 1995: p. 35).

In short, *becaks* were not 'invented' for tourism, were in local use before the advent of tourism; tourism is only a small part of their use and tourist use is viewed positively by the drivers themselves. The status of *becak* drivers is not high in Javanese society but that is as a result of Javanese society, not tourism. The emic approach provides a more positive perspective which may be regarded as perhaps more valid than comments based on 'foreign' Western values (Berno, 1996).

This is not to deny that tourism may not be destructive but rather that the factors to take into account in examining and attempting to evaluate the socio-cultural effects of tourism are numerous. Increasingly, tourism research has focused on the need to undertake much more detailed empirical case studies to elucidate the particular because the social class, ethnic group or community which is being studied will reveal different aspects about the nature of host–visitor relations. Generalizations must be approached cautiously. It is a well-established principle that

people from different socio-economic strata and different gender are impacted differently by tourism, are exploited by it or are able to take advantage of it according to their circumstances. 'Within a single community a range of different impacts or responses may be recorded' (Hitchcock *et al.*, 1993: p. 7).

For example, a recent field study of two mountain communities in Nepal by Sofield (1998) revealed that tourism development was in fact an inadvertent vehicle contributing to increasing class differentiation in village societies. Lodge owners, already having comparatively higher living standards than farming households, were drawn further apart as the recipients of government and donor agency assistance under tourism development projects. Even when projects were integrated into community development with specific action to strengthen backward linkages into the local economy, provide village water supplies and each household with toilets, the weight of the benefits accruing to the community fell to the lodge owners. In terms of returns for investment of time and labour and where the bulk of grants were spent, the lodge owners were perceived to be the major recipients of direct monetary and infrastructural benefits, with some villagers missing out completely on both accounts. For example, while all villagers would benefit from improved sanitation, the only ones for whom this was turned into direct *monetary* gain were perceived to be the lodge owners who could charge trekkers an extra one dollar per day because of the new toilets. The result was strongly divided communities, and sustainability was at risk.

Reconceptualizing culture, tradition and authenticity in the context of tourism

Much of the research and debate on tourism development in Asian countries 'has focused on whether its effects are beneficial or negative and whether they are developmental or anti-devel-opmental' (Hitchcock *et al.*, 1993: p. 5). Increas-ingly, a number of analysts of tourism development are querying the simplistic asser-tions of those from Jafari's cautionary platform that tourism is destructive of culture. Such criti-cism is characterized by the 'billiard ball model' (Wood, 1993). In this model the cue constitutes the interests of tourism (big business, investors, government planners). These are the forces behind the white ball (tourism) which strikes a static (red) ball, culture. The red ball can only move in the direction dictated by the white ball at a pace determined by the white ball: it has no control over its own movement. A limitation of this approach is that it attributes passivity to the host community, thus denying that community the capacity to respond creatively to the presence of tourism within its social space. Such critics attempt to proscribe change away from tradition and assert the destruction of pre-exist-ing social structures and the degradation of cultural integrity and cultural pollution as due to the impact of the hedonistic, materialistic consumerism and demonstration effect of tourism. Under this rubric, as MacCannell (1994: p. 163) stated: 'anything and anyone that does not participate in "authentic" (behaviour or artistic expression) can be classed as a "victim" of development, abject and inauthentic'. Yet socio-cultural change is difficult to measure accurately and interpret objectively, and the use of terms such as cultural 'degradation', cultural 'corruption', loss of tradition and ethnicity, may defy rational measurement. Picard and Wood (1997: p. x) suggest that 'it no longer makes sense to conceive of tourism as a force external to contemporary societies, impacting them from the outside. What needs to be studied is how tourism has become institutionalised in different states and societies and how tourism alters incentives and opportunities for local actors in ways that unleash new and unique processes of change'.

When culture is conceived of as static entity, lacking the dynamics of change, the actions, motivations and values of local community members are ignored. To respond to the tourist desire for souvenirs and exotic experiences, emphasis is placed on the production of 'authen-tic native handicrafts', 'traditional artefacts' and 'traditional time-honoured ceremonies': but this very emphasis often results in a stultifying of natural creativity (MacCannell, 1994: p. 161). And in any case, the criticism is made that because it is produced for the tourist it cannot be authentic, having lost its original purpose. Even that which faithfully reproduces the origi-nal is held to be not authentic: it is fake, it has lost its original significance and therefore demeans its makers because expressions of art-istic creativity have been commoditized and modernized. To be authentic the object of exami-nation for the tourist gaze had to take place with its traditional symbolism untainted by contem-porary values, its meaning embedded in the society's heritage. To incorporate elements of external influence was not interpreted as a sign of creativity (which, one hastens to add, is the norm in the world of Western art) but as evidence of 'neo-colonialism', of cultural degra-dation, of the artists demeaning their culture and being demeaned themselves in the process. Tourists often take part in this unconscious hegemony: they may describe a piece of Balinese or Makonde tribal art as being 'just like a Modigliani', thereby denying the fact that it was the Italian artist who drew his inspiration from the indigenous art forms of Indonesia and East Africa.

What such an etic approach overlooks is the fact that tourism cannot be isolated from many other aspects of culture, that in treating tourism as an exogenous force commentators run the risk of ignoring how tourism may become part of the local reality (Hitchcock *et al.*, 1993: p. 9). But as our understanding of the complexities of community responses to tourism develops, increasingly we find that many societies are in fact resilient and have exhibited a capacity to avert the dominance of the outside force; they have put tourism to work for them rather than working for tourism, and so have incorporated it into their social space.

A crucial factor to emerge from studies of tourism development in Asian countries is that to survive (be sustainable) a system must be adaptable, incorporating elements of both continuity and change (Harrison, 1996). Many social scientists (perhaps the best known of whom is Talcott Parsons) have considered adaptation as a defining feature of their concepts of social systems (Black, 1961). Adaptation may be described more or less objectively but when the impacts of adaptation to tourism are examined and said to be 'positive' or 'negative' the argument often becomes subjective, related 'more to ideology than logic' (Harrison, 1996: p. 76).

The studies also raise the question, particularly in considering socio-cultural factors related to sustainable development, of just what is to be sustained. An examination of the development processes at work in less developed countries has brought about a reconceptualization of such key concepts as 'culture' and 'authenticity'. They stress that each generation redefines its heritage in response to new understandings, new experiences and new inputs from an ever-increasing range of contacts from 'outside', especially in the context of globalization (Kymlicka, 1995). There is a 'new diversity (of cultural expression) based relatively more on interrelations and less on autonomy' (Hannerz, cited in Clifford, 1988: p. 17). Handler and Linnekin (1984) describe this as a shift from a 'naturalistic' to a 'symbolic' concept of tradition. The former assumes that tradition 'is an objective entity, a core of inherited culture traits whose continuity and boundedness are analogous to that of a natural object' but in reality there is an 'ongoing reconstruction of tradition in the present ... which is not natural but symbolically constituted' (Handler and Linnekin, 1984: p. 273). What is 'traditional' for one generation may be reshaped by later generations, and indeed different 'traditions' may coexist; change in all societies is part of an inevitable and evolutionary process. Who, then, is to decide which of the traditions is authentic and is to be 'saved'? Harrison (1996) warns against academics imposing their ideologically driven views on societies and communities under their scrutiny, and Berno (1996) notes that the 'imposed' etic approach often involves judgmental statements about what is 'right' and 'good' for others.

Adaptation to tourism

Sanger (1988, cited in Hitchcock *et al.*, 1993) provides an example of the interface between tourism and traditional culture with an emic analysis of changes to the *barong* dance dramas of the village of Singapadu in Bali. *Barong* performances have been adapted in a variety of ways to suit tourist needs. They have been shortened from more than three hours to about one hour. They include new sequences and slapstick moments which transcend linguistic boundaries to enhance enjoyment for tourists. Women have been introduced to play female roles which traditionally only men had played. Trance sequences with *kris* (daggers) and the eating of live chickens have been omitted because of tourist disapproval.

However, the villagers have not interpreted these changes in terms of cultural denigration (Sanger, 1988). First, they have maintained the traditional prayers and offerings at the beginning of each performance and continue to treat the *barong* with great respect. Second, the oldest and holiest *barong* costume is not used for commercial performances so it is not desecrated. Third, the villagers maintain that the *barong* likes to dance whatever the circumstances. Fourth, 'ownership' of the *barong* provides a resource which the villagers can utilize for much-needed cash income and, since the tourist revenue is distributed communally, the charge of individual greed is inaccurate. Finally, the *barong* reinforces community solidarity in much the same way as the *vilavilairevo* of Fiji and Sanger records that during the monsoons the villagers miss the opportunity it provides to come together during the tourist season. In this instance, commoditization of culture may be reversed and considered as a process of 'culturizing commercialism' (Pere, 1985: p. 139), since local traditions have not been supplanted by the imperatives of the tourist trade but have been modified in culturally acceptable ways. 'Original' traditions now exist with 'new' traditions in the same time and space and 'touristic culture is very much part of the reality' (Hitchcock *et al.*, 1993: p. 11).

Another example of the 'imposed etic' (Berry, 1990) may be found with reference to Bali, where numerous analyses have criticized tourism as a destructive agent of change (e.g. Hanna, 1972; Boon, 1977; Turnbull, 1982; Francillon, 1989). However, the research of Picard and MacKean *inter alia*, both working independently in Bali over a twenty-year period, demonstrates that by using a more actor-oriented (emic) approach the interrelationship between tourism change and culture change cannot be viewed as a 'one-way street'; the host communities adapt to and in turn modify the tourism which takes place within their social space. Picard has termed this 'touristic culture': through tourism, culture has been transformed into the main economic resource of Bali and by the same token Balinese culture has become a major bargaining point with the central Indonesian Government, tourism authorities and tourist operators (Picard, 1993: p. 86).

Picard has chronicled the way in which the Balinese elite responded to the imposition of a tourism development plan from Jakarta which was based on an 'outsider' view of their culture by defining and refining in a comprehensive way their 'Balinese-ness'. Over a period of eight years, from 1971 to 1979, they held a series of seminars under the joint auspices of the Directorate General of Culture and the Directorate General of Tourism which resulted in the formulation of the 'doctrine of cultural tourism' for Bali and the signing of an agreement between the two Directorates General. This established the Balinese Commission of Cooperation for the Promotion and Development of Cultural Tourism *(Komisi Kerjasama Pembinaan dan Pengembangan Wisata Budaya)* whose chief objectives were to:

i) increase and extend the use of culture for the development of tourism; and
ii) to use the proceeds of tourism development for the promotion and development of culture (Picard, 1993: p. 88).

As a manifestation of this new approach, the Balinese Regional Government launched the Bali Arts Festival in 1979 at the opening of a new Arts Centre in Denpasar. Since its inception this month-long festival has been regarded by the Balinese as evidence of the Island's cultural renaissance, yet 'it would be mistaken to consider this event as primarily a tourist attraction as over the years it has proved so popular with the Balinese that they make up nowadays the major part of its public' (Picard, 1993: p. 91). Many of the offerings at the annual Festival could not be termed traditional under the anthropological definition of something old, something performed in its traditional physical setting with its age-old values and purposes intact; but they are indisputably of Balinese origin, drawing upon the long continuous history of Balinese creative expression and, as such, they are authentically Balinese.

Since Balinese tourism relies upon Balinese culture, if tourism were to destroy Balinese culture it would destroy Balinese tourism. The result is that the Balinese, having been compelled to define their cultural heritage, in the process have put tourism to work for Bali rather than the Balinese working for tourism. The key difference in the analyses of Picard and McKean lies in their emic approach, as distinct from the etic approach of many others. This conclusion recalls Wilson's (1981: p. 477) insistence that tourism analyses will benefit by 'a thoroughly empirical research strategy which seeks hermeneutic understanding in terms of the knowledge possessed by the participants themselves – their definitions, goals, strategies, decisions, and the perceived consequences of their actions'. It includes their 'on-going symbolic construction of tradition and authenticity' (Wood, 1993: p. 60).

Ethnicity, culture and tourism

Tourism has played a major role in the 'imaging' and 're-creation' of 'national cultures' and ethnicity in many Asian countries (Graburn, 1997: p. 210). Cultural heritage may be claimed and its ownership utilized to bestow legitimacy on those with the power and authority to present it in a desired form to both insiders and outsiders. Nation-states in Asia have been active in devising tourism policies to support ideologically driven definitions and symbols of national identity and ethnicity. Richter (1989: p. 44) suggests that the Philippines under Marcos was 'the classic case of using tourism development politically' in an attempt to add legitimacy to his regime. Leong (1989) also undertook an incisive study of Singapore and the way in which the Government has channelled its many different ethnicities into four official CMIO 'races' (Chinese, Malays, Indians, Others) and then portrayed ('manufactured') artificial stereotypes for tourism, the underlying political objective being the need to maintain harmony between its ethnic divides, as emphasized in Chapter 1.

Indonesia is another case in point where, until the past two to three generations at most, its many peoples considered themselves not as Indonesians but as Sumatrans or Javanese, or as smaller units such as the Redjang of Sumatra. Many Irianese still today do not consider themselves as Indonesians. The Indonesian government has attempted to use tourism to present ethnic and cultural differences in benign, non-threatening forms to prevent communalism from getting out of hand (Kipp, 1993). *Taman Mini Indonesia* (Beautiful Indonesia in Miniature), a theme park constructed near Jakarta by the Indonesian government in 1975, is a manifestation of this policy. Each of the twenty-seven provinces has a representative architectural pavilion or similar, 'occupied' by different ethnic groups garbed in traditional dress. The park is aimed mainly at a domestic audience, and is promoted in Bahasa Indonesian tourism literature and school textbooks as the place to learn about all of Indonesia. Many more Indonesians than international tourists visit the park. It is ironic that Indonesia's largest ethnic minority, and the one which has been the focus of much communal violence and unrest, is not represented in *Taman Mini Indonesia*, its Chinese nationals.

China provides another example of the involvement of the state in determining ethnic identity and presenting 'acceptable' manifestations of minorities cultures for tourism. It officially recognises fifty-five 'minorities' who number about 100 million people, a total which is larger than the population of 75 per cent of the countries of the globe although is only one-twelfth of China's population (Mackerras *et al.*, 1994). Whilst their numbers are comparatively small, they occupy about 65 per cent of China's total area. Their territories include much of China's border areas so the minorities enjoy a strategic importance well beyond their numbers (Mackerras, 1994). Policy formulation towards the minorities is therefore bound up in foreign affairs, defence and national security, as well as economic development, education, health and social welfare. The state in China has used tourism as a powerful tool to assist in bringing the minorities into the mainstream by promoting and developing tourism activity based on their cultural heritage (Oakes, 1997; Sofield and Li, 1998a).

Tourism policies and development have played a key role in China in assisting the state to manage the tensions generated between the Chinese Government's determination to maintain political stability under the Chinese Communist Party (CCP) and attempts to find the appropriate mix of traditional Chinese culture, socialist culture and 'modern' culture (the latter necessarily incorporating Western values and systems). The interface between politically driven goals of power and government, the preservation of a nation's cultural heritage, sustainable environmental values and tourism development are problematic for many countries. In the People's Republic of China (PRC) these issues are fundamental not only to the place of tradition in a society which is modernizing its economy at a rapid rate, but they also present very real challenges to the legitimacy of the government. A primary cornerstone of the ideology propounded by the CCP since its inception in 1921 concerned the need to reject the cultural past as a whole and its replacement with a new Chinese socialist culture. Under this policy massive destruction of China's rich and varied built heritage occurred and there were sustained attacks on its cultural (living) heritage (Sofield and Li, 1998a). This totalistic iconoclasm, however, is at odds with the contemporary embrace of heritage as perhaps the major element of China's burgeoning tourism product. Owing to its ideological sensitivity, the approach to heritage in its many forms has tended to be carefully controlled by the State; and its use for tourism has often been driven by ideological tenets of politics – in this case, socialism as defined by the Chinese government. Yet in spite of the ambivalence and complexities which can be discerned in the attitude of the CCP to the past, tourism and its use of heritage continues to expand as the policies of the current leadership of China distance the CCP from its founding roots. It has used a vast and diverse array of symbols and markers, both for international tourism and domestic tourism, to pursue its objective of maintaining unity and claiming some aspects of its culture for all Chinese citizens, regardless of ethnicity.

Tourism utilizes symbolism in many different ways, e.g. iconography (famous sites, buildings, people or places) to represent an entire country. In terms of imaging, the Great Wall of China is one of the most universally recognized icons of national identity for any country in the world, certainly ranking with the pyramids of Egypt, the Parthenon of Athens, the Eiffel Tower of Paris and the Basilica of Rome. For many tourists those five words (the-Great-Wall-of-China) are a

synecdoche and encapsulate all that is Chinese, moving the symbol from the concrete (a wall built for military purposes) to the cultural history of that nation and its people. Globally the Wall, as one of the wonders of the world, symbolizes all humankind's heritage, the one man-made object visible, it is claimed (erroneously), from the moon and outer space. It is a compelling tourist symbol for visitation both by Chinese (akin to a pilgrimage) and by international tourists. Symbolically, it has elements of both the sacred and the secular (Sofield and Li, 1998b).

However, the Great Wall, like a traditional Chinese multi-tiered cake box filled with abundant offerings, has many layers and numerous images conveyed by different representations at different times by different actors with different histories. The varied interpretations of the same symbol is contextual, and symbols are an inherent part of the socialization process of a culture (Norbert, 1991). Tourism intervenes to take symbolism beyond the duality of signification and representation to a triadic relationship because of the insertion of a third factor – the interpretant presentation of sign and object. Each interpretation strives to present its own story, locked in combat for proclaiming the truth, so that the reality of the Wall is a veritable whirlwind of myth and legend, historical fact and fantasy, obscured, obfuscated, dependent upon political power or drawing its vision from metaphysical poetry. Throughout time visitors to the Wall have carried with them preconceived ideas and images and the sign of the Wall has meant different things to them. Images are put in place of reality, as presentations of reality. The Wall is Urry's (1990) tourist gaze magnified and multiplied. Like bees to honey it attracts MacCannell's army of semioticians searching for the essence of Chineseness. Yet the Great Wall is a recent construction, its current 'imaging' by the Chinese Government at odds with its actual history. It is a representation of more than 150 different walls, constructed at different times stretching back over 2200 years. The Great Wall which is the object of the tourist gaze of the twentieth century is of relatively recent origin, having been constructed less than 500 years ago, and stretching for perhaps only one-third of the mythical single Great Wall. Regardless of the historical record, however, in contemporary China, the Great Wall is an icon which constitutes a fusion of the authentic and the marker for both Chinese and international tourists. As Urry (citing Baudrillard) states: 'what we increasingly consume are signs or representations ... This world of sign and spectacle is one in which there is no originality, only what Eco terms "travels in hyper-reality"' (Urry, 1990: p. 85). However, Urry argues that sites which have been made into attractive spectacles are not necessarily inauthentic, but rather that there is no one simple 'authentic reconstruction of history'; instead there are various kinds of interpretation and reinterpretation with their own validity (Urry, 1990: p. 156). A visit to the Great Wall, in whatever form, is an example of Nuryanti's 'individual journey of self-discovery' coupled with, for the Chinese, a re-affirmation of the Chinese-ness of the participant observer.

Thailand represents an opposite case to China in the context of its ethnic minorities. Its hill tribes live in strategically sensitive border areas but, whereas the Chinese government has a deliberate policy of engaging its minorities in various forms of tourism, the growth in hill tribe tourism has developed outside official Thai government planning. The Thai government has attempted military intervention to assert its control in the past, although it now appears to accept that tourism could provide the means by which the hill tribe ethnic groups could be assimilated (Dearden and Harron, 1992). However, it still demonstrates little interest in sanctioning, preserving or promoting ethnic cultural diversity. As with the Great Wall, however, it has reconstructed its past (inaccurately) with the excavation and remaking of the ancient capital of Ayutthaya and (more accurately) Sukothai, originally for *farang* (foreign) tourists, but now making a significant contribution to the Thai perception of their own nation, identity and cultural history (Phillips, 1990).

Conclusion

There is a need for more research into tourism in Asia, undertaken from the knowledge-base platform with greater objectivity and incorporating local perspectives on leisure and travel and the place of tourism within the social space of receiving communities. The stereotype of the decadent Western tourist bringing cultural degradation and environmental pollution in his/her wake, as typified by much of the literature from the cautionary platform, is overly simplistic and the place and role of domestic tourism in development and change needs urgent attention. Tourism continues to have major effects on and implications for society and culture in Asian countries and the 'billiard ball model' with its deterministic uni-directional assertion about the impacts of tourism needs to be replaced with a more sophisticated model based on our new perceptions of culture, heritage, authenticity and tradition as processes rather then static objects. Resilience and adaptation with concurrent benefits to host communities may be more prevalent than negative reactions to tourism; but the current state of research does not allow definitive conclusions to be drawn about how the relationship between host and guest, resident and tourist, is translated into particular behavioural patterns and forms of social interaction and how, or indeed if, these encounters change tourist and resident images, views and prejudices. Tourism to Asian countries will continue to grow but there is a major mismatch between the resources devoted to this sector in comparison with most other sectors, despite the fact that in many Asian countries it is in the 'top three' in terms of generation of foreign exchange, creation of employment and the multiplier effect. As arguably the world's largest industry it requires much more multi-disciplinary effort and research if its effects in Asian countries are to be understood, adverse impacts minimized and positive outcomes enhanced.

References

Banskota, K., Sharma, B., Neupane, I. and Gyawali, P., *A Rapid Assessment of the Quality Tourism Project*, CREST, Kathmandu, 1995.

Berno, T., 'Cross-cultural research methods: content or context? A Cook Islands example', in R. Butler, and T. Hinch (eds), *Tourism and Indigenous Peoples*, International Thomson Business Publishing, London, 1996, pp. 376–395.

Berry, J., 'Psychology of acculturation: understanding individuals moving between cultures', in R. Brislin (ed.), *Applied Cross Cultural Psychology*, Sage, Newbury Park, CA, 1990, pp. 232–253.

Black, M. (ed.), *The Social Theories of Talcott Parsons: A Critical Examination*, Prentice-Hall, Engelwood Cliffs, NJ, 1961.

Boon, J., *The Anthropological Romance of Bali, 1597–1972*, Cambridge University Press, Cambridge, 1977.

Butler, R., 'Alternative tourism: the thin edge of the wedge', in V.L. Smith and W.R. Eadington (eds), *Tourism Alternatives: Potentials and Problems in the Development of Tourism*, University of Pennsylvania Press, Philadelphia, PA, 1992.

Clifford, J., *The Predicament of Culture: Twentieth Century Ethnography, Literature and Art*, Harvard University Press, Cambridge, MA, 1988.

Cohen, E., 'Rethinking the sociology of tourism', *Annals of Tourism Research* 6(1), 1979, pp. 18–35.

Contours, 7, 7, 1996. Ecumenical Coalition on Third World Tourism, Bangkok.

Dearden, P. and Harron, S., 'Tourism and the hilltribes of Thailand', in B. Weiler and C.M. Hall (eds), *Special Interest Tourism*, Belhaven Press, London, 1992, pp. 95–104.

Francillon, G., 'The dilemma of tourism in Bali', in W. Beller, P. d'Ayala and P. Hein (eds), *Sustainable Development and Environmental Management of Small Islands*, UNESCO, Paris, 1989, pp. 267–272.

Graburn, N.H.H., 'Tourism and cultural development in East Asia', in S. Yamashita, K. Din and J.S. Eades (eds), *Tourism and Cultural Development in Asia and Oceania*, Penerbit Universiti Kebangsaan Malaysia, Selangor, 1997, pp. 194–213.

Greenwood, D., 'Tourism as an agent of change: a Spanish Basque case', *Ethnology* 11, 1972, pp. 80–91.

Handler, R. and Linnekin, J., 'Tradition, genuine or spurious?', *Journal of American Folklore* 97(385), 1984, pp. 273–290.

Hanna, W.A., *Bali in the Seventies: Cultural Tourism*, American Universities Field Staff, New York, 1972.

Harrison, D., 'Sustainability and tourism: reflections from a muddy pool', in L. Briguglio, B. Archer, J. Jafari and G. Wall (eds), *Sustainable Tourism in Islands and Small States: Issues and Policies*, Pinter, London, 1996, pp. 69–89.

Hitchcock, M., King, V. and Parnwell, M. (eds), *Tourism in South-East Asia*, Routledge, London, 1993.

International Bank for Reconstruction and Development, *Bali Tourism Project: Appraisal Report*, IBRD, Washington, DC, 1966.

Jafari, J., 'Research and scholarship: the basis of tourism education', *Journal of Tourism Studies* 1(1), 1990, pp. 33–41.

Kipp, R., *Disassociated Identities: Ethnicity, Religion and Class in an Indonesian Society*, University of Michigan Press, Ann Arbor, MI, 1993.

Kymlicka, W., *The Rights of Minority Cultures*, Oxford University Press, Oxford, 1995.

Leong, W., 'Culture and the state: manufacturing traditions for tourism', *Critical Studies in Mass Communication* 6, 1989, pp. 355–375.

MacCannell, D., 'Tradition's next step', in: S. Norris (ed.), *Discovered Country. Tourism and Survival in the American West*, Stone Ladder Press, Albuquerque, 1994.

Mackerras, C., *China's Minorities. Integration and Modernization in the Twentieth Century*, Oxford University Press, Hong Kong, 1994.

Mackerras, C., Taneja, P. and Young, G., *China Since 1978. Reform, Modernization and Socialism with Chinese Characteristics*, Longman Cheshire, New York, 1994.

McKean, P., 'Tourists and Balinese', *Cultural Survival Quarterly* 6(3), 1982, pp. 32–33.

Norbert, E., *The Symbol Theory*, Sage Publications, London, 1991.

Nuryanti, W., 'Heritage and post modern tourism', *Annals of Tourism Research* 23, 1996, pp. 249–260.

Oakes, T., 'Ethnic tourism in rural Guizhou: sense of place and the commerce of Authenticity', in M. Picard and R. Wood (eds), *Tourism, Ethnicity and the State in Asian and Pacific Societies*, University of Hawai'i Press, Honolulu, 1997, pp. 35–70.

Pere, B., 'Commercialising culture or culturising commerce?', in Institute of Pacific Studies, *Pacific Tourism as Islanders See It*, University of the South Pacific, Suva, 1985, pp. 139–145.

Phillips, H., *The Integrative Art of Modern Thailand*, Lowrie, Berkley, CA, 1990.

Picard, M., 'Cultural tourism in Bali: national integration and regional differentiation', in M. Hitchcock, V. King and M. Parnwell (eds), *Tourism in South-East Asia*, Routledge, London, 1993, pp. 71–98.

Picard, M. and Wood, R. (eds), *Tourism, Ethnicity, and the State in Asian and Pacific Societies*, University of Hawai'i Press, Honolulu, 1997.

Richter, L., *The Politics of Tourism in Asia*, University of Hawai'i Press, Honolulu, 1989.

Sanger, A., 'Blessing or blight? The effects of touristic dance drama on village life in Singapadu, Bali', in *The Impact of Tourism on Traditional Music*, Jamaica Memory Bank, Kingston, 1988.

Soemanto, R., 'Low cost transportation and tourism. A profile of the Becak's role in tourism development in Surakarta, Central Java', in T. Sofield and M. Sri Samiati Tarjana (eds), *A Profile of Javanese Culture. Its Significance and Potential for Tourism Development*, James Cook University, Townsville, 1995, pp. 33–36.

Sofield, T., *An Independent Evaluation of Nepal's Partnership for Quality Tourism Project*, UNDP, Kathmandu, 1998.

Sofield, T. and Li, F., 'China: tourism development and cultural policies', *Annals of Tourism Research* 25(2), 1998a, pp. 362–92.

Sofield, T. and Li, F., 'Heritage, history and tourism: Is the Great Wall of China the Great Wall of China?, Paper presented at the 14th World Congress of the International Sociological Association, Montreal, August 1998, 1998b.

Turnbull, C., 'Bali's new gods', *Natural History* 1, 1982, pp. 26–32.

Urry, J., *The Tourist Gaze: Leisure and Travel in Contemporary Societies*, Sage, London, 1990.

Wilson, D., 'Comment', *Current Anthropology* 22(5), 1981, p. 477.

Wood, R.E., 'Tourism, culture and the sociology of development', in M. Hitchcock, V.T. King and M.J.G. Parnwell (eds.), *Tourism in South-East Asia*, Routledge, London, 1993, pp. 48–70.

Wood, R., 'Tourism and the state: Ethnic options and constructions of otherness', in M. Picard and R. Wood (eds), *Tourism, Ethnicity and the State in Asian and Pacific Societies*, University of Hawai'i Press, Honolulu, 1997, pp. 1–34.

4

Transport and infrastructure issues in Southeast and South Asian tourism

Stephen Page

Introduction

Transport provides the major element in the tourist's ability to travel because without transport, most forms of travel and tourism could not occur. Transport is the dynamic element which links tourists from origin areas with destination areas, and research has explored the tourist–transport interface in some detail (Hoyle and Knowles, 1992, 1998; Page, 1994, 1998, 1999). Yet, within the literature on Southeast Asian and South Asian tourism, most recent syntheses (e.g. Hitchcock *et al.*, 1993; Go and Jenkins, 1997) have failed to discuss the vital role of transport and infrastructure development as facilitating and potentially constraining factors in the development of tourism within the region (Leinbach and Chia, 1989). It is also important to emphasize that transport has been one of the hidden factors that has assisted the dynamic economies in Southeast Asia to develop export markets (Islam and Chowdhury, 1997), a feature emphasized by Dixon and

Smith (1997). This has been inextricably linked to the development of international trade, regional integration, the expansion of Extended Metropolitan Regions (Douglass, 1995) and the related growth triangles (Tang and Thant, 1993) discussed in Chapter 1. For example, the Johor–Singapore–Riau growth triangle is served by well-developed transport and infrastructure provision, as well as access to ports. Most tourism studies with a focus on Southeast Asia tend to assume that transport is a passive agent despite its obvious role in wider processes of economic development (e.g. Pye and Lin, 1983). Tourism researchers tend to view transport and infrastructure provision as the responsibility of the state or private sector even though transport is a vital ingredient in tourism development. They often fail to acknowledge the key role transport plays in development, ignoring the growth triangles experience which could not function effectively without access, communications and land-based transport networks. In this context, fundamental research in economic geography, planning, transport and development studies has not permeated or greatly influenced tourism research, despite the analogy that economic growth is dependent upon transportation as one of the critical success factors facilitating rapid development. As a result much of the published research on tourism in Southeast and South Asia has been devoid of any critical discussion of the role of transport in economic development in general and tourism in particular. Tourism is not any different in this context to other forms of economic development, since the rapid growth in domestic and international tourism flows and activity at different spatial scales require transportation and associated infrastructure provision to enable the realization of the latent potential demand. In this respect, the supply of transportation and infrastructure is a fundamental requirement for the orderly and efficient development of tourism. It is frequently overlooked, despite the recent publication of specialists' studies on air transport (Findlay *et al.*, 1997), airport development (O'Connor, 1996) as well as private sector reports on aviation (Air Transport Action Group (ATAG), 1997) and other specialist aspects of transportation research on areas related to aviation published in journals such as the *Journal of Air Transport Management*. One of the reasons why aviation has been the focus of much of the existing research relates to the scale and diversity of destinations within the region and the significance of airport hubs and regional air services to manage the distribution and flows of tourists into and within the region. As Wheatcroft (1998: p. 159) argues 'the tourism industry in many countries of the world has been profoundly shaped by the development of air services' a statement which is particularly relevant in the case of Southeast Asia. In fact, the development of air services in Malaysia in the 1950s and the Vietnam conflict in the 1960s and early 1970s had a significant impact on air services in the region. For example, in the case of the Vietnam conflict, the rest and relaxation function provided for American troops in Thailand and the Philippines

contributed to the early development of resorts such as Pattaya and Chang Mai and sex tourism in both Bangkok and Manila (Hall, 1994). In the case of Vietnam, there is also the similar pattern of development occurring to that which occurred in the Pacific Islands after the Second World War, where former American air bases provided the focal point for the development of present-day aviation infrastructure. In some senses, it could be argued that the historical antecedents of former military activity form the nucleus of a neo-colonial stage of economic and transport development in Southeast Asia, utilizing former infrastructure to accommodate tourism demand.

Yet as Hilling (1996) observes, at a global scale, a transport gap exists in terms of the developed regions of the world (North America, Europe and Australasia) and developing countries. For example, in the case of Asia, 'Japan accounts for 64 per cent and 67 per cent, respectively, of Asia's commercial and passenger vehicles [if Japan were] excluded from the totals [it] leaves that area with a grave deficiency' (Hilling, 1996: p. 2). This is exemplified in Hilling's (1996) survey of Indonesia, where advances in transport have been dramatic since the 1960s but provision still remains behind many other developed countries. For example, between the late 1960s and early 1990s, the number of buses increased by 2600 per cent but the base level was low to start with. Indonesia probably mirrors the experience of more advanced countries in Southeast Asia where provision of rail and sea transport for domestic travel has lagged behind, despite road building programmes and the growth in air transport provision for domestic and inbound tourism in the 1980s and 1990s. Underinvestment in public transport networks in urban areas and state railway networks also remains a pressing issue for many countries in the region such as Indonesia. Many of the existing transport networks are still a function of the former economic geography of colonial production systems which were not designed with tourist use in mind. One consequence is that in some states in Southeast Asia, domestic tourism was constrained until domestic airlines services improved, as in the case of Indonesia in the 1980s. In a rural context, Rigg (1997: pp. 169–170) argues that

> Governments have built the roads, while private entrepreneurs have provided the means to galvanise a latent productive resource – roads – into an agent of rural development ... [and] ... It is difficult today, in the countries of Asean, fully to appreciate the transport revolution that has occurred. Partly the problem was a simple lack of roads and consequent inaccessibility. But in some areas the state also limited mobility through decree and control. As is still the case in Myanmar, and until quite recently in Vietnam, Laos and Cambodia, a mobile population was viewed as a potentially dangerous and destabilising one.

As a result, the experience of Indonesia and the wider considerations of infrastructure, development, government policy and funding allocations in the region have had a profound impact on domestic and, to a lesser degree, international tourist travel. In simple terms, the provision and availability of infrastructure have combined with government policy and decrees to shape the patterns of domestic tourism as well as the location and distribution of international tourist patterns of travel (see Gunawon, 1996, on the situation in Indonesia and Oppermann, 1994, for an example of tourist travel patterns in Malaysia). This chapter will examine the significance of transport and infrastructure issues within Southeast and South Asia but, owing to lack of space, it is only possible to identify indicative patterns of demand and supply within the region together with the problems associated with infrastructure constraints. Given that air travel is a dominant feature of tourist travel within the region, the chapter focuses on that dimension of tourist transport rather than the diverse range of modes of travel. For this reason, a more detailed assessment of tourist transport in the region can be found in Page (1999).

This chapter does not consider the role of land-based transport and sea transport, the latter vital for inter-island travel in the Philippines and Indonesia. Likewise, the roles of tourist rail travel and tourist travel in urban areas are not considered owing to the constraints of space. One should also recognize the significance of the historical antecedents of colonial development and subsequent urban development in the present location of the gateway cities and airport hubs within the region, a feature evident from research by Fisher (1964) and more recently Raguraman (1997) in relation to Malaysia and Singapore. Furthermore, the significance and complexity of tourist travel in the emerging Extended Metropolitan Regions in Asia (EMRs) discussed in Chapter 1, are also not explored here. The chapter commences with a detailed discussion of air travel in the region, examining demand and supply issues. This is followed by a review of airport development and the problems facing many of the region's gateways and an examination of the role of government policy and the rise of privatization in Asian aviation.

Determinants of the demand and supply of tourist transport in Asia

In a regional context, Dempsey and O'Connor (1996) argue that it is important to make an essential link in the explanation of the factors shaping the economic geography of the area, of which tourism is an integral part of the service economy. Ioannides and Debbage (1998) also reinforce the argument by highlighting the need to link the regional economic context to the development of tourism in terms of consumer services such as air travel and those activities which tourists consume. As a result, Dempsey and O'Connor (1996: p. 24) outline four key forces shaping the economic landscape of the region:

i)   the offshore investment of Japanese, Korean and Taiwanese companies;

ii) the emergence of China as a market and a production location;

iii) rising levels of personal income in the region; and

iv) the rapidly expanding global role of the cities within the region.

Therefore, even without imposing the tourism demand for travel to and within the region, it is apparent that exogenous factors are influencing economic growth and are fuelling a major demand for air travel which is resulting in an axis shift: O'Connor (1995) argues that in terms of air travel there has been a demand shift from the Europe–Asia trunk routes to a north–south axis in Asia fuelled by the growth of the above factors resulting in city–city travel, of which tourism has been a part. However, in a tourism context, Dempsey and O'Connor (1996: p. 27) argue that in the 1990s, recreational travel has become a more significant part of the daily lives of the Asian population. In fact, one could argue that the previous experience of the Japanese impact of wealth and prosperity on the global outbound tourism market and consequences for air travel, is indicative of what may occur once other Asian markets begin to travel throughout the region (Hall, 1997). While transport researchers may point to the need to develop complementary modes of transport infrastructure to permit substitutability in tourist travel within the region, the reality is that air transport is the only real alternative for the efficient movement of people and tourists over substantial distances. This is particularly the case in Southeast Asia because of the locations of resorts, destinations and airport hubs. This is supported by research by Rimmer (1991) which investigated the potential for the development of high-speed rail corridors in the region. Rimmer (1991) concluded that the only feasible rail links that could substitute for air travel would be; in Japan, as an expansion to the existing network, between Hong Kong, Shanghai and Beijing and between Singapore, Kuala Lumpur and Bangkok. Yet even these new networks would only cater for a small proportion of air travel. In fact, O'Connor (1996) and Clarke (1995) observe that a pattern of

linear air corridors have developed in Southeast. Asia. These are a function of the patterns of economic development, where a 300 km wide corridor exists from Japan/Korea in the north through to Sumatra and Java in the south. Thus, future patterns of travel within the region for business and for tourism will be very dependent upon the capacity of the existing air transport system to accommodate growth, particularly within the highly developed transport corridor.

Patterns of demand and supply in Asian air travel

The main data sources for assessing the demand for tourist travel in the region have been reviewed by Hall and Page (1999) and Page (1994, 1999) and comprise the World Tourism Organization (WTO) annual arrival statistics by country and region which were discussed in Chapter 1, and need not be reiterated here. In the case of transport, probably one of the best sources of data, given the predominance of air travel and the statistics, are the reports generated by the International Civil Aviation Organization (ICAO) and the International Air Transport Association (IATA).

These data sources have recently been synthesized by the Air Traffic Action Group (ATAG, 1997) which is the most detailed, publicly available analysis of air travel in the region. Although many of the region's airlines have detailed market intelligence, such data remains highly sensitive because of its commercial value and is usually unavailable to researchers. In terms of growth, ATAG (1997) recorded 386 million passenger trips by scheduled aircraft in 1995 (including domestic. and international passengers). Prior to the Asian crisis, the growth forecast by ICAO was 7.4 per cent growth per annum. If these growth forecasts reach their potential, then the Asia–Pacific region would 'record almost as many passengers as there were throughout the world in 1995' (ATAG, 1997:

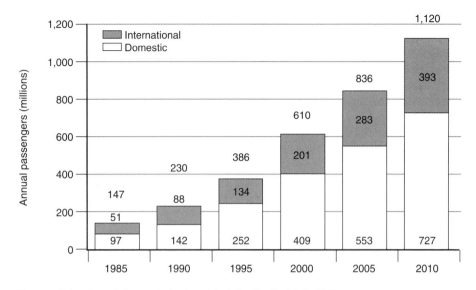

Figure 4.1   *Growth forecasts for travel in Asia–Pacific 1995–2010*

p. 5) by the year 2010. Such growth forecasts are very dynamic as Figure 4.1 shows, which reflects almost double the growth rates of travel throughout other parts of the world. Some of the key factors acting as growth drivers in travel in Asia are:

- strong economic growth (prior to the Asian economic crisis);
- rising disposable income for discretionary spending on travel and tourism;
- periods of relative political stability (prior to the Asian crisis);
- progressive lifting of travel restrictions in Asian countries;
- ethnic and cultural ties between Asian countries which promotes intraregional travel;
- a continued increase in short-haul travel;
- increased travel opportunities promoted by the early stages of air transport liberalization in the region;
- countries with a low base of travel (e.g. China) recognizing and engaging in domestic and international travel;
- the development of new airports and gateways at Kuala Lumpur, Macau and Osaka.

In terms of the Asia–Pacific region, ATAG (1997) identifies five principal areas of activity (Figure 4.2).

i)   *Central Asia*, comprising Kazakhstan, Tajikistan, Turkmenistan and Uzbekistan;

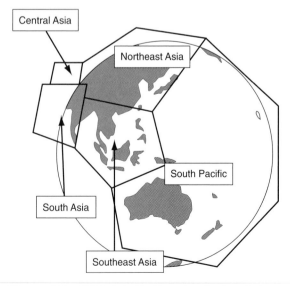

Figure 4.2   *ATAG Asia–Pacific regionalization of air transport*

ii) *South Asia*, comprising Afghanistan, Bangladesh, Bhutan, India, the Maldives, Nepal, Pakistan and Sri Lanka;

iii) *Northeast Asia*, comprising China, Hong Kong, Japan, Macau, Mongolia, Democratic People's Republic of Korea (North Korea), Republic of Korea (South Korea), the Russian Federation (East of the Urals) and Taiwan (Chinese Taipei);

iv) *Southeast Asia*, comprising Brunei-Darus-salam, Cambodia, Indonesia, Lao People's Democratic Republic, Malaysia, Myanmar, The Philippines, Singapore, Thailand and Vietnam;

v) *South Pacific*, comprising Australia, New Zealand, Papua New Guinea and the island nations of the Pacific including Hawai'i.

Within these sub-regions, the major countries for future growth in tourism markets are likely to be:

• China, which is set to become the leading country for scheduled domestic and international travel by 2010. Its total share of Asia–Pacific air traffic is estimated to increase from 5.3 per cent in 1985 and 16 per cent in 1995 to 26 per cent in 2010. China is expected to supplant Japan as the leading market;

• Japan, which was the largest market for air travel in 1995 with 30.8 per cent of traffic is expected to decrease to 20.1 per cent in 2010.

In numerical terms, the forecast growth in traffic will mean an additional 230 million passengers travelling to/from and within China in 2010 over the 1995 level. Other countries such as Vietnam are also expected by IATA to increase their volume of air traffic from 3.6 million passengers in 1995 to 28.4 million in 2010. The implications of such growth forecasts are that for 1995, 65 per cent of Asia–Pacific traffic was spatially concentrated within North-east Asia and within the Northeast–Southeast Asia region, since average travel distances by air were under 5000 km. The most important inter-continental travel flows by air are Europe–Asia

and these will remain a dominant feature of the region as:

• the principal flows are UK–Japan, with 1.2 million passenger trips in 1995, which are forecast to increase to 3.2 million by 2010;
• UK–Malaysia flows in Southeast Asia, with 755 000 passenger trips in 1995, which is expected to rise to 2.7 million in 2010.

These two dominant flows reflect the prevailing pattern of Europe–Asia travel, where the UK, Germany, France and the Netherlands accounted for 74.7 per cent of Europe–Asia–Pacific travel in 1995. This is a function of previous colonial links, business travel and a rapidly expanding medium to long-haul Europe–Asia vacation. In terms of scale, Japan–Europe passenger flows equated to 4.4 million passengers in 1995 which expanded by 13.3 per cent per annum between 1985 and 1995, and is forecast to rise to 10.4 million passengers by 2010, albeit at a lower growth rate of 5.9 per cent per annum.

Tables 4.1 and 4.2 summarize the patterns of air travel and forecast growth rates for individual countries. In terms of the type of demand and likely shape of travel patterns, Figure 4.3 illustrates that much of the growth will occur in terms of medium- and long-haul travel to and from the region, reflected in the investment patterns of many of the airline carriers serving the region. The continued purchase of medium- to long-haul fleet capacity (e.g. Boeing 767–300s with extended range capabilities, Airbus 340s and the new Boeing 777) reflect the expected pattern of growth. For example, Table 4.3 shows that on the basis of IATA forecasts, average rates of growth exceeding 5 per cent per annum are likely to occur on most routes to and from Asia, although some of the higher rates of growth may need revising downwards in the short term owing to the impact of the Asian crisis. However, given the distances involved for both intra-regional travel, Figure 4.4 highlights both the forecast growth rates and a model of traffic flow for the period 1995–2010. In the case of

Table 4.1 Patterns of air travel in Asia–Pacific 1985–2010 (figures are annual passenger trips in millions)

	1985			1995			2010		
	Domestic	International	Total	Domestic	International	Total	Domestic	International	Total
China	6.0	1.9	7.8	51.2	10.4	61.6	229.1	62.3	291.5
Japan	43.8	16.3	60.1	78.1	40.7	118.8	134.0	91.6	225.6
Chinese Taipei	5.9	4.8	10.7	28.7	15.8	44.6	104.1	52.8	156.9
Korea	3.3	4.2	7.6	21.0	14.3	35.3	54.0	54.9	108.9
Australia	13.1	5.5	18.7	23.5	12.8	36.3	61.4	32.5	93.9
Thailand	1.4	5.4	6.8	6.3	15.8	22.1	22.3	49.1	71.4
Hong Kong	0.0	9.3	9.3	0.0	27.3	27.3	0.0	70.8	70.8
India	8.6	4.8	13.4	12.3	9.1	21.3	38.3	22.1	60.4
Singapore	0.0	8.6	8.6	0.0	21.6	21.6	0.0	56.1	56.1
Indonesia	2.6	2.4	5.0	8.2	7.6	15.7	22.6	28.8	51.4
Malaysia	3.3	3.4	6.7	7.5	10.0	17.5	13.0	33.5	46.5
Philippines	3.3	3.1	6.4	4.7	6.7	11.4	17.4	18.3	35.7
Vietnam	n.a.	0.1	0.1	1.5	2.1	3.6	11.3	17.1	28.4
New Zealand	2.7	2.2	5.0	4.0	4.6	8.6	8.2	10.9	19.1
Pakistan	2.3	2.7	5.0	4.6	4.0	8.6	10.9	7.4	18.4
Sri Lanka	0.0	1.1	1.1	0.0	2.1	2.1	0.0	4.1	4.1

Notes
n.a., not available.
For the sake of consistency in trend analyses, traffic to and from Hong Kong has been considered separately from traffic to and from China, even though Hong Kong is part of China after June 1997.

Source: ATAG (1997) based on IATA data for the Asia–Pacific region and forecasts for 1980–2010.

Table 4.2 *Forecast rates of growth in air travel (domestic and international) in Asia–Pacific*

	Average annual rates of growth (%)	
	1985–1995	1995–2010
Vietnam	40.9	14.8
China	22.9	10.9
Chinese Taipei	15.4	8.8
Indonesia	12.0	8.2
Thailand	12.6	8.1
Philippines	6.0	7.9
Korea	16.7	7.8
India	4.7	7.2
Malaysia	10.1	6.7
Singapore	9.6	6.6
Hong Kong	11.3	6.5
Australia	6.9	6.5
New Zealand	5.7	5.4
Pakistan	5.5	5.2
Japan	7.0	4.4
Sri Lanka	7.3	4.4

Note
For the sake of consistency in trend analysis, traffic to and from Hong Kong has been considered separately from traffic to and from China, even though Hong Kong is part of China after June 1997.

Source: ATAG (1997) based on IATA data for the Asia–Pacific region.

intraregional traffic, Northeast Asia will remain a dominant high-traffic area followed by Southeast Asia. However, Figure 4.5 illustrates the principal flows and dominance of the Northeast–Southeast Asia–South Pacific Region (including Australasia). The major flows in 1995 for interregional travel were generated by the China–Thailand, Hong Kong–Thailand and Japan–Singapore routes, as Figure 4.6, a schematic diagram of the major city–city (trunk routes) flows, shows. Hong Kong–Taipei was the dominant flow in 1995, with a volume of passengers in excess of the London–Paris route. Figure 4.6 highlights the growing significance of gateways to the region. The consolidation and concentration of traffic in these trunk routes is reflected in the increase of city pairs with flows in excess of 1 million passengers. In 1993, eight international city-pairs had over 1 million passengers, while in 1995 this had risen to twelve city-pairs (ATAG, 1997). This poses the question – how will airlines respond to the growing demand and accommodate such growth?

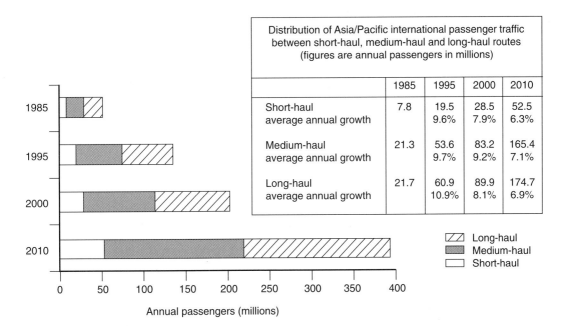

Figure 4.3 *The growth of air travel in Asia–Pacific in terms of short-, medium- and long-haul travel 1995–2010*

Table 4.3   *Air travel by scheduled aircraft between Asia–Pacific and other regions 1985–2010 (figures are annual passengers in millions)*

Main world regions to and from Asia–Pacific	1985	1995	2000	2010
Europe to Asia–Pacific	6.9	20.7	30.1	57.8
Average annual growth		11.6%	7.8%	6.8%
Transpacific	5.1	15.5	22.8	45.3
Average annual growth		11.8%	8.1%	7.1%
Middle East to Asia–Pacific	5.8	9.6	12.4	19.1
Average annual growth		5.09%	5.4%	4.4%
Africa to Asia–Pacific	0.3	1.0	1.5	3.2
Average annual growth		12.7%	9.5%	7.6%

Source: ATAG (1997) based on IATA forecasts for Asia–Pacific air travel 1980–2010.

ATAG (1997) outlines a number of strategies for airlines to meet the long-term demand for capacity growth. Firstly, by increasing load factors (this is the technical term to describe the percentage of seats filled on each flight with fare-paying passengers). Airlines are unlikely to offer more than a limited improvement to overall capacity as, prior to the Asian Crisis, Asia–Pacific loadings were high even on the Europe–Asia routes. Load factors on these routes remain around 76 per cent. The option of increasing seat densities on medium- to long-haul flights is also not a particularly attractive one for many airlines which are seeking to attract passengers in all classes of travel. In fact, with many airlines increasing the space allocated to business class seating, the density of seating will continue to be reduced. Probably the most viable options are to increase the number of flights through improved utilization of aircraft and the acquisition of additional aircraft. Yet, as ATAG (1997) show, even if the existing carriers increased flights by 200 per cent, they would still be unable to serve the 149 city-pairs (sources of demand) in the region on a daily basis. Therefore, the three main options available to airlines are:

- to open new routes;
- to increase frequencies on routes of high demand;
- to rationalize multi-stop flights and replace them with non-stop flights.

Some improvement in capacity may also arise from the delivery of the new generation of wide-bodied aircraft to carriers serving the region. In numerical terms, ATAG (1997) expect the number of aircraft movements to increase on the Europe–Asia–Pacific routes from 79 000 in 1995 to 185 000 in 2010. Likewise on North America–Asia–Pacific, the number of aircraft movements will increase from 64 000 in 1995 to 145 000 in 2010, which will pose major challenges for airports and the provision of airspace to accommodate rates of growth in excess of 5 per cent per annum. For this reason it is pertinent to consider the issue of airport development and the ability of the infrastructure to cope with such demand.

Airport development in Asia: challenges and prospects

The literature on airports, airport development and the management of traffic growth is highly specialized and limited within the tourism field (see Page, 1999, for an overview). What is clear from the literature is that with the growth in tourism and recreational travel in Asia during the

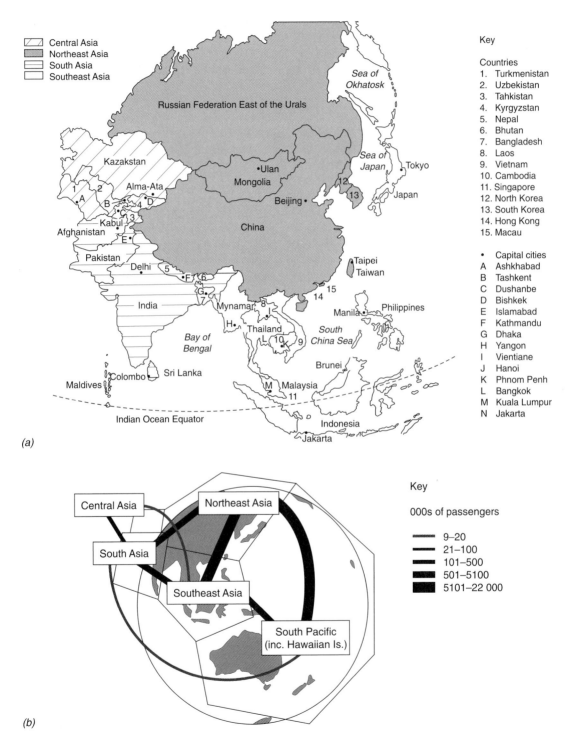

Figure 4.4   *(a) ATAG regions (b) traffic flows in Asia–Pacific 1995–2010 (Source: IATA Asia–Pacific Transport Forecasts 1980–2010, January 1997)*

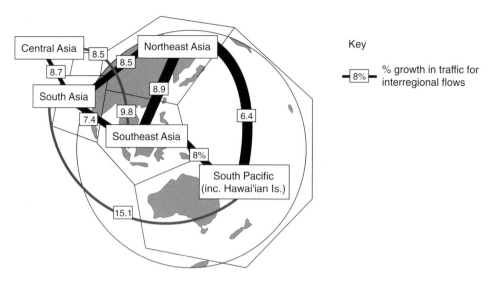

Figure 4.5   *Percentage annual growth in interregional Asia–Pacific traffic flows in air travel 1993–2010 (Source: IATA Asia–Pacific Transport Forecasts 1980–2010, January 1997)*

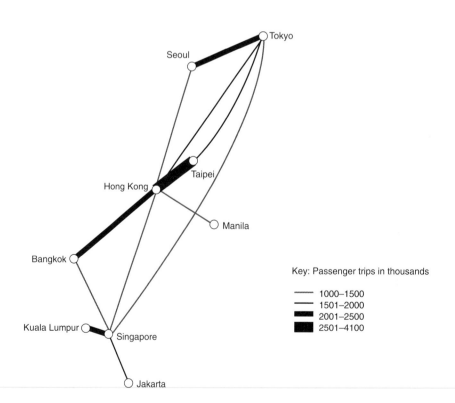

Figure 4.6   *Principal passenger flows in Southeast Asia in 1995*

1980s and 1990s, there has been increasing concern over the ability of the region's airports to accommodate the expected increase in traffic. ATAG's 1997 report is one of a series which have questioned the ability of some gateways and hubs to cope with forecast growth. Despite the 'planned spending of more than US$200 billion on airport infrastructure through to 2005, many of Asia's airports will be unable to cope with air traffic growth' (Anonymous, 1998: p. 1). Even accommodating the dampening effect of the Asian economic crisis for tourism in South Korea, Indonesia and Thailand, 'economists generally expect recessionary conditions to persist for two to three years' (Anonymous, 1998: p. 2). A recent IATA (1998) report argued that the Asian economic crisis should lead to a reduction in Asia–Pacific air traffic from 7.7 per cent for 1997–2001 to 4.4 per cent, implying a reduction in passengers from 207 million to 176 million. While this may pose some fiscal problems for existing airports in Hong Kong, Seoul, Bangkok and Jakarta, ironically it may help the region's airports to cope with demand in the short term. IATA have recently revised their forecast for Asia–Pacific air travel from an average growth rate of 7.7 per cent until 2001 to 4.4 per cent, although it has not revised its long-term forecasts (IATA, 1998). However, this is likely to be short-lived with a renewed period of growth expected during 2005–2010 (Anonymous, 1998). In fact, recent studies by the Asia–Pacific Economic Cooperation Conference's (APEC) Transportation Working Group recognized that most key airports in Southeast Asia would all experience different degrees of capacity constraints (APEC Transportation Working Group, 1996). For this reason, it is useful to examine the recent new airport developments on greenfield sites in the region and other modernization programmes.

New airport development projects

As Page (1999) shows, since the opening of the US$15 billion Kansai International Airport in Osaka, Japan, other developments include the US$1.2 billion Macau International Airport, the opening of Chep Lap Kok in Hong Kong and Kuala Lumpur International Airport, Sepang, Malaysia. Furthermore, the government in Thailand has also approved a further airport construction project for Bangkok, with further modernization planned for the Philippines, Indonesia, Vietnam, Singapore, China and Taiwan. In the case of China, ten new international airports are planned over the next decade. Further modernization plans are also planned for China's other 140 airports. As the recent report in *Travel and Tourism Analyst* indicated, 'Asia is the centre of an unprecedented number of expansion and modernisation projects at existing facilities, including enlargement of terminal buildings and cargo handling capacity, runway additions and updating of air traffic control (ATC) equipment' (Anonymous, 1998: p. 9). It is clear that Singapore's Changi Airport is recognized as the region's principal hub, a position which may be challenged in the foreseeable future. For example, in 1997 it handled 25.2 million passengers, up from 24.5 million in 1996 and, to accommodate future growth to retain its competitive position, the Civil Aviation Authority of Singapore is spending US$300 million on Terminal 1 to provide a further fourteen air bridges, raising the number of air bridges to sixty-seven by the end of 1999 (Anonymous, 1998). Work has also commenced to increase the airport's capacity to 65 million passengers a year by the year 2005, while land reclamation work has started so that a third runway can be built by the year 2015 (Anonymous, 1998).

The role of government policy and rise of privatization in Asian aviation

Oum (1997) indicates that the Asia–Pacific region is one of the world's fastest growing regions for scheduled air travel and Li (1998) discusses recent developments and the implications of policy change for ASEAN countries. In

Table 4.4   *Airline privatization in the Asia–Pacific region 1985–1995*

Airline	Country	Pattern of ownership			
		1985		1995	
		Private	Public	Private	Public
American Airlines	USA	X		X	
Aeromexico	Mexico		X	X	
Aero Peru	Peru		X		20%
Air Canada	Canada		X	X	
Air China	China		X		100%
Air Lanka	Sri Lanka		X		100%
Air New Zealand	New Zealand		X	X	
Air Nugini	Papua New Guinea		X		100%
Air Pacific	Fiji		X		79.6%
Air India	India		X		100%
Air Nippon Airways	Japan	X		X	
Ansett Australia	Australia	X		X	
Avianco	Colombia	X		X	
Biman Bangladesh	Bangladesh		X		100%
Canadian Air International	Canada	X		X	
Cathay Pacific Airways	Hong Kong	X		X	
China Airways	Taiwan	X		X	
Continental Airways	USA	X		X	
Delta Airlines	USA	X		X	
Garuda	Indonesia		X		100%
HAL (Hawaiian)	USA	X		X	
Indian Airlines	India		X		100%
Japan Air Systems	Japan	X		X	
Japan Airlines	Japan		X	X	
Korean Air	South Korea	X		X	
Ladeco	Chile	X		X	
Lan Chile	Chile			X	X
Malaysia Airlines	Malaysia		X		30%
Merpati	Indonesia		X		30%
Mexicana	Mexico		X		35%
Northwest Airlines	USA	X		X	
Pakistan International	Pakistan		X		57.4%
Philippine Airlines	Philippines		X		33%
Qantas	Australia		X		75%
Royal Brunei	Brunei		X		100%
Saeta Air Ecuador	Ecuador	X		X	
Singapore Airlines	Singapore		X		54%
Thai International	Thailand		X		93.7%
United Airlines	USA	X		X	
Vietnam Airlines	Vietnam		X		100%

Source: modified from Forsyth, 1997.

the period 1980–1990, commercial air traffic expanded by 7.95 per cent per annum compared with 5.8 per cent growth per annum in North America. Forecasts from IATA indicate that passenger traffic in Asia–Pacific will rise by 31 per cent of world scheduled traffic in 1990 to 41 per cent in the year 2000 and 51 per cent in 2010.

While the currency crisis in Asia in 1997–1998 may impact upon these forecasts, it is evident that the region will become the world's most important airline market during the next century (Boeing Commercial Airplane Group, 1996). Oum (1997: p. 1), however, argues that 'even though the major airlines of Asia belong to the world's fastest growing airline market, they have remained relatively small in terms of network size, traffic volume and operating revenue, compared with major carriers in the United States and Europe'. Part of this is related to the restrictive bilateral agreements which also protect the home market. There has been considerable research in the aviation sector which compares the productivity of airlines under government control with privately owned enterprises. Most of the studies indicate superior performance under conditions of privatization (Findlay and Forsyth, 1984; Oum, 1995) although not in every case (Oum and Yu, 1995). Even the former Eastern Europe is privatizing its national flag carriers as central state planning is removed (Hall, 1993).

Table 4.4 indicates that prior to 1985 there were isolated cases of privatization but much of the privatization occurred post-1985. For example, while the case of Singapore Airlines indicates that the government remains the majority shareholder, it is largely a private airline. In Oceania, the majority of airlines are privately owned but many of the smaller airlines of the Pacific Island states remain state-owned to retain a degree of control over tourist arrivals (Forsyth and King, 1996) and for strategic reasons related to accessibility and independence of major carriers. In Pacific South American States, airlines have been privatized as have those in North America, Canada and Mexico. In Asia, the situation is mixed. While some states have privatized their airlines and others have intentions to do so, a considerable number remain state-owned. Most of the privatized companies are large successful airlines. As Forsyth (1997: p. 53) observes, 'there is a strong correlation between per capita income levels and private ownership. In the richer countries in the region, such as Japan, Korea, Singapore, Taiwan, Malaysia, along with the former colony of Hong Kong, all the airlines are privately owned. By contrast, there are a few examples of private ownership of airlines in the poorer countries', while a number of governments have allowed the introduction of private airlines (e.g.

Asiana in Korea, Sempati in Indonesia and Dragonair in Hong Kong) to compete on international routes.

Where privatization has occurred, it can take a number of forms:

- listing on the stock market (JAL and Singapore Airlines);
- sale to industrial groups in the home country;
- sale to strategic shareholders.

Privatization also allows overseas investment in airlines by direct investment by shareholders and equity holdings through strategic alliances. The exception to the rule is Philippine Airlines which went bankrupt in 1998 after a number of profitable years as a privatized airline. As Table 4.5 shows, a profit of US$1.1 million in 1991–1992 slipped into the red in 1993–1994. Philippine Airlines was the backbone of tourist transport in the 7100-island archipelago, and is one of the latest casualties of the Asian crisis and its impact on Asian carriers.

In contrast, there has been less interest in the privatization of airports in Asia with only Australia and New Zealand taking Britain's lead in privatizing many of its airports and devolving government ownership from central to state and local government. The argument advanced to justify privatization of airlines is the efficiency gains which will result. In the case of airports, it is widely recognized that the greatest proportion of costs are capital as opposed to operating costs. Therefore the potential for efficiency gains

Table 4.5 *Profitability of Philippine Airlines 1991–1999*

Year	US$ profit/loss (millions)
1991–1992	1.1
1992–1993	1.02
1993–1994	−0.45
1994–1995	−0.84
1995–1996	−1.7
1996–1997	−2.18
1997–1998	−8.08
1998–1999	−2.2

Source: Lopez, 1998.

is limited. Some of the aspects of airport operation which private firms may perform efficiently:

- terminal operation;
- retail outlet operation;
- building and operating runways;
- contracted-out services.

However, Forsyth (1997: p. 62) maintains that 'investment policy, and ownership of the main facilities may best be left to the public sector'. In an Asia–Pacific context, privatization has certainly opened up the opportunities for the region's airlines to become part of a global aviation industry through foreign investment, alliances and cooperation, motivated by commercial motives in the absence of state policies to protect state airlines. As Wheatcroft (1994: p. 24) argues 'in the long term, the privatisation of airlines seems certain to contribute to a reduction in protectionism in international aviation policies' and these changes are beginning to affect Southeast Asia.

Summary

In terms of the recent Asian crisis, the impact on tourism has been a concern for intraregional visitor arrivals, although Li (1998) has looked at the positive aspect – a rise in inbound tourism from non-ASEAN countries owing to depreciation of Asian currencies although, of course, this is not so clear-cut given the political turmoil in various countries which could have deterred some international trips. For airlines, the immediate consequence is the

> escalation of debt service and lease costs and operating costs. Four flag carriers in ASEAN, namely, Garuda, Malaysia Airlines, Philippine Airlines and Thai Airways International, are experiencing most difficulties. Home-based air travel has drastically decreased as a result of dramatic currency depreciations (Li, 1998: p. 143).

The following comments serve as a useful summary of the situation prevailing in 1998/1999 and offer both short- and long-term strategic advice to both governments and policy makers associated with transport provision for tourism as

> whilst most airport projects are unlikely to be affected by the economic crisis there is a danger that infrastructure programmes in the pipeline, or those which might have been expected to get underway soon, may be postponed or even cancelled. This would be short-sighted. It is essential that the region's airport and ATC [Air Traffic Control] infrastructure continues to be improved and expanded, not only to overcome an existing shortfall but to prepare for future growth, which will be substantial in the medium to long term (Anonymous, 1998: p. 21).

This advice also has a more specific application to the broader context of urban tourism associated with megacities in Asia. As Shah (1996) argues

> Rapid urban growth, particularly in megacities puts enormous demands on transport systems capable of moving large numbers of passengers ... at affordable costs. In most megacities this demand is not met, leading to the familiar problems of air pollution and congestion, magnified in their impact in megacities because of the prevailing high densities of land use, shortage of roads, and inadequacies of public transport (Shah, 1996: p. 14).

Shah's argument has a direct concern for tourism, particularly when one considers the environmental concerns of Ross and Thandanti (1995: p. 287) in relation to Bangkok, where it 'will become increasingly inhospitable and its [environmental] excesses will leak into the surrounding countryside. Foreign companies will leave and investment will dry up. Tourism will turn down'. The negative impacts of rapid industrialization and urban development and the significance for tourism in Thailand were also highlighted by Ratanakomut (1995: p. 92) in that 'the positive impact of the growth of tourism has been the development of infrastructure in provincial towns such as Chiang Mai, Chiang Rai and Phuket. But tourism also brings problems. For example, it might create overall economic instability, increased resource leakages through import demand and environmental problems'. Furthermore, in relation to Bangkok and the mounting problems of traffic congestion and a declining environmental quality, Ratanakomut (1995: p. 94) argues that 'This would make Bangkok a less attractive place and lead tourists to shorten their stay. The growth of tourism areas such as Pattaya and Phuket is reaching its limit in terms of water supply and waste-water treatment'. Therefore, whilst this chapter has predominantly emphasized the significance of air travel and tourism, there are other major infrastructure and land transportation concerns affecting megacities with a thriving tourism trade such as Bangkok. This experience is not dramatically different from the situation in other rapidly expanding urban areas in Southeast Asia. As a result, the future viability of urban tourism markets could be jeopardized, although this is not specific to urban tourism, as Ross and Thandanti (1995: p. 273) suggest that

> *Tourist infrastructure such as hotels and access roads, and recreation facilities such as golf courses, contribute to the clearing of land and entail a very high per-capita consumption of water. Because of the lack of planning controls, particularly in Pattaya and Phuket, untreated sewerage discharge has been allowed to pollute beaches, rivers and the corals at Phuket ... This in turn has affected tourist numbers.*

Yet ironically, Rimmer (1995: p. 185) argues that in the case of Bangkok, 'foreign trade, investment and tourism were crucial in the development of Bangkok's role as an international transport and communications hub' with the megacity status of the Bangkok metropolitan region propelling the national economy as 'the economic growth of Bangkok is indistinguishable

from Thailand as a whole' (Rimmer, 1995: p. 183). Rimmer (1995) points to Bangkok's competition with other megacities in Pacific Asia for supremacy and tourism has become one element of the government's pursuit of this supreme status. Rimmer's (1995) analysis of Singapore and Bangkok's air traffic markets highlighted Singapore's dominance in short-haul traffic from within Southeast Asia and Bangkok's stronger performance in East Asia and South Asia. However, while 'Over longer distances, Singapore was foremost in Australasia and North America while Bangkok was foremost in the Middle East ... In 1990 Bangkok handled more European passengers than Singapore – a reflection of its function as a fuelling base on the one-stop Australia–Europe flights'. Thus, the megacity role of many of Southeast Asia's primary cities perform a significant gateway function. This highlights their existing and future potential for urban tourism in many of the core areas of economic development of Southeast Asia (see Chapter 1 for a discussion of the pre- and post-colonial stages). It is also a major factor in any initial explanation of the geographical distribution of international and, to a lesser degree, domestic visitors throughout the region as travel is conditioned by the availability of transport infrastructure routes and networks which are focused on the highly urbanized pattern of development.

In the case of transport, the relationship with environmental pollution and the significance of the tourism–transport interface in terms of declining environmental quality in cities and resort areas is becoming an issue of growing concern in Southeast Asia. In fact Parnwell and Bryant (1996) highlight the current flaws in the economic and ecological approaches to development in Southeast Asia and the importance of political processes in relation to sustainable development. The political dimension of sustainable development is a feature subsequently analysed by Hirsch and Warren (1998) now that the environment has become an issue of public debate in the region. In recent years it is evident that transport has become a critical factor in the spatial transformation of Southeast Asia, particularly in tourism, connecting the various regions into a series of economic communities. It is notable that such developments within and outside the primary cities of the region now reflect the earlier comments by Fisher (1964). The following comments by Fisher (1964) are interesting:

> *Moreover, partly because of their wartime experiences, which were unparalleled in other colonial lands, many of the South-east Asian peoples have been particularly thorough-going in their rejection of Western affiliations. Thus, while the South Asian successor states – India, Pakistan and Ceylon – remained in the Commonwealth, Burma opted out in 1948, the national states of Indochina-Cambodia, Laos and Vietnam – found little satisfaction in the offer of associated statehood within the French Union, ... [and] ... Accordingly, where formerly there existed a series of colonial dependencies, each tied politically and in varying degree also economically to a particular Western power.*

Indeed Fisher (1964) implicitly documented the rejection of the former colonial ties in the post-war period. It is ironic that Fisher's (1964) argument has now been supplanted in a tourism context by the former colonists returning as tourists. In fact, some commentators have examined the contention that the arrival of the Western tourists in Southeast Asia may herald the 'shock troops' of modernity (Oakes, 1997). What is clear in the thirty or more years since Fisher's (1964) seminal study of Southeast Asia is that an economic transformation has occurred in the region, with the development of an export-based economy founded on primary and manufactured products. This has been complemented by the development of a service sector with a strong tourism dimension as

> *the distance from the major tourist supply areas of the United States and Europe may ... have been a disadvantage, although the rapid development of the wide-bodied jet airliners has to a large degree offset this problem, while the rapid growth of*

> *incomes in the Asia Pacific region has substantially increased the potential supply of tourists* (Walton, 1993: p. 214)

despite the temporary setback to intraregional travel induced by the Asian crisis. Thus, the transport revolution and expansion in both domestic and international tourism (both long- and short-haul) has really only been possible through the facilitating role which transport has played over the last twenty years in expanding and developing Southeast Asia's tourism industry (Wood, 1979). There is very little doubt that Wood's (1997: p. ix) comments are contestable: 'the region has the fastest growing tourism industry – both domestic and international – in the world' and transport has been one of the principal catalysts aiding this development. Indeed, the future prospects for further growth in tourism will be contingent upon regional cooperation to assist in the greater integration and development of transport modes upon which the region's tourism industry relies (Elek, Findlay, Hooper and Warren 1999).

References

Anonymous, 'Asian airport development', *Travel and Tourism Analyst* 2, 1998, pp. 1–21.

Asia–Pacific Economic Cooperation Conference Transportation Working Group, *Congestion Point Study Phase II – Final Report Volume 1 – Executive Summary; Volume 2 – Air Transport*, APEC Secretariat, Singapore, Maunsell Pty. Limited, 1996.

Air Transport Action Group, *Asia/Pacific Air Traffic Growth and Constraints*, ATAG, Geneva, 1997.

Boeing Commercial Airplane Group, *1996 Current Market Outlook*, Boeing Commercial Airplane Group, Seattle, 1996.

Clarke, R., 'Air transport system congestion in East Asia', *Transportation Quarterly*, 49(3), 1995, pp. 31–42.

Dempsey, S. and O'Connor, K., 'Air traffic congestion and infrastructure development in the Pacific Asia region', in C. Findlay, C. Lin and K. Singh (eds),

Asia Pacific Air Transport: Challenges and Policy Reforms, Institute of South East Asian Studies, Singapore, 1997, pp. 23–48.

Dixon, C. and Smith, D. (eds), *Uneven Development in South East Asia*, Ashgate, Aldershot, 1997.

Douglass, M., 'Global interdependence and urbanisation: Planning the Bangkok mega-urban region', in T. McGee and I. Robinson (eds), *The Mega-Regions of Southeast Asia*, UBC Press, Vancouver, 1995, pp. 45–77.

Elek, A., Findlay, C., Hooper, P. and Warren, T., 'Open skies or open clubs? New issues for Asia Pacific economic cooperation', *Journal of Air Transport Management*, 5(3), 1999, pp. 143–51.

Findlay, C. and Forsyth, P., 'Competitiveness in internationally traded services: The case of air transport', *Working Paper No 10*, ASEAN–Australian Joint Research Project, Kuala Lumpur and Canberra, 1984.

Findlay, C., Sien, C. and Singh, K. (eds), *Asia Pacific Air Transport: Challenges and Policy Reforms*, Institute of South East Asian Studies, Singapore, 1997.

Fisher, C., *South East Asia*, Methuen, London, 1964.

Forsyth, P., 'Privatisation in Asia Pacific aviation', in C. Findlay, C. Sien and K. Singh (eds), *Asia Pacific Air Transport: Challenges and Policy Reforms*, Institute of South East Asian Studies, Singapore, 1997, pp. 48–64.

Forsyth, P. and King, J., 'Competition, cooperation and financial performance in South Pacific aviation', in G. Hufbaner and C. Findlay (eds), *Flying High: Liberalising Aviation in the Asia Pacific*, Institute for International Economics and Australia–Japan Research Centre, Washington and Canberra, 1996, pp. 99–176.

Go, F. and Jenkins, C. (eds), *Tourism and Economic Development in Asia and Australasia*, Cassell, London, 1997.

Gunawon, M., 'Domestic tourism in Indonesia', *Tourism Recreation Research* 21(1), 1996, pp. 65–69.

Hall, C. M., *Tourism in the Pacific Rim*, First Edition, Longman Cheshire, Melbourne, 1994.

Hall, C.M., *Tourism in the Pacific Rim*, Addison Wesley Longman, Melbourne, 2nd edition, 1997.

Hall, D.R., 'Transport implications of tourism development' in D.R. Hall (ed.), *Transport and Economic Development in the new Central and Eastern Europe*, Belhaven, London, 1993, pp. 206–225.

Hall, C. M. and Page. S. J., *The Geography of Tourism and Recreation: Environment, Place and Space*, Routledge, London, 1999.

Hilling, D., *Transport and Developing Countries*, Routledge, London, 1996.

Hirsch, P. and Warren, C. (eds), *The Politics of Environment in Southeast Asia*, Routledge, London, 1998.

Hitchcock, M., King, V. and Parnwell, M. (eds), *Tourism in South East Asia*, Routledge, London, 1993.

Hoyle, B. and Knowles, R. (eds), *Modern Transport Geography*, Belhaven, London, 1992.

Hoyle, B. and Knowles, R. (eds), *Modern Transport Geography*, John Wiley and Sons, Chichester, 2nd edition, 1998.

International Air Transport Association, 'The impact of recent events on the Asia Pacific aviation market and prospects for future growth to 2001', IATA, Montreal, March 1998.

Ioannides, D. and Debbage, K. (eds), *The Economic Geography of the Tourist Industry: A Supply-Side Analysis*, Routledge, London, 1998.

Islam, I. and Chowdhury, A., *Asia Pacific Economies: A Survey*, Routledge, London, 1997.

Leinbach, T. and Chia, L., *Southeast Asian Transport: Issues in Development*, Oxford University Press, Singapore, 1989.

Li, M., 'Air transport in ASEAN: Recent developments and implications', *Journal of Air Transport Management* 4, 1998, pp. 135–144.

Lopez, A., 'Back from the grave', *AsiaWeek* 9 October 1998.

Oakes, T., 'Ethnic tourism in rural Guizhou: Sense of place and the commerce of authenticity', in M. Picard and R. Wood (eds), *Tourism, Ethnicity and the State in Asian and Pacific Societies*, University of Hawai'i Press, Honolulu, 1997, pp. 35–70.

O'Connor, K., 'Airport development in South East Asia', *Journal of Transport Geography* 3(4), 1995, pp. 269–279.

O'Connor, K., 'Airport development: A Pacific Asian perspective', *Built Environment* 22(3), 1996, pp. 212–222.

Oppermann, M., 'The Malaysian tourism system', *Malaysian Journal of Tropical Geography* 25(1), 1994, pp. 11–20.

Oum, T., 'A comparative study of productivity and cost competitiveness of the World's major airlines',

Discussion Paper No 363, Institute of Social and Economic Research, Osaka University, Osaka, 1995.

Oum, T., 'Challenges and opportunities for Asian airlines and governments' in C. Findlay, C. Sien and K. Singh (eds), *Asia Pacific Air Transport: Challenges and Policy Reforms*, Institute for South East Asian Studies, Singapore, 1997, pp. 1–22.

Oum, T. and Yu, C., 'A productivity comparison of the world's major airlines', *Journal of Air Transport Management* 2(3/4), 1995, pp. 181–195.

Page, S.J., *Transport for Tourism*, Routledge, London, 1994.

Page, S.J., 'Transport for recreation and tourism', in B. Hoyle and R. Knowles, (eds), *Modern Transport Geography*, John Wiley and Sons, Chichester, 2nd edition, 1998.

Page, S.J., *Transport and Tourism*, Addison Wesley Longman, Harlow, 1999.

Parnwell, M. and Bryant, R. (eds), *Environmental Change in Southeast Asia*, Routledge, London, 1996.

Pye, E. and Lin, T. (eds), *Tourism in Asia, the Economic Impact*, National University of Singapore, Singapore University Press, 1983.

Raguraman, K., 'Airlines as instruments for nation building and national identity: Case study of Malaysia and Singapore', *Journal of Transport Geography* 5(4), 1997, pp. 239–256.

Ratanakomut, S., 'Industrializing the service sector, with special emphasis on tourism', in M. Krongakaew (ed.), *Thailand's Industrialization and its Consequences*, Macmillan, Basingstoke, 1995, pp. 85–98.

Rigg, J., *Southeast Asia: The Human Landscape of Modernization and Development*, Routledge, London, 1997.

Rimmer, P., 'Megacities, multilayered networks and development corridors in the Pacific Economic Zone: The Japanese ascendancy', in T. Hutton (ed.), *Conference Papers on Transportation and Regional Development*, Centre for Human Settlements, University of British Columbia, Vancouver, 1991.

Rimmer, P., 'Urbanization problems in Thailand's rapidly industrializing economy', in M. Krongakaew (ed.), *Thailand's Industrialization and its Consequences*, Macmillan, Basingstoke, 1995, pp. 183–217.

Ross, H. and Thandanti, S., 'The environmental costs of industrialization' in M. Krongakaew (ed.), *Thailand's Industrialization and its Consequences*, Macmillan, Basingstoke, 1995, pp. 267–288.

Shah, A., 'Urban trends and the emergence of the megacity', in J. Stubbs (ed.), *The Future of Asian Cities: Report of the 1996 Annual Meeting Seminar on Urban Management and Finance*, Asian Development Bank, Manila, 1996, pp. 11–32.

Tang, M. and Thant, M., *Growth Triangles: Conceptual Issues and Problems, Economics*, Staff paper Number 54, Asian Development Bank, Manila, 1993.

Walton, J., 'Tourism and economic development in ASEAN', in M. Hitchcock, V. King and M. Parnwell (eds), *Tourism in South East Asia*, Routledge, London, 1993, pp. 214–233.

Wheatcroft, S., *Aviation and Tourism Policies*, Routledge/World Tourism Organization, London, 1994.

Wheatcroft, S., 'The airline industry and tourism' in D. Ioannides and K. Debbage (eds), *The Economic Geography of the Tourist Industry: A Supply-Side Analysis*, Routledge, London, 1998, pp. 159–179.

Wood, R., 'Tourism and underdevelopment in Southeast Asia', *Journal of Contemporary Asia* 9(3), 1979, pp. 274–287.

Wood, R., 'Tourism and the state: Ethnic options and constructions of otherness', in M. Picard and R. Wood (eds), *Tourism, Ethnicity and the State in Asian and Pacific Societies*, University of Hawai'i Press, Honolulu, 1997, pp. 1–34.

5

Tourism and politics in South and Southeast Asia: political instability and policy

C. Michael Hall and
Alfred L. Oehlers

... tourism may decline precipitously when political conditions appear unsettled. Tourists simply choose alternative destinations.

Unfortunately, many national leaders and planners either do not understand or will not accept the fact that political serenity, not scenic or cultural attractions, constitute the first and central requirement of tourism

(Richter and Waugh, 1986: p. 231).

After years of not so 'benign neglect' (Richter, 1983), the political dimensions of tourism are starting to receive considerable attention in the tourism research literature (e.g. Richter, 1985, 1989; Richter and Richter, 1985; Lea and Small, 1988; Buckley and Klemm, 1993; Hall, 1994; Burns, 1995; Hall and Jenkins, 1995; Pizam and Mansfield, 1996). An appreciation of the political context of tourism is critical to an understanding of the complex nature of tourism, particularly in South and Southeast Asia where political effects have dramatically affected

tourism flows, investment, development and policy decisions. Issues of political stability and political relations within and between states are extremely important in determining the image of destinations in tourist-generating regions and, of course, the real and perceived safety of tourists (e.g. Brackenbury, 1995; Hall and O'Sullivan, 1996; Pizam and Mansfield, 1996). 'Tourism is ... very much part of the competition for and consumption of scarce resources, the seeking of which *must* surely lead one to the essential elements of the politics of tourism: *Politics is about power, who gets what, where, how and why*' (Hall, 1994: p. 195). Indeed, as several chapters in this book indicate, a number of countries in the region have been dramatically affected by actual and perceived dangers to tourists in 1997 and 1998, to the substantial detriment of their tourism industries. Undoubtedly, there are a small number of tourists for whom travel to the world's danger spots represent the ultimate in adventure tourism (see

Fieldings's Dangerfinder® http://www.field-ingtravel.com/df/index.htm). However, for the vast majority of travellers personal safety, security and economic and political stability are primary considerations in selecting a destination or even in choosing to travel at all. This chapter provides a brief overview of various dimensions of the relationship between tourism and politics and includes a case study of tourism and politics in Singapore. Subjects discussed include tourism and underdevelopment, political stability, tourism and terrorism, human rights and policy development.

Tourism, development and imperialism

At the macro-political level, broader issues surrounding the nature of development and relationships between nations are of substantial importance for tourism (Harrison, 1992). The notion of dependency has been influential in the understanding of the tourism development process in the less developed nations, particularly those with a colonial legacy. Several commentators emphasized the need to examine the nature of capital and tourist movements between the core and periphery of the tourist system and the resultant impacts on the host society (e.g. Turner, 1976; Hoivik and Heiberg, 1980; Britton, 1982; Richter and Richter, 1985; Nash, 1989). For example, Crick (1989: p. 322) argued that the manner in which the tourism industry is planned and shaped with respect to the attraction of international tourists, 'will recreate the fabric of the colonial situation'. Indeed, Crick went on to argue that tourism was a form of 'leisure imperialism' and represented 'the hedonistic face of neo-colonialism' (1989: p. 322). The insights of Britton, Crick, Nash and others with respect to neo-colonial relationships have had substantial influence in understanding the manner in which tourism contributes to development processes, the manner in which it may serve to reinforce the power of particular elites

in society and the nature of the relationship between metropolitan powers and the periphery (Harrison, 1992). However, it would also be true to say that these insights have tended to be restricted primarily to anthropological and socio-logical approaches to the study of tourism as opposed to a wider understanding of tourism development processes within the mainstream tourism studies literature which have tended to ignore issues of power relationships (Harrison, 1992; Hall, 1994; Hall and Page, 1999). Nevertheless, such insights are useful in understanding tourism in South and Southeast Asia.

Political dimensions of sex tourism

The connection between the developed and the less developed worlds that tourism provides has meant that sex tourism has been likened to a form of imperialism (Graburn, 1983; Nash, 1989). Sex tourism consists of a series of linkages that 'can be conceptualised as one between a legally marginalized form of commoditization (sexual services) within a national industry (entertainment), essentially dependent on, but with a dynamic function in, an international industry (travel)' (Thanh-Dam, 1983: p. 544). From the perspective of political economy, sex tourism may be regarded as a result of shifts in the international division of labour and the spread of consumerism to the Third World. As Lanfant (1980: p. 15) observed, 'Tourism is not, as is often claimed, a spontaneous phenomenon. It does not occur in a disorderly way, as a result of uncontrollable demand. It is a product of will. It unfolds under the impetus of a powerful tourist promotion mechanism, supported at the highest level'. Therefore, it is the movement of capital and tourists which ultimately determines the economic, social and environmental impacts of tourism on the host region. As Graburn (1983: p. 442) argued:

> ... the phenomenon of prostitution in the third world is particularly crucial because of the

economic power differential between the buyer and the seller. Furthermore there is a direct analogy between prostitution in the Third World and that in the metropolitan resort centers where the prostitutes are disproportionately drawn from disadvantaged sections of the population who may have similar economic problems illuminating forms of 'internal colonialism' commonly found in stratified, industrial societies.

The flow of capital and visitors to less developed countries have led several commentators to conclude that tourism is prostitution (International Shipping Information Services (ISIS), 1979; Sousa, 1988) and an inevitable consequence of mass Western tourism, 'the nature and character of modern tourism which is strongly centred around (an) unquenchable (thirst for) profit and the sexual gratification of men from the First World cannot but breed and perpetuate the prostitution of deprived and dispossessed women and children of the Third World' (Rogers, 1989: p. 20). However, as noted above, the occurrence of sex tourism at certain destinations is perhaps as much related to broader political and economic relationships and issues of development than to simply the desire of the First World for sexual relationships with members of a specific society (Hall, 1992). Nevertheless, tourism issues such as sex tourism illustrate the manner in which politics serves to connect the global and local dimensions of tourism.

Tourism and political instability

Political instability refers to a situation in which the political legitimacy of conditions and mechanisms of governance and rule are challenged by elements operating from outside the normal operations of the political system. When challenge occurs from within a political system and the system is able to adapt and change to meet demands placed on it, it can be said to be stable (e.g. India). When

forces for change are unable to be satisfied from within a political system and such non-legitimate means as protest, violence, or even civil war are used to seek change, then a political system can be described as being unstable (Hall and O'Sullivan, 1996) (e.g. Indonesia in 1998 and Pakistan in 1999).

Political stability is not a value judgement as to the democratic nature, or otherwise, of a state. Indeed, it may well be the case that certain authoritarian states which limit formal opposition to government may provide extremely stable political environments in which tourism may flourish. By their very nature, authoritarian regimes do not have to undertake the public consultation measures which are in place in most Western democracies (Hall, 1994). Therefore, tourism development can be fast-tracked through any local, provincial, or national planning system that is in place. The role that authoritarian states have played in tourism development highlights the importance of government, media and tourist perceptions of destinations in determining attitudes towards the political characteristics of the destination and the creation of its tourist image. Figure 5.1 provides a model of the factors leading to the creation of images of the political stability of a destination region. Three main elements are identified: returning tourists through word-of-mouth reporting of their experiences, the media and the government of the tourist-generating region. Governments, through their foreign policy settings, can have a dramatic impact on perceptions of potential destinations. Travel flows between nations may be suspended if political relations are poor, as has happened between India and Pakistan at various times. Indeed, international tourism policy is intimately related to foreign policy objectives. As Richter (1984: p. 614) observed: 'the time is rapidly approaching when travel trade restrictions on the part of one country may in fact constitute an act of war against a small nation heavily dependent on the tourist trade'. Government policy is certainly important in regulating tourist flows and also influencing tourist visitation through

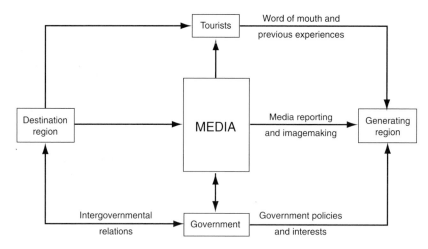

Figure 5.1   *Political instability, violence and the imagemaking process (Source: Hall and O'Sullivan, 1996)*

the articulation of national government policies towards current or potential tourist destination regions. However, it is the media which has the greatest influence on the creation of destination images in tourist-generating regions (Hall and O'Sullivan, 1996).

Media, through books, magazines and newspapers, has always had a substantial influence on images of destination areas. More recently, the telecommunications revolutions of the late twentieth century have created a visual immediacy to image creation unmatched in human history. Thanks to satellites and cable links events in countries and regions far away from the viewer can now be seen as they happen. Indeed, as this chapter is being finished we could watch the conflict between Pakistan and India over the disputed Kashmir Territory.

The manner in which the media and, to a lesser extent, government mediates as an image filter between the tourist destination and generating regions is therefore critical in influencing images of political stability and safety in a destination. Sometimes the filter will emphasize particular issues or events; at other times events may be ignored. Either way, the media will be a major force in creating images of safety and

political stability in the destination region. As Hall and O'Sullivan (1996: p. 108) observed:

The media is not a passive portrayer of events. The media select particular representations and interpretations of places and events amid a plethora of potential representations in terms of time, content, and images. Therefore, it is the portrayal of political instability rather than political instability itself which becomes uppermost as a factor in tourist destination choice behaviour. Nevertheless, political instability clearly does exist.

Political instability occurs in a number of forms. A number of different dimensions of political instability can be identified within international tourism: international wars, civil wars, coups, terrorism, riots and political and social unrest and strikes (after Lea and Small, 1988). Examples of these different types of political instability are illustrated in Table 5.1. Nevertheless, warfare, coups and political strikes or protests may make tourism development or the attraction of visitation problematic but they do not by themselves constitute a direct threat to tourists. For example, in the case of Sri Lanka, Sinclair (1994: p. 13) reported that 'no visitor has ever been involved in the communal strife'. However, terrorism constitutes

Table 5.1 *Dimensions of political instability*

Dimension	Examples
International wars	Iraqi invasion of Kuwait and consequent invasion of Iraq in 1990–1991 had massive impact on international travel. Even though at a great distance from the conflict, countries such as Thailand and Malaysia were deemed by American authorities to be dangerous areas for Americans to travel, subsequently affecting American tourist numbers and travel patterns
Civil wars	Civil wars have had a major impact on tourism in Cambodia and Sri Lanka in recent years
Coups	Political or military coups may have a major impact on tourism. For example, the 1998 coup in Cambodia had a dramatic impact on visitor numbers
Terrorism	Terrorist attacks have severely affected tourism in Kashmir and Cambodia in recent years because of their effect on visitor safety. Foreign travellers may also be targeted as kidnap victims because of the possibilities for wide media coverage and/or ransom. Several foreigners have been abducted and executed in the Cambodian countryside in recent years and foreigners often are robbed at gunpoint in Phnom Penh and on the highways
Riots/political protests/social unrest	Following the crushing of the political protests in T'iananmen Square in 1989 the total number of overseas arrivals in China fell by 22.7 per cent (Hall and O'Sullivan, 1996)
	Political and social unrest may also occur in direct response to tourism development. For example, if the local community were opposed to the development of a tourist resort, golf course or tourist infrastructure such as an airport (e.g. see IRIP News Service, 1996)
Strikes	Labour disputes may have a substantial impact on transport networks and will substantially affect quality of service at destinations

a different nature of threat to tourists because in this instance, tourists may constitute the target for terrorist activity.

Philippines

The Philippines provides a good example of some of the problems which political instability poses for tourism development. One of the wealthiest countries in Asia in the immediate post-Second World War period, the Philippines has since stumbled under a series of political, economic and natural disasters. Although the Philippines had suffered under a succession of seemingly inept and possibly corrupt regimes during the late 1950s and the 1960s it was the declaration of martial law by President Ferdinand Marcos in September 1972 that heralded the worst period of tourism-related corruption and incompetence in the country's history.

Shortly after declaration of martial law, tourism became a priority industry for the Marcos regime. A number of reasons can be put forward for this initiative, including the use of tourist arrivals as a form of legitimisation for the regime; using tourism to create a favourable image for the government, including the perception of a safe place for tourists to visit; and using tourism development as a means to provide business opportunities for Marcos's supporters (Richter, 1989). Techniques used by the regime to promote tourism, include the hosting of events such as Miss Universe and boxing title fights to create positive images and the hosting of an International Monetary Fund–World Bank Conference, which included the fast-track development of twelve luxury hotels. Ironically, it was a failed bombing attempt on Marcos at the 1980 American Society of Travel Agents Conference which attracted international attention to the corruption of the Marcos regime and illustrated the deep political instability that had developed in the country as a result of Marcos's abuse of power. The bombing attempt obviously had a dramatic impact on visitation from the

USA and also helped undermine the level of support for Marcos in the American government. However, even with the removal of Marcos from power and the appointment of Corazon Aquino to the Presidency in 1986 the long years of Marcos's misrule have had a substantial affect on tourism, severely affecting the country's image but, perhaps more importantly, providing for a misallocation of tourism infrastructure in a country virtually bankrupted by the corrupt Marcos regime (Richter, 1989; Hall, 1997).

Cambodia

Cambodia also provides a useful example of problems of political instability and violence against tourists; the number of visitors to Cambodia increased by an annual average of 30 per cent from 1993 (when a UN peace-keeping force organized an election) to 1996. Tourism then fell by 16 per cent in 1997 to 218 843 visitors (see Chapter 13). According to Jean-Pierre Kaspar (cited in Eng, 1998), general manager of the Hotel Sofitel Cambodiana, a five-star hotel in the capital Phnom Penh,

> *Our occupancy averaged 74 per cent over the first six months of 1997. Since then, [it has been] around 20 per cent. Some tourists are coming back, but it's negligible. We need more ... CNN especially was detrimental to us. You saw refugees, rockets, tanks on the streets. These images – people don't forget them. But the fighting affected very few areas.*

Similarly, Pierre Jungo of Diethelm Travel, one of the largest tour operators in the country, commented that the problem was that Cambodia 'just gets too much attention compared to other countries' (cited in Eng, 1998). Nevertheless, an upsurge in violent crimes, armed robberies and clashes between rival political factions in Phnom Penh in March and April of 1998 led to warnings being issued about trouble within the country (US State Department extends caution announcements on Cambodia,

April 8, 1998, http://www.cnn.com/TRAVEL/NEWS/9804/08/cambodia.announce/index.html). With Eng (1998) noting, 'Foreigners in particular are targeted. In many cases, the assailants appear to be policemen or soldiers. In mid-March, the *Cambodia Daily* reported a 40-member police unit that had been created two years ago to stop crimes against foreigners, was being disbanded because it was committing crimes against foreigners'. While in July 1998, the US State Department again issued a warning for Americans in Cambodia, saying 'politically motivated violence' and a dramatic increase 'in the number of armed robberies and assaults' have made travel in that country risky (US warns against travel to Cambodia, July 30, 1998, http://www.cnn.com/TRAVEL/NEWS/9807/30/cambodia.warning/index.html). However, 'Ironically, the streets of Phnom Penh are otherwise becoming more pleasant. Workers have been installing badly-needed street and traffic lights, planting grass and flowers, repairing roads and the promenade along the river, and sprucing up Wat Phnom, the hill-top temple that gives the capital its name'.

Tourism and human rights

Pacific Area Travel Association (PATA) delegates have generally praised Burmese efforts in opening up the once hermit nation. They praised Burmese authorities for improving customs and immigration procedures, constructing quality hotels and opening up large areas of the country once off-limits to foreigners. And, of course, not a single word was spoken on the social costs and impact of 'Visit Myanmar Year' (VMY). For them, money is more important than human rights (Oo and Perez, 1996: n.p.).

Despite the potential for tourism in Burma, with natural beauty, friendly people, culture and historical wonders, its future is tenuous owing to the political instability that is deep-rooted in the country. For poor, isolated and repressive regimes, foreign tourists represent

Figure 5.2 *People's Park: the united 'races' poster, Myanmar (Copyright: John Monin)*

both opportunity and threat. The government of Myanmar is accentuating the positive. The New Light of Myanmar, the mouthpiece of the ruling military junta, bluntly editorialized in 1995 that tourism 'can bring foreign exchange in large amounts in a short period' (in Hall and O'Sullivan, 1996). But the junta knows it can also bring foreign ideas and headaches for the secret police. Burmese leaders are therefore in two minds when it comes to foreigners. Some fear that exposure to outside ideas will undermine the government and possibly erode Burmese culture, yet they also desperately want the economic returns to buy weapons which will strengthen the ruling military regime (Figure 5.2).

Economic returns are not the only factor important to the government body controlling tourism, an international presence and approval is also important. In 1994 the tourism body was filing for membership of PATA and participating in the World Travel Market in London.

Goodwill promotion trips have been increased and cultural delegations have been sent to Japan, China and Korea to raise awareness of Burma in this part of the world. The Myanmar Trade Fair 1994 was attended by 1500 visitors from twenty-one countries. The local products on display brought in sales of US$17 million (Asia Travel Trade, 1994a, in Hall and O'Sullivan, 1996b). More recently, in April 1996, the Myanmar government hosted a 'World Economic Forum' and a conference on environment, cultural heritage and tourism, in an attempt to create a positive image, attract investors and give an impression of normality. It is perhaps therefore ironic that at the latter conference, the Minister for Foreign Affairs, U Ohn Gyaw, emphasized the role of cultural and natural heritage as essential factors for beneficial and sustainable tourism (Nyunt, 1996, in Hall and O'Sullivan, 1996), unfortunately, very little was stated about the social and political dimensions of sustainability.

The final word on tourism in Myanmar and VMY in particular should most appropriately come from the legitimately elected leader of Burma, Aung San Suu Kyi. In an interview with John Pilger (1996), she declared, '... They (tourists) should stay away until we are a democracy. Look at the forced labour that is going on all over the country. A lot of it is aimed at the tourist trade. It's very painful. Roads and bridges are built at the expense of the people. If you cannot provide one labourer you are fined. If you cannot afford the fine, the children are forced to labour'. With Burma being one of the last remaining countries in the world to be relatively untouched by outside influence, where men have resisted wearing trousers and still dress in the traditional sarong and where Western influence is minimal, 'tourism poses another threat to the preservation of ancient and unique traditions. But Myanmar's are resilient. If they can survive the junta, they can survive Visit Myanmar Year' (*The Economist*, 1995).

The SLORC [State Law and Order Council] *government is well-known for its track record in human rights violations. For over seven years now (it seized power through a bloody coup in 1988), it has been arresting, detaining, torturing, killing and conscripting into slave labour the Burmese people. But it is desperate to make 'Visit Myanmar Year' a success. It hopes to generate enough income to boost a failed economy from the tourists and foreign investors who have poured in $1 billion to hotel construction. And more importantly, it hopes to project a 'good image' internationally* (Oo and Perez, 1996: n.p.).

Burma faces a plethora of obstacles to tourism development. In the middle of VMY 1996 widespread media coverage was given to the attempts of the Nobel Peace winner, Aung San Suu Kyi, in heading a congress with her National League for Democracy (NLD). The main objective of the conference was to promote meaningful negotiation with SLORC. More than 200 NLD members were taken into custody, including Aung San Suu Kyi's personal assistant

and her adopted Uncle, Leo, an Australian citizen who has since died whilst in military custody. As may be imagined, these events were covered by the international press and, in Australia in particular, was not conducive to encouraging tourists to visit the country.

The main deterrent to tourism development is the poor image that Burma faces through its abject human rights record. As many as 10 000 people were thought to be killed by the army in the 1988 pro-democracy demonstrations. In 1990 the NLD, lead by Aung San Suu Kyi, won 82 per cent of seats in the election. The junta simply imprisoned those who tried to establish the government.

In January 1995, the BBC reported that slave labour was being used to build roads and other infrastructure needed to support the tourism industry. This claim was further documented by John Pilger, 'Inside Burma: land of fear' screened in June 1996 (Pilger, 1996). The documentary showed children and chain gangs being used as slave labour to build roads, bridges, airports, railways, the imperial palace in Mandalay and other tourist attractions. According to Oo and Perez (1996) some 2 million Burmese including women and children have been used as slave labourers in the beautification campaign for VMY. Human rights groups, such as Amnesty International, also charged that forced and prison labour were being used to develop Myanmar's infrastructure and people were being forced to relocate from slum areas so that tourists do not see them. The Director-General of Myanmar's Directorate of Hotels and Tourism categorically denied such allegations, calling those advancing such notions as 'against the government' and 'out of touch with what is really happening in Myanmar'.

Burma's opposition leader, or more appropriately, legitimately elected leader, Aung San Suu Kyi, has joined human rights groups in calling on tourists to boycott the country in protest against the use of forced labour and other human and political rights abuses (Oo and Perez, 1996). She is not anti-tourism, but urges people deciding to visit her country to hold off until the country is democratic and children are not put in life-threatening situations in the name of tourism development. She believes people who visit Burma are supporting one of the cruellest regimes in the world.

Tourism in Burma is being developed with little or no regard to its people. In 1990, 4000 people living in Pagan, one of the last wonders of the ancient world; equivalent to Ankor Wat in Cambodia, were forced to leave their homes as the city was being opened up to mass tourism. Only guides and the staff of a planned strip of hotels were permitted to stay. The people's homes were bulldozed – all in the name of tourism. Last year, the International Confederation of Free Trade Unions reported that a million people had been forced from their homes in Yangon alone, in preparation for tourism and foreign investment (Pilger, 1996).

The wide network of intelligence means that communication between Burmese and tourists is limited and remains on a superficial level. Free Independent Tourists (FITs) who manage to get off the tourist track are almost immediately approached by government intelligence and sent back to the nearest tourist town. A group of cyclists had their tour derailed by authorities in January 1996 as they were thought to be close to a military-sensitive area (*Trade Travel Gazette Asia*, 22–28 March 1996, in Hall and O'Sullivan, 1996). Even though they had permission from the government tourism body to be in the area and had paid for special permits, they were stopped from going any further. The government has expressed interest in attracting more adventure travel groups, including cyclists, it remains to be seen if special interest tourism in Burma will be developed. The paranoid government would ideally like all tourists to be on group tours led by a government official who can present a completely glowing and false representation of the country.

Tourism and policy

Public policy 'is whatever governments choose to do or not to do' (Dye, 1992: p. 2). This definition

covers government action, inaction, decisions and non-decisions as it implies a deliberate choice between alternatives. Tourism public policy is therefore whatever governments choose to do or not to do with respect to tourism (Hall and Jenkins, 1995). Pressure groups (e.g. tourism industry associations, conservation groups, community groups), community leaders and significant individuals (e.g. local government councillors), members of the bureaucracy (e.g. employees within tourism commissions or regional development agencies) and others (e.g. academics and consultants), all influence and perceive public policies in significantly and often markedly different ways. However, there is increasing scepticism and uneasiness about the effectiveness of government, and the intended consequences and impacts of much government policy, including with respect to tourism. For example, Richter (1989: p. 21) reported that 'critics of current tourism policies are becoming aware and are more than a little cynical about the excesses and 'mistakes' occasioned by national tourism development schemes'. The following case study serves to illustrate some of the ways in which tourism has been put to broader political ends in the case of Singapore.

Case study: tourism and politics in Singapore

When the Peoples' Action Party (PAP) assumed office following Singapore's first general election in 1959, it was not totally convinced of the merits of tourism development. The party, indeed, harboured strong suspicions, fearing that tourism may engender a process of cultural erosion (Lim, 1979: p. 27). This position, however, soon changed, particularly following Singapore's expulsion from the Federation of Malaysia in 1965. In the wake of this tumultuous event, tourism was identified as one of the key sectors that would contribute to the economic development of Singapore. Accordingly, through a special statutory authority (the Singapore Tourist

Promotion Board), as well as a succession of detailed plans, this sector was groomed to assume a critical role in the economy. These efforts, by all accounts, have been highly successful. Tourism-related activities in Singapore are now significant contributors to foreign exchange earnings. In addition, they are also a very important source of employment, with tourism receipts responsible for a sizeable proportion of Singapore's gross domestic product.

While primarily concerned with its economic contribution, the PAP was also aware that tourism could be used to pursue a variety of political goals. Thus, together with detailed blueprints charting the role of tourism in the economy, the development of the sector was also carefully tailored to complement and support broader political objectives as elaborated by the party. This section highlights some instances where tourism has been used in this manner. As it will be shown, tourism has been instrumental to the PAP in its pursuit of political goals on both an internal as well as external plane. Internally, tourism was, for example, a critical tool in efforts to forge a national identity. It has also been an essential aspect of the PAP's efforts to manage the domestic political scene to its own advantage. Externally, tourism has emerged as an important aspect of foreign policy, serving, for instance, to counter Western criticisms of Singapore's authoritarian politics. It has also been integral to efforts to position Singapore within the region, spearheading a drive to gain economic advantage over neighbouring countries.

The internal setting: tourism as politics

It is now well recognized that there is a distinct political dimension to tourism. Regardless of their ideological disposition, governments have frequently used tourism as a vehicle to advance all sorts of political agendas (Richter, 1989). With specific reference to Singapore, it is possible to identify at least two instances where the PAP has used tourism to influence domestic political developments. The first of these relates to the

PAP's attempts to create a multicultural national identity to unify an ethnically diverse population. The second revolves around the party's efforts to demonstrate its centrality to the successful development of Singapore and thus secure its pre-eminent position in Singaporean politics.

Creating a multicultural national identity

Following its electoral victory in 1959, the PAP governed a population that was deeply divided along racial and socio-linguistic lines. Owing to a liberal colonial immigration policy, there existed alongside the indigenous Malays, Indians, Chinese, as well as a multitude of other races (e.g. Europeans, Eurasians, Arabs). Each racial group tended to live in a cluster, maintaining its own education systems, economic functions, myths, legends, heroes and history (Vasil, 1992). Accentuating the divisions within Singapore society, each was fragmented into further socio-linguistic sub-groups. Within the Chinese, for example, there were as many as sixteen sub-groups with their own unique dialect, customs and rituals. The Malays were similarly divided, with at least seven such groups, while within the Indian community there were at least twenty-one (Leong, 1989).

As the government of a fledgling nation-state, one of the principal challenges facing the PAP was the unification of these diverse ethnic groups for the task of national development. To achieve such unity and establish social and racial harmony the PAP adopted the principle of multiculturalism. Under this principle, cultural tolerance was preached, as was an acceptance of differences in religious practices, customs and traditions. Each community, moreover, was not to be discriminated against and was to be accorded equality before the law and equal opportunity for advancement (Chan and Evers, 1978: p. 123). In a sense, therefore, the very diversity of Singapore's population was to serve as a unifying force. Chinese, Indians, Malays and 'others' were to symbolize the new national identity and give meaning to being 'Singaporean' (Ang and Stratton, 1995).

This principle of multiculturalism was pursued at all levels of government and found expression in a wide range of policies. Tourism was no exception. In guiding the development of this sector, the PAP took care to craft a specific tourism image that supported its political objective of fostering racial harmony. Thus, for much of the 1960s and 1970s, the Singapore Tourist Promotion Board (STPB) portrayed Singapore as an exotic island where many cultures and ethnic groups lived harmoniously together. This theme was emphasized constantly in publicity material and media advertisements. In a monthly newsletter (*Singapore Travel News*) distributed to tourists, travel agents, hotels and locals, for example, the multicultural theme was featured on no less than forty-four occasions between 1969 and 1978 (Chang, 1997: p. 550). Racial harmony was a consistent theme, with the following excerpts being typical fare:

At the cross-roads of Asia, Singapore has become the home of the three main races of the area – Malay, Chinese, Indian – and the home of their culture and traditions. Today, they live together in harmony participating in and enjoying the many festivals (July 1964: p. 2).

The people of Singapore may come from different ethnic backgrounds but they are united in one identity as Singaporeans, knowing no ethnic divisions, only that this exciting clean, green and progressive city of Singapore is their country and home. (June 1973: p. 6).

Singapore is a world within a world. Where so many ethnic groups have come together to make it one of the world's great melting pots of different races. It's a place where one can see a Malay wedding, a Chinese opera and an Indian dance all in one day. Where one can eat Chinese noodles, Malay 'satay' (barbecue) and Indian 'murtabak' (pancake) in a coffee shop and hear a dozen languages and dialects spoken just walking in the city. One may see Eurasian, Chinese and Indian people walking together or enjoying a meal at the food-stalls and it will be no rare sight in Singapore (March 1976: p. 6).

The objective of such promotional material is more than evident: 'The aim is clearly to affirm in the minds of tourists (and residents) the harmonious mix of races in the country' (Chang *et al.*, 1996: p. 300). This was an essential stepping stone towards the realization of a multicultural national identity. As Boorstin (1992: p. 198) notes, once such images are affixed, they have a strong tendency to become 'self-fulfilling prophecies'. After all, with time, '[w]hat is successfully presented for consumption by outsiders also redefines the parameters of legitimacy and authenticity for indigenous audiences' (Simpson, 1993: p. 170). Eventually, a belief will take hold within the indigenous population: 'This is what tourists are looking at and, therefore, that must be what we are' (Simpson, 1993: p. 170).

For the PAP, thus, tourism was an important instrument in efforts to create a national identity to unify the population. As Chang (1997: p. 552) points out:

[B]y projecting Singapore as a multi-ethnic destination to the world, the state was ... making a public statement on local society and culture while fulfilling the political goal of nation building. Tourists' fascination with the country's ethnic composition would foster a sense of civic pride, which in turn would help knit the ethnically diverse people together.

Managing domestic politics

The PAP has ruled Singapore without interruption since 1959. By any standards, this is no mean feat, and is testament to the enormous success and achievements of the party. As others have pointed out, however, while the popularity of the PAP is no doubt an important factor, its longevity may as much be due to its political astuteness and use of an extensive apparatus of intimidation, coercion and control (see, e.g. Rodan, 1989; Tremewan, 1994; Lingle, 1996). According to the latter view, the PAP has remained in power for so long mainly because it has been able to engineer or manage the political scene to its own advantage. The instruments that have been used to achieve this have been chronicled elsewhere (see especially Tremewan, 1994, Lingle, 1996). Of note, though, is the fact that tourism may have had some role to play in this, as the following two examples will attempt to illustrate.

Following their stay in Singapore, tourists often compliment the island for its cleanliness, efficiency and remarkable achievements. All these compliments, of course, are thoroughly well deserved. Singapore is nothing but spotless, runs as efficiently as clockwork and boasts a formidable range of social and economic accomplishments. Local residents are well aware of these fine traits. When they are recognized by foreign tourists, however, they take on a special significance. As the local state-owned media never fails to point out, these comments by tourists confirm that Singapore ranks amongst the best in the world. This privileged position, moreover, is due wholly to the capable leadership of the PAP. In a sense, therefore, tourism takes on a propaganda role in this context, showcasing Singapore to foreigners for the purposes of instilling pride and loyalty amongst Singaporeans to the ruling PAP. Through tourism, a political climate favourable to the party is created, ensuring any challenge to its supremacy is unlikely to succeed.

The multicultural theme that has been a hallmark of tourist promotion strategies is another example of how tourism may help reinforce and justify the pre-eminent position of the PAP in Singapore politics. According to Leong (1989: p. 373): 'As a philosophy of the nation-state, multiculturalism does not seek to create a single culture out of a blend of other cultures (the melting pot model); rather, it aims to create a culture of tolerance of other cultures (the salad bowl model in which the ingredients remain unchanged but are tossed alongside each other)'.

This has inherent dangers. As Leong (1989: p. 373) observed, 'when operationalised ... [multiculturalism] can institutionalise ethnic boundaries' and even promote a process of 'cultural involution or ethnic retribalisation as individuals are pressured to identify with an ethnic group, to search for their ethnic past, and to act according to the official stereotypes of their cultural traditions'. Consequently, 'Singapore's multiracialism puts Chinese people under pressure to become more Chinese, Indians more Indian, and Malays more Malay, in their behaviour ... [E]ach culture turns on itself in a cannibalistic manner, struggling to bring forth further manifestations of its distinctiveness' (Benjamin, 1976: pp. 122, 124). Thus, far from blurring the distinctions between races, multiculturalism throws these into ever sharper contrast. An environment is created where the cultural uniqueness of each group is aggressively celebrated, often in a chauvinistic manner and, as a result, ethnic tensions are heightened (Wood, 1984).

While this is seemingly contrary to PAP policy, it does have its usefulness. Any escalation in ethnic tensions permits the PAP to create a climate of fear and manufacture a sense of anxiety or crisis. Hence, under the veneer of ethnic harmony, there simmers an antagonistic and irreconcilable conflict between the races that threatens to explode at any moment. That this has been avoided at all is largely attributable to the genius of the PAP – its foresight, pragmatism and capable leadership. For Singaporeans, the lesson to be learned is clear: remove the PAP at your peril. To avoid a repetition of ethnic conflicts of the past and the wholesale unravelling of Singapore society, the retention of the PAP is essential.

The external setting: tourism as foreign policy

Apart from playing a political role in the domestic context, tourism has also been used by the PAP to pursue a number of foreign policy objectives. Two recent examples stand out. The first arose in the midst of the 'Asian values' debate when tourism was used to counter and deflect Western criticisms about the authoritarian nature of politics in Singapore. The second relates to the PAP's ongoing attempts to position Singapore within the Southeast Asian region and integrate the island with the economies of its neighbours.

The 'Asian values' debate

It is difficult to pinpoint with any accuracy the exact origins of this debate. For the purposes of this chapter, this is probably not critical, nor is a blow-by-blow account of how it unfolded essential (the interested reader is referred to Lingle, 1996, for an account). It should suffice to note the broad contours of the debate and the role tourism assumed within this.

Towards the mid-1980s, the PAP began to promote its own unique version of 'Asian values' as an ideology to be embraced by all Singaporeans. This emphasized, amongst other things, teamwork, cooperation, honesty, diligence, thriftiness, respect for authority, and a devotion to society and nation (Wilkinson, 1988; Kuah, 1990; Tremewan, 1994). The promotion of these values would probably have stirred little contention in the international arena, but for a series of unfortunate events that focused international attention on Singapore. An American teenager was found guilty of vandalism and sentenced to receive a number of strokes from the fearsome *rotan* (cane). A massive outcry against this followed, with a large number of Western nations expressing disappointment over the nature and severity of the sentence. Led, as one would expect, by the USA, Singapore was labelled a barbaric country where human rights were trampled on by an authoritarian government. When the popular press in the USA joined the fray, these accusations spread. The independence of the judiciary was called into question, as was the proud record of the PAP. The party, according to these accounts, was running nothing more than a despotic dictatorship, where dynastic politics, nepotism and cronyism ran rampant, all of which were camouflaged and legitimized by the 'Asian values' ideology.

In typical fashion, the PAP responded aggressively, confronting its critics head-on. Through a series of speeches, interviews and articles, government ministers and high-ranking civil servants stoutly defended the PAP's policies and practices, going further in many instances to draw attention to many of its Western critics' own chequered records. Litigation against publishers and individuals was also frequently resorted to in an effort to counter negative publicity (prompting the International Commission of Jurists to note that this amounted to a new form of censorship and oppression in Singapore), while consistently troublesome publications such as the *Far Eastern Economic Review* were banned, or had their circulation drastically reduced.

To complement this heavy-handed response, efforts were also made to present Singapore in a softer, more favourable light. In this respect, tourism had a critical role to play. In 1996, a new marketing tagline was adopted by the STPB to promote Singapore as a holiday destination: 'Singapore – So Easy to Enjoy, So Hard to Forget'. Under this theme, marketing campaigns depicted Singapore as an island paradise where numerous pleasurable activities and pursuits could be enjoyed, presumably with utter freedom and without any intrusive intervention by the state. This served to counter the harsh authoritarian image of Singapore frequently encountered in the international press. In addition to the new marketing campaign, concerted efforts were made to encourage foreign dignitaries to visit Singapore and comment on the political situation. In June 1997, for example, the Singapore International Foundation feted a delegation from the US Conference of Mayors to a six-day, all expenses paid visit. After sampling the delights on offer, one delegate was sufficiently moved to declare: 'The images of coercion that perhaps some others have, I haven't sensed ... Since coming here, I've been very impressed'. Another, while admitting an awareness of media commentaries on authoritarianism in Singapore, readily offered a dissenting opinion to these reports: 'When you get here, you find out that there is definitely not a dictatorship' (*Singapore Bulletin*, 1997: p. 3).

Jockeying for position in the region

In 1985, Singapore suffered its worst recession since emerging as an independent republic. In response, a high-level committee was appointed by the government to identify the causes of the recession, suggest immediate remedies and, perhaps most importantly, chart the future direction of the economy. One of the central findings of the committee was that Singapore was losing its competitive edge in production-based manufacturing. Its strength lay, instead, in high-value-added, service-oriented activities. The report also recommended the establishment of much closer links with the economies of immediate Southeast Asian neighbours. In particular, by assuming an intermediary role in the region and providing these fast-growing economies with a wide range of sophisticated services, it was felt the future of Singapore's development would be assured (Economic Committee, Ministry of Trade and Industry, 1986; see also Rodan, 1989; Chang, 1997; Yeung, 1998).

To successfully carve itself such an intermediary role, however, a number of obstacles had to be overcome. In many neighbouring countries, the intermediary role that Singapore aspired to was viewed with considerable caution. As development on the island had largely been underwritten by Western capital and expertise, there was a strong perception that Singapore was not really a part of Asia at all. Socially, culturally and economically, it had more in common with Western nations than it did with its Asian neighbours. In the context of a major global recession and where economic tensions between Asia and the West were escalating rapidly, this gave rise to doubts over the true loyalties of Singapore.

This problem was complicated further by Singapore's overwhelmingly Chinese population. Indeed, when looked at in ethnic terms, Singapore was (and remains) essentially a Chinese society (McKie, 1972; Vasil, 1992). This placed it in a highly advantageous position to exploit opportunities then emerging in China.

The very same trait, however, was a major drawback in dealings with other neighbours. In these countries, Singapore was perceived as a Chinese enclave. Given the animosity felt towards Chinese by indigenous populations (especially in Malaysia, Indonesia and Vietnam), the overtures from Singapore could not always be assured a warm reception.

Various efforts were made by the PAP to overcome these obstacles and establish Singapore's legitimacy in the region. The determination and vigour with which the 'Asian values' debate was pursued was one aspect to this. Through this, the PAP sought to conclusively demonstrate where its loyalties lay. Beyond this, it also took a leading role in discussions concerning the definition of the 'region'. As Jayasuriya (1994) notes, this encompassed a variety of interpretations, ranging from economic, security, to cultural. All, however, emphasized the inclusion of Singapore, if not its centrality. Finally, efforts were also made to demonstrate the useful and lucrative role Singapore could play in the region. This was designed specifically to overcome any apprehensions about the intermediary role Singapore sought to occupy. In this last respect, tourism had an important role to play.

To support the broader 'regionalization' effort, tourism development in Singapore was to have two distinct goals. Firstly, the export of tourism-related services to neighbouring countries was to be actively promoted. Secondly, Singapore was to be developed into a gateway to other Southeast Asian destinations, functioning as 'the centre of a spatial division of tourist flows' (Chang, 1997: 557). These twin objectives were neatly summarized by the STPB. According to the statutory authority, '[i]n addition to taking Singapore into the region', under this strategy, 'the region could be brought into Singapore' (*The Straits Times Weekly Edition*, 26 June 1993).

In accordance with this new philosophy, investments in tourism-related activities in neighbouring countries were aggressively promoted. The development of hotels, in particular, soon emerged as highly significant, with major projects in countries such as Burma, Cambodia, Vietnam, Indonesia and Malaysia. At the same time, attempts were made to forge strategic alliances with operators in neighbouring countries to provide what the Minister for Trade and Industry described as, a 'collective tourism product' (*The Straits Times Weekly Edition*, 22 April 1995). For the Minister, the rationale behind such alliances was simple. By partnering countries 'with abundant beach resorts, scenic landscapes and exotic native cultures', it would immediately be apparent that tourism could be 'mutually beneficial'. Indeed, when the entire picture was considered, taking into account both the outward investments from Singapore as well as its role as a tourist hub to the region, this would conclusively demonstrate that tourism need not be a competitive and 'negative process and zero-sum game'. As with any venture where Singapore would be permitted an intermediary role, all could be enriched in the process.

Conclusion

It is impossible to separate tourism strategies and images from the 'interests, values and power of those who formulate them' (Hall, 1994: 172). These strategies and images will invariably be coloured by the particular interests and political agendas of governments. Singapore probably ranks as one of the best examples of this. As has been shown in this chapter, tourism in Singapore has been profoundly influenced by the political priorities of the ruling PAP. Whether in the field of domestic politics or the arena of foreign relations, tourism has been moulded and marshalled over the years to support the party's political initiatives.

The Singapore case clearly demonstrates how political tourism can be. While it may be said that the situation in Singapore is fairly extreme, the wider lesson to be learned from it nevertheless remains valid. In an increasingly complex world, tourism cannot be understood in a vacuum. A proper understanding of this important activity must situate it within, and refer constantly to, the social, economic and political context in which it is rooted.

References

Ang, I. and Stratton, J., 'The Singapore way of multiculturalism: Western concepts and Asian cultures', *Sojourn: Journal of Social Issues in Southeast Asia* 10, 1995, pp. 65–89.

Benjamin, G., 'The cultural logic of Singapore's multiracialism', in R. Hassan (ed.), *Singapore: Society in Transition*, Oxford University Press, Kuala Lumpur, 1976.

Boorstin, D., *The Image: A Guide to Pseudo-Events in America*, Vintage House, New York, 1992.

Brackenbury, M., *Managing the Perceptions and Realities of Physical Safety and Security in Tourism Destinations*, PATA Occasional Papers Series No. 13, Pacific Asia Travel Association, San Francisco, CA, 1995.

Britton, S.G., 'The political economy of tourism in the Third World', *Annals of Tourism Research* 9(3), 1982, pp. 331–358.

Buckley, P.J. and Klemm, M., 'The decline of tourism in Northern Ireland', *Tourism Management* June, 1993, pp. 185–194.

Burns, P., 'Sustaining tourism under political adversity: the case of Fiji', in M.V. Conlin and T. Baum (eds), *Island Tourism: Management Principles and Practice*, John Wiley & Sons, Chichester, 1995, pp. 259–272.

Chan, H.C. and Evers, H., 'National identity and nation building in Singapore', in P. Chen and H. Evers (eds), *Studies in Asian Sociology*, Chopmen Enterprises, Singapore, 1978.

Chang, T.C., 'From "instant Asia" to "multi-faceted jewel": urban imaging strategies and tourism development in Singapore', *Urban Geography* 18(6), 1997, pp. 542–562.

Chang, T.C., Milne, S., Fallon, D. and Pohlman, C., 'Urban heritage tourism: the global-local nexus', *Annals of Tourism Research* 23(2), 1996, pp. 284–305.

Crick, M., 'Representations of international tourism in the social sciences: sun, sex, sights, savings, and servility', *Annual Review of Anthropology* 18, 1989, pp. 307–344.

Dye, T., *Understanding Public Policy*, 7th edn, Prentice Hall, Englewood Cliffs, NJ, 1992.

Economic Committee, Ministry of Trade and Industry, *The Singapore Economy: New Directions*, Singapore National Printers, Singapore, 1986.

Eng, P., 'Election wrecks tourism hopes', *South China Morning Post*, Focus, 2 April 1998.

Graburn, N.H.H., 'Tourism and prostitution', *Annals of Tourism Research* 10, 1983, pp. 437–456.

Hall, C.M., 'Sex tourism in South-East Asia', in D. Harrison (ed.), *Tourism and the Less Developed Nations*, Belhaven Press, London, 1992, pp. 64–74.

Hall, C.M., *Tourism and Politics: Policy, Power and Place*, John Wiley & Sons, Chichester, 1994.

Hall, C.M. and Jenkins, J., *Tourism and Public Policy*, Routledge, London, 1995.

Hall, C.M. and O'Sullivan, V., 'Tourism, political stability and violence', in A. Pizam and Y. Mansfield (eds), *Tourism, Crime and International Security Issues*, John Wiley & Sons, Chichester, 1996, pp. 105–122.

Hall, C.M., *Tourism in the Pacific Rim*, 2nd edn. South Melbourne: Longman, Australia, 1997.

Hall, C.M. and Page, S.J., *The Geography of Tourism and Recreation: Environment, Place and Space*, Routledge, London, 1999.

Harrison, D. (ed.), *Tourism and the Less Developed Countries*, Belhaven Press, London, 1992.

Hoivik, T. and Heiberg, T., 'Centre–periphery tourism and self-reliance', *International Social Science Journal* 32(1), 1980, pp. 69–98.

IRIP News Service, 'Beaches and broken bones', *Inside Indonesia* 47, July 1996.

International Shipping Information Services, *Tourism and Prostitution*, International Bulletin 13, ISIS, Geneva, 1979.

Jayasuriya, K., 'Singapore: the politics of regional definition', *The Pacific Review* 7(4), 1994, pp. 411–420.

Kuah, K.E., 'Confucian ideology and social engineering in Singapore', *Journal of Contemporary Asia* 20, 1990, pp. 371–383.

Lanfant, M., 'Tourism in the process of internationalization', *International Social Science Journal* 32(1), 1980, pp. 14–43.

Lea, J. and Small, J., Cyclones, riots and coups: tourist industry responses in the South Pacific, paper presented at Frontiers in Australian Tourism Conference, Australian National University, Canberra, Australia, July 1988.

Leong, W.T., 'Culture and the state: manufacturing traditions for tourism', *Critical Studies in Mass Communication* 6, 1989, pp. 355–375.

Lim, V.C.H., A History of Tourism in Singapore 1950–1977, unpublished honours dissertation, Department of History, National University of Singapore, 1979.

Lingle, C., *Singapore's Authoritarian Capitalism: Asian Values, Free Market Illusions and Political Dependency*, Edicions Sirocco, Barcelona, 1996.

McKie, R., *Singapore*, Angus and Robertson, Sydney, 1972.

Nash, D., 'Tourism as a form of imperialism', in V. Smith (ed.), *Hosts and Guests: The Anthropology of Tourism*, 2nd. edn., University of Pennsylvania Press, Philadelphia, PA, 1989, pp. 37–52.

Oo, A.N. and Perez, M., 'Behind the smiling faces', *Newsletter – The International Communication Project*, no. 28, 1996. http://www.comlink.apc.org/fic/newslett/eng/28/page_36.htm

Pilger, J., 'The land of fear', *The Sydney Morning Herald, Spectrum*, 1 June, 1996.

Pizam, A. and Mansfield, Y. (eds), *Tourism, Crime and International Security Issues*, John Wiley & Sons, Chichester, 1996.

Richter, L.K., 'Tourism politics and political science a case of not so benign neglect', *Annals of Tourism Research* 10, 1983, pp. 313–335.

Richter, L.K., 'A search for missing answers to questions never asked: reply to Kosters', *Annals of Tourism Research* 11, 1984, pp. 613–615.

Richter, L.K., 'State-sponsored tourism: a growth field for public administration', *Public Administration Review* 45(6), 1985, pp. 832–839.

Richter, L.K., *The Politics of Tourism in Asia*, University of Hawaii Press, Honolulu, 1989.

Richter, L.K. and Richter, W.L., 'Policy choices in South Asian tourism development', *Annals of Tourism Research* 12, 1985, pp. 201–217.

Richter, L.K. and Waugh, W.L., Jr., 'Terrorism and tourism as logical companions', *Tourism Management* December 1986, pp. 230–238.

Rodan, G., *The Political Economy of Singapore's Industrialisation: National State and International Capital*, Macmillan, London, 1989.

Rogers, J.R., 'Clear links: tourism and child prostitution', *Contours* 4(2), 1989, pp. 20–22.

Simpson, B., 'Tourism and tradition: from healing to heritage', *Annals of Tourism Research* 20, 1993, pp. 164–181.

Sinclair, K., 'Colombo's hotels are on the move', *Asian Hotelier* July 1994, pp. 12–13.

Singapore Bulletin, August 1997: p. 3.

Singapore Travel News, various issues, Singapore Tourist Promotion Board, Singapore.

Sousa, D., 'Tourism as a religious issue', *Contours* 3(5), 1988, pp. 5–13.

The Economist, 11 November, 1995.

The Straits Times Weekly Edition, June 26 1993.

The Straits Times Weekly Edition, April 22 1995.

Thanh-Dam, T., 'The dynamics of sex-tourism: The cases of Southeast Asia', *Development and Change* 14(4), 1983, pp. 533–553.

Tremewan, C., *The Political Economy of Social Control in Singapore*, St. Martin's Press, New York, 1994.

Turner, L., 'The international division of leisure: tourism and the third world', *World Development* 4(3), 1976, pp. 253–260.

Vasil, R., *Governing Singapore*, Mandarin Paperbacks, Singapore, 1992.

US State Department extends caution announcements on Cambodia, April 8 1998, http://www.cnn.com/TRAVEL/NEWS/9804/08/cambodia.announce/index.html

Wilkinson, B., 'Social engineering in Singapore', *Journal of Contemporary Asia* 18, 1988, pp. 165–188.

Wood, R.E., 'Ethnic tourism, the state and cultural change in Southeast Asia', *Annals of Tourism Research* 11, 1984, pp. 355–374.

Yeung, H.W.C., 'The political economy of transnational corporations: a study of the regionalisation of Singaporean firms', *Political Geography* 17(4), 1998, pp. 389–416.

6

Tourism and the environment: problems, institutional arrangements and approaches

C. Michael Hall

ASEAN ministers believe that economic development need not be at the expense of our precious environment. Yeo Cheow Tong, Singapore's Health and Environment Minister,

quoted in Porter (1997).

Introduction

The natural environment is a major focal point for the selling of Asia to tourists. As has already been noted in earlier chapters (see Chapter 1), romantic images of a pristine environment – sun, sand, sea and palm trees – and exotic cultures have been at the forefront of images of the 'orient' in Western eyes. It is perhaps for this reason that fears of tourism's impacts on the natural environment have often been at the forefront of debates surrounding tourism development in the Asia–Pacific region (Minerbi, 1992).

Unfortunately, tourism's impacts on the natural environment have likely been exaggerated, given that the impacts of tourism are often hard to distinguish from the effects of other exploitative industries such as logging and fishing, or of agriculture and urban development. This is not to say that tourism has not affected the environment. However, what is often at issue are aesthetic or cumulative impacts rather than effects that can be isolated as solely resulting from tourism development. To focus on tourism as a form of negative impact on the natural environment may be to miss the far greater environmental problems which face the region: global warming, sea-level rise, depletion of forest resources, the need to maintain biodiversity and overpopulation (see Earth Summit+5, 1997, for Asian state of the environment profiles). Indeed, the World Bank (1998) has noted the enormous environmental problems facing the region:

The region's emphasis on economic growth without equal attention to the environment has resulted in widespread environmental damage. The costs of air and water pollution and soil degradation are large even in simple economic terms. The region's costs from environmental degradation are above 5% of annual GDP, and in China may be as high as 10%. The poor suffer most from the consequences of environmental neglect.

Asian countries are learning that the trade-offs between effective environmental action and economic growth have changed. Economic progress around the world is proving to be beneficial for the environment as it generates resources for better environmental protection and promotes new and environmentally efficient technologies. Better education and higher incomes are crucial to reducing environmental damage. In spite of these new possibilities, however, Asia's most vexing environmental problems continue to intensify.

The cost of such environmental damage is substantial. The World Bank (1998) estimates that an additional US$30–40 billion a year would be needed by the year 2000 alone for environmental restoration and improvement programmes, through such measures as:

- policy and pricing reform to improve the rate of return on infrastructure investments;
- improving the private sector's access to information and government incentives;
- aggressive regulation enforcement; and
- environmental education to create wider participation in the management process.

The relationship between tourism and the state of the environment in the region was brought into sharp focus in the latter half of 1997 when much of Southeast Asia was covered by a smoke haze as a result of massive forest fires in Indonesia, a result of a combination of drought conditions, unscrupulous land clearance for agriculture and the action of loggers. The forest fires and the subsequent smoke haze was not only a major ecological disaster for the tropical forests and the creatures which inhabit them, such as the orangutan, but also dramatically affected visitor numbers to countries and destinations in the region (see Chapters 10 and 11). Furthermore, the

fires were extremely significant in terms of environmental management strategies as it was clear that an international effort was required to prevent such a disaster happening in the future. As a consequence, Southeast Asian environment ministers gathered for a special ASEAN summit in December 1997 to sign a regional haze action plan which set out for the first time a co-operative and definitive programme to prevent and control land and forest fires in the region (Porter, 1997). The forest fires therefore put into sharp relief the way in which local environmental problems become international issues in the Asia region and vice versa.

This chapter is divided into two main sections. The first section discusses the institutional arrangements which surround the environmental impacts of tourism in the region, while the second examines the way in which coastal zone tourism may be managed. The chapter concludes by noting that the internationalization of environmental issues and difficulties in implementing environmental regimes pose major challenges to tourism and the environment in the region.

Impacts and institutional arrangements

That tourism can have harmful impacts on the physical environment has now become well recognized within the tourism literature (e.g. Mathieson and Wall, 1982). However, that tourism automatically has a negative effect has now become something of a truism in much of the contemporary travel literature. Undoubtedly, unplanned and poorly managed tourism development can damage the natural environment, but the overall understanding of the interaction between tourism and the environment is quite poor, with debates over the impacts of tourism development often dealing in generalities rather than in the outcomes of scientific research on tourist impacts on a specific environment or on a specific species (Hall, 1997).

There has been little systematic study of the environmental impacts of tourism over the region as a whole. Data and information is highly fragmented. Baseline data, i.e. information regarding the condition of the physical environment prior to tourism development, is invariably lacking (Carpenter and Maragos, 1989; Minerbi, 1992; Economic and Social Commission for Asia and the Pacific (ESCAP), 1994, 1996b). In addition, development-specific reports, such as environmental impact statements or environmental statements, may be extremely brief overviews of development impacts, if they are called for at all.

The lack of information on the environmental impacts of tourism has arisen for several reasons. First, substantial public, and hence, business and political concern over environmental conditions has only emerged in recent years. Second, many of the governments of the region have placed far greater priorities on economic development (World Bank, 1998). Third, and as a partial consequence of the above two factors, the resources and scientific expertise was not generally available to undertake the vast amount of research required. Nevertheless, the latter situation is changing substantially, particularly through United Nations and overseas aid programmes (e.g. Commission On Sustainable Development, 1996) and through a growing awareness of the need for more sustainable forms of tourism development (ESCAP, 1994). As the ESCAP Intergovernmental Meeting on Tourism Development recommended:

for sustainable tourism development, countries in the region should give more attention to planning, coordination and monitoring by government agencies and should create awareness in the mass media, with the general public and with international tourists about protecting and preserving the environment (ESCAP, 1996a).

One of the most significant difficulties of effective environmental management in the region is the establishment of appropriate and effective institutional arrangements for managing the relationship between tourism and the environment. The internationalization of environmental issues is apparent when one notes the plethora of relevant legislation from the international (e.g. Agenda 21) through to the local scale (e.g. local government site regulations and planning schemes). However, there are very few legal agreements which deal specifically with tourism and the environment (Hall, 1999). Instead, the relationship between tourism and the environment tends to be managed within general environmental and planning law. Table 6.1 identifies the various levels at which such legal frameworks operate from the international through to the national and the sub-national level.

A number of international conventions operate in the region. These conventions range from international agreements on oil pollution and the Law of the Sea, which is clearly of major importance to the cruise ship industry and marine tourism; to the World Heritage Convention, which serves to establish World Heritage listing for cultural and natural heritage sites of universal significance (e.g. Taj Mahal in India, Sagarmatha in Nepal and Angkor Wat in Cambodia) which are typically of great significance as visitor attractions; and to provisions for the conservation of fauna and flora (e.g. the Ramsar Convention which governs habitat for migratory birds) which may also serve as important ecotourism attractions.

International agencies have also been strongly involved in regional environmental programmes which have tourism components or implications. The Regional Seas Programmes of the UN Environmental Programme (UNEP) have been promoted to protect common resources including the East Asian Seas and South Asian Seas Regions, while the UN Development Programme (UNDP) has given specific focus to the regional programmes on energy and the environment, marine pollution protection and management and urban management. It also supported joint resource management for cross-border cooperation for the Mekong River Commission and the Himalayan Eco-regional Initiative of Bhutan,

Table 6.1 *Legal framework for tourism and the environment in South and Southeast Asia*

A. International Conventions relating to tourism and the environment in South and Southeast Asia

1969	International Convention on Civil Liability for Oil Pollution Damage (Brussels)
1969	International Convention relating to Intervention on the High Seas in Cases of Oil Pollution Damage (Brussels)
1971	Convention on Wetlands of International Importance especially as Waterfowl Habitat (Ramsar)
1972	Convention concerning the Protection of the World Cultural and Natural Heritage (Paris)
1972	Convention on the Prevention of Marine Pollution by Dumping of Wastes and Other Matter (London)
1973	Convention on International Trade in Endangered Species of Wild Fauna and Flora (Washington)
1973	International Convention for the Prevention of Pollution from Ships (MARPOL) (London)
1978	Protocol of 1978 relating to the International Convention for the Prevention of Pollution from Ships, 1973 (London)
1979	Convention on the Conservation of Migratory Species of Wild Animals (Bonn)
1982	United Nations Convention on the Law of the Sea (Montego Bay)
1985	Convention for the Protection of the Ozone Layer (Vienna)
1989	Convention on the Control of the Transboundary Movements of Hazardous Wastes and their Disposal (Basel)
1990	International Convention on Oil Preparedness, Response and Cooperation (London)
1992	Framework Convention for Climate Change (New York)
1992	Convention on Biological Diversity (Rio de Janiero)

B. Regional International Conventions

1985	Agreement on the Conservation of Nature and Natural Resources (Kuala Lumpur)
Parties:	The Government of Brunei
	The Government of the Republic of Indonesia
	The Government of Malaysia
	The Government of the Republic of the Philippines
	The Government of the Republic of Singapore
	The Government of the Kingdom of Thailand
	Member States of the Association of South East Asian Nations (ASEAN)

C. National Legislation and Regulations

Malaysia	Environmental Quality Act, 1974 (127, Am.: A636)
	Fisheries Act, 1985 (317)
	Land Conservation Act, 1989 (385)
	Land Development Act, 1991 (474, Am: 474, 478, A818)
	National Forestry Act, 1984 (313, Am.: Pu(A) 82/86, A864)
	National Parks Act, 1980 (226, Am.:A571)
Singapore	National Parks Act
	Parks and Trees Act
	Preservation of Monuments Act
	Planning Act
	State Lands Act
	State Lands Encroachment Act
	Urban Redevelopment Authority Act
	Water Pollution Control and Drainage Act
	Wild Animals and Birds Act

D. Provincial Legislation and Regulations

E. Local Regulations

China, India, Myanmar, Nepal and Pakistan for biodiversity conservation and management (ESCAP, 1998). The Asian Development Bank (ADB) has also promoted the Greater Mekong Subregion (Vietnam, Thailand, Laos and Cambodia) for the development of infrastructure, energy, trade and protection of the environment. The projects include environmental strategy, poverty reduction and environmental improvements in remote watersheds, protection and management of Tonle Sap Lake and the wetlands of the lower Mekong basin, environmental monitoring and information systems, and environmental training and education (ESCAP, 1998).

One of the most significant pieces of regional environmental international law is the Agreement on the Conservation of Nature and Natural Resources signed in Kuala Lumpur in 1985. Signatories to the Agreement were the then member states of the Association of South East Asian Nations (ASEAN): Brunei, Indonesia, Malaysia, Philippines, Singapore and Thailand. The fundamental principle of the Agreement is that the signatories

> ... within the framework of their respective national laws, undertake to adopt singly, or where necessary and appropriate through concerted action. The measures necessary to maintain essential ecological process and life-support systems, to preserve genetic diversity, and to ensure the sustainable utilization of harvested natural resources under their jurisdiction in accordance with scientific principles and with a view to attaining the goal of sustainable development.
>
> ... To this end they shall develop national conservation strategies, and shall co-ordinate such strategies within the framework of a conservation strategy for the Region (Article 1).

The Agreement was also designed to encourage signatories to set aside protected areas. Under Article 13 the protected areas (national parks and reserves) were to be established for the purpose of safeguarding:

a. the ecological and biological processes essential to the functioning of the ecosystems of the Region;
b. representative samples of all types of ecosystems of the Region;
c. satisfactory population levels for the largest possible number of species of fauna and flora belonging to those ecosystems;
d. areas of particular importance because of their scientific, educational, aesthetic, or cultural interests; and taking into account their importance in particular as:

a. the natural habitat of species of fauna and flora; particularly rare or endangered or endemic species;
b. zones necessary for the maintenance of exploitable stocks of economically important species;
c. pools of genetic material and said refuge for species, especially endangered ones;
d. sites of ecological, aesthetic or cultural interest;
e. reference sources for scientific research;
f. areas for environmental education.

Furthermore, signatories undertook to develop plans of management, buffer zones (where appropriate), undertake impact assessments (Article 14), while protected areas established pursuant to the Agreement were to be regulated and managed in 'such a way as to further the objectives for the purpose of which they have been created. Contracting Parties shall, wherever possible, prohibit within such protected areas activities which are inconsistent with such objectives'. Nevertheless, while such a regional agreement is important and provides a useful declaration of intention with respect to conservation activity, it remains dependent on national legislation and, perhaps more importantly, a clear implementation regime for it to be effective (Hall, 1999).

At the national level, a number of legislative instruments may affect the relationship between tourism and the environment. For example, Table 6.1 notes some of the relevant laws in Malaysia and Singapore. However, because of its nature, it must be emphasized that tourism development will be influenced by an extremely wide variety of laws and regulations, particularly when national tourism organizations are usually responsible for tourism promotion and marketing rather than tourism's impacts. Nations with federal structures, such as those of Malaysia and India, will also have a range of provincial/state laws and regulations that will affect tourism, while within most countries decisions taken at the local level in the form of development permissions and local plans will also have a major effect on the environmental impacts of tourism development and tourist activities.

The multiscale institutional arrangements which surround tourism and the environment are only one aspect of the difficulties of managing tourism's impacts, probably the other key aspect is the manner in which tourism is related to other factors affecting use of the environment in any given area, thereby creating multi-dimensional environmental problems. Perhaps nowhere is this better seen than in the case of the coastline.

Coastal tourism

Of all the activities that take place in coastal zones and the near-shore coastal ocean, none is increasing in both volume and diversity more than coastal tourism and recreation. Both the dynamic nature of this sector and its magnitude demand that it be actively taken into account in government plans, policies, and programs related to the coasts and ocean. Indeed, virtually all coastal and ocean issue areas affect coastal tourism and recreation either directly or indirectly. Clean water, healthy coastal habitats, and a safe, secure, and enjoyable environment are clearly fundamental to successful coastal tourism. Similarly, bountiful living marine resources (fish, shellfish, wetlands and coral reefs) are of critical importance to most recreational experiences. Security from risks associated with natural coastal hazards such as storms, hurricanes, tsunamis, and the like is a requisite for coastal tourism to be sustainable over the long term (National Oceanic and Atmospheric Administration, 1997).

Coastal tourism is an important aspect of tourism in the Asia–Pacific region (Minerbi, 1992; Hall, 1997). The concept of coastal tourism embraces the full range of tourism, leisure and recreationally oriented activities that take place in the coastal zone and the offshore coastal waters. These include coastal tourism development (accommodation, restaurants, food industry and second homes), and the infrastructure supporting coastal development (e.g. retail businesses, marinas and activity suppliers). Also included are tourism activities such as recreational boating, coast- and marine-based ecotourism, cruises, swimming, recreational fishing, snorkelling and diving (Miller and Auyong, 1991; Miller, 1993). The selling of 'sun, sand and surf experiences', the development of beach resorts and the increasing popularity of marine tourism (e.g. fishing, scuba diving, windsurfing and yachting) has all placed increased pressure on the coast, an area for which use may already be highly concentrated in terms of agriculture, human settlements, fishing and industrial locations (Miller, 1993; UNEP et al., 1996; and many chapters within this book). Because of the highly dynamic nature of the coastal environment and the significance of mangroves and the limited coral sand supply for beaches in particular, any development which interferes with the natural coastal system may have severe consequences for the long-term stability of the environment (Cicin-Sain and Knecht, 1998). The impact of poorly developed tourism projects on sand cays (coral sand islands), for example, has been well documented:

- near-shore vegetation clearing exposes the island to sea storm erosion and decreases plant material decomposition on the beach, thereby reducing nutrient availability for flora and fauna;
- manoeuvring by bulldozer (instead of hand clearing) results in scarring and soil disturbance and makes sand deposit loose and vulnerable to erosion;
- excessive tapping of the fresh ground-water lens induces salt water intrusion which then impairs vegetation growth and human water use and renders the cay susceptible to storm damage and further erosion;
- sewage outfall in shallow water and reef flats may lead to an excessive build-up of nutrients thereby leading to algal growth which may eventually kill coral;
- seawalls built to trap sand in the short-term impair the natural seasonal distribution of

sand resulting, in the long run, in a net beach loss and in a reduction of the island land mass; and

• boat channels blasted in the reef act as a sand trap; in time they fill with sand which is no longer circulating around the island; in turn this sand is replaced by other sand eroded from the vegetated edges, changing the size and shape of the island and in time threatening the island's integrity (Baines, 1987).

Another component of the coastal environment which can be substantially affected by tourism is the clearing and dredging of mangroves and estuaries for marinas and resorts. Mangroves and estuarine environments are extremely significant nursery areas for a variety of fish species. The loss of natural habitat resulting from dredging or infilling may therefore have dramatic impact on fish catches. In addition, there may be substantial impacts on the whole of the estuarine food chain with a subsequent loss of ecological diversity. A further consequence of mangrove loss is reduced protection against erosion of the shoreline thereby increasing vulnerability to storm surge. Removal of mangroves will not only impact the immediate area of clearance, but will also affect other coastal areas through the transport of greater amounts of marine sediment (Clarke, 1991; Minerbi, 1992; Hall, 1997). Excessive nutrients from sewage and fertilizers associated with tourism developments may also damage coastal environments. While both of these types of pollution may come from non-tourism sources it should be noted that septic tanks or inadequate sewage systems at resorts, or fertilizer run-off from golf courses may substantially impact reef systems (Kuji, 1991).

In concluding his examination of the impacts of tourism development on Pacific islands, Minerbi (1992: p. 69) was scathing in his criticism of the environmental impacts of tourism:

Resorts and golf courses increase environmental degradation and pollution. Littering has taken place on beaches and scenic lookouts and parks.

Marine sanctuaries have been run over and exploited by too many tourists.

Resorts have interfered with the hydrological cycle by changing groundwater patterns, altering stream life, and engaging in excessive ground water extraction. Coastal reefs, lagoons, anchialine ponds, wastewater marshes, mangroves, have been destroyed by resort construction and by excessive visitations and activities with the consequent loss of marine life and destruction of ecosystems. Beach walking, snorkelling, recreational fishing, boat tours and anchoring have damaged coral reefs and grasses and have disturbed near shore aquatic life ...

Tourism has presented itself as a clean and not polluting industry but its claims have not come true ...

Given the potential impacts of tourism on the coastal environment it is therefore not surprising that organizations such as ESCAP (1995a, b, 1996c, d) have been trying to encourage sustainable forms of coastal development in Asia and the Pacific. Sustainable development of coastal tourism is recognized as being dependent on:

1. good coastal management practices (particularly regarding proper siting of tourism infrastructure and the provision of public access);
2. clean water and air, and healthy coastal ecosystems;
3. maintaining a safe and secure recreational environment through the management of coastal hazards (such as erosion, storms, floods), and the provision of adequate levels of safety for boaters, swimmers, and other water users;
4. beach restoration efforts that maintain the recreational and amenity values of beaches; and,
5. sound policies for wildlife and habitat protection (NCAA, 1997).

However, such a statement fails to reflect the complexities and difficulties of the management and regulation of tourism with respect to the physical environment. Despite the litany of damage noted by Minerbi (1992), it must be emphasized that the environmental impacts of tourism may actually be less than other industries such as agriculture, fishing, forestry and mining. There is complexity of causation with respect to the different uses of the coastal zone and problems of the complexity of cumulative impact. Other forms of 'indigenous' impact such as overpopulation, inappropriate urban development and land clearance may be far more significant but are perhaps not so easy to blame as an industry as visible as tourism, particularly when businesses are often owned by foreigners (Hall, 1997).

Unfortunately, there usually is no coordination between programmes that promote and market tourism and those that manage coastal and marine areas. Environmental or planning agencies often fail to understand tourism, while tourism promotion authorities tend not to be involved with the evaluation of its effects or its planning and management. Implementation strategies often fail to recognize the interconnections that exist between agencies in trying to manage environmental issues, particularly when, as in the case of the relationship between tourism and the environment, responsibilities may cut across more traditional lines of authority. Therefore, one of the greatest challenges facing coastal managers is how to integrate tourism development within the ambit of integrated coastal management, and thus increase the likelihood of long-term sustainability of the coast as a whole (Cicin-Sain and Knecht, 1998). Nevertheless, solving such dilemmas will clearly be of importance to many countries in the region which has substantial emphasis on marine and coastal tourism, particularly when environmental quality becomes another means to achieve a competitive edge in the tourism marketplace.

Conclusion

This chapter has highlighted some of the difficulties in creating appropriate management frameworks for the relationship between tourism and the environment. From an ecological perspective, tensions exist in our understanding of the relationship because a detailed knowledge of the impacts of tourism on the environment in Asia, and on specific ecosystems and species in particular, does not exist. Furthermore, understanding of the complex series of institutional arrangements which surround tourism in the region is limited, and attention to the difficulties of implementing such arrangements even more so.

Sustainable tourism means conserving the productive basis of the physical environment by preserving the integrity of the biota and ecological processes and producing tourism commodities without degrading other values, including socio-cultural and economic values.

Tourism, like other industries, is an agent of development and change and must be recognized as such. It is consumptive like any other industry and the level of consumption is determined by the scale and style of tourism development. At low levels and with careful design, tourism may be able to operate at a sustainable level. However, controlling the level and style of development over the long term presents challenges which, to this point, have not been successfully met. Because of its potentially high impact, tourism should be considered in the same manner as any other industry and should be subjected to the same environmental and social impact assessment processes during the planning stages (Woodley, 1993: p. 137).

It therefore becomes important that, not only for the sake of the environment and the laudable goals of the agreements and legislation which has been enacted but also for ensuring high-quality environments for the development of sustainable forms of tourism, governments in the region should begin to undertake the relevant environmental impact assessments and monitor and develop appropriate planning strategies (see Chapter 7). However, in addition, it is essential that governments adopt a whole-of-government strategy whereby planning frameworks and communication structures within and between government agencies reflect the synergistic and cumulative nature of the environmental impacts of human activities.

References

Baines, G.B.K., 'Manipulation of islands and men: sand-cay tourism in the South Pacific', in S. Britton and W.C. Clarke (eds), *Ambiguous Alternative: Tourism in Small Developing Countries*, University of the South Pacific, Suva, 1987, pp. 16–24.

Carpenter, R.A. and Maragos, J.E. (eds), *How to Assess Environmental Impacts on Tropical Islands and Coastal Areas*, South Pacific Regional Environment Programme (SPREP) Training Manual, Environmental and Policy Institute, East–West Center, Honolulu, 1989.

Cicin-Sain, B. and Knecht, R.W., *Integrated Coastal and Ocean Management: Concepts and Experiences*, Island Press, Washington, DC, 1998.

Clarke, W.C., 'Time and tourism: an ecological perspective', in M.L. Miller and J. Auyong (eds), *Proceedings of the 1990 Congress on Coastal and Marine Tourism*, National Coastal Research and Development Institute, Honolulu, 1991, pp. 387–393.

Commission on Sustainable Development, *Progress in the Implementation of the Programme of Action for the Sustainable Development of Small Island Developing States: Report of the Secretary-General*, Commission On Sustainable Development, Fourth session, 18 April–3 May 1996, Addendum, Document E/CN.17/1996/20/Add.3 of 29 February 1996, Geneva, 1996.

Earth Summit+5, *Special Session of the General Assembly to Review and Appraise the Implementation of Agenda 21, New York, 23–27 June 1997*, Country Profiles – Asian States http://www.un.org/esa/earthsummit/asia-cp.htm, 1997.

Economic and Social Commission for Asia and the Pacific (ESCAP), *Review of Tourism Development in the ESCAP Region*, ESCAP Tourism Review No. 15, United Nations, New York, 1994.

ESCAP, *Guidelines on Environmentally Sound Development of Coastal Tourism*, ST/ESCAP/1371, ESCAP, Bangkok, 1995a.

ESCAP, *Planning Guidelines on Coastal Environmental Management*, ST/ESCAP/1316, ESCAP, Bangkok, 1995b.

ESCAP (Tourism Unit), *Intergovernmental Meeting on Tourism Development, Bangkok, 11–13 December 1996: Recommendations, Major Conclusions and Decisions of the Intergovernmental Meeting on Tourism Development*, ESCAP, Bangkok, http://unescap.org/tctd/rpt_int.htm, 1996a.

ESCAP, *Guidelines on the State of Environment Reporting in Asia and the Pacific*, ST/ESCAP/1707, ESCAP, Bangkok, 1996b.

ESCAP, *Coastal Environmental Management Plan for Pakistan*, ST/ESCAP/1360, ESCAP, Bangkok, 1996c.

ESCAP, *Coastal Environmental Management Plan for Macajalar Bay Area, the Philippines* (2 vols and summary), ST/ESCAP/1359, ESCAP, Bangkok, 1996d.

ESCAP, *Selected Issues with Reference to the Work of the Committee on Environment and Natural Resources Development: Subregional Cooperation for Environmental Programmes* (Item 4 (a) of the provisional agenda), Economic and Social Commission for Asia and the Pacific Committee on Environment and Natural Resources Development, First session, 21–23 October 1998, E/ESCAP/ENRD/1.

Hall, C.M., 'Tourism and the environment', in C.M. Hall and S.J. Page (eds), *Tourism in the Pacific*, International Thomson Business Publishing, London, 1997.

Hall, C.M., *Tourism Planning*, Prentice Hall, Harlow, 1999.

Kuji, T., 'The political economy of golf', *AMPO, Japan–Asia Quarterly Review* 22(4), 1991, pp. 47–54.

Mathieson, A. and Wall, G., *Tourism: Economic, Physical and Social Impacts*, Longman, London, 1982.

Miller, M., 'The rise of coastal and marine tourism', *Ocean and Coastal Management* 21(1–3), 1993, pp. 183–199.

Miller, M. and Auyong, J., 'Coastal zone tourism: a potent force affecting environment and society', *Marine Policy* 15(2), 1991, pp. 75–99.

Minerbi, L., *Impacts of Tourism Development in Pacific Islands*, Greenpeace Pacific Campaign, San Francisco, CA, 1992.

National Oceanic and Atmospheric Administration (NCAA), *1998 Year of the Ocean – Coastal Tourism and Recreation* (Discussion paper), http://www.yoto98.noaa.gov/yoto/meeting/tour_rec_316.html, 1997.

Porter, B., 'Environment ministers sign haze action plan', *South China Morning Post* 24 December 1997.

Woodley, A., 'Tourism and sustainable development: the community perspective', in J. Nelson, R. Butler, and G. Wall, (eds), *Tourism and Sustainable Development: Monitoring, Planning, Managing*, Heritage Resources Centre Joint Publication Number 1, University of Waterloo, 1993.

World Bank, *Asia and the Pacific*, http://www-esd.worldbank.org/html/esd/env/envmat/vol2f96/asiapac.htm, 1998.

United Nations Environment Programme, World Tourism Organization, and Foundation for Environmental Education in Europe, *Awards for Improving the Coastal Environment: The Example of the Blue Flag*, United Nations Environment Programme, Paris, France; World Tourism Organization, Madrid, Spain; and Foundation for Environmental Education in Europe, Kobenhaum, Denmark, 1996.

7

Tourism planning and development in Southeast and South Asia

Russell Arthur Smith

Introduction

It is now recognized that tourism planning is a fundamental component of the development and management of tourism in any location, and South and Southeast Asia are no exception to this. Throughout the region the concern for the existing and future management of tourism assumes an important role, since each destination is at a different stage of development, contains different opportunities and constraints and requires a distinctive approach to the management and development of its tourism industry. The South and Southeast Asia region has experienced strong, though not uniform, tourism growth since the early 1970s. Many countries in this region have had economic growth that has expanded business travel in the region, particularly through intraregional travel. Each destination has an abundance of outstanding natural, historic and cultural resources which has formed a basis for attracting increasing numbers of international and intraregional holiday makers. Domestic tourism has also expanded. The governments of some countries have been proactive in developing tourism. For many other countries, ineffectual planning for tourism development has been common.

Commencing in 1997, a regional economic crisis dramatically changed the former patterns of tourism demand. In the resultant fierce competition for tourism market share, effective tourism development became an imperative. This was particularly important when many destinations were receiving considerably fewer tourists than previously. Compounding the difficulties was the degraded condition of many destination areas. A classic, but by no means only, case was Pattaya, Thailand (Smith, 1992a). Over three decades from 1970, the number of hotel rooms in Pattaya expanded from 400 to 24 000.

Concentration of development in one place and over a short period of time had many serious negative impacts. Loss of trees, devastation of terrestrial wildlife and other natural features resulted in a sterile and harsh urban environment. Off-shore islands were similarly affected by pollution and degraded coral reefs. The sea became badly polluted and unsafe for swimming. Congestion was commonplace and informal (that is, unapproved or illegal) development was a widespread problem. Water supply shortages plagued the area. Major social and political conflicts arose. The original ambience of the natural resort was totally lost. Not surprisingly, the appeal of the area to tourists declined. After peaking in 1988, tourist arrivals at hotels declined sharply. Only after exceptional attention was given to some of the more glaring problems was this negative demand trend reversed, with the first subsequent year-on growth recorded in 1993. By 1994, the previous 1988 peak in tourist arrival numbers had been exceeded (Tourism Authority of Thailand (TAT), 1996). It had taken six years to regain the earlier level of tourism demand. In this period, the tourism business losses were considerable. The transformations witnessed in Pattaya typify the developmental evolution of many destination areas in the South and Southeast Asian region. These are the results of poor and inadequate tourism planning. Such outcomes are not inevitable, as has been demonstrated in some countries that have developed attractive and sustainable tourism destinations. This has been achieved through competent tourism planning. Planning in general is undertaken as urban and regional planning, for which the theory and practice is well developed (see, for example, Harvey, 1992; Kaiser *et al.*, 1995; Chatterji, 1997; Levy, 1997). Tourism planning is an emerging specialization of planning, particularly in developing countries, and in many cases is undertaken by planners who have little explicit knowledge or understanding of the nature of tourism and a dynamic business activity with its own peculiarities.

The rationale for tourism planning

As with any form of development, a primary concern of tourism development will be economic benefits for individual enterprises, related communities and the country as a whole. Tourism development does generate wealth and, in areas of unemployment, create jobs. There is also considerable potential for community development, the conservation of historic and natural sites and the development of the arts related to tourism. Tourism may, however, be responsible for extensive social and environ-

mental damage; and economic gains are not always assured. The intent of planning for tourism development is to maximize the positive benefits of tourism development while minimizing any negative impacts in a sustainable manner. Planning for tourism development is the systematic process of determining ideal future conditions. Tourism planning extrapolates future development situations from existing conditions and trends and seeks to optimize the likely development outcomes that may otherwise have been undesirable. Tourism planning provides for managed intervention of tourism development so as to correct the undesirable and enhance the beneficial.

The planning process strives to be rational but is subject to the distortions of imperfect operational conditions. Weaknesses of planning in practice relate to insufficient data (which is a major and common problem in developing countries), unforeseen future change in the development context, political interference, poorly defined planning scope, inadequate coordination and insufficient resources for planning (such as budget, expertise and time).

Despite these problems, real benefits have been achieved with tourism development that has arisen from effective tourism planning. Not that perfect tourism projects have resulted in these cases. The complexity of tourism development and the diversity of the vested interests of the actors involved ensures that not all will agree that desirable development objectives have been adequately achieved. Tourism planning should result in sustainable tourism development that satisfactorily fulfils most objectives to a high degree and does not disadvantage communities or degrade resources. In short, tourism planning seeks to enable sustainable tourism development.

The planning hierarchy and activity

Tourism planning operates at many levels that may be classified in any of several ways (Gunn, 1994; Inskeep, 1991, 1994). A common hierarchy is based on a geo-spatial scale. For this, generally there are five levels of planning activity: international, national, regional, destination area and project-specific.

International planning

This level involves the governments of two or more countries and is common, for example, with international air service development, but much less so in physical development projects. In the latter case, physical proximity of compatible resources can be the catalyst. The development of the large integrated beach resort (23 000 ha) in the north of Bintan Island, Riau, Indonesia, has been planned jointly by the Indonesian and Singapore governments. Essentially, Indonesia supplies prime coastal resources, land and labour, while Singapore supplies infrastructure (Changi International Airport in Singapore is only 45 minutes away by fast catamaran ferry), expertise in development and management and investment security. Sources from both countries have financed the project. Tourism policy lobbying by the international agencies, such as the World Travel and Tourism Council and the Pacific Asia Travel Association, should not be confused with tourism planning; though it is acknowledged that some of these organizations do undertake tourism planning, but typically at the lower levels of this hierarchy.

National planning

Many countries have found benefits in preparing national tourism plans. Because of the normally large spatial dimensions, such plans tend to be strategic or conceptual. Those with a strategic intent formulate development plans based, in part, on a review of the available resources and the strategic advantage of applying these to the likely future competitive market of the region. National plans should consider all resources (natural, infrastructure, existing facilities, labour and demand) in a comprehensive manner for rationalization of resource. These plans become the basis for national tourism policy on, for example, tourism taxation, national and international transport, education and training, allocation of resources over time and the delineation of project types and their locations.

When completed, a national tourism plan would normally be endorsed by the national government executive, such as the cabinet. National tourism plans of this type then become frameworks for coordination and management of tourism development at the other levels, where the planning timeframe may be up to 20 years. It is important that regional political considerations are not allowed to bias recommendations. An example is the Malaysia Comprehensive National Tourism Development plan (Government of Malaysia (GOM), 1987). This plan reviewed existing tourism facilities and other resources suitable for tourism from a national perspective and proposed development in the best interest of the nation. Under this plan, because of their limited resources or potential, some Malaysian states received little or no support for tourism development, which was the proper outcome of an objective planning process.

Regional planning

At the sub-national level, tourism plans are normally initiated by regional governments, i.e. state or provincial. Plans may cover the entire area of jurisdiction of the regional government, but more often they have a smaller area of study. Definition of the study area in geo-spatial terms depends on the study objectives. Commonly the intent of a regional tourism plan is to develop tourism in relation to specific resources or groups of mutually compatible resources. Ideally, regional governments would generally follow broad strategies and concepts in the national plan in preparing their own tourism plans as the national plan prioritizes tourism development. Support from the national government is then more likely. Coordination of the preparation of these plans is typically undertaken by the state's economic planning unit, national tourism office or the urban and regional planning department.

There is likely to be a steering committee which comprises representatives of relevant state and national organizations who meet to review the preparation of the plan at designated stages. The final plan would have to be endorsed by the state government.

In Malaysia, the Perak State Government coordinated a tourism plan for Pangkor Island, related islands and the nearby mainland. The study area boundary coincided with local government boundaries; specifically those of the adjacent Districts of Lumut and Perak Tengah (GOM, 1994). This arrangement facilitated subsequent implementation and management of the plan by the respective district councils. A similar case is the plan for the tourism development of Phetchaburi and Prachuap Khiri Khan Provinces near Bangkok, Thailand (TAT, 1987). Regional tourism plans are also a guide for investors and developers to the tourism projects that will be supported in one way or another by government. A contrasting Malaysian example is the Pahang Coastal Tourism Development Plan for the entire 200 km of the state's coastline that was initiated by the Pahang State Government. This plan ignores local government boundaries and focuses completely on the future success of coastal marine tourism development in the state. The onus here was on the Pahang Government to coordinate the development (Smith, 1997).

Destination area planning

Commonly referred to as master planning, destination area planning is concerned with the delineation of physical and related development within specific geographical contexts. Whole resort areas may be planned for new tourism destinations. In Indonesia, the Bali Tourism Development Corporation, a government agency, prepared a plan for the development of a completely new beach resort where only farming and fishing villages had existed. This plan for Nusa Dua, Bali, is discussed in the section 'Integrated strategy', below. Alternatively existing destination areas, such as cities or resorts, may be planned for rejuvenation or expansion of their tourist functions. One example

is the tourism plan for Singapore: Tourism 21. This plan seeks to build on past tourism success through rejuvenation of existing tourism development and the addition of new facilities (Singapore Tourism Promotion Board (STPB), 1996). The institutional arrangements for preparation of these plans will depend on several factors, of which control of land will play a large part. Where a private-sector development organization owns the land in the planning area, then this organization will convene and coordinate its own planning team. Where there is government land involved or there are several land owners, the regional government is likely to take the lead role. This latter situation is more common where the land area under study is large, primarily because only the government can coordinate the necessary development of infrastructure. In most cases, endorsement of tourism development plans lies with the regional government.

Project planning

At the project level there is planning for individual hotel and other tourism developments. This is the final stage – the cumulative output – of all the previous planning undertaken at the preceding levels. In the case of Nusa Dua, the plan for this development included sites for the hotels, each of which was sold to different developers. Thus each site became a tourism project with its own project plan. In this case, the output is physical buildings. The planning process requires inordinate attention to physical detail and is often, on account of its nature, referred to as design. In cities, unique urban areas may be planned with tourism development in mind. This was the case for the historic Chinatown area of Singapore when a plan was prepared to restore the old shophouses (Smith, 1988).

Planning linkages and outcomes

Ideally, the hierarchy described here should follow sequentially from the strategic national level through to the detailed project level. The advantage is that the benefits of systematic planning will more likely be realized. Foremost amongst these will be coordinated tourism development and therefore more efficient, rational allocation of resources and appropriate phasing of development. Economic and other benefits of tourism development will then be maximized. In practice, this does not always occur. Development opportunities may arise which cannot wait for the completion of tourism plans. Political imperatives may also interfere with systematic planning. Generally there are three types of plan produced: statutory, management and construction. While the names given to these types will vary in different circumstances, here these names reflect their intent. The degree of detail contained in these will be determined by their hierarchical level: the lower the level, the more detailed the recommendations.

Statutory plans have formal roles under relevant legislation. Planning legislation often calls for the preparation of plans that are usually displayed for community comment prior to formal adoption. Once finalized, these plans have specific roles under the legislation and become part of the legal framework for the management of development. Few tourism plans are of this type as statutory plans typically are multi-sectoral where tourism is one among many. In such cases, tourism planning is undertaken as an integrated component of the overall plan formulation. This underscores the fact that tourism is only one sector competing for limited resources.

Most tourism plans at the national, regional and destination area levels are non-statutory plans that are prepared primarily as management tools. Once one of these plans has been endorsed by government, regardless of whether it has been prepared by the public or private sectors, it becomes a guideline for tourism implementation and facility operation. Government officers and non-government managers in different organizations thus have a common reference for tourism development in a particular area. A comprehensive tourism plan will identify the potential for tourism development qualitatively and quantitatively. This will include the projected demand change for international and domestic segments and their estimated expenditures over time. The spatial distribution for physical development and the related project types will be described. Essentially there are two types of project: hardware and software. Generally hardware includes physical projects that involve the development of accommodation, theme parks, airports and so forth. Supporting infrastructure such as water supply, highways and telecommunications along with housing and community facilities for the resident population, where relevant, are also hardware. Software projects, for example, may relate to institutional development such as establishment of government tourism units, marketing and promotion programmes for the developed tourism product, training of tourism industry workers and initiation of new tour packages. Feasibility analyses and recommendations on the sources and quantum of investment finance may also be included, though the latter is often a separate exercise, especially in public-sector planning.

Some tourism plans focus on a few of these aspects only; for example, tourism development potential, human resource development or marketing. In all situations, vertical integration with tourism development at higher and lower hierarchical levels is critical for coordinated resource allocation and resultant development. Similarly, horizontal integration will be needed to create the necessary linkages between regions and related destination areas for coordinated infrastructure provision and marketing programs. Central to the success of any tourism plan will be its implementation. An important facet of this is provision of guidelines for those who manage the implementation and operation of tourism projects. Government officers need guidelines that provide a framework for approval of projects for implementation, the regulation of implementation and project operation. Guidelines also assist developers, building contractors and facility operators to understand the parameters and requirements for project implementation and operation. A comprehensive tourism plan will include guidelines for each project – both hardware and software. Physical development guidelines, for example, may impose limits on the maximum height of buildings in a resort, the distance of buildings from one another and the site boundary and the types and colour of construction materials so as to create a controlled resort ambience. Construction guidelines may, for example, impose limits on the extent of cutting of hills in mountainous areas to prevent slope collapse and silt traps to limit silting of rivers and streams. Operational guidelines may require the on-site treatment of wastewater from kitchens and bathrooms to prevent the pollution of the sea and may impose limits on foreign employment to provide jobs and training for residents. As is indicated by these few samples, guidelines must be all-encompassing and strive to provide a clear framework for effective management of tourism development. Construction plans elaborate in considerable detail on the concepts of elements of destination area plans to facilitate their construction. Designs by architects, landscape architects and engineers are detailed as tender drawings for construction. While an important and indispensable part of the tourism planning and development process, this activity is not normally considered to be planning but a post-planning activity.

Spatial issues

The spatial distribution of tourism is planned in macro terms through delineation of destination areas. Strategic concepts are reflected in structure plans where major elements of all forms of development are coordinated for entire regions. Structure plans would normally include the proposed future development condition at some distant point in time. Major concentrations of tourism are coordinated with infrastructure, service centres and transport. It also becomes important to separate land uses where there is likely to be a conflict of use; for example, to

separate tourism from heavy industry and mining. At a more detailed development scale, spatial allocation is determined by land use controls. The intent is to encourage rational development that maximizes the allocation of resources, especially related to capital investment by both public and private sectors, while separating incompatible land uses. In this way tourism becomes a designated land use that is tied to specific land areas or sites, which may be large or small. For each designated tourism site, other controls may be assigned. In the Bukit Bendera Local Plan, for the mountain resort in Penang, Malaysia, each development site had regulatory controls for new buildings in terms of height of building, percentage of the site permitted to be covered by buildings, retention of large trees, limiting of cutting of hill slopes, external finishes (i.e. the construction material) of buildings and form of roof. These controls were intended to conserve and reinforce the prevailing historic hill heritage character (GOM, 1993).

Strategies for development planning

As has been demonstrated with the case of Pattaya, unplanned and unregulated tourism development fails in many ways. If this is the characteristic pattern and outcome of unmanaged tourism development, the question becomes one of how to avoid these problems. There are four basic strategic approaches to tourism development and management: *ad hoc*, *limited growth*, *integrated* and *comprehensive*. These strategies differ in intent, procedure and end result. All four have merits, though the specific developmental and managerial conditions of the region recommend the comprehensive approach over the others.

Ad hoc

This is unfettered and poorly controlled tourism development for which plans are not prepared or, if they are, not followed. Development proceeds in a project-by-project process with little or no attention to overall objectives, long-term consequences, linkages to other sectors or appropriate allocation and conservation of resources. The de facto objective is maximization of short-term gains as found in sharply increasing demand and related expansion of revenues. This strategy works in the short term but fails beyond that time-frame (Smith, 1991).

Limited growth

In an attempt to conserve natural resources and to limit social impacts on communities, tourism development may be capped through, for instance, the imposition of a maximum capacity for tourist accommodation. While this strategy has been implemented in developed countries, in the Third World informal development is likely to occur to neutralize artificially imposed caps as latent demand increases. The lure of short-term financial gains and the general weakness of institutionalized development management will result in any artificial limits ultimately being ignored. Initially this strategy is likely to work, however over time the development process will revert to ad hoc.

Integrated

As a reaction to the manifold problems of ad hoc tourism development, attention has shifted to integrated approaches, particularly for resort projects. Integrated development is applied to large destination areas and results in totally planned tourism facilities. In resorts, there will be a number of hotels that share elements of infrastructure, recreational features and other facilities such as second homes, marinas and retail outlets. Central to the integrated strategy is control. With a large land area and a number of tourism features, it is possible to create a totally planned environment that brings together all of the best resort elements in a programmed manner which excludes incompatible activities and land uses. Coordination of

resort planning and development creates a consistent ambience for the area as a whole (Stiles and See-Tho, 1991). The first integrated tourism development in Southeast Asia was Nusa Dua, Bali. Planning for this 350-ha beach resort commenced in 1971 under the direction of the Bali Tourism Development Corporation. The first hotel opened in 1983 and now Nusa Dua has ten high-quality beachfront hotels. Common facilities include an 18-hole golf course and a large central shopping precinct. More integrated developments have either been completed or are planned throughout the region. Nusa Dua is a major improvement over other beach resorts that evolved in ad hoc ways. Only well maintained tourism facilities are to be found in the integrated resort, where the common areas – the roadways, footpaths and beach fronts – are well planted with trees and shrubs. Centralized wastewater treatment has helped avoid the perennial sea pollution found in other resorts. Litter is also rarely seen as solid waste is collected and removed for landfill. Outside of the Nusa Dua integrated resort boundary in the adjacent village is a contrasting world of inadequate streets, crowded housing, clogged open sewers, piles of solid waste and a polluted ground water supply. In addition, development of tourism facilities is occurring in an ad hoc manner along the beach outside of the integrated project boundary. Lateral spread of the resort is continuing to the north as hotels, guest houses and other tourist facilities are constructed. Physical deterioration and environmental degradation of the areas around the integrated project means that, in time, the larger Nusa Dua area is likely to resemble other unplanned resorts except for the central core (Smith, 1992b).

Comprehensive

The comprehensive strategy is the recommended approach for tourism development. It maximizes the benefits of the integrated strategy while avoiding the pitfalls of the ad hoc and limited growth approaches. With balanced planning, designated integrated development areas are coordinated with other tourism projects and priority is given to development and conservation of related, non-tourism functions. Through these processes, tourism benefits are maximized and negative impacts minimized. The prime characteristics of this approach are: identification of suitable sites for integrated development; zonation of the remaining land for appropriate tourism, community and other uses; designation of environmental protection areas; policy formulation that addresses tourism development in a comprehensive manner; institutional development; and enactment of regulatory instruments and their enforcement.

Planning processes

The process of tourism planning should follow a logical procedure that addresses relevant development opportunities and problems. It should propose future scenarios that meet the objectives of interest groups. Generic planning procedures are well documented in the literature (Inskeep, 1991; Gartner, 1996; Cooper *et al.*, 1998). In practice, planning contexts and objectives will determine the actual form of a particular process. Typically, planning commences with the delineation of the planning parameters and objectives. A systematic procedure then follows a step-by-step process resulting in a set of recommendations that are endorsed by the client. In Southeast Asia, much tourism planning is initiated by government. A typical planning procedure, where government is the client, is as follows.

Conceptualization: Definition of objectives, study area, scope, time frame and outcomes by the client. Preparation, by the client, of the Terms of Reference (TOR) which record this information.

Assembly of study team: Appointment of experts by the client to undertake the planning study. Composition of the team will be determined by the nature of the study but generally will include expertise in tourism project development and marketing, planning, transportation, infrastructure (e.g. water supply and waste disposal), environment, economics and institutional management. If circumstances warrant, other expertise may be included, such as finance, recreation, sociology, law, population, landscape, coastal management, conservation, heritage or others. Each area may be covered by a single individual or there may, if necessary, be several experts; for example, separate experts may be engaged for water supply and power supply. Also there may be several planners, such as urban, land use and regional. The study team should be headed by someone with considerable tourism planning expertise. Increasingly this expert is a professionally qualified urban and regional planner who has special training and experience in tourism development. For plans with narrow scopes, the team leader's expertise is more likely to reflect the focus for the study. If the exercise is initiated by government, then the experts may be drawn from the private sector, government or both. All team members must be familiar with developing county contexts if their contribution is to be of use to the work of the study team.

Inception: The study team is briefed and undertakes a preliminary field survey. The objective of this phase is to quickly review the TOR to ensure that they are workable. An Inception Report is produced and presented to the client in committee. This report includes a proposed timetable for completion of the study. Sometimes the study team recommends adjustment to the TOR such as to modify the study area by inclusion or exclusion of some physical features or the modification of a study objective. If not, this stage is a formality.

Interim study: This phase may produce an Interim Report, a Sectoral Report or a Technical Report; all of which are similar in intent. In all cases, this is a major part of the study during which the existing conditions are analysed in detail and significant opportunities and problems identified. Previous studies are examined, extensive fieldwork is undertaken in connection with existing tourism development and resources with potential for tourism, surveys are conducted and numerous strategic, statistical and other analyses are completed. Essentially the study team needs to delineate the nature of and extent for future tourism development. Projections are made for future tourism demand and supply, often for 20 years into the future. Typically a range of scenarios are prepared: high, medium and low growth. Part of the work involves the difficult task of allowing for future change, especially for committed development projects. New infrastructure and accommodation supply will certainly impact forecasts, as will significant upgrades. These have to be allowed for.

Interim review: The draft report is sent to the client for circulation to interested government organizations prior to presentation in committee. Comments are given to the study team and a revised report has to be prepared and submitted for re-circulation and re-presentation. This circular process continues until the client is satisfied with the report and it is endorsed. Where the client is government, it is common for this phase to take considerably longer than the preceding phase, a fact which is almost never allowed for in the study timetable. A major reason for this delay is the difficulty in convening meetings when there are numerous government organizations that need to comment, as well as coordinating their comments. A government client committee commonly includes representatives from the national tourism office, the regional tourism unit, the economic planning unit, the urban and regional planning department, the forestry department, the national parks office, the department of parks and recreation and the departments of health, water, electricity, drainage, fire and police. (Even with a private-sector client, a major tourism proposal would have to be vetted by these bodies before being allowed to proceed.)

Final study: The first task of this phase is to define an appropriate tourism development strategy. The strategy must properly address the opportunities and problems identified at the interim stage. Based on this, a programme of appropriate tourism projects is proposed as new enterprises and as modifications to or expansions of existing facilities. This programme for tourism development needs to be integrated and coordinated internally as well as externally with relevant facilities and proposed projects. The implementation of the programme must be phased over time. The implementation agencies have to be identified along with the operators. This point is important in developing countries as there is frequent confusion over the most suitable roles for the parties to tourism development. It therefore becomes critical to identify the roles for which government is most suitable and those most suited to the private sector. Some development projects benefit from a joint venture between public and private sectors. The feasibility of individual projects needs to be demonstrated. Comprehensive management and monitoring guidelines are included for the implementation and operational stages of each project.

Final review: The Draft Final Report is submitted and reviewed. The review process is similar to that described at the interim review stage, however the focus of the review is firmly on the programme of projects and their implementation. Once the report has been endorsed, a Final Report is produced for limited distribution. These are occasionally made available to the public. Each country follows its own policy on this. In Thailand, there has been a tradition of public release of final, and even interim, reports but much less so in Malaysia.

Parallel with or subsequent to this process may be other tourism planning studies that address a narrow set of issues. Examples are environmental or social impact assessment, which identify the type and degree of positive and negative impacts that specific projects may have. Ordinarily these concerns would be covered by the main tourism planning exercise, but for statutory or political reasons, an appraisal by a third party may be called for.

Actors

In the developing countries of South and Southeast Asia, the key actors in approving tourism plans are politicians, government officers and private developers. Even though, ultimately, the plan is endorsed by a ranking government politician, the interactions between these three parties actually determine the outcome. Developers supply capital investment and seek to maximize financial returns on their investments. Government politicians (for example, ministers) have considerable power to guide developers' funds, albeit indirectly, and have acute short-term objectives. In general, government officers (for example, heads of ministries or statutory bodies) seek to fulfil the missions of their respective organizations which continuously puts them in conflict with both the developers and their nominal superiors, the government politicians. Planning study teams will report directly to either the government officers or the developers, as the case may be. The objectivity of the team may thus be constrained by the interests of the client.

Unlike many developed country contexts, where public participation in planning is a major force, public involvement in planning in South and Southeast Asia has been comparatively insignificant. The judiciary has also not been a major actor. The wild card in the tourism planning and development equation is individual communities, which have in the past tolerated major change as a result of tourism development. Occasionally, a proposed tourism project may incite strong community resentment that is expressed in highly visible protests, blockades or violence. Such events typically derail tourism development that may be

cancelled or subject to review and change. Instances of this have not been frequent, but recent political turmoil in several Southeast Asian countries may lead to a more formal community involvement in the planning process.

Expertise

A major limitation on tourism planning in South and Southeast Asia is the shortage of relevant expertise. Because of this shortage, qualifications generally take a pre-eminent position in developing countries, with experience and ability coming a poor second. The private sector attracts most of the best experts as it pays better than government. For the experts who work in government, the best jobs are at the federal level and the least desirable with local government. The prime reason for this is the relative budgets of the levels of government and, for many local government jobs, remote locations. Shortage of expertise at the local level leads to weak local government that impacts tourism plan preparation and the management of the implementation of these. The comparatively low pay of government officers can inject the need to supplement incomes, which introduces another distortion into the tourism planning, approval and implementation process.

Prospects

At the time of writing, the regional economic crisis of the late 1990s shows no signs of abating. With some countries also experiencing dramatic social and political turmoil, the full effects of the crisis have perhaps not yet been fully felt. That this is a period of change is indisputable: the challenge is to capitalize on this change. In a time of renewal, planning for future success is a key objective. Several actors in the tourism industry have already taken steps in that direction. Government agencies in some countries and several private-sector organizations are repositioning and restructuring for future growth. As we have seen here, an essential component of successful tourism development will be effective planning. The real challenge for the regions is to assess future growth prospects and to attempt to provide infrastructure, accommodation and other services which meet both the demand and ability of the area to cater for tourist needs. All too often, tourism development plans are confined to paper and political objectives prevent sound and rational plans from being implemented or monitored owing to the possible repercussions for investment and constraints on further development. The rapid growth in visitor arrivals experienced in some countries of South and Southeast Asia and the demands being placed on destinations (reviewed in the chapters focused on specific countries in this book) underlines the need for tourism planning at various levels from the national to the local. Only through a rationally organized and systematic assessment of tourism prospects and long-term goals, can both the environment and host population be harmonized with the political objectives which many governments in the region have attached to a thriving inbound and domestic tourism industry.

References

Chatterji, M. (ed.), *Regional Science: Perspectives for the Future*. St. Martin's Press, New York, 1997.

Cooper, C., Fletcher, J., Gilbert, D. and Wanhill, S. (edited by Rebecca Shepherd), *Tourism: Principles and Practice*. Longman, Harlow, 1998.

Gartner, W., *Tourism Development: Principles, Processes, and Policies*. Van Nostrand Reinhold, New York, 1996.

Government of Malaysia (GOM), *Malaysia Comprehensive National Tourism Development*. Government of Malaysia, Kuala Lumpur, 1987.

GOM, *Bukit Bendera Local Plan*. Government of Malaysia, Georgetown, Penang, 1993.

GOM, *Pangkor Tourism Development Study*. Government of Malaysia, Ipoh, Perak, 1994.

Gunn, C., *Tourism Planning: Basics, Concepts, Cases*, 3rd edn. Taylor and Francis, Washington, DC, 1994.

Harvey, J., *Urban Land Economics*. Macmillan, Basingstoke, 1992.

Inskeep, E., *Tourism Planning: An Integrated and Sustainable Approach*. Van Nostrand Reinhold, New York, 1991.

Inskeep, E., *National and Regional Tourism Planning*. Routledge, London, 1994.

Kaiser, E., Godschalk, D. and Chapin, S., *Urban Land Use Planning*. University of Illinois Press, Urbana, IL, 1995.

Levy, J., *Contemporary Urban Planning*. Prentice Hall, Upper Saddle River, NJ, 1997.

Singapore Tourism Promotion Board, *Tourism 21: Vision of a Tourism Capital*. STPB, Singapore, 1996.

Smith, R.A., 'The role of tourism in urban conservation – The case of Singapore', *Cities* 5(3), 1988, pp. 245–259.

Smith, R.A., 'Beach resorts: A model of development evolution', *Landscape and Urban Planning* 21(3), 1991, pp. 189–210.

Smith, R.A., 'Coastal urbanization: Tourism development in the Asia Pacific region', *Built Environment* 18(1), 1992a, pp. 27–40.

Smith, R.A., 'Review of integrated beach resort development in Southeast Asia', *Land Use Policy* 9(3), 1992b, pp. 209–217.

Smith, R.A., 'Resort landscapes of the Asia Pacific', *Landscape East* 5, 1997, pp. 14–16.

Stiles, R.B. and Wilke See-Tho, 'Integrated resort development in the Asia Pacific', *Travel and Tourism Analyst* 3, 1991, pp. 22–37.

Tourism Authority of Thailand (TAT), *Master Plan for the Development of Phetchaburi Province and Prachuap Khiri Khan Province. Volumes 1 and 2*. TAT, Bangkok, 1987.

TAT, *Statistical Report 1995*. Tourism Authority of Thailand, Bangkok, 1996.

Part Two

Tourism in Southeast Asia

8

Singapore: tourism development in a planned context

Peggy Teo and T.C. Chang

Introduction

Singapore offers a case study of tourism development in a planned context. In a country with limited land space, a history that dates only to the early nineteenth century and relatively few natural and cultural attractions, its achievements in tourism stand as a testimony to careful planning and marketing. In 1997, Singapore attracted 7.19 million visitors. Tourism receipts in 1996 reached US$9.4 billion, ranking it eleventh in the world, ahead of larger countries such as Australia, Thailand and Canada (World Tourism Organization (WTO), 1997). In 1995, Singapore was also Asia's top convention destination and was ranked sixth in the world. Singapore's enviable status in tourism has been the result of proactive state policies. Reflecting on Singapore's tourism achievements, Senior Minister Lee Kuan Yew commented in 1993:

Why should anybody come to Singapore to begin with? What did we have? ... We only had a name, then Raffles Hotel, and what? A few quaint habits and customs and the mediums and the temples, and the Indian with his kavadi *walking over heated charcoal ... that is not going to bring in six million [tourists]. [Instead], we* created the

attraction. *We created the interest that brought the six million tourists. We developed a marketing strategy ... [a]nd made ourselves useful to the world.* (cited in The Straits Times Weekly Edition, *16 June 1993*) (emphasis inserted by the editors).

'Creating interest' and being 'useful' to the world are the principles by which Singapore has been able to sustain itself in tourism, ever since the Singapore Tourism Board (STB)[1] was set up in 1964. This chapter is concerned with the role of the state in promoting tourism. It argues that tourism development is essentially a state-led phenomenon spearheaded by conscious attempts at 'inventing resources' to meet the needs of global travellers, and to augment both real and perceived shortcomings in its resource endowment. This argument will be empirically substantiated as we show how assets are built up to enhance the country as an attractive destination area. Before doing so, an introduction to the extraordinary growth of tourism is outlined.

[1]Originally called the Singapore Tourist Promotion Board (STPB), the name was changed to better reflect the additional but vital role of developing the tourism industry beyond merely the promotion of tourist attractions and arrivals.

Tourism: phenomenal growth in the face of local constraints

Following Singapore's independence in 1965, tourist arrivals had been increasing at an average growth rate of 12 per cent until 1983. The first decline occurred in 1984 when arrivals fell 3.5 per cent over the previous year. Fortunately, the trend reversed and the numbers continued to escalate again at an average of 9.6 per cent per annum until 1994 (Table 8.1). At last count, there were 7.19 million visitors to Singapore in 1997, dropping slightly from 7.29 million in 1996. The decline is attributed to the region's current economic crisis and its environmental haze (*The Straits Times*, 11 February 1998).

While the numbers grow continuously, the profile of Singapore's visitors has not been as stable. The main bulk of visitors in the decade of the 1960s and the early 1970s was from the USA, UK and Australia; since the late 1970s, Asians constitute the bigger market with Japan topping the list in 1997 (16.1 per cent), followed by Indonesia, Malaysia and Taiwan (Table 8.2). Other growing Asian markets include South Korea, Hong Kong, China and India. This augurs well for Singapore as most analysts agree that leisure growth is expected to be greatest in the Asia–Pacific region where, not only is the demographic potential good, but where disposable income has also been increasing (Go, 1997; WTO, 1997; Qu and Zhang, 1997).

The only significant setback in Singapore's tourism growth has been the average length of stay of visitors, which declined from 3.5–4 days in the 1970s to the current 3.3 days (STB, 1996: p. 4). The decline is mainly due to the fact that Singapore is often a stopover point for many tourists. They pass through Singapore on their way to more exotic locations such as Bali or Chiangmai. Moreover, it is widely accepted that Singapore does not have the wide range of natural, historical or cultural attractions offered by surrounding destinations. In some ways, a short length of stay is also a reflection of the purpose for visiting Singapore: the number who come for holiday rather than for business has declined from 68.7 per cent in 1986 to only 53.2 per cent in 1996. Concomitantly, the number who came for business has risen from 9.5 per

Table 8.1   *Visitor arrivals to Singapore 1965–1997*

Year	Number
1965	111 892
1970	521 624
1975	1.32 million
1980	2.82 million
1985	3.03 million
1990	5.32 million
1995	7.13 million
1997	7.19 million

Source: Singapore Tourism Board (STB), various years.

Table 8.2   *Main visitor markets 1971–1996*

1971	%	1977	%	1985	%	1990	%	1996	%
Indonesia	14.0	Australia	14.3	ASEAN	33.3	ASEAN	27.0	Japan	16.1
UK	13.4	Japan	12.6	Japan	12.5	Japan	18.0	Indonesia	14.6
USA	12.7	Malaysia	8.5	Australia	9.9	Australia	9.0	Malaysia	9.6
Australia	10.8	USA	7.8	India	7.2	UK	6.0	Taiwan	7.3
Malaysia	10.2	UK	5.2	USA	5.8	USA	5.0	S. Korea	5.3
Japan	9.6	Hong Kong	2.9	UK	5.2	Taiwan	4.0	USA	5.1
India	4.1	New Zealand	2.9	Hong Kong	3.2	India	4.0	Australia	4.8
Taiwan	2.6	West Germany	2.6	Taiwan	2.7	Hong Kong	4.0	UK	4.3
West Germany	2.6	Thailand	2.4	West Germany	2.4	West Germany	3.0	Hong Kong	4.0
Hong Kong	1.9	Others	40.8	New Zealand	1.9	S. Korea	2.0	Thailand	3.5
Others	18.2			Others	15.9	Others	18.0	China	3.1
								India	2.8
								Others	16.5

Source: STB, various years.

Table 8.3 *Purpose of visit for international visitors to Singapore 1976–1996 (%)*

Purpose	1976	1986	1996
Holiday	65.1	68.7	53.2
Business	12.5	9.5	14.6
Business and holiday	–	4.0	2.9
In transit	–	0.2	9.4
Visiting friends/relatives	–	–	4.3
Convention/exhibition	–	0.3	1.1
Education	–	0.4	0.4
Others	–	7.9	3.9
Not stated	–	–	10.2

Source: STB, various years.

cent to 14.6 per cent in the same period (Table 8.3).

A history of self-invention

A large part of Singapore's economic growth can be attributed to the unfettered efforts at making the island 'useful to the world'. Dating back to 1819 when a British official was tasked with the job of finding a suitable location for the Empire to establish a 'factory'[2] so that it could effectively compete with the Dutch for a stronghold in the East Indies trade, Singapore was deemed to have potential to meet this challenge. Over time, as the Empire's naval power in the east expanded, Singapore's strategic importance for the Straits of Malacca grew to the point that Lord Canning, the Secretary of Foreign Affairs, described the island as 'the *unum necessarium* for making the British Empire in India complete' (Wong, 1991:p. 31). A century and a half later, historical events have proved the description of 'strategic importance' apt for Singapore. It has limited natural resources but the city-state is highly globalized and clearly embedded in international business and services. Originally the gateway to the East for the British yearning for spices and silks, today Singapore engages the world not only in industry and commerce but

[2]A 'factory' is a European trading post in an Eastern port.

also in the financial and communications sectors. The legendary transformation of Singapore to become one of the four 'tigers' (Smith *et al.*, 1985: p. 1) has not been wholly spontaneous. Chua (1995) attributes the successful push towards capitalist industrialization to the ideology of communitarianism in which the state legitimates its policies by claiming them to be 'pragmatic' and necessary for the 'survival' of Singapore (Chua, 1995: p. 37). Working for the 'common good' necessitated the co-operation of all Singaporeans and was applied to many arenas of life, including housing, job creation, education, birth control, pluralism, religious freedom (for a fuller discussion, refer to Sandhu and Wheatley, 1989; Chua, 1995, 1997; Teo and Ooi, 1996) and, last but not least, tourism.

Inventing resources for tourism

In Singapore's guided programme towards economic take-off, the consensus of the population was sought to develop an infrastructure of communications, schools, healthcare, housing and industry. Personal sacrifices, such as smaller family size, were promoted along with the ideology of racial harmony and the freedom of worship. In addition, virtues such as hard work were embodied in the meritocratic system built into the education system and work force. These became the basic framework onto which was founded the Singapore landscape. As for tourism, creative ways were sought to improve Singapore's tourism product base. The potential of tourism as a cheap and quick means to boost foreign exchange earnings was recognized in the 1960s, and was officially promoted as one avenue to economic development. This intention is realized in three ways: (a) the creation of an economic infrastructure which capitalizes on Singapore's geographic location; (b) the reconfiguration of environmental resources in order to sustain nature-based tourism; and (c) the refashioning of cultural attributes to project Singapore as a 'Global City for the Arts'.

Through this tripartite strategy, Singapore's tourism resources are constantly adapted so as to remain 'relevant' to the needs of visitors. Today, emerging niche markets such as business travellers, eco-tourists and arts buffs are also being courted as the government believes in their growth potential in the new millennium.

Economic resources: creating infrastructure for tourism

The importance of the service sector in many countries has grown in absolute and relative terms in the recent decades. In the USA, for example, there was a 12 per cent increase in the proportion of all employment in this sector between 1947 and 1980 (Knox and Agnew in Shaw and Williams, 1994: p. 9). De-industrialization comes about as a later stage of economic development and is only possible if an infrastructure is in place. In Singapore, tourism is a significant component of this process, generating over 162 000 jobs (9.5 per cent of the work force), thus producing 12 per cent of Gross Domestic Product in 1996 (World Travel and Tourism Council (WTTC), 1996: pp. 1, 6). It stands to reason, then, that efforts to create that necessary infrastructure would start early. As a country with very limited resources on 646 km² of land, Singapore has a very serious problem of creating a support base to attract visitors. Without many physical or scenic resources as attractions, the state resorted to redefining resources, recognizing that good infrastructure, such as a world-class airport and an excellent networked communications structure, would provide Singapore with a competitive edge. Currently, the island has two air terminals with a third being built. Services are so efficient that the airport has won many accolades. Singapore also has one of the busiest airports in the world. In January 1996 alone, nearly half a million visitors landed in Singapore by air, an achievement made possible by the complex air linkages it has all over the world. Over 1500 flights per week arrived in Singapore in January 1996, representing a total seat capacity of 350 000 (STB, 1996: p. 20).

The development of economic resources in Singapore is the result of close co-operation between the state and statutory boards set up by the state. For example, in civil aviation Singapore Airlines, which runs the national carrier, works closely with the Singapore Tourism Board (STB) and the Civil Aviation Authority of Singapore (CAAS) which is in charge of the running of the air terminals. In addition, STB works closely with the Urban Redevelopment Authority (URA) to oversee the grant of land to build airports, hotels and tourist attractions. In the 1990s, in an attempt to diversify the tourist product, STB has become close partners with the Economic Development Board (EDB) to produce lifestyle products and to seek overseas investments for such projects as the building of resorts, hotels and other leisure attractions in regional locations in China, Vietnam and Myanmar. STB also works closely with the Ministry of Communications and with the Ministry of Information and the Arts to attract arts and cultural enterprises to invest in the country. Overall, therefore, the state has created a symbiotic relationship between all organizations on the one hand, and with the people of Singapore on the other. Land and money have been heavily invested in the infrastructure of Singapore with the promise that it would generate jobs, wealth and growth for the nation. In many respects, these have been delivered and today that infrastructure is almost taken for granted (Teo and Ooi, 1996) (Figures 8.1–8.4). The efforts of STB in inventing tourism resources have a number of different phases, starting with the 1970 Dillingham Report which was subsequently modified in 1980. Dillingham, an American real estate company, proposed the development of Sentosa, an off-shore island, as a tourist haven, complete with restaurants, hotels, a beach resort, golf course, museum, shopping areas and a theatre. This would add to the limited number of attractions that Singapore was perceived to have. In 1986, a new plan, the

Figure 8.1   *Singapore Convention Centre: the MICE sector is an important component of Singapore's positioning as the business, tourism and shopping hub of Southeast Asia*

Figure 8.2   *Riverside Point shopping complex on the Singapore River*

Figure 8.3   *Boat Quay on the Singapore River has been converted from shophouses to restaurants and cafes. It is one of the focal points of Singapore's annual food festival*

Figure 8.4   *Restoration of the Stamford House complex combined with the creation of a restaurant and outdoor eating area*

Tourism Product Development Plan, was introduced (Ministry of Trade and Industry (MTI), 1986). This plan aimed to crystallize tourism promotion into a much more comprehensive approach, including both the main island and offshore developments. Under this plan, the state aimed to 'revitalize the city' based on five themes: Exotic East, Colonial Heritage, Clean and Green Garden City, Tropical Islands Resorts and International Sports Events. The Exotic East theme aimed to preserve Singapore's unique cultures by conserving and revitalizing historical areas such as Chinatown and Little India.

The Colonial Heritage theme focused on the island's history as a British colony, while the Tropical Islands theme provided the core for the development of offshore islands, beach resorts and marinas. Clean and Green is the logo showcasing how a highly urbanized society can enjoy a high quality of life with green lungs dotted throughout the city. Over S$1 billion[3] investments were planned.

In 1996, another assessment took place which identified a number of problems facing Singapore as a destination: insufficient variety of attractions; insufficient high-yield visitors (convention and incentive travellers); and the need for more market diversification (MTI, 1996 in Wong, 1997: p. 263). An initiative by various committees resulted in the Tourism 21 Plan, which is even more ambitious (STB, 1996). Its vision is Singapore as a 'tourism capital', and six strategic plans will be used to achieve this:

- *redefining tourism*: tourism will no longer be defined on the measure of visitor arrivals alone; instead, the state aims to make Singapore a tourism business centre and a tourism hub;
- *reformulating the product*: attractions will no longer be developed as stand-alone attractions but will be regrouped into thematic zones in order to enhance the product that Singapore already has to offer (eleven zones were identified in total);
- *developing tourism as an industry*: in order to create a meeting point for tourism entrepreneurs, clusters of functions such as travel agencies, cruise companies, airlines and hotels, will be developed further. Gaps in their services will be plugged so that horizontal integration of services can develop spontaneously. Monies for their development into world-class organizations will be sought both within Singapore and abroad. To make Singapore a tourism business centre and hub, the operating environment will be enhanced: for example building a 60 000 m² covered exhibition hall

as well as an international passenger terminal. A competent tourism workforce and supporting IT will be addressed;
- *reconfiguring tourism space*: develop Singapore's complementarity with the region so as to create new tourism space. The strategy of 'Tourism Unlimited' will see Singapore breaking out of its traditional geographical boundaries and forming economic and cultural ties with its neighbours;
- *partnering for success*: partnering with private enterprise inside and outside of Singapore to raise funds for the development of the industry, as well as a regional approach for the marketing of Singapore as a tourism business centre and hub;
- *championing tourism*: developing a resource centre and working with the department of statistics to research tourism and raise its profile.

As tastes and markets change, Singapore constantly strives to recreate its resources in order to remain competitive. Policy shifts reflect the government's changing focus over time; from the development of local resources in the 1986 plan to the creation of a 'regional tourism economy' in the 1996 blueprint (Chang, 1998). However, one constant which the government has consistently emphasized over the years is Singapore's location. As an air travel hub, a business centre and a node for tourism/lifestyle companies, the foundation of Singapore's ability to survive in the tourism business is to take advantage of its sophisticated infrastructure to position itself as a gateway. Whether for its own attractions, or as a facilitator and organizer for others, Singapore must constantly rework its resources and promote them well if it desires a sustainable tourism industry.

Environmental resources: reconfiguring new space

Despite the scarcity of land and virtual lack of breathtaking natural scenery in Singapore, environment-based tourism has nevertheless been promoted. Outlets for an 'urban eco-tourism'

[3]S$1 is equivalent to approximately US$1.72 at 1998 prices.

Figure 8.5   'Tourism space': the Indonesia–Malaysia–Singapore growth triangle
as a single destination area

experience are created in two ways: through the
enlargement of Singapore's tourism space to
embrace the natural delights of its neighbouring
countries, and through the innovative adaptation
of natural attractions to suit the urban setting of
Singapore.

Using neighbouring natural resources

Environmental resources are invented for tourism
by laying claims to the natural wonders of neighbouring countries such as Malaysia and Indonesia.
According to the STB, one of its strategic aims for

the millennium is to 'configure new tourism space'
so that Singapore 'can tap the tremendous potential of the region and complement her own city
resort attractions with select destinations in the
region' (STB, 1996: p. 6). This configuration of new
economic space is best demonstrated by the Singapore government's endorsement of the Indonesia–Malaysia–Singapore Growth Triangle in which
cross-border collaboration between Singapore, the
Malaysian state of Johor and the Indonesian
islands of the Riau Archipelago is encouraged
(Figure 8.5). To this end, joint projects in manufacturing, oil refining, telecommunications, resort

management and agribusiness have been forged between the three countries (Wong, 1993). The Growth Triangle strengthens Singapore's position as a tourist destination because it makes up for the scarcity of land by providing an extended hinterland. The Triangle serves as a single destination area where tourists can enjoy Singapore's urban attractions in tandem with the beach resorts, golf courses, forest lands and other scenic sites of its neighbours. By forging links with immediate countries, Singapore's natural resource base is immediately widened and a 'new, more attractive and mutually beneficial collective tourism product' emerges (*The Straits Times Weekly Edition* 22 April 1995).

By borrowing neighbouring natural scenery, Singapore is able to promote environment-based tourism such as cruise and eco-tourism. With its sophisticated air and sea port facilities, Singapore acts as an embarkation point for visitors travelling on to Malaysia and Indonesia. This adoption of natural attractions is undertaken through various means. In logistical terms, the government established a Cruise Development Department within the STB in 1988 to promote and market regional cruise tourism. In terms of infrastructure, a S$50 million World Trade Centre Cruise Terminal was constructed in 1992 and the Tanah Merah Ferry Terminal was opened to service visitors travelling in the Triangle. Plans are also underway to simplify immigration and even to introduce the possibility of non-passport clearance while travelling within the region. In investment terms, the Growth Triangle provides immense opportunities for Singapore entrepreneurs to reap economies of scale. To promote the Growth Triangle as a destination, the Singapore government and the private sector have entered into many joint ventures with their Indonesian and Malaysian counterparts. The most ambitious scheme is the Bintan Beach International Resort, to be developed by a consortium of Singaporean and Indonesian private-sector companies and the government. After its initial development phase the resort was opened in June 1996, with plans to further expand the complex which is expected to take fifteen years to complete. It will comprise over 23 000 ha of land, ten hotels and numerous golf courses. By early 1998, four Singapore companies had opened hotels, including the Banyan Tree and the Sedona Resort.

The innovative adaptation of natural attractions

A second strategy in inventing environmental resources focuses on devising innovative nature-based sites in Singapore. Towards this end, man-made natural environments are ingeniously created as 'natural' attractions. Examples include the creation of the world's first night safari; an open zoological garden; a gigantic aviary and bird park with the world's tallest man-made waterfall; theme parks using 'water' as their selling point; and the conversion of nature reserves and water catchment areas into jungle attractions for Singaporeans and tourists. The inability to create space-consuming attractions has resulted in new conceptions of 'nature'. The innovative night safari is the best example. Opened in 1994 at a cost of S$60 million, the park simulates the open spaces of Africa and South America through its use of grazing lands where nocturnal animals are allowed to roam freely, framed by lushly landscaped grounds and ingenious use of waterways and moats which serve as fences. Tram rides, walking trails and jungle walks are created throughout a compact 40 ha of undulating land, and eight themed areas are designated to represent the various 'parts of the world' from which the animals originate. Despite its size, the safari boasts over 1200 animals and birds from 100 species, and its simulated natural environment has even won it the prestigious ASEANTA best new tourist attraction in ASEAN award in 1995.

What is defined as 'natural' need not always emerge from the reworkings of the physical environment. In fact, some attractions have little to do with the environment apart from being broadly 'natural' in flavour. A case in point are the theme parks for which Singapore is famous and which capitalize on notions of nature such as 'water', 'aquatic life' or 'volcanoes'. Sentosa is home to many quasi-nature attractions such as 'Volcano Land', 'Underwater World' and 'Fantasy Island'. Volcano Land, for example, features a gigantic fibreglass volcano in which visitors can travel to the centre of the earth, while Fantasy Island offers multiple water rides which simulate the white-water rapids of wild rivers. In Underwater World, visitors are taken into the depths of the ocean through a glass-enclosed travellator. Promoted as an idyllic respite and a 'natural getaway' from urban Singapore, Sentosa is anything but 'natural'. Urry (1990: p. 63) described the island as an 'wholly artificial environment' where its colonial buildings and natural scenery are 'plastic', and where its sandy beaches are filled with sand imported from Indonesia. Criticisms aside, quasi-natural attractions are Singapore's most popular tourist sites. According to the STB's 1996 survey of tourists, Sentosa is the top tourist site attracting 35.0 per cent of all visitors. Underwater World was ranked second; Volcano Land fourth; Night Safari eighth and Fantasy Island tenth. Reinventing notions of nature and embellishing them with technological touches have indeed produced highly successful attractions in Singapore.

Cultural resources: reformulating notions of culture

Local cultures and ethnic traditions in Singapore have been modified, revalorized and redefined in ever-changing forms to meet the fluctuating needs of tourists. Reformulating culture to attract visitors is demonstrated in various ways from the time of independence, when Singapore was marketed as 'Instant Asia', until today, when it is positioned as a 'Global City for the Arts' (Chang, 1997). In the decades of the 1960s and 1970s, Singapore was depicted as exotic 'Instant Asia'. Comprising a mixed population of Chinese, Malays, Indians and 'others' of Eurasian descent, the government promoted Singapore as a melting pot of Asian traditions, manifested in dress, cuisine, festivities, craft souvenirs and ethnic districts. According to Leong (1997), this depiction of culture through the 'CMIO' (Chinese, Malay, Indian and others) model is a formula intended to discipline Singapore's disparate and often divisive ethnic communities into a state-conceived model which is amenable to tourism promotion on one hand, while conveying an image of ethnic harmony on the other. In reality, the CMIO model camouflages the complexities of the ethnic groups in Singapore which vary tremendously in dialect, religious affiliation and diet. For example, within the Chinese community, there exists as many as sixteen sub-ethnic groups. For the Malays, there are seven different groups and as many as twenty-one for the Indians. By collapsing these boundaries, the government had hoped to unite the people while providing a simplified and easy-to-remember tourism marketing image. As Leong (1997: p. 93) explains, 'mass tourists are not anthropologists who seek a textured understanding of another culture; rather, they often want a formula of an abbreviated culture'.

In the 1990s, Singapore's marketing image shifted from 'Instant Asia' to 'New Asia', and Singapore has been repositioned as a country which embraces the modern dynamism of Asia while proudly proclaiming its traditional Asian heritage. Towards this end, culture is reinterpreted with a higher degree of elasticity. Above and beyond the narrowly defined CMIO categories, cultural tourism now embraces the whole of Asia as a vast storehouse of treasures, drawing in both Eastern and Western influences. From inward-looking 'Instant Asia' to outward-looking 'New Asia', Singapore aspires to be the cultural hub of Asia and a 'Global City for the Arts'. Apart from the CMIO categories, cultural tourism in the 1990s also embraces attractions which have little to do with Singapore's history, apart from being broadly Asian in theme. A case in point is the Chinese theme parks of Tang Dynasty City and the Haw Par Villa Dragon

World. While the former simulates the city of Chang-An, the ancient capital of China, the latter is styled as a Chinese mythological theme park complete with Disney-inspired rides (Yeoh and Teo, 1997). Both attractions claim to commemorate Chinese culture and to showcase tradition but what is being marketed is actually a canonized Chinese mythology based on images of dragons, fairy maidens, deities and dynasties with little or no suggestion of Singaporean heritage. Theme parks such as these clearly arise from the reworkings of culture to capture the imagination of tourists regardless of their links to local society and history.

Another way in which cultural resources have been refashioned is the STB's reassessment of what constitutes cultural tourism. Instead of confining itself to just Asian cultures, there has been an increasing effort to even embrace cultures from the West. Towards this end, non-traditional, non-Asian and non-historic elements, such as arts fairs, antique exhibitions, auctions, Western performing arts and operas, have been staged as tourist attractions. Singapore is marketed as a 'Global City for the Arts' and it has played host to mega-events such as the annual Tresors Fair of fine art and antiques, Broadway performances of *Cats* and *Les Miserables*, as well as prestigious art auctions and exhibitions by Christie's and Sotheby's. Even the Singapore International Film Festival and concerts by jazz and new-age performers such as Wynton Marsalis and Kintaro in 1998 have been marketed as 'cultural feasts' for visitors.

In broadening the cultural palate, the state realizes the immense opportunities offered by the 'arts'. Arts tourism provides a means of showcasing the artistic heritage of Singaporeans while also promoting the country as a 'must visit' cultural destination in the same league with 'Europe's Cultural Capitals'. Embracing the arts allows Singapore to capture new niche markets while remaining competitive with other cultural cities. Cultural tourism thus takes on a new meaning as Singapore is developed as a 'reputable base for fine art and antique dealing and auctioning, a theatre gateway to the region,

and an exciting cultural and entertainment destination' (STB, 1995: p. 9).

Conclusion

In resource-scarce localities, tourism development hinges on the dual strategy of inventing resources and capturing new niche markets. In a country where the ingredients popularly associated with tropical exotic islands are missing, inventing resources becomes a necessary tool to position Singapore as an attractive destination. Towards this end, economic, environmental and cultural resources are constantly being invented or refashioned to suit evolving tourist needs. In inventing tourism resources, the STB's *modus operandi* has been multi-faceted. On the economic front, the government has capitalized on Singapore's geographic location and traditional strength as a business centre. Building up transportation and communication infrastructure and developing Singapore as a tourism business centre and regional hub are the chosen strategies. On the environmental front, the STB has supplemented its lack of land by embracing the natural attractions of the region and marketing them as part of Singapore. Reworking nature-inspired theme parks within an urban setting has also enhanced the country's image as a garden city. On the cultural dimension, Singapore has redefined notions of 'culture'; in the 1960s through the 'rationalization' of cultural boundaries and in the 1990s through the celebration of local, regional and Western art forms.

As the economic crisis looms larger in the region in the final years of the 1990s and into the new millennium, the public has certainly reduced its consumption and countries throughout Southeast Asia are reporting declines in tourist arrivals. This runs contrary to many depictions of a 'New Asia' which is economically buoyant and dynamic. The challenge posed by the economic crisis has made the need for adaptability and creativity even more apparent. Singapore had the foresight to realize that the island itself may be sufficient for regional markets in the short term, but certainly inadequate for international markets which it must now attract. By expanding its tourism space by forging links with overseas tourism development in places like Australia, China and India, the country may be able to avoid some of the scars expected from the regional crisis. Theme parks, even if they are artificial representations of nature (e.g., the Night Safari and the Singapore Zoological Gardens), together with the promotion of world-class art shows and theatrical performances, will make Singapore more attractive to the world market, especially if these are packaged together with other destinations in the region. As the tourist becomes more sophisticated and demands an eclectic mix of attractions characteristic of the post-modern era, Singapore must rise to meet this challenge. The island's tourism development demonstrates a case of planned development and shrewd marketing which can withstand rapid transformations. The dearth of natural and cultural resources, and the lack of geographic space have not prevented tourism development because of the emphasis on resource invention. How well Singapore continues to upgrade its economic infrastructure, market its environmental attractions and refashion its cultural attributes will determine its tourism future.

References

Chang, T.C., 'From "Instant Asia" to "Multi-faceted Jewel": Urban imaging strategy and tourism development in Singapore', *Urban Geography* 18(6), 1997, pp. 542–562.

Chang, T.C., 'Regionalism and tourism: Exploring integral links in Singapore', *Asia Pacific Viewpoint* 39(1), 1988, pp. 73–94.

Chua, B.H., *Communitarian Ideology and Democracy in Singapore*, Routledge, London, 1995.

Chua, B.H., *Political Legitimacy and Housing: Stakeholding in Singapore*, Routledge, London, 1997.

Go, F., 'Asian and Australasian dimensions of global tourism development' in F.M. Go and C. Jenkins (eds), *Tourism and Economic Development in Asia and Australia*, Cassell, London, 1997, pp. 3–34.

Leong, L.W.T., 'Commodifying ethnicity: state and ethnic tourism in Singapore' in M. Picard and R. Wood (eds), *Tourism, Ethnicity and the State in Asian and Pacific Societies*, University of Hawaii Press, Honolulu, 1997, pp. 71–98.

Ministry of Trade and Industry, *Tourism Product Development Plan*, MTI and Singapore Tourist Promotion Board (STPB), Singapore, 1986.

Qu, H. and Zhang, H.Q., 'The projection of international tourist arrivals in East Asia and the Pacific' in F. Go and C. Jenkins (eds), *Tourism and Economic Development in Asia and Australia*, Cassell, London, 1997, pp. 35–47.

Sandhu, K.S. and Wheatley, P., *Management of Success: The Moulding of Modern Singapore*, Institute of Southeast Asian Studies, Singapore, 1989.

Shaw, G. and Williams, A.M., *Critical Issues in Tourism: A Geographical Perspective*, Blackwell, Oxford, 1994.

Singapore Tourism Board, *Annual Report on Tourism Statistics*, STB, Singapore, various years.

Singapore Tourism Board, *Global City for the Arts*, STB, Singapore, 1995.

Singapore Tourism Board, *Tourism 21: Vision of a Tourism Capital*, STB, Singapore, 1996.

Smith, M., McLoughlin, J., Large, P. and Chapman, R., *Asia's Industrial World*, Methuen, London, 1985.

Teo, P. and Ooi, G.L., 'Ethnic differences and public policy in Singapore' in D. Dwyer and D. Drakakis-Smith (eds), *Ethnicity and Development: Geographical Perspectives*, John Wiley, Chichester, 1996, pp. 249–269.

The Straits Times, various issues.

The Straits Times Weekly Edition, various issues.

Urry, J., *The Tourist Gaze: Leisure and Travel in Contemporary Societies*, Sage Publications, London, 1990.

Wong, L.K., 'The strategic importance of Singapore in modern history' in E.C.T. Chew and E. Lee (eds), *A History of Singapore*, Oxford University Press, Singapore, 1991, pp. 17–35.

Wong, P.K., 'Economic co-operation in the Southern Triangle: a long-term perspective' in M.H. Toh and L. Low (eds), *Regional Cooperation and Growth Triangles in ASEAN*, Times Academic Press, Singapore, 1993, pp. 119–133.

Wong, P.P., 'Singapore: tourism development of an island state' in D. Lockhart and D. Drakakis-Smith (eds), *Island Tourism: Trends and Prospects*, Pinter, London, 1997, pp. 248–267.

World Tourism Organization, *Yearbook of Tourism Statistics*, WTO, Madrid, 1997.

World Travel and Tourism Council, *Singapore Travel and Tourism*, WTTC, London, 1996.

Yeoh, B.S.A. and Teo, P., 'Remaking local heritage for tourism', *Annals of Tourism Research* 24(1), 1997, pp. 192–213.

9

Thailand: prospects for a tourism-led economic recovery

James Higham

Introduction

Thailand lies at the geographical heart of Southeast Asia, sharing borders with Myanmar (Burma), Laos, Cambodia, and Malaysia. The geography of Thailand comprises four main regions (Figure 9.1). The northern mountainous region includes many cultural ruins, temples and distinct ethnic hill tribes set around the ancient city of Chiang Mai. The semi-arid Korat Plateau is set in the northeast region of Thailand. Here the Mun and Chi rivers drain into the Mekong river which forms the border with Laos. This is the least visited region in Thailand but one with an intriguing blend of Thai, Lao and Khmer cultural influences. The central region, Thailand's most fertile and populous, is located at the lower Chao Phraya river catchment. To the south, set on the Chao Phraya river delta, is the capital, Bangkok. The southern region, which occupies much of the Malay Peninsula, offers visitors the opportunity to experience outstanding coastal and beach resort destinations (Interknowledge Corp., 1996). Each of these diverse regions present contrasting resources for tourism. However, such is the integration of Thailand within Southeast Asia, economically, politically and

geographically, that the oscillations of the Thai tourism industry generally mirror those of the wider east and southeast Asian nations. Never was this more true than in 1998.

Economic dimensions

The economies of northeast, east and southeast Asia have enjoyed many years of economic growth and prosperity (Parnwell, 1996; Dixon, 1999). Hanging on the coat tails of Japanese post-war economic development, the Taiwanese and Korean, and latterly the so-called 'Tiger' economies of the ASEAN member states (Thailand, Malaysia, Myanmar, Laos, Indonesia, Philippines, Singapore, Vietnam and Brunei) have generated impressive rates of economic growth. Lan Li Wei Zhang (1997) recognizes that the industrialization of the Thai economy resulted in the increased export value of tourism as well as of textile products, rice and rubber, particularly during the 1980s (Table 9.1). Increased disposable income and an expanded middle class have been precursors to the emergence of societies more disposed to business and leisure travel in these countries

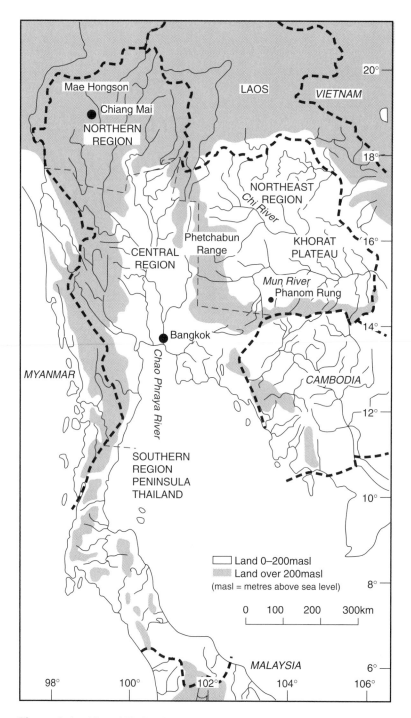

Figure 9.1   *Map of Thailand*

Table 9.1   *Revenue generation from Thailand's export industries (1981–1989) (US$)*

Rank	1981		1983		1985		1987		1989	
	Export	Value	Export	Value	Export	Value	Export	Value	Export	Value
1	Rice	26 367	Tourism	25 050	Tourism	31 768	Tourism	50 024	Tourism	96 383
2	Tourism	21 455	Rice	20 157	Textiles	23 578	Textiles	48 555	Textiles	74 036
3	Tapioca	16 446	Tapioca	15 387	Rice	22 524	Rice	22 703	Rice	45 462
4	Textiles	12 531	Textiles	14 351	Tapioca	14 969	Tapioca	20 661	Rubber	26 423
5	Rubber	10 840	Rubber	11 787	Rubber	13 567	Rubber	20 539	Tapioca	23 974

Source: Lan Li Wei Zhang, 1997.

(Hall, 1997). The expectation of continued economic growth in Asia is implied by predictions that the Chinese economy will prove to be the sleeping giant of the Asia–Pacific economies (World Tourism Organization, 1998).

Much has been written about the fast-growing economic and tourist destination status of Thailand in the 1980s. The Visit Thailand Year (VTY) launched in 1987 succeeded in stimulating annual increases in visitor arrivals of 20 per cent through to the end of that decade (Hall, 1997). Whilst VTY was an undoubted success in these terms, the sustainability of this course of tourism development has, in hindsight, been questioned. A general shortage of hotel accommodation in the wake of VTY resulted in a period of intense hotel development in 1989, induced quite deliberately by government tax incentive policies. Between 1986 and 1990 the Thai hotel sector experienced a 44 per cent increase in room availability (Lan Li Wei Zhang, 1997). This, according to Hall (1997), resulted in an oversupply of accommodation in the 1990s which, in combination with domestic and international political instability, resulted in the 1991 Thai tourism slump. In 1991 international visitor arrivals declined by 4 per cent, but more urgently still, tourism revenue fell by 10 per cent on the previous year.

Slowing economic growth, chronic congestion and pollution in Bangkok, environmental degradation and a raft of social problems (Cohen, 1996) hindered the prospect of continued economic growth. Reference is now made to the party of the 1980s and the hangover of the 1990s. However, in 1992 international tourist arrivals

and revenue from tourism resumed the growth patterns of pre-1991. The shallow nature of the slump is attributed by Lan Li Wei Zhang (1997) to the continued economic growth of the Asia–Pacific economies. As a consequence East Asian countries assumed greater importance as a source of international arrivals, at the expense of Europe and the USA, in terms of market share, average tourist expenditure and revenue generation. Double digit percentage growth in the Malaysian and Singaporean visitor markets, combined with a 33 per cent increase in Taiwanese visitors and a 29 per cent increase in South Korean arrivals, provided the tonic to the hangover of 1991. The lifting of Thai immigration restrictions in 1993, with the consequence of creating new sources of inbound tourists, also contributed to this end. The dramatic rise of Chinese visitor arrivals, for example, began in 1993; China was Thailand's ninth largest source of international arrivals in that year (Jariyasombat, 1997a; Tourism Authority of Thailand (TAT), 1993).

However, while it may have seemed that the duration of the 'boom' heavily outweighed the pain of the 'bust', social, economic, environmental and political problems remained largely unresolved. The ascent of Thai tourism continued into the mid-1990s, but the economic growth of the Thai economy came to an instantaneous, jarring halt in May 1997. Economic growth propped up by investment speculation and impossible commercial and business loans created an economic house of cards in Korea and Thailand, more so than in any other Asian countries. The crashing demise of the Korean

Table 9.2 *Thailand's Economic Recovery Plan*

Action	Impact
• Obtain US$20 billion in loans and stand-by credits from the IMF, World Bank, Asian Development Bank and Bank for International Settlements	• Restore confidence in Thailand's economic stability • Finance the balance of payments gap
• Raise VAT from 7% to 10% • Reduce government spending by 59 billion Baht without slashing education/infrastructure/ social welfare programmes • Control inflation at 8–9% in 1997	• Balance the budget • Reduce current account deficit to 3% of GDP in 1998 • Enable government to maintain Treasury reserves of at least 1% of GDP
• Retain managed float of the Baht rate	• Permit market forces to determine the exchange • Eliminate the draining of foreign reserves to control the exchange rate
• Close insolvent finance firms • Require additional capitalization of remaining financial institutions	• Encourage mergers and acquisitions by healthy firms • Encourage injections of capital from overseas investors
• Install safeguards to prevent recurrence of unregulated lending • Strengthen regulations of lending institutions • Require institutions to establish adequate levels of bad-debt reserves	• Rebuild confidence in Thai financial institutions • Ensure prudent fiscal management • Increase public disclosure of financial information • Increase lending credibility
• End subsidies to State Enterprises • Require State Enterprises to increase fees to cover expenses	• Accelerate privatization in areas such as energy, transportation, infrastructure and communications • Create dynamic opportunities for foreign investment

economy in 1997 set in motion a domino effect that saw no Asian economy survive unscathed.

Most economic profiling data relating to the Thai economy were rendered obsolete by the 1997 Asian Economic Crisis (AEC), triggered by a catalogue of bad loans among banking institutions and financial companies (*Economist*, 1997a,b,c,f). The collapse of the stock and property markets, spiralling local inflation and the consequent devaluing of the Thai Baht have left the Thai economy, like most in Asia, in a state of crisis. In August 1997 the International Monetary Fund (IMF) and World Bank became involved in an attempt to save the ailing Asian economies from complete collapse. In October 1997 Thailand unveiled a plan to meet the terms of a $17.2 billion bailout by the IMF (*Economist*, 1997d: p. 13) as part of a broader Economic Recovery Plan (Table 9.2). The Thai Economic Recovery Plan (ERP) aims to restore confidence, attract foreign business interests and investment and create a credible economy. A likely effect of this is to promote the importance of tourism as

a means of earning foreign exchange. The weakened Thai Baht supports this probability as exchange rates act as an incentive for inbound tourism and a disincentive for outbound tourism. If the ERP can create stability, employment and social and political calm then this also augurs well for the prospects of tourism playing a role in Thailand's economic recovery.

Some suspect that Thailand's Economic Recovery Plan may be a quick-fix solution to a problem that requires a closer examination of the issues that caused the crisis. By early 1998 it seemed that the crisis had passed but signs of a recovery remain faint. The *Economist* (1997d: p. 13) reported that Southeast Asians 'could only dare to think their smog-filled air and the worst of their currency problems may be dispersing'. While many suspect that the AEC need not end in absolute disaster (Hall, 1998), the causes and magnitude of the problems suggest that the difficulties may become worse before they show signs of getting better (*Economist*, 1997h). The causes included political denial, misrepresentation of private and foreign debt and the cartels and monopolies bred from an economy propped up by political connections, nepotism and greed (Mayston, 1998).

The effects of the AEC on Thai tourism have been severe. Visitor arrivals for 1997 showed a downturn on a scale not seen since the Gulf crisis. Thailand's integration with the national economies of Asia has contributed to this decline in various ways. These include the collapse of travel agents and tour operators in Japan and Korea, steep increases in exit taxes in Indonesia, fare wars throughout the region, airline layoffs in Hong Kong, hotel redundancies (*Bangkok Post*, 1998a) and a proposed (but later shelved) increase in petrol prices in Thailand (*Economist*, 1997e).

The only evidence of a silver lining to the cloud of the AEC, from the perspective of inbound visitors, has been the foreign exchange rate advantages of the devalued Thai Baht. Thailand has been effective in countering the flood of bad news by promoting its cost attractiveness, particularly to the European markets: an obvious consequence of a currency in decline (Cockerell, 1997; WTO, 1998). While tourists may have been lured to Asia in 1998 by advantageous currency exchange rates, the WTO (1998: p. 1) claims that this 'will not offset travel industry losses caused by Asia's financial crisis'. While this may be the case, Thailand has proceeded with a two-year promotional campaign, particularly of cultural attractions, in an attempt to encourage both international and domestic tourist activity.

Cultural dimensions

In December 1997 the 'Amazing Thailand' tourism promotional campaign was launched in Bangkok. This campaign used Thai culture as a vehicle for attracting 16 million tourists and 580 billion Baht to the Kingdom of Thailand in 1998–1999 (Inchukul and Svasdivat, 1997). 'Amazing Thailand' extended over two years

Figure 9.2 *Phnom Rung, Thailand*

with cultural performances, handicraft displays, traditional dancing and processions throughout. The Tourism Authority of Thailand (TAT), who promoted 'Amazing Thailand' internationally through its seventeen international offices, coordinated the launch of the campaign.

Many Thai festivals are linked to the Buddhist temples (Figure 9.2), rituals and the lunar calendar. Songkran, the Thai New Year celebration, takes place in mid-April. This is one of many festivals that have a definite domestic tourism component. Indeed, the magnitude of the domestic tourism component of Songkran in 1998 surprised many in the Thai travel industry (Jariyasombat and Sivasomboon, 1998) with most hotels and resorts in major provincial

Table 9.3   *Outbound Thai tourism destinations 1996–1997*

Destination	1997		1996		Change 1996/97 (%)
	Number	% Share	Number	% Share	
East Asia	1 272 846	77.7	1 424 680	77.9	−10.47
ASEAN	664 353	40.5	726 428	39.8	−8.6
Europe	155 661	9.5	174 241	9.6	−10.66
The Americas	59 303	3.6	69 693	3.8	−14.9
South Asia	25 720	1.6	25 770	1.4	−0.2
Oceania	63 462	3.9	75 978	4.2	−16.47
Middle East	57 524	3.5	52 374	2.9	9.8
Total all outbound	1 637 595	100	1 823 676	100	−10.2

Source: TAT, 1998a.

destinations operating at capacity. This has been widely attributed to the weakened Thai Baht which resulted in Thais who usually travel abroad opting for domestic holidays instead (Table 9.3). Both the Thai Railway Authority and Thai Airways International were required to schedule extra services during the five-day Songkran period in 1998 to cater for extra demand.

While culture clearly represents an important aspect of the Thai tourism product there is wide concern that Thai culture is being diluted through tourist interaction. This concern is exemplified by the case of the Padaung refugees of Myanmar being held prisoners in Thai/Myanmar (northern region) border villages. Police raids in April 1998 exposed the enslavement of Padaung women by Thai entrepreneurs seeking to profit from them as cultural tourism attractions (Gray, 1998). The Padaung tribeswomen of Myanmar adorn their necks with brass coils which have the effect of elongating the neck by up to 10 cm. Having fled the political upheavals in Myanmar, they have been held in three border camps in Mae Hong Son Province. An estimated 10 000 tourists visited these camps in 1997, paying an entrance fee to photograph the Padaung women. The so called 'Giraffe Women' have become a symbol to attract tourists to the region. However, they have also become a symbol of violated human rights. The tourist potential of the 'human zoo'

(Gray, 1998) has also resulted in the abandonment of agricultural practices, so that now most male villagers are idle. The tradition of neck coiling has also been diluted; previously only Padaung girls born during the full moon were destined to wear neck coils. This tradition has been abandoned in an attempt to profit from tourist demand. The damaging impacts of tourism, so often associated with the Thai tourism industry, apply equally in the context of the environment.

Environment

The tourism sector relies on the management of natural environments more so than most industries. The connection between tourism and the state of the natural environment is one of interdependence (Tisdell, 1998). While there exists much interest in ecotourism in Thailand, rapid industrialization, particularly during the 1980s, has created a legacy of environmental degradation (Lan Li Wei Zhang, 1997). Environmental problems in both urban and rural areas have been the consequence of rampant industrialism and exploitation of natural resources, particularly the logging of native forests. In tourism terms, the degradation of resort destinations and beaches has been the result of poor planning in combination with overwhelming rates of growth. Pattaya, once billed the Queen of Southeast Asia's beach resorts, has been transformed from a tranquil fishing village to a 3 million visitor per annum pleasure resort within the space of two decades. An obvious consequence has been the neglect of environmental considerations in favour of economic interests. The causes and consequences of this calamitous course of tourism development have been widely published (Cohen, 1996; *Economist*, 1997g; Hall, 1997; Lan Li Wei Zhang, 1997).

In 1989, an important year in Thai environmental politics, the Environmental Protection Act was legislated. A National Environment Board was created and charged with designating protected areas and designing pollution control measures commensurate with their conservation (Lan Li Wei Zhang, 1997). In the same year a nationwide logging ban was enacted. While these developments offered some hope for an ecologically sustainable future in Thailand, that remains an illusive reality. An immediate consequence of the 1989 logging ban was the announcement by the Forest Industry Organization (FIO) of a plan to develop ecotourism interests in national parks to meet revenue shortages. This has taken place with the full support of the Agriculture Ministry, particularly in the parks of the northern region, despite reservations surrounding the FIOs ability to manage tourism in sensitive environments. Indeed one may question the compatibility of ecotourism and the cash-strapped FIOs obvious money-making principles underpinning this initiative. Despite these well intentioned developments, illegal logging threatens the remaining vestiges of Thailand's forest resources (Hongthong and Tangwisutijit, 1997), much of which is connected to political corruption (Nontarit and Ridmontri, 1998). The degradation of forest areas, particularly in the mountain environments of the Chao Phraya catchment, has rendered Thailand more flood-prone in all areas adjacent to rivers (including Bangkok).

Despite these problems, ecotourism offers real possibilities for a new direction in Thai tourism. Hvenegaard (1998) describes the outstanding bird watching ecotourism resources of Doi Inthanon National Park, visited in 1993 by 900 000 tourists, in the northern region of Thailand. He argues the case that ecotourism offers the Thai government the opportunity to improve its management of natural resources while also providing economic incentives to protect Thailand's natural heritage. Appropriate management and planning to achieve these goals may help overcome the budget constraints that currently hinder environmental protection programmes in Thailand.

Thailand's integration within the wider ASEAN region extends to environmental issues. The southern region was marginally affected by the late 1997 Indonesian smog crisis. Whilst Thailand was not affected to the same extent as Malaysia and Indonesia, the perception, particularly among the long-haul European markets, was somewhat different to the reality (Cockerell, 1997). In the wake of this environmental crisis, the European travel markets effectively did not distinguish between Thailand and Malaysia and Indonesia. This illustrates the point that Thai tourism is influenced by broader regional as well as national environmental issues.

Tisdell (1998) presents a case in support of regional cooperation in meeting the challenges of sustainable ecotourism development. He argues, for example, that the setting of environmental standards for all APEC member nations will create environmental standards for foreign investors. This represents a measure of protection against relaxing environmental concerns in order to attract foreign investment. While this may be so, sound environmental policy, a restructuring of environmental administration and limiting political corruption is necessary on a domestic front as a prerequisite to regional cooperation.

There is perhaps some hope that out of the adversity of the financial crisis may come a 'new beginning' for tourism in Thailand. The necessity of political and constitutional restructuring prior to the reality of a financial recovery presents the opportunity to refocus the future of Thai tourism. Should this be so, a fundamental

Table 9.4 *International tourist arrivals to Thailand by country of residence, January–December 1997*

Country of residence	1997		1996		Change 1996/97 (%)
	Number	% Share	Number	% Share	
East Asia	4 568 837	62.64	4 513 315	62.30	+1.23
ASEAN	1 739 015	23.84	1 689 328	23.32	+2.94
Brunei	6 938	0.10	6 668	0.09	+4.05
Indonesia	89 110	1.22	85 757	1.18	+3.91
Malaysia	1 046 029	14.34	1 056 172	14.58	−0.96
Philippines	76 727	1.05	77 732	1.07	−1.29
Singapore	492 089	6.75	437 103	6.03	+12.58
Vietnam	28 122	0.39	25 896	0.36	+8.60
China	439 795	6.03	456 912	6.31	−3.75
Hong Kong	472 325	6.48	396 679	5.48	+19.07
Japan	965 454	13.24	934 111	12.89	+3.36
Korea	411 087	5.64	488 669	6.75	−15.88
Laos	28 301	0.39	24 288	0.34	+16.52
Taiwan	448 280	6.15	447 124	6.17	+0.26
Others	64 580	0.89	76 204	1.05	−15.25
Europe	1 585 915	21.74	1 605 113	22.16	−1.20
Austria	39 731	0.54	40 555	0.56	−2.03
Denmark	52 080	0.71	47 521	0.66	+9.59
Finland	34 094	0.47	31 246	0.43	+9.11
France	202 643	2.78	205 466	2.84	−1.37
Germany	342 329	4.69	353 677	4.88	−3.21
Italy	104 778	1.44	114 803	1.58	−8.73
Netherlands	77 296	1.06	78 744	1.09	−1.84
Norway	31 868	0.44	27 172	0.38	+17.28
Russia	48 516	0.67	53 206	0.73	−8.81
Spain	31 947	0.44	36 420	0.50	−12.28
Sweden	99 368	1.36	84 409	1.17	+17.72
Switzerland	97 253	0.33	110 459	1.52	−11.96
UK	287 664	3.94	286 889	3.96	+0.27
East Europe	31 287	0.43	30 434	0.42	+2.80
Others	65 222	0.89	64 090	0.88	+1.77

reconsideration of environmental protection and management is a move that would augur well for the Thai tourism sector. If tourism is to play a prominent role in the resurrection of the Thai economy it is imperative, as Jenkins (1997) observes, that sound environmental policies are developed and implemented.

The tourism market

An analysis of Thailand's tourism markets is, once again, punctuated by the AEC. Prior to this, despite the hangover of 1991–1992, most

Thai inbound markets continued to grow, aggregating in 1995 to 6.95 million visitors, up 12.7 per cent on the previous year (*Bangkok Post*, 1996). In that year, Malaysia contributed over 1 million visitors for the first time. No Asian markets recorded a decline in 1995, while the Middle East (led by strong growth in Israeli arrivals) rebounded strongly from its 1991 decline. The fastest growing markets in that year were United Arab Emirates (57.6 per cent) albeit on a small base, and China which, most significantly, sounded its potential with growth of 45.9 per cent.

Thailand's National Economic and Social Development Plan for 1997–2001 published in

Table 9.4   *Continued*

Country of residence	1997		1996		Change 1996/97 (%)
	Number	% Share	Number	% Share	
The Americas	388 190	5.32	383 925	5.30	+1.11
Argentina	4 107	0.06	3 061	0.04	+34.17
Brazil	6 249	0.09	6 389	0.09	−2.19
Canada	57 336	0.79	56 886	0.79	+0.79
USA	311 081	4.26	308 573	4.26	+0.81
Others	9 417	0.13	9 016	0.12	+4.45
South Asia	229 571	3.15	271 269	3.74	−15.37
Bangladesh	20 911	0.29	46 272	0.64	−54.81
India	135 121	1.85	129 762	1.79	+4.13
Nepal	14 141	0.19	17 739	0.24	−20.28
Pakistan	35 151	0.48	53 071	0.73	−33.77
Sri Lanka	18 981	0.26	19 630	0.27	−3.31
Others	5 266	0.07	4 795	0.07	+9.82
Oceania	271 442	3.72	251 876	3.48	+7.77
Australia	233 781	3.21	215 074	2.97	+8.70
New Zealand	35 431	0.49	33 669	0.46	+5.23
Others	2 230	0.03	3 133	0.04	−28.82
Middle East	126 427	1.73	119 198	1.65	+6.06
Egypt	3 829	0.05	3 534	0.05	+8.35
Israel	49 666	0.68	46 675	0.64	+6.41
Kuwait	9 482	0.13	9 317	0.13	+1.77
Saudi Arabia	8 522	0.12	8 877	0.12	−4.00
UAE	20 451	0.28	20 295	0.28	+0.77
Others	34 477	0.47	30 500	0.42	+13.04
Africa	50 963	0.70	47 449	0.65	+7.41
S. Africa	25 702	0.35	25 043	0.35	+2.63
Others	25 261	0.35	22 406	0.31	+12.74
Sub total	72 612	1.00	52 255	0.72	+38.96
Grand total	7 293 957	100.00	7 244 400	100.00	+0.68

Source: TAT, 1998a.

1996 outlines three tourism goals for that quinquennium:

- foreign currency income to increase by an average of no less than 14 per cent per year for all five years of the plan;
- the number of foreign tourist arrivals to increase by an average of no less than 6 per cent per year for all five years; and
- the number of Thai tourists travelling in Thailand to increase by an average of no less than 2 per cent per year.

These goals have clearly been truncated by the AEC. The effect to date has been the stagnation of inbound tourism generally, the demise of several key inbound markets and the growth of domestic Thai tourism. Specifically, the implications of the AEC for the Thai tourism markets have been (Table 9.4):

- the overall stagnation of the East Asian markets. The demise of the Korean market (−15.9 per cent) has been offset by slight growth in the Hong Kong, Singapore, Laos and Vietnam markets;
- the collapse of the South Asian markets. Only India recorded an increase in visitor arrivals to Thailand while most fell significantly;

- an overall decline in European arrivals, albeit slight (–1.2 per cent). This despite strong growth in the Scandinavian market; and
- continued growth in Middle Eastern markets.

Since the publication of TAT visitor statistics (TAT, 1998a) the Japanese inbound market has fallen by 11.2 per cent. The Southeast Asian haze and the bird flu scare in Hong Kong, as well as the domestic economic situation, are likely causes of the downturn in Japanese outbound tourism within the Asian region (*Bangkok Post*, 1998b). The TAT seeks to reverse this trend through aggressive marketing in association with falling package-tour prices and airfares that have resulted from this decline. However, Jariyasombat (1997b) reports a deeper problem identified by the Thai–Japan Tourism Association. This agency identifies a lack of new tourism products that may appeal to repeat visitors from the lucrative Japanese market. These sentiments, in combination with the economic fallout of the AEC in Japan, indicate a genuine threat to the future potential of inbound tourism from Japan.

Thailand's tourism markets are likely to change further in the post-AEC era. Thailand's efforts to act as a hub of tourism in Southeast Asia, particularly Indochina, have assumed heightened priority (*Bangkok Post*, 1996). In April 1996 Thailand hosted the Mekong Tourism Forum during which it was confirmed that the Secretariat that will coordinate the group's development plans will sit in Bangkok. Growth plans developed by this Forum include the establishment of road and rail networks throughout Indochina, more border checkpoints, the streamlining of visitor formalities and hotel and airport developments. These efforts should see Thailand orientate increasingly towards the Laos, Vietnam, Cambodia and Yunan markets, whilst serving as an international gateway to these destinations. The strengthening of tourism ties with China, in an attempt to serve a gateway function to one of the world's fastest growing destinations, indicates further change in Thailand's tourism markets. These conclusions are confirmed by TAT's (1998b) tourism statistics (January–April 1998) which report 114.7 per cent and 84.6 per cent increases in visitor arrivals from Laos and Vietnam, respectively.

Marketing and promotion

The marketing and promotion of Thailand is undertaken by the TAT which was established in 1960. The TAT is responsible for the promotion of tourism, the collection of tourism statistics, the development of plans for tourist areas and for personnel resource development in Thailand (TAT, 1998a). The thrust of TAT's recent promotional efforts focus on 'Amazing Thailand' for which a budget of 2.67 billion Baht was initially approved. The goals of this campaign have been expressed in visitor arrival and foreign exchange terms but the overriding objective of 'Amazing Thailand' is to attain status as the Southeast Asian tourism hub. 'Amazing Thailand' promotional efforts are currently coordinated through twenty-two domestic and seventeen international TAT offices. In 1997 the TAT requested an additional budget of 1.13 billion Baht to prepare the marketing strategy to promote 'Amazing Thailand' (Amnatcharoenrit, 1997). These figures leave little doubt that the focus of most TAT energies falls upon the generation of inbound travel activity.

TAT has been criticized for committing too many resources to tourism promotion while overlooking the havoc being wreaked upon Thailand's natural and cultural attractions (Techawongtham, 1997). Indeed, Janviroj (1997) refers to the 'unethical and morally reprehensible marketing hype and commercialisation' that has contributed to the debasing of Thailand's cultural and environmental tourism resource base. There is little doubt that the tourism sector in Thailand has been over-promoted and under-managed. Janviroj (1997) speculates that the 'Amazing Thailand' promotional campaign may replicate the problems experienced in Thailand as a result of the VTY 1987.

The role of government

The role of government in Thai tourism has, since the 1970s, been guided by a series of five-year Tourism Development Plans (TDPs). In 1977, as a result of recognition of the contribution made by tourism to the Thai economy, the first TDP (1977–1981) was published. The promotion of Thailand in an attempt to increase foreign exchange earnings was the principal focus of that document. Subsequent TDPs have concentrated energies on marketing, market research, advertising and public relations (1987–1991) and the renovation, restoration and maintenance of tourism resources (1992–1996). Despite a commitment to the sustainable management of tourism resources in the fourth TDP, the course of tourism development during the fifth five-year plan (1997–2001) is likely to be influenced by the harsh realities of the AEC. The probable outcome is a return to the deliberate economic growth goals of the first three TDPs. In the economic melee of 1997–1998, the Thai government placed greatest priority in the agricultural and tourism sectors to lead Thailand's economic recovery. The rationale underlying the high hopes placed in the tourism sector is documented in Table 9.5.

Thai government policy relating to the future of the tourism sector also recognizes the strategic opportunity linking Thailand to China, specifically performing the function of a gateway. The Pacific Area Travel Association (PATA) and the WTO document the potential of both inbound and outbound Chinese tourism. Indeed, the WTO predicts that China will succeed the USA as the world's single largest tourist-generating nation by 2017, when 100 million outbound Chinese tourists are forecast (Cockerell, 1997). This is by no means a new Thai initiative. Since the development and success of cooperative marketing campaigns such as Visit ASEAN Year (1990) the Thai government has actively sought to cement Thailand's status as the tourist hub of Southeast

Table 9.5   *A tourism-led economic recovery in Thailand: theory and practice*

Theory behind Government support for tourism in developing nations	The role of tourism in the Thai economic recovery process
Tourism is a growth sector. Since the 1950s tourism has had a growth rate that has been higher than world trade	Attractive option in any development strategy and in economic recovery strategies
Major consumers of international tourism are residents of the developed countries of the world	Attracts hard currencies
Relative absence of trade barriers and tariffs	New opportunities are being presented to Thailand via the lifting of travel restrictions in countries such as Taiwan, Republic of Korea and People's Republic of China
Labour intensive service sector	Generates employment in economies that have been devastated by the AEC. Also population growth skewed towards the young who need to be absorbed into the workforce
Attractions for international tourism relate to climate, beaches, wildlife and other natural and cultural attractions and festivals	Despite management problems these are tourism resources that play to the advantage of Thailand. Very saleable to the international tourism market
Wealth of intermediate technology	Appropriate for developing countries but also applicable to economic recovery
Future of the tourism sector. Evidence suggests that (a) people protect their holiday discretionary income even in times of deteriorating economic climates, (b) tourism flows generally recover quickly after crises, (c) air transport developments will further modify time, cost and distance barriers (Jenkins, 1997)	Currently the global economic climate seems set to deteriorate further, or at the very least recover slowly (WTO, 1998). In Asia as well as Russia and Latin America (Haq, 1998) tourism poses as a logical option for governments to pursue economic growth

Figure 9.3   *Phnom Rung, Thailand*

Figure 9.4   *Tropical forest, northern Thailand*

Asia (Hall, 1997). The effect of the AEC has been to steel the Thai government's resolve to position Thailand generally, and Bangkok specifically, as the gateway to China, as well as to Cambodia, Laos, Vietnam and Myanmar.

If this goal is to be achieved there remains an urgent need for the Thai government to address the infrastructural requirements of the tourism sector. The pace of Thailand's economic growth since the 1980s has been such that Thailand's public utilities, amenities, transport, communications and energy infrastructures have been unable to keep pace (Lan Li Wei Zhang, 1997). The ramifications for Thai tourism have been significant, particularly in Bangkok, in terms of average length of stay, room rates, investment and income from tourism in shops and restaurants. This scenario has also had implications for the environment in cases such as Pattaya and Phuket where the development and upkeep of public utilities and amenities have fallen behind tourism growth.

Furthermore, if Thailand is to achieve tourist hub status for Southeast Asia (a stated objective of 'Amazing Thailand') then the fact that Don Muang International Airport has met its operational capacity, in both aircraft landing and passenger handling terms (Janviroj, 1997), has not been adequately addressed. When set alongside the twenty-first century aviation facilities of Changi International Airport (Singapore) and Kuala Lumpur International Airport (Malaysia), this tourism objective seems doomed to fail. Indeed, Singapore's competitive advantage in terms of safety, cleanliness, infrastructure and convenience (Lan Li Wei Zhang, 1997) stands in stark contrast to the Thai situation.

Conclusions

The recent history of tourism development in Thailand has clearly been a chequered one. Hall (1998) notes that the stability provided by political regimes considered unacceptable in the West has provided an environment of economic stability in ASEAN. This has played a significant part in achieving economic growth, a stable economic climate for investment and, as a consequence, the tourism successes of the 1980s. However, the AEC of May 1997 casts a dark shadow over the short-term future of the Thai tourism industry and its ability to rejuvenate the Thai economy.

While the IMF bailout is widely considered to have political and constitutional implications, the region's policy makers continue to avoid the central issues that gave rise to the crisis. It is expected that the financial collapse will result in at least two years of harsh austerity. This is most likely to hurt the urban poor who will suffer unemployment as development stagnates in centres such as Bangkok (*Economist*, 1997a). In mid-October 1997 protesters took to the streets of Bangkok calling for the resignation of General Chavalit. Such factors do not augur well for the future of the Thai tourism sector, or its prospects for earning foreign currencies and leading the economic recovery. Furthermore, evidence of the social upheaval that is likely to result has already been manifest in civil unrest and the alienation of ethnic Chinese, in Thailand and other ASEAN states such as Indonesia (Hall, 1998).

High interest rates, currency instability and the costs of servicing debts are also likely causes of social and political instability which, as Hall (1998) suggests, do not serve the best interests of the tourism sector. Tourism is widely recognized as the sector most likely to lead a recovery. However, the magnitude of the crisis, and its likely social and political consequences, will blunt this prospect. Corruption continues to disfigure the Thai political scene. While efforts are being made to put an end to bad investments, negotiated tenders rather than competitive bidding, and the cosy relationships between banks, businesses and governments in the region, the legacy of this political environment remains. It seems, therefore, that the social, political and economic upheaval of the last eighteen months may be insurmountable in the short and medium terms. The gravity of the crises in tourism terms is perhaps best illustrated by the WTO (1998) which states that compared with estimates made before the crisis through the year 2000, some 11–12 million potential tourist arrivals will not materialize in the Asia–Pacific region, representing a loss of earnings of some 10 per cent.

1997 has generally been reviewed as having two halves in tourism terms, with strong growth in the first and 'tough going' in the second (*Bangkok Post*, 1998a). The same in reverse is expected to be the case in 1998. Doubt, however, remains as to the degree of recovery that was achieved in the latter half of 1998 and the speed of the recovery thereafter. More realistic, perhaps, is the WTO (1998) prediction that 'tourism in East Asia and the Pacific could suffer for three more years due to the financial crisis'. Whilst the Thai government places great stock in tourism as a source of foreign exchange the AEC should be observed as a new beginning from which a slower, more controlled and sustainable course of development can be pursued. However, the pressures of the AEC seem set to entrench Thailand's recent course of tourism development. As such, Thailand essentially remains a 'quantity driven, mass tourism destination, mainly owing to strong promotions backed by low prices and surplus air seat and hotel room capacity' (*Bangkok Post*, 1996). The Asian economic crisis, 'Amazing Thailand' and the priority given to tourism as a source of stable foreign currencies act only to confirm this conclusion.

Acknowledgements

The author acknowledges permission to use Figures 9.1, 9.2 and 9.3 from Professor Charles Higham.

References

Amnatcharoenrit, B., 'TAT request extra Bt 1 billion', *The Nation*, 1997. http://203.146.51.4/nation-news/1997/199707/19970705/14180.html (accessed 2.9.1998).

Bangkok Post, Economic review, June 1996. http://bkkpost.samart.co.th/news/BParchive/my er/myer96tourism.html (accessed 31.7.1998)

Bangkok Post, February 23 1998a

Bangkok Post, 'Tourism: TAT out to reverse decline from Japan. Aggressive marketing targets key sectors', 22 June 1998b. http://bkkpost.samart. co.th/news/BParchive/BP19980622/220698/Busin ess.html (accessed 31.7.1998).

Cockerell, N., 'Issues and trends, Pacific Asia travel December 1997, PATA Research. http://www. pata.org/patanet/dec97.html http://www.pata.org/patanet/dec97.html (9.7.1998).

Cohen, E., *Thai Tourism: Hill Tribes, Islands and Open-ended Prostitution*, White Lotus Press, Bangkok, 1996.

Dixon, C., *The Thai Economy: Uneven Development and Internationalisation*, Routledge, London, 1999.

Economist, 'Asia: Thailand gets the bill'. 9 August 1997a, pp. 21–22.

Economist, 'Thailand's economic package: What the doctor ordered'. 9 August 1997b, pp. 22–23.

Economist, 'Thailand: Reaching for the moon'. 20 September 1997c, pp. 39–40.

Economist, 'South-East Asia in denial'. 18 October 1997d, p. 13.

Economist, 'Asia: The blind, the deaf and the dumb'. 18 October 1997e, pp. 27–28.

Economist, 'Asia: Thailand: More questions than answers'. 18 October 1997f, p. 95.

Economist, 'Asia: Dirty air, dirty seas'. 25 October 1997g, p. 30.

Economist, 'Asia: The relegation of Thailand'. 25 October 1997h, p. 29.

Gray, D.D., 'Long necked tourism: Human zoo or boon to the poor?', Cnews features, 31 March 1998. http://www.canoe.com/CNEWSFeatures-Archive/mar31_zoo.html (accessed 2.9.1998).

Hall, C.M., *Tourism in the Pacific Rim: Developments, Impacts and Markets*, 2nd edn. Longman, Melbourne, 1997.

Hall, C.M., *Tourism in the Pacific Rim: Past, Present and Future*. In *Tourism in the Pacific Rim*, Proceedings of the Second International Students Conference. August 1998. Tourism Club, University of Otago, 1998.

Haq, F., 'Finance – Russia: fears of global crisis as economic woes spread'. World News Interpress Service, 1998. http://www.oneworld.org//ips2/ aug98/03_21_008.html (accessed 4.9.1998).

Hongthong, P. and Tangwisutijit, N., 'Forest lands face threat from tourism'. *Nation News*, Sport Section, 1997. http://203.146.51.4/nationnews/ 1997/199704/19970405/3918.html (accessed 2.9.1998).

Hvenegaard, G., 'Ecotourism in Northern Thailand: The risks and benefits of ecotourism in Northern Thailand', 1998. http://www.idrc.ca/books/reports.1996.html (accessed 2.9.1998).

Inchukul, K. and Svasdivat, P., 'Amazing Thailand: Tourists flock to cultural feast', *Bangkok Post*, 28 December 1997. http://bkkpost.samart.co.th/ news/Bparchive/BP971228/281297_News.html (accessed 31.7.1998).

Interknowledge Corp., 'Introduction to Thailand', 1996. http://www.interknowledge.com/thailand/index. htm (accessed 3.6.1998).

Janviroj, P., 'Is it going to be Amazing Thailand? Towards the millennium', *The Nation*, 1997. http://203.146.51.4/nationnews/1997/199707/199 70714/14505.html (accessed 2.9.1998).

Jariyasombat, P., 'Thailand to be a door to China: Millions of Baht to be spent on promoting the Kingdom in five cities', *Bangkok Post*, 25 April 1997a. http://bkkpost.samart.co.th/news/BParchive/BP9 70425/2504_busi1.html (accessed 31.7.1998).

Jariyasombat, P., 'Amazing Thailand. Japanese bored by same old places'. *Bangkok Post*, 14 October 1997b. http://bkkpost.samart.co.th/news/BParchive/BP9 71014/1410_bus1.html (accessed 31.7.1998).

Jariyasombat, P. and Sivasomboon, B., 'Travel demand surprises many businesses: Songkran gives kiss of life to hotels, tour firms', *Bangkok Post*, 6 April 1998. http://bkkpost.samart.co.th/ news/Bparchive/BP19980406/060498_Business.ht ml.

Jenkins, C.L., 'Impacts of the development of international tourism in the Asian region', in F.M. Go and C.L. Jenkins (eds), *Tourism and Economic Development in Asia and Australasia*, Cassell, London, 1997, pp. 48–66.

Lan Li Wei Zhang, 'Thailand: the dynamic growth of Thai tourism', in F.M. Go and C.L. Jenkins (eds), *Tourism and Economic Development in Asia and Australasia*, Cassell, London, 1997, pp. 286–303.

Lonely Planet Guide, *Destination Thailand*, 1998.

http://www.lonelyplanet.com.au/dest/sea/thai.htm (accessed 3.6.1998).

Mayston, B., 'Thailand: Solidarity in the land of the idle crane', *Otago Daily Times*, Business Section, 21 October 1998, p. 20.

Nontarit, W. and Ridmontri, C., 'Salween Scandal: Log tycoon holds the key, says Prawat', *Bangkok Post*, 5 March 1998. http://www.bangkokpost.net/today/050398_News03.html (accessed 6.3.1998).

Parnwell, M., *Uneven Development in Thailand*, Avebury, Aldershot, 1996.

Techawongtham, W., 'My hat goes off to the TAT', *Bangkok Post*, 28 August 1997. http://bkkpost.samart.co.th/news/BParchive/BP970828/2808_news2.html (accessed 31.7.1998).

Tisdell, C., 'Tourism in the APEC region and its promotion in an ecologically sound way through regional cooperation', APRENet On-line Library, 1998. http://www.nautilus.org/aprenet/library/apec.html (accessed 30.7.1998).

Tourism Authority of Thailand, *Thailand Tourism Statistical Report 1993*. TAT, Bangkok, 1993.

Tourism Authority of Thailand, 'International travel arrivals to Thailand by country of residence', 1998a. http://tourismthailand.org/stat/december/res-jan-dec.html (accessed 4.8.1998a).

Tourism Authority of Thailand, 'Tourist Authority of Thailand index', 1998b. http://www.tat.or.th/tat/index.html (accessed 30.7.1998).

World Tourism Organization, 'Asia slowdown could last three years. WTO revises forecasts', *WTO News*, March–April 1998. http://www.world-tourism.org/newslett/marapr98.asiacrsis.html (accessed 27.8.1998).

10

Tourism in Malaysia

Ghazali Musa

Introduction

Tourism was virtually unknown in Malaysia until the late 1960s. Since then it has developed very rapidly into a major industry and makes an important contribution to the country's economy. The government has played a significant part in the development by allocating substantial funds to the promotion of tourism and provision of infrastructure. Less attention has been given to the establishment of sound policies for sustainable tourism and their management. The impact of tourism development on the environment has received insufficient consideration. Added to this, recent economic changes and political events are also having an effect on the international perception of Malaysia as a tourist destination. This chapter will examine the tourism industry in Malaysia. It will also deal with the tourism development in Malaysia, tourist arrivals, tourism products, marketing and promotions, domestic tourism and special issues including the economic downturn beginning in 1997, negative factors affecting tourism in 1997/1998, and the environmental impact of tourism. The causes of the Asian economic downturn and its effects on the tourism industry and the government's plan for tourism development according to The National Economic Recovery Plan, 1998 will also be examined. Environmental issues associated with the problems of managing coastal and marine tourism in Malaysia are discussed, given the emphasis placed on these resources in promoting Malaysia's tourism.

Tourism development

Human settlement in Malaysia probably dates back over 5000 years (Information Malaysia, 1998). The early settlement and later colonization of the country by the European powers were largely determined by Malaysia's strategic position as one of the world's major crossroads, which serves as a meeting place for traders from the East and West (Figure 10.1). Malaysia has a land area of 330 434 km^2 and is a federation of thirteen states. Peninsular Malaysia contains eleven states, while Sabah and Sarawak are the remaining two states in the northern part of Borneo. The country's population is 21.2 million (*Asiaweek*, 1998). It is a multi-racial country: Malays and other *bumiputra* (indigenous people) constitute 59.0 per cent, Chinese 32.1 per cent, Indians 8.2 per cent and other races 0.7 per cent of the total population (Information Malaysia, 1998).

In the 1970s, the Malaysian government began to develop tourism to fulfil several development objectives, such as increasing foreign exchange earnings, increasing employment and income levels, fostering regional development, diversifying the economic base and increasing government revenue (Khalifah and Tahir, 1997). Following the racial tension in 1969, there was an urgent need for

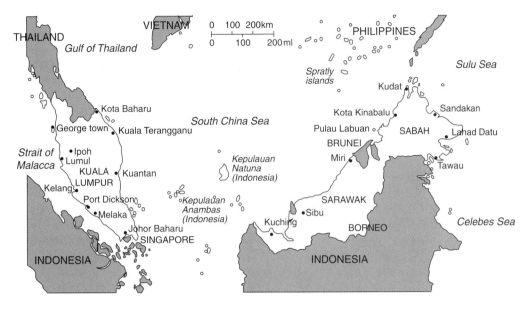

Figure 10.1 *Map of Malaysia (Source: http://geography.miningco.com/library/maps/blmalaysia.htm)*

stronger socio-cultural integration and a greater sense of unity. Tourism is seen as one of the keys to promote a greater understanding of the various cultures and lifestyles of the multi-ethnic population. During this period the government concentrated on providing basic tourism infrastructure, such as highways, airports and tourist sites in each state. It occasionally acted as entrepreneur and guarantor for overseas investment.

In the 1980s, the government began to encourage private-sector tourism development. More incentives were given to the private sector for development of accommodation, visitor centre facilities, manpower development and encouraging the participation of native Malays in the tourism industry (Khalifah and Tahir, 1997). During the Fifth Malaysian Plan 1986–1990, apart from developing the primary tourist nodes such as Kuala Lumpur and Penang, the development of secondary tourist nodes was also emphasized, especially the coastal resorts (Wong, 1990). In the 1990s, the Seventh Malaysia Plan 1996–2000 provided for extensive development of tourism products, marketing and promotion, private-sector involvement and local participation (Hall,

1997). The important economic contribution of tourism to the country was evidenced by the establishment of the Ministry of Culture and Tourism in 1987 which, in 1990, was renamed the Ministry of Culture, Arts and Tourism. Since then, the industry has had full support in terms of funding, planning, coordination, regulation and enforcement. Government commitment to the tourism industry in Malaysia is also reflected in the increasing spending on the development of tourism infrastructure, marketing and promotions during each Malaysia Plan, from RM17.2 million in the Second Malaysia Plan to RM966 million in the Seventh Malaysia Plan (Hall, 1997; Khalifah and Tahir, 1997).

Tourism products

The different ethnic groups are diverse in culture which is reflected in festivals, religious events, languages, variety of architecture, choices of cuisine and lifestyles. This feature is the main selling point of Malaysia to the outside world, as promoted by the Malaysia Tourism and Promotion Board (MTPB). Historical buildings in Melaka, Kuala Lumpur and Penang have been restored and are being promoted as tourist attractions. More recent landmarks of interest to tourists are the Petronas Twin Towers (the world's tallest building), the Shah Alam Mosque, the Bukit Jalil Commonwealth Sports Complex and shopping complexes such as Sunway Pyramid, Kuala Lumpur City Centre and the Mall. Hotels in Kuala Lumpur, Penang and Langkawi have equipped themselves with sophisticated convention facilities to attract the MICE (Meetings, Incentives, Conventions and Expositions) market.

Mega-events often act as a catalyst to urban developments. Extensive sporting facilities were built for the Commonwealth Games 1998. In Kuala Lumpur, the government spent US$5 billion (RM21 billion) on the combined cost of the mega-projects including the Kuala Lumpur International Airport, roads, stadia and other facilities such as the International Broadcasting Centre in conjunction with the Commonwealth Games (Yusof, 1998).

Recent statistics reveal that nature-based activities are the fastest growing tourism product in Malaysia (Hashim, 1998). It is estimated that 10 per cent of Malaysia's tourism revenue in the year 2000 will be from ecotourism (Hashim, 1998). Malaysia is blessed with many attractive beaches and just over 1000 offshore islands. Tioman, Langkawi, Redang, Perhentian and Pangkor are among others which are attracting not only domestic but also international tourists. There are a variety of activities, such as scuba diving, snorkelling, picnicking and camping. The Malaysian jungles have remained virtually untouched by man for more than 100 million years and are older than those found in the Amazon and Africa. There are nineteen National Parks in Malaysia; among the widely known are Taman Negara, Endau Rompin, Mulu and Kinabalu National Parks. Activities available are fishing, swimming, bird watching, mountain climbing, limestone caving, camping and many others.

Hill stations were initially developed as sanatoria for colonials living in the hot humid climates (Smith, 1995), to provide a cooler climate away from the heat of the lowlands. In the post-colonial period, many of these places are commoditized as tourist attractions with the development of hill resorts. Among these are Genting Highlands, Fraser's Hill, the Cameron Highlands, Maxwell Hill and Penang Hill.

Malaysia's theme parks generally combine a mixture of water activities, adventure, futuristic experiences, games, rides and sometimes a place for relaxation and sightseeing. Genting Highlands, which is situated at 2000 m above sea level was the first Malaysian theme park. It is also known as the 'City of Entertainment'. Other theme parks are Sunway Lagoon, Gold Mine, the Mines Resort, Wet World, A Famosa Waterworld and Bukit Merah.

A total of RM5.2 billion was invested in hotel and tourism projects in 1997 (Malaysia Hotel Supply and Statistics (MHSS), 1998). Competition in the hotel industry is very strong, especially in the Klang Valley where the construction of new hotels was concentrated for the 1998 Commonwealth Games. The Multimedia Super Corridor (MSC) project and the positioning of Kuala Lumpur International Airport (KLIA) as a regional hub of the major airlines are expected to increase the volume of travel to Malaysia in the future. Furthermore, with the economic downturn which began in 1997, Malaysians have been expected to take more holidays within the country. The government has encouraged the building of more budget hotels to cater for the domestic market. The hotel growth in Malaysia has been increasing annually by between 8.0 and 15.9 per cent from 1991 to 1998 (MHSS, 1998). At the time of the Commonwealth Games in September 1998, Malaysia was expected to have 1471 hotels throughout the country with 130 536 hotel rooms. By the end of the century, it is estimated that Malaysia will have another eleven hotels.

Tourist arrivals

In 1990, 7.5 million tourists visited Malaysia. This was attributed to the increased government spending (RM137 million) on overseas promotion in conjunction with Visit Malaysia Year 1990. This figure represented an increase of 55.5 per cent on the previous year (4.8 million). However, in 1991, tourist arrivals dropped dramatically by 21.5 per cent as a result of the Gulf War and the economic recession in many tourist-generating countries. In the subsequent years, the arrival rate increased steadily again, and when Malaysia launched its second Visit Malaysia Year in 1994 the tourist arrivals reached 7.2 million. However, in 1996, even though the tourism receipts increased from RM9.2 million in 1995 to RM10.3 million, tourist arrivals reduced again.

Tourist arrivals in Malaysia have no distinct pattern of seasonality. The weather pattern in Malaysia is stable throughout the year except for the east coast of Peninsular Malaysia which is affected by the monsoon season from November to March. Table 10.1 shows that most spending among tourists is on accommodation (34.7 per cent), shopping (21.5 per cent) and food and beverages (18.7 per cent). The spending on organized tours dropped by 39.2 per cent in 1997 compared with 1996, which signifies the moving away of organized tours to Free and Independent Travellers (FIT).

The ASEAN countries' main markets are those of its own members (Peat Marwick, 1993; Hall, 1997; Khalifah and Tahir, 1997). This is due to the rapid economic development which changed people's attitude towards leisure travel and ease of transport and visa access. Singapore has long been the most important market for Malaysia, with 56.2 per cent of tourist arrivals in 1997. This is followed by Thailand (7.8 per cent), Japan (5.0 per cent) and Indonesia (3.7 per cent) (Table 10.2).

Table 10.1 *Distribution of tourist expenditures 1996–1997*

Type of expenditure	1997		1996		% Change 1996/97
	RM mil.	% Share	RM mil.	% Share	
Accommodation	3365.8	34.7	3686.1	35.6	−8.7
Food and beverages	1813.8	18.7	1905.2	18.4	−4.8
Shopping	2085.4	21.5	2008.7	19.4	3.8
Organized tours	465.6	4.8	766.2	7.4	−39.2
Local transportation	805.0	8.3	786.9	7.6	2.3
Domestic airfares	426.8	4.4	486.6	4.7	−12.3
Entertainment	349.2	3.6	445.2	4.3	−21.6
Others	388.0	4.0	269.2	2.6	44.1
Grand total	9699.6	100.0	10354.1	100.0	−6.3

Source: Tourism Malaysia, 1997.

Table 10.2 *The top ten tourism generating markets for Malaysia in 1995, 1996 and 1997*

1997 (n=6 210 921)		1996 (n=7 138 452)		1995 (n=7 468 749)	
Countries	%	Countries	%	Countries	%
1. Singapore	56.2	1. Singapore	58.2	1. Singapore	60.8
2. Thailand	7.8	2. Thailand	7.9	2. Thailand	7.1
3. Japan	5.0	3. Japan	4.9	3. Japan	4.4
4. Indonesia	3.7	4. Taiwan	3.3	4. Taiwan	3.9
5. Taiwan	3.3	5. Indonesia	3.2	5. Indonesia	3.1
6. Brunei	2.9	6. Brunei	2.8	6. Brunei	2.5
7. UK	2.6	7. UK	2.3	7. UK	2.2
8. China	2.6	8. Australia	2.1	8. Hong Kong	2.0
9. Australia	2.1	9. Hong Kong	2.0	9. Australia	1.8
10. USA	1.5	10. China	1.9	10. China	1.4

Source: ASTR, 1996, 1997 in Musa 1998.

In 1997 Malaysia earned a total of RM9.7 billion from 6.2 million tourists visiting, representing a decrease of 6.3 per cent from RM10.4 billion in 1996. However, the average per capita expenditure increased by 8.2 per cent from RM1443.9 in 1996 to RM1561.7 in 1997. Among the highest per capita spenders were Italy (RM2783), the UK (RM2585) and Belgium and Luxembourg (RM2476). Tourists from Singapore were the highest daily spenders (RM446.2), followed by Brunei (RM397.5) and Taiwan (RM367.9). The average length of stay in 1997 was 5.3 nights, a small drop from the 5.4 nights recorded in 1996.

ASEAN and non-ASEAN markets recorded an average length of stay of 4.4 nights and 7.4 nights, respectively. Generally, tourist arrivals from many countries reduced substantially in 1997 except from China (+16.9 per cent), Vietnam (+13.6 per cent), Sweden (+9.4 per cent), Finland (+10.7 per cent), Argentina (+10.8 per cent), Russia (+5.9 per cent) and the Philippines (+3.5 per cent). Tourist arrivals from Singapore have reduced by 16.1 per cent. China is the most promising emerging market in Malaysia. There has been a rapid increase from 7000 visitors in 1990 to 100 000 in 1994 and is now the eighth biggest market to Malaysia, exceeding other secondary markets

such as the USA, South Korea and Germany. Another valuable source of visitors to Malaysia is the MICE market. Despite the downward trend of tourist arrivals, foreign participants attending meetings and conventions increased by 6.8 per cent to 115 768 (2 per cent of the tourist market).

Figure 10.2 illustrates that 52.7 per cent of the tourists visited Malaysia on holiday. This was followed by visiting friends and relatives (VFR) (13.5 per cent), transit (11.5 per cent), business (6.7 per cent), conference (2 per cent) and others (13.6 per cent). Some 75.1 per cent of the tourists in Malaysia come as FITs, while 15.1 per cent are on organized tours. This figure is influenced by ASEAN tourists who feel comfortable travelling in Malaysia independently, especially Singaporeans, as well as experienced European travellers. However, more than 50 per cent of tourists from China, Taiwan and South Korea are on organized tours.

1997–1998 – a painful period for Malaysian tourism

Tourism in Malaysia was substantially affected by a series of unfortunate events in 1997; together they contributed to a drop in tourist arrivals of 13

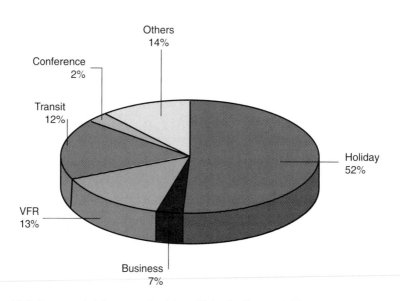

Figure 10.2 *Purpose of visits among tourists to Malaysia (Source: ASTR, 1997 in Musa 1998)*

per cent in that year. The year began with the tense relationship between Malaysia and Singapore (Malaysia's biggest inbound market) over agreement on railway services and tourism promotion. Soon after that a Dengue fever outbreak struck the second most important tourist city in Malaysia, Penang. Coxsackie B virus killed more than forty children in Sarawak, while Sabah was hit with a cholera epidemic (Soon, 1998).

In May 1997, Malaysia was covered by a pall of smoke, which also affected other countries in Southeast Asia. This was caused by the burning of forest to create agricultural estates in Indonesia. Despite its effect over the whole region, Malaysia received most coverage in the international media. The country experienced a 30–40 per cent holiday cancellation rate by foreign tourists, while hotels suffered a similar drop in occupancy rates (Chik, 1998a). Even though Malaysia was declared smoke-free on 2 October 1997, low tour bookings continued to be recorded for the first quarter of 1998 because of the uncertainty over whether the haze might recur (National Economic Recovery Plan (NERP), 1998).

In July 1997, Malaysia faced the toughest challenge in its economic history. After decades of prosperity, the economy suddenly experienced a downturn. Shocked at the sudden crisis, Dr Mahathir Mohamad, Malaysia's Prime Minister, hinted at a Jewish conspiracy (*The Economist*, 1997). In response to this, thirty-four US Congressmen accused the Prime Minister of anti-Semitism and demanded that Dr Mahathir apologize or relinquish his position. In 1998, Malaysia's image as a tourist destination was further tarnished after the bombings in Kenya and Tanzania which killed 250 people. Following the incident, the USA listed Malaysia as one of the countries where terrorism may occur and issued a safety directive to all its citizens to be extra careful in Malaysia (McNulty, 1998). The warnings may have frightened off tourists, investors and even those who wanted to attend Malaysia's biggest international event, The Commonwealth Games.

In the midst of the overwhelming success of the Commonwealth Games in Kuala Lumpur, Dr Mahathir sacked and later had the Deputy Prime Minister, Anwar Ibrahim, arrested on various charges of alleged corruption and sexual misconduct. This was in response to the call for political reformation led by the Deputy Prime Minister and the elimination of corruption, nepotism and cronyism. During his detention Anwar was ill-treated by the police and appeared in court with a blackened left eye. Since then, riots and demonstrations for political reformation by Malaysians have become regular events in Kuala Lumpur and have received substantial international media attention. As a result, tourist arrivals in Malaysia dropped by 80 per cent in September 1998 (Chik, 1998b). Those incidents triggered an avalanche of international criticism, from Washington to Sydney (Larimer, 1998). The criticism culminated, during APEC meetings in November 1998, with the Malaysian government being urged by the Vice-President of the USA to listen to the cry of Malaysians for more democratic government. Unfortunately, these events have detracted from the favourable international impression and the national self-esteem created by the Commonwealth Games (Frei, 1998).

On 1 September 1998, the government announced capital restrictions (McCarty, 1998). These require all travellers to declare all currencies which they bring into or take out of the country and place a limit on the amount taken out. Malaysia, which was until recently the thirteenth largest trading nation in the world with imports and exports more than one-and-a-half times GDP, has fallen off the radar screen of most foreign investors (McCarty, 1998). To some (e.g. McCarty, 1998), the go-it-alone economic policy gives Malaysia a similar image to that of North Korea and Myanmar.

The economic downturn (an analysis from the National Economic Recovery Plan 1998)

The causes

In the 1980s and 1990s, the sluggishness of the West's economy stimulated the movement of private international capital to East Asia, where economies were booming, in order to earn greater profits from investments. The rapid economic growth in Malaysia was not due to an improvement in efficiency, but was primarily brought about through augmenting input; this is an unsustainable situation in the long term (NERP, 1998). Of greater concern was that a significant proportion of this input (both capital and labour) was imported. In addition, certain characteristics of the Malaysian economy and government policies increased Malaysia's vulnerability. Increasing non-performing loans, excessive outside borrowings, a possibility of political instability (Colmery, 1998), misallocation of investment resources and opaque banking systems all caused foreign investors to doubt whether the country would be able to service its debts. The loss of confidence in the financial system resulted in the withdrawal of foreign investments and this is the main cause of the economic downturn.

The effects on tourism

The National Economic Recovery Plan (1998) identified tourism as the key sub-sector of the service sector in generating foreign exchange earnings for the country. With the worsening of the economic downturn, Malaysia's tourism industry is left with many issues to be faced. There is increasing competition from developing countries such as Vietnam, Cambodia, China and India for market share in the tourism industry. At the same time, Thailand, Singapore and Hong Kong have launched aggressive promotions to attract tourists, especially from Europe. Even though Chik (1998a) argues that the Ringgit depreciation can be looked upon as a blessing in disguise for tourism (weaker currency attracts more tourists), there is a time lag between promotional efforts and decisions by tourists on their holiday destinations. Furthermore, as currency depreciation has also hit the main Malaysian markets such as South Korea, Japan, Thailand and Indonesia, tourist arrivals from these regions are inevitably

affected. Tour operators face a slowdown in both inbound and outbound travel: 85 per cent of tour bookings for September to December 1997 were either postponed or cancelled (NERP, 1998). Tourists remain concerned about the haze and personal safety as portrayed in the foreign media. In 1998, there was an oversupply of hotel rooms in the Klang Valley. The government also reduced the budget for tourism promotion from RM79 million in 1997 to RM63 million in 1998. Since previous experience indicated a strong relationship between the expenditure for tourism promotion and tourist arrivals, the number of inbound travellers to Malaysia may be affected.

Tourism development planning in the National Economic Recovery Plan 1998

Under the Recovery Plan Malaysia will place more emphasis in promoting the country to the markets that are not so affected by economic downturn, such as Australia, Hong Kong, Taiwan, India, China, Europe, the USA and the Middle East. Bilateral and speedy efforts to prevent the recurrence of the smog have been introduced and implemented in Malaysia and Indonesia. Even with limited financial resources, effective promotion is expected to be optimized by the use of electronic media and the avoidance of duplication among promoters. Domestic tourism will also be encouraged in order to support the country's tourism industry and prevent the loss of foreign exchange from overseas travel. Malaysia also plans to promote itself as a 'shopping paradise' and MICE destination. As a part of its fiscal measures, the government is also aiming to discourage people from travelling abroad, including the possibility of introducing a travel exit tax. The government also plans to review various regulations and procedures. Among them are the ease of visa applications from potential markets such as China and India. In view of the glut of hotels in

Klang Valley, further proposals for development are likely to be rejected.

Marketing and promotion

National Tourism Organizations (NTOs) in the Pacific Rim are among the highest spenders on tourism promotion, ranging from 18 per cent of the tourism budget in the Philippines to 59 per cent in Thailand (Oppermann, 1997). In Malaysia, the Tourism Development Corporation (TDC) was created through an Act of Parliament in 1972 with the aim of coordinating, developing and promoting tourism in Malaysia. Currently, the task is given to the Malaysia Promotion and Tourism Board (MPTB) (1996). In accordance with the Malaysia Tourism Promotion Board Act 1992, functions of the Board are:

- to stimulate and promote tourism to and within the country;
- to stimulate, promote and market Malaysia, internationally and domestically, as a tourist destination;
- to coordinate all marketing and promotional activities relating to tourism conducted by any organization, government or non-governmental agencies; and
- to offer recommendations as to the adoption of appropriate methods, measures and programmes to facilitate or stimulate the development and promotion of the tourism industry in Malaysia. Where approved, to implement or assist in the implementation of these recommendations.

Following the success of Visit Thailand Year 1987, Malaysia decided to launch its 'visit year' in 1990. A total of 107 events including festivals, sport tournaments and cultural shows were planned for the whole year (Hall, 1997). Despite the late distribution of the Calendar of Events (Iskandar, 1989) which resulted in scepticism as to whether the Visit Malaysia Year 1990 would be a success, 7.5 million tourists visited Malaysia in 1990. However, the growth in arrivals was not sustained long term: in 1991, it dropped by 21.9 per cent. It may be that Malaysia promoted its tourism products internationally before the necessary laws, management plan, facilities and manpower were in place (Wong, 1996). Peat Marwick (1993) argued that Malaysia has the tendency to promote an image and product that the country is largely unable to deliver once tourists arrive. Nevertheless, one of the main obstacles to Malaysian success in marketing and promotion is the lack of a strong image. Malaysia does not have a similar appeal to the entertainment city of Bangkok or the shopping cities of Singapore and Hong Kong. As with Singapore, Malaysia often sells itself as a multi-ethnic country with cultural diversity. However, many other countries have a similar advantage. A study on the Malaysian image in various countries is required to facilitate effective promotion and marketing. A false image may result in dissatisfaction in the tourist experience. For example, Sarawak Iban culture is frequently promoted as head-hunting in Australian brochures although it is an outmoded practice. Yet a study by Zeppel (1997) indicated that tourists preferred social interaction with Iban people rather than looking for evidence that the Iban was, or is, a head-hunter.

In 1994, Malaysia launched its Second Visit Malaysia Year, which again saw the arrival of over 7 million tourists. Even though domestic tourism has been promoted since the early 1980s (Din, 1982), it was not until the Second Visit Malaysia Year that it received equal emphasis with foreign tourism by the government (Hall, 1997). Efforts to promote the growth of domestic tourism were reinforced by organizing several annual events such as the Malaysia Fest, the Flora Fest and Shopping Carnivals. To ensure Malaysia continuously attracts tourists, 1998 was announced as the Sports and Recreation Year which has the same function as Visit Malaysia Year (Chik, 1998a). The one-year programme highlighted Malaysia as an ideal international sporting venue and haven for recreational activities. A total of 217 events were planned throughout the year in all states. Sports and Recreation '98 was historic, as Malaysia was the first Asian country to host the Commonwealth Games. The Games, with seventy participating countries, were expected to attract an estimated 60 000 overseas visitors and a worldwide TV audience of 500 million (Hashim, 1997). The sum of RM200 million was spent on the promotion alone (Chik, 1998a). Among the legacies of the Games are the magnificent sports complexes, gardens and other developments which are intended to serve local needs, foster local tourism and attract the international tourist (Emmanuel, 1998).

MPTB and the private sector participate in many trade shows overseas to promote Malaysian tourism products. The government, making use of current technology, has also introduced the Tourism Malaysia Homepage (http://tourism.gov.my) to facilitate international marketing and promotions.

Malaysia is also making efforts to promote itself as a 'medical tourist' destination (Rajendran, 1998). According to the Health Minister, Malaysia is at the forefront within the region in using the latest state-of-the-art technology in medical and health care. Malaysian medical and hospital treatment charges compare favourably with charges for comparable treatment elsewhere. The immigration requirements for patients and their relatives from other countries have been relaxed. To encourage a longer stay in the country for the recuperating patients, the government also provides retirement villages for the patients and their relatives.

Domestic tourism

In Malaysia domestic tourism has a role engendering local awareness of cultural matters and national identity and heritage, and enhancing national pride and commitment, while receipts from domestic tourism are estimated to be rising at a rate of 15 per cent per year (Khalifah and Tahir, 1997). In 1993, 25 million person trips

were made by domestic travellers each spending an average of RM230 (Khalifah and Tahir, 1997). Domestic tourism is expected to boom further owing to the depreciation of the Ringgit, changes in government policies, an improvement in transportation and an increase in incomes. There were 26 164 712 outbound travellers in 1997 (ASTR, 1997 in Musa 1998) which represents a considerable financial loss to the country. Efforts to promote domestic tourism appeared in the Parliamentary Budget Speech 1998 wherein the sum of RM38 million was budgeted for the construction of medium-cost hotels, improvement of basic tourist facilities, cleaning of beaches, establishing camping sites and so forth (Ibrahim, 1998). Persuading Malays to take a holiday in the country is a difficult task. Often a great deal of prestige is involved in taking holidays overseas. The outbound travel markets also perceive that tourism facilities in Malaysia are lacking and rather expensive for what is provided. Malaysian travellers always want the best at the cheapest price (Hall, 1997).

The Marketing Plan 1994 (MPTB), in conjunction with the Second Visit Malaysia Year, promoted domestic tourism by encouraging people to 'Buy Malaysia', creating awareness of the products available, attractively pricing tour packages, teaching tourism as a subject in school and encouraging private and public sectors to conduct MICE-orientated activities locally (Khalifah and Tahir, 1997). The media and film makers are encouraged to use the features of tourist destinations in their publications or productions. Motorists travelling the North–South highway will be entertained by cultural shows and exhibitions and traditional demonstrations of local games and traditional cooking at highway rest areas (*New Straits Times*, 1998b). This is intended to attract not only domestic but also international tourists, especially Singaporeans and Thais who use the highway frequently. An extensive study of domestic tourism is being undertaken by the University Kebangsaan Malaysia with funding from MPTB in fifteen major towns nationwide, in order to determine the travelling habits of local people (Tourism Malaysia, 1998), with knowledge of motivation and preferences being regarded as crucial in developing tourist products and services.

Environmental dimensions

Tourism has become the second biggest foreign exchange earner and employs 102 833 people in Malaysia (Tourism Malaysia, 1997). Culturally, tourism development has, to a certain extent, been influenced by the perceived conflict between secular tourism and Islamic values (Hall, 1997). Even though it is widely accepted that tourism acts as a catalyst to economic development and employment creation, it also has potentially disruptive impacts on the local community (Hall, 1997). Din (1982, 1997) stresses that tourism development in Malaysia often ignores the importance of local participation and urges researchers and tourism developers to include this element for a more sustainable form of tourism development. Economic and cultural impacts are areas which can be managed with sound policies. However, the impact of tourism development on the environment can be catastrophic and is often irreversible.

It may be said that Asia remains relatively immature in the tourism sector owing to the lack of infrastructure, human resources, knowledge and political will to confront environmental problems. For example, various studies have been conducted on the impact of tourism development in Marine Park areas in Malaysia (Mohd and Japar, 1992; Mohd *et al.*, 1993; Lim and Spring, 1995; Lim, 1996; Wong, 1996; Musa, 1998). Among physical impacts seen are:

• increased sedimentation owing to infrastructural development;
• improper sewage and solid disposal;
• chemical pollution such as pesticide, fertilizer and oil spillage; and
• over-development.

Tourists may be exposed to pathogens such as giardia and cholera in surrounding waters such as Port Dickson and Batu Ferringgi (Wong, 1990). Lim and Spring (1995), in their study of sixty-seven divers in Tioman island, found the majority of divers were alarmed at the extent of coral damage. This is echoed in the speech by the Malaysian Education Minister, where he stated 70 per cent of coral life in Sabah had been destroyed (Najib, 1998). Scuba diving activities have not been proven to directly contribute to the coral damage (Wood *et al.*, 1995), however fish-bombing, which is still being practised in Sabahan waters, and improper and over-development of the islands or beaches could cause an environmental disaster. This is indicated in the study by Musa (1998) on divers' satisfaction with Sipadan Island (Sabah). Of 314 divers interviewed, 85 per cent were extremely concerned with haphazard and over-development of the island and the resulting problems of litter, noise and crowding. Despite the overwhelming satisfaction which is mainly due to the island's outstanding marine biodiversity, easy access and the friendliness and efficiency of staff and dive-masters, divers are left to wonder whether the island's attributes will be there in the future judging by the rate of exploitation of this small fragile ecosystem for hard currency.

Hiew and Yaman (1996) identified two main problems of the Marine Parks management in Malaysia: the lack of environmental conservation awareness and the unintegrated management of natural resources. Thirty-eight offshore islands in Malaysia have been gazetted as Marine Parks under the Fishery Act 1985, from the low watermark to two nautical miles offshore. The responsibility for the development, administration and management of these Marine Parks was given to the Department of Fisheries. Even though two offshore nautical miles of the Marine Parks are protected, the islands themselves are under the jurisdiction of the individual states. Contradiction in management is often seen. The Park's authorities (under the federal government) have no power to stop the over-development of the islands as the state government permits it.

Environmental issues and the concept of sustainable management are relatively new, and developers and policy makers are lacking in this specialist knowledge. Many decisions pertaining to the use of land are at the local or state level and are heavily influenced by immediate economic gain. Major infrastructure projects are likely to have environmental consequences despite the requirement of Environmental Impact Audits (Jenkins, 1997). However, Japar and Lim (1997) observe that even the combination of uncontrolled small resort development and expansion at Pasir Panjang beach (Redang Island) has been seen to produce an environmental impact comparable with the up-market Berjaya Resort development.

Since 1988, Environmental Impact Assessment (EIA) has become a mandatory requirement for tourism projects in Malaysia through the 1985 amendment of the Environmental Quality Act of 1974. Developers of tourism projects are required to submit an EIA to the Department of Environment (DOE) to be passed prior to their approval by the relevant federal, state or local authorities. This is only for the building of resorts and hotels at the seaside which exceed the capacity of eighty rooms and the development of tourism attractions and recreational areas in National Parks (Khalifah and Tahir, 1997). However, many projects are exempted from this requirement and, even if it is carried out, the enforcement is weak owing to the lack of man-power and the poor understanding of the standardized measurement criteria. Scientific research is often conducted on an ad hoc basis. The result is either difficult to access or often ignored by developers and government.

The Redang development is a notorious example of how environmental recommendations are being ignored. Despite a thorough EIA, which warned that the major resort development would cause serious impact on natural ecosystems, the state government sanctioned the project. Following the resort's construction, slope erosion resulted in siltation which subsequently killed many coral species and affected the water visibility (Manning and Dougherty, 1995).

However, greater environmental awareness and knowledge are growing among environmentalists and non-governmental organizations such as the Malaysian Nature Society, and World Wide Fund for Nature (WWF) in Malaysia. These organizations educate people and influence government to change policies towards conservation in order to gain sustainable tourism development. A National Ecotourism Plan is being prepared by WWF Malaysia for the Ministry of Culture, Arts and Tourism. Efforts to preserve Malaysian heritage have also been indicated by an application for the listing of three National Parks and four cultural sites in UNESCO's World Heritage (*New Straits Times*, 29 July 1998a).

Conclusion

The government had projected that 12.5 million tourists would visit Malaysia by the year 2000 (Hall, 1997). In view of the current economic situation, the present unfavourable image of Malaysia, and the 1997 lacklustre performance of tourist arrivals, the target arrival for 1998 has been revised to 6.8 million, 7 million in 1999 and 7.5 million in the year 2000 (Sooi, 1998). Emphasis will be placed on persuading tourists to stay longer and spend more. The present government has built many impressive tourism landmarks and organized a great number of successful international events, such as the Commonwealth Games 1998. However, the pattern of overspending, weak banking policies and misallocation of investment funds has affected the economy and led to withdrawal of foreign investment.

Malaysia has yet to resolve the internal political situation. One may argue that the authoritarian way of governing a country provides stability which permits healthy growth of the tourism industry. This may hold true if the population remains docile and accepts such a government. With the emergence of an educated middle-class society in Malaysia, it seems that authoritarianism is being increasingly questioned. Both economic and political instabilities are known to jeopardize the tourism industry in many countries, and this is currently affecting Malaysia.

Further, the policies to develop and maintain tourism have paid little attention to the negative impact which growth can have on the environment, especially in coastal and marine areas. For growth in tourism to be sustainable, it is essential to preserve unharmed the features which attract the tourist. There is a dichotomy between federal policies and state practices. Tourism management should be more integrated between the government and various stakeholders involved in the development of tourist resources. The government is yet to equip itself with human resources, knowledge and a sustainable tourism development policy. Heavy spending on marketing and promotion should be reviewed against these criteria.

Despite the economic downturn in Malaysia and the region, the political concern and the lessons yet to be learned about tourism policies and management, the country has much to offer in its beauty, natural resources, excellent communications, colourful and friendly people and ample and attractive accommodation for visitors at affordable prices. The present troubles will pass and tourism will revive and take its place as a major factor in the life of the country.

References

Asiaweek, 'Bottom line', *Asiaweek*, August 1998, p. 58.

Chik, S., 'Tourism rules despite setbacks – an interview with the Minister of Culture, Arts and Tourism Yb. Dato' Sabbaruddin Chik', http://tourism.gov.my/magazineJan-Feb98/page_10.html, 1998a.

Chik, S. 'Tourist arrivals drop by 80 per cent', *The Straits Times*, 2 November 1998b, p. 17.

Colmey, J., 'Heir today, gone', *Asiaweek*, August 1998.

Din, K.H., 'Tourism Malaysia: competing needs in a plural society', *Annals of Tourism Research* 9, 1982, pp. 453–480.

Din, K.H., 'Indigenization of tourism development: some constraints and possibilities', in M. Opper-mann (ed.), *Pacific Rim Tourism*, CAB International, Wallingford, 1997.

The Economist, 'South East Asia in denial', *The Economist* 18 October 1997: p. 13.

Emmanuel, T., 'Turn games village into tourist draw, agencies urged', *News Straits Times* (Malaysia), 7 August 1998.

Frei, M., 'Black eye could floor Mahathir', *The Weekly Telegraph*, 1998, p. 376.

Hall, C.M., *Tourism in the Pacific Rim: Developments, Impacts and Markets*, 2nd edn, Addison Wesley Longman, South Melbourne, 1997.

Hashim, A., *Malaysia Tourism*, a bimonthly publication of Malaysia Tourism Promotion Board, Malaysia, September–October 1997.

Hashim, A., 'An interview with the Director General of Tourism Malaysia Ybhg. Datoi Dr. Arshad Hashim', http://tourism.gov.my/magazine/vol2/page_5.html, 1998.

Hiew, K.W.P. and Yaman, A.R.G., 'The Marine Parks of Malaysia: objectives, current issues and initiatives'. Paper presented at the workshop on impact management in Marine Parks, Kuala Lumpur, 13 and 14 August 1996.

Ibrahim, A., 'Parliamentary Budget Speech', HYPERLINK http://www.treasury.gov.my/budget/ http://www.treasury.gov.my/budget/_Htdocs/speech/budget/apdx/fvmain.html, 1998.

Information Malaysia, *Year Book*. Berita Publishing Sdn. Bhd. Malaysia, 1998.

Iskandar, T., 'The early campaign lures the tourist?' *Asia Travel Trade*, October 1989.

Japar S.B. and Lim, L.C., 'Assessment of the impact of large scale development on the coastal environment of Pulau Redang'. Report produced under project MYS 320/95, 1997.

Jenkins, C.L., 'Impact of the development in international tourism in the Asian region', in F. Go and C.L. Jenkins (eds), *Tourism and Economic Development in Asia and Australasia*, Cassell, London, 1997.

Khalifah, Z. and Tahir, S., 'Malaysia: tourism in perpective', in F. Go. and C.L. Jenkins (eds), *Tourism and Economic Development in Asia and Australasia*, Cassell, London, 1997.

Larimer, T., 'Blackest hours', *Time: The Weekly Newsmagazine*, 12 October 1996.

Lim, L.C., *Tourism, Pollution and Marine Environment*

in Malaysia, WWF Malaysia Report, produced under project MY 941/97, 1996.

Lim, L.C. and Spring, N., 'The concepts and analysis of carrying capacity: a management tool for effective planning, Part 3, case study: Pulau Tioman', WWF Malaysia, produced under project MY0058, 1995.

Malaysia Hotel Supply and Statistics, update 1997–2000, official publication, Tourism Malaysia, Malaysia.

Manning, E.W. and Dougherty, T.D., 'Sustainable tourism: preserving the golden goose', *Cornell Hotel and Restaurant Administration Quarterly* April 1995, pp. 29–42.

McCarty, T., 'It's Dr. M's economy now', *Time: The Weekly*, 5 October 1998.

McNulty, S., Malaysians gear up for the big marketing push', *Asia Travel Trade*, October 1998.

Mohd, I.H.M. and Japar, S.B., *Development Impact on Coral Reefs and Mangroves of Pulau Redang*, Faculty of Fisheries and Marine Sciences, University Pertanian Malaysia, Malaysia, 1992.

Musa, G., 'Sipadan: a survey of the geographical aspects of divers' satisfaction on Sipadan Island'. Unpublished dissertation, Centre for Tourism, University of Otago, Dunedin, 1998.

Najib, R., '70 per cent of coral life in Sabah destroyed', *News Straits Times*, Malaysia, 24 July 1998.

National Economic Recovery Plan, *Agenda and Action*, National Economic Action Council, Economic Planning Unit, Prime Minister's Department. Malaysia, August 1998.

News Straits Times, 'Seven sites for Unesco's Heritage List', *News Straits Times*, 29 July 1998a.

News Straits Times, 'Entertainment at highway rest area', *News Straits Times*, 3 September 1998b.

Oppermann, M., 'The future of tourism in the Pacific Rim', in M. Oppermann, (ed.), *Pacific Rim Tourism*, CAB International, Wallingford, 1997.

Peat Marwick, *Tourism Policy Study. A Marketing Report*, prepared for the Ministry of Culture, Arts and Tourism, Government of Malaysia, Kuala Lumpur: Peat Marwick Consultants Sdn. Bhd., 1993.

Rajendran, S., 'Steps taken to promote medical tourism', *News Straits Times*, Malaysia, 25 August 1998.

Smith, R.A., 'Book review: Imperial Belvederes: The Hill Stations of Malaysia', *Annals Tourism Research* 22(4), 1995, pp. 941–943.

Sooi, C.C., 'Island resorts with a lot to offer', *News Straits Times*, Malaysia, 3 August 1998.

Soon, T., 'Reflections of 1997 – from prosperity to austerity', *The Star*, http://thestar.com.My/archives/yearend1997/31yrn9.html, 1998.

Tourism Malaysia, *Annual Tourism Statistical Report*, Tourism Malaysia, Kuala Lumpur, 1997.

Tourism Malaysia, 'Local tourism industry to be further developed', *Tourism Malaysia Highlights*, http://tourism.gov.my/magazine/Jan-Fe_b98/page5.html, 1998.

Wong, J.L.P., *Marine Parks Malaysia: Tourism, Impact and Conservation Awareness*, Maritime Institute of Malaysia (MIMA), Kuala Lumpur, 1996.

Wong, P.P., 'Coastal resources management – tourism in Peninsular Malaysia', *ASEAN Economic Bulletin* 7(2), 1990.

Wood, E., Wood, C., George D., Dipper, F., and Lane, D., *Pulau Sipadan: Survey and Monitoring 1995*, WWF project number MYS 319/95, 1995.

Yusof, R., 'Dr M: Funds for Games facilities well spent', *News Straits Times* (Malaysia), 25 August 1998.

Zeppel, H., 'Headhunters and long-house adventure: marketing the Iban culture in Sarawak, Borneo', in M. Oppermann (ed.), *Pacific Rim Tourism*, CAB International, Wallingford, 1997.

11

Tourism in Indonesia: the end of the New Order

C. Michael Hall

Introduction

It has long been recognized that tourism growth is reliant on a perception of economic, political and social stability. Many of the countries in South and Southeast Asia have seen their tourism fortunes rise and, more recently in some cases, fall as a result of their national stability and stability within the region overall (Go, 1997). Indonesia provides a useful case study of some of the difficulties which instability causes for tourism development and the measures which may be used to overcome consumer perceptions.

Indonesia has experienced positive economic growth almost without exception since the beginning of Suharto's New Order in 1996. Growth of around 7 per cent per year, inflation below 10 per cent and strong export growth was the norm (Van Klinken, 1998). However, in the wake of the Southeast Asian economic crisis, Indonesia has seen a dramatic collapse in the value of its currency, substantial decline in its foreign reserves and increased levels of foreign debt. The effects of the financial collapse have rippled through the economy creating unemployment, with an estimated 10 million jobs being lost; lowering living standards with more than 50 million people falling below the poverty line and affecting the supply of food in

a country in which, according to the World Bank, some 39 per cent of Indonesian children were malnourished before the economic catastrophe (Miah, 1998). The same World Bank Report stated that 'no country in recent history, let alone the size of Indonesia, has ever suffered such a dramatic reversal of fortune' (cited in Miah, 1998: n.p.).

This chapter will therefore examine the factors which have created instability in Indonesia and their implications for tourism.

Growth in tourism

Tourism has long played a major role in the Indonesian government's economic and regional development priorities with activities geographically focused on centres such as Bali (Denpasar, Nusa Dua), western and central Java (Jakarta, Yogyakarta, Bogor, Bandung, Surabaya), northern Sumatra (Banda Aceh, Medan, Danau Toba) and Sulawesi (Toraja land) (Economist Intelligence Unit, 1991; Hall, 1997; Wall, 1997). Bali is the focal point for leisure-oriented travel, although the Indonesian government has attempted to spread international tourist development around the country in recent years (Hall, 1997).

Table 11.1 *Arrivals to Indonesia, 1985–1997*

Year	Arrivals (000)	% change
1985	749	
1986	825	10.15
1987	1060	28.52
1988	1301	22.70
1989	1626	24.95
1990	2178	33.92
1991	2570	18.02
1992	3064	19.22
1993	3403	11.06
1994	4006	17.72
1995	4324	7.9
1996	5034	16.4
1997	5185	3.0

Source: after Hall, 1997; Badan Pusat Statistik, 1998.

Since the 1960s the focal point of Indonesian economic development has been a series of five-year development plans known as Repelita. Repelita VI began in April 1994. During Repelita IV, at the end of 1987, inbound visitation hit the 1 million mark for the first time (see Table 11.1). During the period 1984–1988, US$918.6 million in foreign money and Rp2.15 billion from local interests funded a total of 264 investments, including 182 hotels, 40 recreational facilities, 21 travel bureaus, 10 marine resorts and 11 restaurants (Teh and Wong, 1989). In 1989 tourism represented 5.8 per cent of exports earnings, compared with 2.8 per cent in 1985 (Economist Intelligence Unit, 1991). In 1989 the Directorate General of Tourism set a target of at least 2.5 million arrivals and US$2.25–3.15 billion in foreign exchange earnings by the end of the Repelita V period. The target of 2.5 million arrivals had been reached by 1991 although they only produced US$969 million in revenue (Hall, 1997). By 1995 Indonesia was attracting over 4.3 million visitor arrivals, producing an estimated US$5.31 billion in revenue (World Tourism Organization, 1996). In 1997 the 5.04 million arrivals, substantially lower than the projected 5.3 million, brought in an estimated US$6.62 billion in foreign exchange earnings (*TravelAsia*, 1998b).

Growth in inbound tourism has meant that Indonesia has become one of the world's top tourist destinations in terms of numbers of tourists attracted. In 1990 Indonesia had 0.8 per cent of the world international tourism arrivals market (ranking 26th), by 1995 this had grown to 1.43 per cent (ranking 19th) (World Tourism Organization, 1996). Indonesia has had substantial growth in inbound visitor arrivals for much of the late 1980s and early 1990s, with an average annual growth rate of approximately 20 per cent for much of the decade. However, this figure dropped dramatically in 1997 and 1998 as will be discussed below. In 1991 Indonesia attracted 2.569 million visitors, over three times the 1986 figure of 825 035 visitors. By 1997 this had grown to almost 5.2 million (Table 11.1).

Not surprisingly given geographical proximity and ease of access, visitors from ASEAN countries account for approximately 30 per cent of the inbound market to Indonesia (Hall, 1997). In 1997 the top ten national markets for Indonesia in order of importance were:

1. Singapore
2. Japan
3. Australia (up from no. 5 in 1996)
4. Malaysia (grew 22.7 per cent in 1997)
5. Taiwan (down from no. 3 in 1996, a decrease of 33.3 per cent)
6. South Korea
7. Germany (up from no. 8 in 1996, an increase of 11 per cent)
8. USA (down from no. 7 in 1996, dropping 13.3 per cent)
9. The Netherlands (up from no. 10 in 1996, with an increase of 18.2 per cent)
10. UK (down from no. 9) (*TravelAsia*, 1998a).

Of the long-haul markets, the major inbound markets are Japan, Taiwan, Australia, the USA, the UK and Germany. The ASEAN market from Singapore, Malaysia and the Philippines is also significant for short-haul travel, particularly weekend breaks (see Table 11.2). Table 11.3 gives a detailed breakdown of visitor arrivals by nationality from 1993 to 1995.

Approximately 75 per cent of international travel to Indonesia is for holidays, with the

Table 11.2 *Visitor arrivals to Indonesia by nationality, 1996–1997*

Nationality	1996	%	Nationality	1997	%
ASEAN	1 832 548	36.4	ASEAN	2 066 857	39.9
Japan	638 287	12.7	Japan	661 214	0.8
Australia	361 234	7.2	Australia	458 733	8.8
Taiwan	527 746	10.5	Taiwan	347 314	6.7
USA	257 138	5.1	USA	230 394	4.4
UK	224 624	4.5	S. Korea	226 327	4.4
Germany	191 723	3.8	Germany	185 861	3.6
The Netherlands	171 084	3.4	UK	170 238	3.3
S. Korea	117 794	2.3	The Netherlands	135 209	2.6
Hong Kong	89 204	1.8	France	107 228	2.1
Others	623 090	12.4	Others	595 868	11.5
Total	5 034 472	100.0	Total	5 185 243	100.0

Source: ASEAN Centre (1998) http://www.asean.or.jp/e_st/etour02.html (accessed 17 December 1998).

Table 11.3 *Number of foreign visitor arrivals to Indonesia by country of residence 1993–1997 (000s)*

Country of residence	1993	1994	1995	1996	1997
USA	155	169	155	198	172
Canada	26	31	31	32	27
Other America	9	12	15	14	10
Total Americas	190	212	201	244	209
Austria	17	22	18	17	12
Belgium	14	18	17	20	22
Denmark	15	20	18	17	13
France	70	72	80	88	108
Germany	133	160	168	168	186
Italy	60	75	56	63	68
The Netherlands	115	135	137	122	145
Spain and Portugal	17	19	15	16	33
Sweden, Norway and Finland	31	36	39	38	41
Switzerland	35	41	44	34	30
UK	133	162	166	145	142
USSR	4	9	7	11	7
Other Europe	17	28	28	14	12
Total Europe	660	799	794	754	820
Africa	7	10	38	29	24
Middle East	30	31	27	24	30
Brunei	7	10	12	11	9
Malaysia	361	371	512	393	482
Philippines	77	78	96	51	51
Singapore	858	1017	1047	1300	1376
Thailand	37	41	39	43	46
Total ASEAN	1340	1519	1705	1799	1963
Australia	288	305	320	380	539
Hong Kong	70	85	93	123	103
India	15	21	32	27	26
Japan	378	476	486	666	707
South Korea	86	104	115	250	246
New Zealand	34	36	28	33	39
Pakistan, B'desh and Srilanka	12	14	19	19	13
Taiwan	244	318	353	607	405
Other Asia–Pacific	51	77	112	78	59
Total Asia–Pacific	1176	1434	1558	2183	2138
Grand total	3403	4006	4324	5034	5185

Source: Badan Pusat Statistik, 1998.

Table 11.4 *Number of foreign visitor arrivals to Indonesia by port of entry (000s)*

Year	Port of entry					Total
	Soekarno Hatta	Ngurah Rai	Polonia	Sekupang Batam	Other port	
1988	538	352	104	228	80	1301
1989	631	426	121	359	89	1626
1990	845	476	129	578	149	2178
1991	845	567	151	607	399	2570
1992	978	741	170	678	497	3064
1993	991	886	185	745	595	3403
1994	1182	1049	189	900	687	4006
1995	1259	1065	218	941	841	4324
1996	1566	1195	225	1048	1000	5034
1997	1457	1294	174	1119	1140	5185

Source: Badan Pusat Statistik, 1998.

remainder being almost completely comprised of business travel (Hall, 1997). In 1993 the average length of stay was over ten days, by far the longest in ASEAN and, hence, important in the relatively high rate of return that Indonesia receives from tourism per tourist (ASEAN Tourism Information Centre, 1996). The three most popular Indonesian destinations are Bali, Jakarta and Yogyakarta. Table 11.4 illustrates the number of foreign visitor arrivals to Indonesia by port of entry with the capital's airport being the most significant, although other airports have clearly shown considerable growth in recent years.

Markets also show different spatial characteristics in their travel patterns. The Korean and Taiwanese markets prefer the Jakarta–Yogyakarta–Bali route with a seven-day average stay. In comparison, the Japanese spend four to five days in Bali and take day trips to Yogyakarta to see Borobudur. Europeans and Australians stay for between twelve and fourteen days and tend to focus their activities on Bali, although they are increasingly moving further afield to areas such as Kalimantan, as part of ecotourism and adventure travel packages. Similarly, the American market had started to venture out to newer destinations such as Toraja, Kalimantan, and Irian Jaya (Hall, 1997).

Indonesia's Ministry of Tourism, Art and Culture revised its target for tourist arrivals

mid-1990s to 5.5 million, 15 per cent lower than the previous projection, with the newly installed minister, Abdul Latief, blaming the negative media coverage of forest fires and the monetary crisis for the declining trend. As with many other countries in the region, Indonesia aimed to prioritize tourism promotion in 1998 in countries not so directly affected by the monetary crisis, including Australia, New Zealand, Japan, Europe and North America (*TravelAsia*, 1998b). However, the relatively positive picture of Indonesian tourism which existed up until mid-1997 has since been shattered by a series of economic and political crises in 1998 and 1999.

Crisis in Indonesia

Events throughout 1998 indicated that Indonesia is a country in crisis. This crisis is fourfold.

1. *The financial crisis*, caused by the currency collapse and consequent capital flight. Indonesia's foreign debt is now estimated at over US$110 billion, banks and most leading firms effectively bankrupt, the rupiah less than a quarter of its pre-crisis value (at the time of writing, 1998) and stock prices just 9 per cent of pre-crisis values. Furthermore, according to one report, 95 per cent of the

country's huge foreign debt is owed by just fifty wealthy individuals (Van Klinken, 1998).

2. *The economic crisis*, with real output estimated to fall 15 per cent in 1998 and a further fall expected in 1999. Tens of millions of Indonesians are unemployed, and real wages have plunged sharply, with inflation running at approximately 10 per cent per month for 1998. The government further predicted in November 1998 that half of Indonesia's 202 million people could fall into poverty if the economic crisis continues (*The Age*, 1998a).

3. *The food crisis*, with drought, hoarding and panic buying driving prices up 100 per cent and 1 kg of rice now costing 4000 rupiah – roughly a day's wage. The crisis was more one of affordability than shortage, but newspaper and media reports suggest that so many people are now out of work that rice is being stolen from fields. The price of rice trebled for most consumers in 1998 despite market control efforts by the government. The *Jakarta Post* reported Minister Saefuddin as saying that 60 per cent of 7.3 million poor families in Central and Eastern Java, or 4.4 million families, were having only one meal a day. According to the Minister, 'Urban poor are especially vulnerable. In many rural areas, people are more used to hardship and can seek alternative ways to cope. Those who demonstrate or loot are usually urban poor' (cited in *The Age*, 1998a). Similarly, *AsiaWeek* (1998) commented, 'nothing is more urgent than food security. If Indonesia's civilian leaders are unable to stave off hunger, social unrest is likely to erupt on a large scale. And that could bring about not only untold devastation, but also the military dictatorship that everyone fears'.

4. *The political crisis*, with widespread protest against the government, violence against ethnic minorities, tensions between the national government and provincial regions, parliamentary and presidential elections not due until mid-1999.

All of the above crises have implications for tourism, but their effects are variable over time and in relation to different facets of the tourism industry. Clearly, the financial and economic crisis has important implications for outbound tourist flows from Indonesia and also for domestic tourism, both of which have been severely affected by Indonesia's economic woes. However, the financial implications of the changes to the Indonesian economy are also considerable in terms of their effect on investment in tourism infrastructure such as accommodation, attractions and transport. The changes in the value of the rupiah, for example, will make the Indonesian tourism industry more reliant on foreign sources for tourism investment. Perhaps paradoxically in some ways, the economic and financial crisis in Indonesia makes the country even more dependent on tourism than ever before, as Indonesia seeks to gain foreign exchange, improve its balance of payments position, repay its huge levels of overseas debt and attempts to generate employment.

The food crisis has an indirect impact on tourism. The potential for food shortages may serve to reinforce the anger felt in some sections of the Indonesian community at the sudden lowering of their standard of living, thereby feeding into existing ethnic and political tensions (Colebatch, 1998). In the longer term, it is also possible that food shortages may lead to negative reactions towards tourists who are perceived to be well off. However, having the most direct and immediate effect on tourism is the political crisis which has beset Indonesia and which has had substantial implications for tourism.

As noted in Chapter 5 which discussed the political dimensions of tourism in the region, political stability and perceptions of visitor safety are vital to tourism. Several countries in the region, notably Burma (Myanmar), Cambodia, China, Philippines and Thailand have all been affected by media images of protest or human rights abuses in recent years. Until recently, Indonesia has been generally

Figure 11.1 *'Beautiful Indonesia in Miniature Park', known in Indonesia as 'Taman Mini', is a theme park designed to reflect the cultures of all of Indonesia's provinces and to assist in the creation of an Indonesian national identity for the large numbers of domestic visitors and educational groups which visit*

Figure 11.2 *Reconstruction of a Kalimantan long house in Taman Mini*

Figure 11.3 *This Disney-like attraction in Taman Mini, especially built as a children's attraction, had a portrait of Mrs Suharto in the entrance. Such an attraction may have served to provide a positive image of the former president's family to the visitor*

unaffected by such images, however that situation has changed markedly in the period leading up to the resignation of President Suharto and in the post-Suharto period.

The cultural, geographical and political structure of Indonesia is one which has long had the potential for major upheaval. Indonesia is a state of many cultures and languages (Figures 11.1 to 11.3) which has been created from the previous colonial structures of the Dutch East Indies and the dominance of a small elite with close ties to the military for much of the post-colonial period. This situation was exacerbated by the nepotistic activities of the family of President Suharto and the military, which served to further concentrate wealth and power. Opposition to Indonesian occupation of a number of cultural and ethnic groups, such as those of Aceh (northern Sumatra), Irian Jaya (West New Guinea) and East Timor (the former Indonesian colony invaded by the Indonesians in 1975 and occupied despite United Nations opposition) were brutally crushed. While Indonesia was experiencing economic growth, the gradual betterment of conditions for the general population provided a cushion for political protest and created a basis, if somewhat tenuous at times, of popular support for Suharto. However, once growth faltered, conditions proved ripe for the encouragement of greater political opposition.

Indeed, the post-Suharto period has provided a reopening of many of the cases of human rights abuse of the 1980s and 1990s. For example, Indonesia's Human Rights Commission reported that there is clear evidence of massacres of civilians by Indonesian troops in the northern province of Aceh, after investigating allegations by locals and human rights groups that thousands of Acehenese had been killed by the military during campaigns of fear and brutality in the late 1980s and early 1990s, and again from 1997 until July 1998 (Williams, 1998a). What is significant in these findings is not only that they represented an 'excessive and brutal' armed deployment against a movement which probably numbered only hundreds at its peak and perhaps about thirty today, but that they contribute to the wider portrayal of abuse of human rights in Indonesia in the West, in addition to images of protests in the streets of Jakarta and violence against ethnic and religious minorities.

Despite attempts by President Habibie to portray himself as a reformer in the West it is increasingly becoming apparent that violence against ethnic groups is continuing to occur and be reported in the Western media. For example, despite a much publicized public withdrawal of Indonesian troops from East Timor earlier in the year as a supposed gesture of reconciliation, Indonesian special forces returned several

weeks later in a move designed to reinforce Indonesian control of the territory (Williams, 1998b). Similarly, Indonesian armed forces killed numerous supporters of the Free Irian Jaya movement in a crackdown on political opposition in the province in October and November 1998 (Murdoch, 1998).

The Indonesian military have long been held responsible for human rights atrocities, including systematic torture and kidnapping of political activists. However, there is a possibility that investigations into such abuses will open a Pandora's box, which may trigger a crisis of confidence and threaten the unity of the security forces just as Indonesia faces a new round of turbulence in the lead-up to general elections. Beyond kidnapping investigations are the court-martialling of eighteen soldiers involved in the killing of four student protesters in the May 1998 street protests, and calls for investigations into past massacres of civilians by troops, such as the 1991 Dili killings and the shooting of protesters in Tanjung Priok in 1984. Indeed, the most troubling possibility in looking at the role of the military in Indonesian society is the apparent split in the Indonesian armed forces and the involvement of one faction in fanning the May riots and lootings and, worse still, attacks on the Chinese ethnic community in an attempt to provide a justification for stronger military controls (Berfield and Loveard, 1998; Williams, 1998c, e).

Long-time autocratic President Suharto was forced to quit in May 1998 after the protests and riots, partly triggered by economic hardship, which resulted in the deaths of 1200 people. However, the May violence in Indonesia had a profound affect on tourist numbers and on the Chinese ethnic market in particular. The armed forces did nothing to protect the victims from the terrible wave of violence that swept Jakarta, and there is evidence that in the lead-up to the crisis, rage against the relatively wealthy Chinese was fanned by senior Suharto government officials and military leaders as a means of deflecting attention from the government (Williams, 1998d, e). It is also apparent that there was a pattern of systematic rape against ethnic

Chinese women and children within a wider rampage against the ethnic Chinese community. The Indonesian Human Rights Commission, in its report on the rape of ethnic Chinese women during the May riots, detailed 168 rapes of women and children and the consequent death of twenty victims, either killed by their assailants, burned to death in their homes or who later died from their injuries. Compiled by the Volunteers for Humanity, which first publicly raised the rape claims, the report says 152 women were raped around Jakarta and another sixteen in provincial towns, between the May riots and the first week of July (Williams, 1998e).

The attacks against ethnic Chinese were extensively covered by the media and led to widespread protest by ethnic Chinese against the Indonesian government from Beijing through to New York (*The Age*, 1998b) and threats from Taiwan to reconsider its economic and trade relationship with Indonesia. Despite guarantees from the Indonesian Police Department regarding the safety of tourists (Susanti, 1998a) and calls from politicians such as Dr Rais, who heads the Islamic mass movement Muhammadiyah and the National Mandate Party (PAN), to reassure 'our Chinese brothers and sisters' (Colebatch, 1998), the riots had an immediate effect on visitor numbers with a collapse in arrivals in May and June and cancellations from Hong Kong, Taiwan and other parts of Asia in particular (Susanti, 1998b). A number of countries, including the USA, the UK, Australia, and the Netherlands issued advice recommending against travel to Indonesia; such warnings were also issued from a number of Asian countries including China, Hong Kong, Taiwan, Japan, India, Malaysia, Korea, Philippines, and Thailand. The travel patterns most affected were:

• all city trips and stopover packages to Jakarta, Yogyakarta and Medan;
• all Java–Bali roundtrips;
• all Java roundtrips; and
• all Sumatra roundtrips (*TravelAsia*, 1998c).

One of the immediate issues facing the tourism industry was to attempt to distinguish between Bali and the rest of Indonesia, and Jakarta in particular, in the marketplace. In response the head of the Bali Tourism Office, Luther Barrung, sent a message to all Bali hotels and foreign consulates based in Bali:

Bali remains peaceful and calm. Any demonstrations that have occurred to-date have taken the form of dialogues which have been orderly and confined to the campus area in the centre of Denpasar. These dialogues have been characterised by a free exchange of opinions with participants from all walks of Balinese society.

Without exception, these dialogues have focused on the issue of political reform and at no time have any of Bali's many tourists and visitors been the focus of any protest.

All hotels, tourist attractions and tours continue to operate in Bali as usual with no interruptions or disturbances in services provided to our valued tourism visitors (TravelAsia, 1998d).

In addition, Bali launched a 'Two years in Bali' campaign in June which provided for cheap flights from key European and Asian markets and a certificate guaranteeing guests three extra nights, which they could use to either extend their stay or use during a return visit anytime before December 1999 (Hamdi, 1998). At the national level, the Indonesian Tourism Promotion Board, under the patronage of the Ministry of Tourism, Arts and Culture, launched a 'Let's Go Indonesia!' campaign to attempt to attract visitors back to the country. The campaign has four components:

1. 'Happy Day', a 'free' day for international visitors;
2. 'Magic Month', a value-driven sales campaign;
3. 'Pasar Wisata', the Indonesia travel trade event;
4. 'The Best of Indonesia', an image-driven campaign of advertising, public relations and cooperative trade marketing from September onwards.

However, the campaign only received marginal support from Bali which sought to pursue a 'Bali first' policy (*TravelAsia*, 1998e). In addition to the promotional campaign, the Indonesian government also undertook a number of other measures to encourage both visitors to return and foreign investment in tourism, including the cutting of bureaucratic red tape by shortening the time required to process development projects (Jarret, 1998); allowing any airlines from their home base to bring tourists direct to any place in Indonesia, with Batam as the western hub and Biak as the eastern hub where airlines could 'refuel and go anywhere'; and promotional costs for tourism, arts and culture would become tax-deductible (Habibie, 1998).

At the time of writing, late 1998, the long-term effectiveness of Indonesia's efforts to attract tourists back remains unknown, particularly when the political situation remains volatile. International inbound arrival figures for Bali showed a drop of 15 per cent, or 91 000 visitors, in the first six months of 1998, compared with the first half of 1997. In June international arrivals in Bali were down 35.7 per cent, almost 40 000 visitors. For Indonesia as a whole, arrivals were down 22.7 per cent in the first half of 1998, almost half a million visitors less than in 1997 (Jarret, 1998).

Conclusion

The manipulation of violence in Indonesia for political ends goes as far back as the colonial period. The establishment of Suharto's New Order in 1965–1966 was marked by one of the most horrifying political purges in modern history, in which up to 500 000 communists and alleged communist sympathizers were massacred, many by their own neighbours. More recently, Indonesia has been marred by violence against street protestors and ethnic minorities. Such political instability, abuse of human rights and violence clearly has substantial implications for tourism. At the time of writing, it appears likely that the political oppression which was such a characteristic of the Suharto regime is continuing under Habibie (Williams, 1998f, g). Experience from elsewhere in Asia, such as the Philippines under Marcos, suggests that an authoritarian state can only manage to convey an image of stability for a short period of time before activists and the media present an alternative image to the marketplace (Hall, 1994). However, there is also considerable evidence to suggest that should a destination have a strong presence in the marketplace then, as with China after the quelling of the democratic movement in 1989 (Hall and O'Sullivan, 1996), it will not be long before growth can continue.

The path for Indonesia is unknown. Although restoration of political and human rights is obviously important, the country clearly has several other pressing financial, economic and food security issues to address. In this context, human resource management issues seem rather insignificant given the political problems facing the country. However, as Guerrier (1993) observed in the context of Bali, such issues are fundamental to the long-term prosperity of the tourism industry and appropriate strategies and training are essential for the development of the tourism workers and managers. Tourism will play an important part in future economic development given its potential for employment generation and attraction of needed foreign exchange. However, its capacity to contribute will obviously depend on the wider political stability of the fragile Indonesian state.

References

The Age, 'Indonesians head into famine crisis', *The Age* 15 September 1998.

The Age, 'Jakarta urged to act on rapes', *The Age* 9 September 1998b.

ASEAN Centre, *Tourism Statistics*, http://www.asean.or.jp/e_st/etour02.html (accessed 17 December 1998), 1998.

ASEAN Tourism Information Centre, *Tourism Statistics*, ATIC, Singapore, http://www.serve.com/ATIC/index.html, 1996.

AsiaWeek, 'Indonesia's flashpoint: Habibie must give top priority to feeding his people', *AsiaWeek* 2 October 1998.

Badan Pusat Statistik (Central Bureau of Statistics), Republic of Indonesia, http://www.bps.go.id/statbysector/tourism/table25.shtml (accessed 14 December 1998), 1998.

Berfield, S. and Loveard, D., 'Ten days that shook Indonesia', *AsiaWeek* 24 July 1998.

Colebatch, T., 'Act or face ruin, Indonesians told', *The Age* 27 September 1998.

Economist Intelligence Unit, 'Indonesia', *International Tourism Reports* 3, 1991, pp. 23–40.

Go, F., 'Asian and Australasian dimensions of global tourism development', in F. Go and C.L. Jenkins (eds), *Tourism and Economic Development in Asia and Australasia*, Pinter, London, 1997, pp. 3–34.

Guerrier, Y., 'Bali', in T. Baum (ed.), *Human Resource Issues in International Tourism*, Butterworth Heinemann, Oxford, 1993, pp. 108–115.

Habibie, B.J., 'Habibie charms', *TravelAsia* 2 October 1998.

Hall, C.M., *Tourism and Politics: Policy, Power and Place*, John Wiley and Sons, Chichester, 1994.

Hall, C.M., *Tourism in the Pacific Rim*, 2nd edn, Addison Wesley Longman, South Melbourne, 1997.

Hall, C.M. and O'Sullivan, V., 'Tourism, political instability and violence', in A. Pizam and Y. Mansfield (eds), *Tourism, Crime and International Security Issues*, John Wiley and Sons, Chichester, 1996, pp. 105–122.

Hamdi, R., '"Two years in Bali" campaign launched', *TravelAsia* 12–18 June 1998.

Jarret, I., 'Indons cut red tape: move aimed at encouraging investment', *TravelAsia* 18 September 1998.

Miah, M., '"Never seen in history" Indonesia's economic titanic', *Against the Current* 8(4), September/October (http://www.labornet.org/solidarity/atc/miah76.html, accessed 15 December 1998), 1998.

Murdoch, L., 'Witness to a bloodbath', *The Age* 14 November 1998.

Susanti, Y., 'Indon guarantees', *TravelAsia* 15 May 1998a.

Susanti, Y., 'Long road to recovery', *TravelAsia* 22 May 1998b.

Teh, S. and Wong, Y., 'Bursting at the Seams', *Asia Travel Trade*, 21 December 1989, pp. 6–7, 10–11.

TravelAsia, 'Tracking trends: top 10 markets', *Travel Asia* 18 September 1998a.

TravelAsia, 'Indonesia revises targets, priorities promotions', *TravelAsia* 24 April 1998b.

TravelAsia, 'Indon woes: cancellations pour in as tension escalates', *TravelAsia* 22 May 1998c.

TravelAsia, 'Bali travel trade acts', *TravelAsia* 22 May 1998d.

TravelAsia, 'Bali cool towards ITBP's new campaign', *TravelAsia* 3 July 1998e.

Van Klinken, G., 'From go-go to yo-yo', *Inside Indonesia* 54, April–June 1998.

Wall, G., 'Indonesia: the impact of regionalisation', in F. Go and C.L. Jenkins (eds), *Tourism and Economic Development in Asia and Australasia*, Pinter, London, 1997, pp. 3–34.

Williams, L., 'Mass graves point to Aceh massacres', *The Age* 24 August 1998a.

Williams, L., 'The endless torment of Timor', *The Age* 17 October 1998b.

Williams, L., 'Military madness', *The Age* 19 August 1998c.

Williams, L., 'Report tells of rioters' ethnic rape rampage', *The Age* 15 July 1998d.

Williams, L., 'Indonesia's new wave of terror', *The Age* 7 November 1998e.

Williams, L., 'Habibie moves to shackle opponents', *The Age* 17 November 1998f.

Williams, L., 'Habibie puts clamp on opponents', *The Age* 12 December 1998g.

World Tourism Organization, *Tourism Trends Highlights 1995*, WTO Tourism Statistics Service, World Tourism Organization, Madrid, 1996.

12

Tourism in Vietnam: Doi Moi and the realities of tourism in the 1990s

Malcolm Cooper

Introduction

In the Vietnam of the 1970s and 1980s, government policy discussions focused on the development of a liberalized market-oriented economy that would bring the country greater prosperity and higher standards of living (*Doi Moi*). Since 1986, restrictions on private investment were gradually lifted and foreign investment and ownership encouraged, in line with similar experiments that were occurring throughout Asia. However, opening up the economy was not easy in the beginning as Vietnam lacked capital, experience, infrastructure and a trained labour force. Moreover, at that time Vietnam was virtually isolated from the outside world as a result of an American embargo on trade. Tourism was seen as a way to gain much-needed foreign exchange and to circumvent the embargo. So effective was the *Doi Moi* strategy that, despite these problems, the country had by 1992 passed into a stage of rapid economic development. At the end of 1994 the American embargo was lifted and, in 1995, Vietnam was accepted as a full member of the ASEAN group of nations.

This chapter investigates the changing character of Vietnam's tourism industry post-1986, discussing the major themes and issues that have emerged since that watershed year. It outlines the economic, cultural and environmental dimensions of tourism in Vietnam, the nature of the tourism market for Vietnam, the approaches taken by the government in developing tourism and the likely future of tourism within and to the country. The chapter concludes by commenting on the current downturn in the flow of international tourists to Vietnam.

Vietnam – at a crossroads

Vietnam, situated in the eastern part of Southeast Asia, is a country of some 75 million people at a point of convergence for many ethnic groups and a cross-roads of different civilizations. It shares borders with Cambodia, Laos and China and has 3260 km of coastline. Its rugged topography adds another factor to ethnic complexity, in that many minority groups now inhabit the highlands, having been displaced from more favourable areas by the dominant Viet population. In economic terms, 20 per cent of the active population is unemployed and 40 per cent is underemployed. Over fifty-four ethnic groups have been identified in Vietnam; the *Kinh* or Viet, the most numerous, account for 87 per cent (65 million) of the total population. Other major groups such as the Tay, Thai, Muong, Hoa, and Khmer number in excess of 1 million each, but others number in the few hundreds only. Of the larger sub-groups, the Muong belong to the Viet language group, the Khmer to the Mon-Khmer group, the Tay and Thai to the Tay–Thai group, and the Hoa speak a local variant of the Han (Sino-Tibetan) language.

Vietnam has considerable potential for tourism development. It has extensive natural resources such as beaches, lakes, forests, mountain ranges, many rare species of fauna and flora and a rich and diverse human cultural heritage. The government has identified four major zones for the development of tourism (Figure 12.1), based on the World Tourism Organization Master Plan released by the government in 1994. These are the Northern, Central, and the South-central and Southern Zones (Vietnamese National Administration of Tourism (VNAT), 1995). Within these zones a number of divisions have been created:

- Sub-Zones (in Zone III – see Figure 12.1);
- Tourist Micro-Zones (provincial level attractions);
- Tourist Centres (i.e. Ha Noi, Ho Chi Minh City, Hue); and
- Tourist Spots.

The Northern Zone comprises twenty-three provinces centred on Ha Noi. In the wider region summer holiday resorts and weekend tourism from Ha Noi, particularly seaside resorts and related activities, are seen as an important focus, especially around Ha Long Bay. In the city itself the focus of tourism is on historical sites and on serving the needs of business travellers, including seminar tourism, conferences, and sports events. The Central Zone comprises five provinces and is centred on the ancestral capital of Hue and the town of Da Nang. In the northern part the focus is on sightseeing, and there is significant potential for linkages with a wider Laotian/Thai tour. Hue, in particular, is a focus for heritage tourism, while the southern part of this zone has greater potential for nature and adventure tourism. Preservation of the environment is identified as a key issue for this area, and there is also a need to preserve historical and cultural relics. The South-central and Southern Zone is centred around Ho Chi Minh City (HCMC – Saigon). This area has the most developed tourism industry of the zones – currently 70 per cent of all tourists visiting Vietnam visit HCMC. The Tourism Master Plan sees a close linkage between both natural and heritage tourism in this zone, with cultural, architectural and historical attractions all playing a key role, along with southern 'nature' treks, both in the highlands and along the Mekong River. In fact the Greater Mekong sub-region is also the focus of intensive tourism development, assisted by the Asian Development Bank, the United Nations Economic and Social Committee for Asia and the Pacific, the Pacific Area Travel Association (PATA) and the World Tourism Organization (WTO). Again the protection of the natural and heritage environment is seen as crucial to tourism development.

Tourism in Vietnam: development, trends and impacts

The history of tourism in Vietnam is linked closely to the country's political experiences of the past 100 years. A limited amount of international adventure and resort tourism had developed during the decades of French colonial control and before, based on hunting wild animals, escaping the lowlands summer heat and observing the lifestyles of indigenous

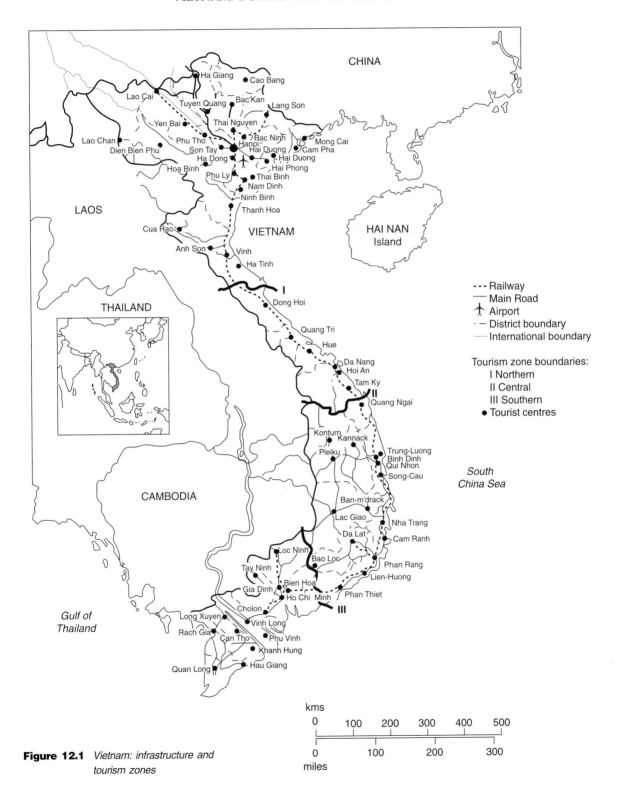

Figure 12.1 *Vietnam: infrastructure and tourism zones*

Table 12.1   *International tourist arrivals in Vietnam, 1990–1997*

Category	1990	1991	1992	1993	1994	1995	1996	1997
USA	10 425	12 510	14 563	102 892	152 176	57 515	43 171	40 409
Australia	n.a.	n.a.	n.a.	33 381	n.a.	n.a.	n.a.	n.a.
France	23 650	28 500	19 204	61 883	111 657	118 044	73 599	67 022
Taiwan	45 000	54 000	70 143	96 257	185 067	224 127	175 486	154 566
Japan	15 975	19 170	19 119	31 320	67 596	119 540	118 310	122 083
China	3 525	4 230	2 738	17 509	14 381	62 640	377 555	405 279
Other	81 500	89 000	233 235	242 602	n.a.	n.a.	546 891	580 369
Total non-Viet Kieu	181 175	217 410	359 142	600 438	816 016	1 096 882	1 408 248	1.5M (est.)
USA	35 142	42 170	2 910	78 024	103 164	n.a.	n.a.	n.a.
Australia	8 968	10 761	3 520	19 904	26 326	n.a.	n.a.	n.a.
France	5 430	6 516	3 840	12 052	15 941	n.a.	n.a.	n.a.
Other	19 285	23 143	70 588	42 830	56 615	n.a.	n.a.	n.a.
Total Viet Kieu	68 825	82 590	80 858	152 810	202 046	261 300	196 907	272 157
Total	250 000	300 000	440 000	670 000	1 018 062	1 358 182	1 607 155	1 715 637

Sources: VNAT, 1997; Nguyen and King, 1998; ASEAN – http://asean.org.

peoples. In addition, a small amount of 'domestic' tourism had developed amongst the indigenous 'leisure classes'. The Japanese invasion during the 1940s and the subsequent attempts by Vietnamese nationals to reclaim their country brought tourism to an end during and immediately after the Second World War. The North–South partition of 1954 and the subsequent war all conspired to arrest the development of international and domestic tourism in Vietnam until the mid-1980s.

After reunification in 1975 Vietnam continued to be cut off from the flow of tourism generated by the non-communist world. As a member of the Council for Mutual Economic Aid (COMECON) though, Vietnam was host to large numbers of visitors from Soviet bloc countries who came for rest and recreation. However, the low purchasing power of these tourists meant that the accommodation provided for them was austere and associated services were limited (King and Fahey, 1993). This legacy is reflected in many of the poorly constructed government 'Guest-houses' still to be found in tourist destinations around Vietnam.

A turning point in the development of tourism in Vietnam was the Sixth Party Congress in 1986, where the *Doi Moi* policies were approved. The

basic problem facing the researcher seeking to reconstruct patterns of tourism in Vietnam is the consistency and reliability of the available statistics. This is confirmed by Anonymous (1997) where the statistics on international arrivals available from the WTO and PATA do not tally. This is a historical problem related to the secrecy which surrounded tourist arrivals during the socialist regime. It also reflects internal disagreements between the immigration and tourism departments over what and who should be recorded in tourist arrivals (Anonymous, 1997). Most arrival statistics are collated at the three principal gateways: Ha Noi, Ho Chi Minh City and Danang. By the early 1990s renewed international interest in Vietnam had led to a surge in visitor numbers, which increased more than fourfold between 1990 and 1994 (Table 12.1). In 1990, the government promoted Visit Vietnam Year which was not overly successful but signalled the country's re-emergence on the international tourist circuit. In 1995 overseas visitors numbered 1.3 million, producing a tourism industry turnover of approximately US$540 million; a tenfold increase over 1990 (*Vietnam News*, 1996). Turnover from tourism is predicted to reach US$1.06 billion by 2000 and to be around US$8 billion in 2010 (in 1989 US$).

Taiwan and Japan dominated the rapid growth of tourism during the early 1990s, with French tourists dominating the European market, especially from 1994 (Table 12.1), and the USA in fourth place. The French are the largest group (16 per cent) of foreign tourists in Ha Noi, whereas in Ho Chi Minh City Taiwanese visitors account for 45 per cent of the total (VNAT, 1997). Significant tourist numbers also come from Australia, the European Community other than France, and other East and Southeast Asian countries. In 1996, 1.6 million international visitors were recorded and Vietnamese planners estimate 3.8 million arrivals by the year 2000 and 8.7 million by 2010. Yet, compared with most other ASEAN countries, tourist arrivals to Vietnam are still relatively low, on a par with the Philippines (1 800 000 in 1995). For the American market, however, the lack of direct flights currently prevents American tourists from travelling to Vietnam. Once direct flights are established – both Delta and United Airlines have started negotiations to obtain landing rights in Ha Noi and Ho Chi Minh City – American tourist arrivals are expected to increase more rapidly. Also, the enumeration of Viet Kieu (Vietnamese living abroad – 21.6 per cent of all tourist arrivals) as a separate traveller category has the effect of depressing the figures for Americans, given the prevalence of their residence in the USA (Table 12.1).

As a consequence of this rapid growth in visitor numbers, coupled with an increase in domestic travel which partly incorporated some elements of leisure and recreation (as distinct from travel to markets or for policy reasons), some elements of the international media and business world saw, by the mid-1990s, a new Asian tiger economy in the making. Other observers were more circumspect (Cooper, 1996; Fforde and de Vydler, 1996; Logan, 1998), noting that the under-developed technological base of the country and restrictions on travellers would force tourism to grow only slowly in the short term. In any event, growth in international visitors to Vietnam, and growth in the

Vietnamese economy in general, slowed in the late 1990s.

The economic impact of tourism

Tourism has impacted quite strongly on the Vietnamese economy, particularly as the government has allowed a liberalization of trade in tourism with overseas companies. For example, in 1992, private companies within Vietnam were allowed to operate in domestic tourism and some overseas companies were allowed to obtain three-year tour operator licences. This was followed by the relaxation of visa restrictions. In December 1993, a licensing system for hotels was established and in mid-1995, a classification system for hotels was begun. In 1994, tourism's contribution to GDP was 3.5 per cent; this grew to 4.4 per cent in 1995 and is predicted to be 12 per cent by the year 2010 (Table 12.2). International tourism receipts in Vietnam have remained fairly static after the initial growth to US$85 million in 1990. In fact, in 1992, receipts dropped to US$80 million, a drop of almost 6 per cent on 1991. Since 1993, minor increases have occurred, with a return to US$85 million for 1993 and 1994 and a slight rise to US$86 million in 1995. As a result, Vietnam ranks eighteenth among the top tourism earners in the WTO East Asia–Pacific region (Anonymous, 1997: p. 83). Furthermore, the tourism sector had created 205 400 jobs by 1995 and it is estimated that it will generate a further 341 400 by the year 2010. As a result, the tourism and

Table 12.2 *Tourism's contribution to Gross Domestic Product in Vietnam*

Year	Share of GDP (%)
1994	3.5
1995	4.4
1996	5.3
1997	9.6
2010	12.0

Source: VNAT, 1997.

Table 12.3   *International-standard rooms in Vietnam*

Year	Number of rooms	Growth rate (%)
1992	13 055	n.a.
1993	16 845	29.0
1994	21 051	25.0
1995	26 000	23.5
1996	31 200	20.0
2000	55 760	15.6
2010	135 200	9.3

Source: VNAT, 1997.

hospitality industry in Vietnam became the focus of international investors in the early 1990s. By the end of 1995, there were 160 joint venture projects with US$4.5 billion capital in the tourism industry, accounting for 26 per cent of the total foreign investment capital in Vietnam. The Vietnamese government especially encouraged investors (both domestic and international) to invest in hotel and entertainment complex construction. By June 1996, there were 50 000 hotel rooms in Vietnam, among them 26 000 rooms of international standard. According to the Master Plan's forecast, by the year 2000 a further 30 000 international-standard rooms will be available and, by the year 2010, another 80 000 (Table 12.3).

Infrastructure and service quality

Despite increased investment in the industry, Vietnam tourism still faces many problems and challenges with respect to general and industry-specific infrastructure. Since the majority of official overseas arrivals use air transport to Vietnam, air services assume a major role. In 1997, Anonymous (1997) reported that twenty airlines served Vietnam, with direct services to twenty-one cities mainly from Asia–Pacific. Yet further expansion is reported as being limited by state protectionism in favour of the state airline – Vietnam Airlines. A number of airlines have been refused traffic rights, although other airlines such as Cathay Pacific have entered into

code-share agreements, with twenty-two flights a week. However, the lack of competition resulting from such protectionism has meant that the cost of air travel to and from Vietnam is high. The Vietnam Airlines Corporation, established in May 1996, had twenty-seven aircraft in 1997, including three dry-leased 767-300s and ten dry-leased Airbus A320s. These are complemented by ATR-72s and Fokker 70 aircraft. In 1996, the airline carried 2.5 million passengers, reporting a consistent growth of 30 per cent each year in passengers. However, as Chapter 4 suggests, in terms of aviation, infrastructure needs to keep pace with the growth in traffic as well as developing modern terminal facilities. The Vietnam Civil Aviation Department is using a master plan to upgrade and expand the number of airports available for international traffic from sixteen in 1997 to thirty-two by 2010 (although the three main gateways dominate patterns of international air traffic). An indication of the investment being committed to aviation is as follows:

- at Ha Noi Airport, US$65 million is being used to develop a new terminal for Noi Bai airport so that it can cater for 2.5 million passengers per year by the year 2000, with plans for a capacity of 5–7 million passengers in 2005. Assistance and aid from the French government has been used and there are also plans for a second international airport at Mieu Mon, southwest of Ha Noi;
- Ho Chi Minh City Airport, which served as a US airbase prior to 1975, has a capacity for handling 3.6 million passengers per year, which may already have been reached. Apart from a newly completed terminal and another terminal planned at a cost of US$180 million, it remains the country's main gateway. By 2010, it is expected to be handling up to 21 million passengers per year;
- Danang Airport, located in central Vietnam, is expected to be upgraded to handle up to 1 million passengers per year (subject to government approval);
- a range of other domestic airports which will be upgraded/renovated are: Dien Phu, Buon

Me Thot, Cat Bi Vinh, Rach Gia and Phu Quoc, of which a number are former US military airbases (after Anonymous, 1997).

The road system in Vietnam comprises 105 600 km of tracks through to dual carriageways. Much of the stock was developed a long time ago and has received little maintenance since the war. The problem is compounded by the climate where erosion and subsidence remain a persistent problem causing road surfaces to deteriorate. Anonymous (1997) reports that while the road network is quite satisfactory in the south of the country owing to US wartime investment, the north suffers from various deficiencies. As a result, tourists have a difficult time in reaching sites of interest outside the major tourism centres (Lonely Planet, 1998). The rail network, in common with many other countries in Southeast Asia, was built during the colonial period (post-1885) and the main route linking Ha Noi and Ho Chi Minh City was built in 1936. The network suffered from extensive damage during the war, and the journey time on the main route has been cut from 58 to 36 hours. Accommodation facilities generally remain in poor condition and many do not meet basic international standards. It is therefore necessary to upgrade and/or build more hotels of international standard in order to attract and accommodate the travellers accustomed to and expecting such facilities. A number of international hotel chains are investing in the country (Sofitel, New World and Century) which is a major turnaround after it was necessary in 1991 for the government to tow in ships and convert them to hotels on the Saigon river (Anonymous, 1997). A current over-supply of quality rooms in Ho Chi Minh City has meant occupancy rates are currently at 45 per cent. However, as Anonymous (1997) shows, in 1996 it was estimated by SaigonTourist that 300 000 international tourists stayed in hotels, a 6 per cent growth on 1995. Ha Noi has a dearth of five-star hotels, with overseas investment being used to construct two- and three-star accommodation. A number of coastal areas are also due to see growth in hotel accommodation up to the year

2010 (e.g. Ha Long, Hue, Danang, Nha Trang and Ba Ria-Vung Tau). The government master plan also seeks to develop another ten to fifteen resort projects by the year 2000 (Anonymous, 1997). The master plan anticipates the need for the supply of accommodation to increase by 25 270 rooms.

At the same time the country needs to solve very pressing problems of basic infrastructure provision (water supply, sewerage, energy, distribution of goods) before such hotels can be realistically serviced. This is currently more difficult than erecting individual buildings and is significantly affecting economic growth. Service *quality* also needs to be improved. The major providers of services to visitors are public companies, often as a sideline to their central product or service. Of these SaigonTourist, founded in 1975 by the HCMC People's Committee is Vietnam's largest tourist operator, with sixty hotels, and also runs the Saigon Tourism School. Other significant operators include Ha NoiTourism, a VNAT-owned company and one of the oldest tourism operators in Vietnam, and OSC Vietnam Tours. Ha NoiTourism operates a car-rental agency and eight hotels in Ha Noi, including the Sofitel Metropole, Ha Noi's only international five-star hotel. OSC Vietnam Tours is a subsidiary of Oil Services Vietnam (OSC), and is a large national company running eighteen hotels (600 rooms are of international standard) and forty villas. Like SaigonTourist, this company also runs a tourism training school, at Vung Tau.

While job skill levels and the salary levels attached to them are set by VNAT, the most recent figures show that, despite the existence of such skill-related pay levels in the tourism and hospitality industry, less than 50 per cent of employees are trained (Table 12.4). One of the reasons (and consequences) for this is that most industry training is done in-house by the tour companies and/or the major hotels. This system cannot physically produce the level of trained labour that will be required if Vietnam is to reach its visitor targets because it does not have sufficient places for students. For Vietnam to be

Table 12.4 *Estimated number and qualifications of state tourism employees, Vietnam, 1994*

Employment category	Number	Level of training	Number
Tourism service	6 000	Technical training	25 000
Hotel service	60 000	On-job training	20 000
Related to hotel service	15 000	University degree	2 000
Management	7 500		
Total employees	88 500	Total trained employees	47 000

Source: VNAT, 1997.

able to provide quality service there is, therefore, a critical need for the *public* post-secondary education system to be involved. To achieve this an integrated system of tourism and hospitality training schools is urgently required.

Environmental and cultural issues

Sustainable tourism development, or tourism that does not erode its resource base or disappoint its customers, is a key goal in Vietnam's Tourism Master Plan (VNAT, 1995), a feature explored in detail by the Economic and Social Commission for Asia and the Pacific (ESCAP) (1992) and later by Theuns (1997). In practice, this approach is heavily tempered by political, social and cultural factors, as can be seen in the proposal to redevelop the National Forest Park located at Ba Vi, 50 km northwest of Ha Noi, at an estimated cost of US$1.2 million. Relocation of 20 000 people into new villages, upgrading of an existing Tropical Agriculture Research Centre, redevelopment of existing tourist facilities and the building of training facilities will turn this Park into an operating example of an integrated economic and social development based on tourism, revitalized agriculture and forestry. The tourist authorities themselves will refurbish a nineteenth-century French hill station retreat, while the tourism product will be based on village/rural tourism and activities within the natural environment.

On the surface, this development could be seen as supportive of the desire to use cultural tourism as a mechanism through which state policy on environmental protection might be implemented. While this was a policy direction expressed to the author on a number of occasions by Provincial and National officials in the North of Vietnam during 1995–1996, there also appears to be a clear desire by the *Viet* authorities to use the cultural and other resources of such ethnic groups for social engineering ends, rather than strictly for tourism. In other words, to bring minority groups under the direct control of lowland authority is actually the primary aim, rather than lofty ideals of 'development' based on cultural tourism (Cooper, 1996).

Indeed, while a great deal is made of ethnic minority cultures and of the many other forms of cultural heritage within Vietnam, the level of involvement by ethnic minority groups and of local communities in general in the control and operation of tourism activities is limited (Mercer, 1994). As a consequence, the promotion of tourism through Vietnamese culture has tended to occur at a fairly superficial level (Gilbert *et al.*, 1998), and the danger is that irreplaceable heritage items and cultural forms will be lost in the desire to modernize (Logan, 1998). Environmentalists have also protested about the proliferation of water and chemical-intensive forms of development such as golf courses, arguing that the tourism boom has the potential to cause widespread ecological damage, while the government has recently deplored the 'social evils' associated with tourism (Gill, 1996).

The role of government in tourism

Tourism was not given priority in national planning during the first 25 years of Vietnam's post-colonial existence. However, with the 1986 *Doi Moi* policies the government's attitude to tourism altered dramatically as the industry's ability to provide economic benefits was increasingly realized. At this time many of the governments in Asia strongly committed themselves to the development of international tourism in the firm belief that to do so would bring substantial economic benefits to their respective countries (Din, 1989; Tisdell and Wen, 1991; Oppermann, 1992; Richter, 1993). In 1992 the Vietnam National Administration of Tourism was established and was placed directly under the Prime Minister, a privilege shared only with the gas and oil industries. As a policy direction, these actions were encompassed in Government Resolution 45/CP on the 'Renovation of tourism management and development', issued on 22 June 1993. This resolution stressed, *inter alia*: 'Concentration on overall planning for tourism development in the whole country, and the setting up of tourist centres with outstanding and attractive products for drawing domestic and foreign investment capital'. With such support, the new national tourism authority began to focus on 'boosting tourism development and turning the traditionally passive business into one increasingly corresponding to the country's great potential' (VNAT, 1995).

Tourism planners were empowered by this change to outline some major strategies for Vietnam tourism until the year 2010 in the above-mentioned Tourism Master Plan. But Vietnam is a strategic planner's paradise – for plans on paper that is. While the strategies were not of themselves controversial: upgrading and diversifying the tourist product, upgrading the quality of service, preservation and conservation of tourism resources and directed priorities for investment, as already noted, the resources do not yet exist to achieve them. A major dilemma thus arises for the government – should it seek to actively promote investment in tourism without being able to service such development properly, in which case the investor may decide to abandon the development – or should it restrict investment until conditions are more favourable, in which case investment capital will definitely be taken elsewhere. Possibly as a result of this, Vietnam has not developed clear actions that go with the strategic approaches, as witnessed by the fact that exit and entry regulations for foreign visitors are expensive, often arbitrary and change sporadically, indicating undeveloped policy and suggesting conflict between different ministries.

In addition to these concerns, the image of Vietnam as an exciting new destination was always going to have limited currency, given the rapid opening-up of a number of other international visitor destinations at roughly the same time, but this fact seems not to have been taken into account in the master plan. For the first time since Vietnam reopened itself to international tourism, official figures in May 1997 registered a decline in the number of foreign visitors from the previous year (Arshall, 1997). The total number of international arrivals fell by 7 per cent and arrivals from the main sources of tourists, Taiwan, Japan and France, declined by 13 per cent. Major hotels reported a decline in occupancy rates, so much so that Vietnam's two major tourist destinations, Ho Chi Minh City and Ha Noi, were experiencing for the first time an oversupply of hotel rooms. Occupancy rates fell to 52 per cent in Ha Noi and 48 per cent in Ho Chi Minh City (Lamb, 1997), forcing a dramatic cut in room tariffs in large state and joint venture hotels and bankruptcies for many smaller private hotels.

A serious decline in tourism is clearly going to cause difficulties for Vietnam since the government throughout the 1990s had promoted the industry as something of a panacea for the country's economic problems (VNAT, 1995). Consequently, the slowdown in 1997 was somewhat unexpected and led VNAT to seek urgent government action to arrest the trend. The actions suggested included an easing of some visa restrictions, an overseas advertising campaign and an expansion of tax exemptions for tourism development. The underlying cause is actually that there was a too-rapid expansion of the luxury end of the tourism market, directed by an unrealistic view of the capacity of the Vietnamese economy to sustain this. While the current hotel room surplus is directly the result of a building boom initiated by international investors in 1992–1993, when Vietnam was a newly opened destination and predictions of tourist arrivals were highly optimistic, for all the reasons outlined earlier Vietnam has not been able to attract enough of the type of tourists these developments require. This has been exacerbated by the economic crisis that struck Thailand, South Korea, Philippines, Malaysia and Indonesia in the second half of 1997. While Vietnam has so far been able to avoid the dramatic economic downturn experienced by its neighbours, it has been affected by a rapid decline in trade and investment from these countries and this has impacted on tourism figures, hotel occupancy rates, restaurant patronage and other tourist activities.

Conclusion

Industry officials and foreign tour operators now recognize that Vietnam will not achieve its planned international visitor targets in the short term (*Vietnam Today*, 1997). In Ha Noi, a construction ban has already been placed on mini-hotels with fewer than twenty rooms and the national government is considering extending the ban to other cities (Lamb, 1997). In Ho Chi Minh City, it has been proposed that foreign investment should be limited to four- and five-star hotels with greater than 200 rooms and that new licences for mini-hotels be restricted (Truong Van Khoi, 1996).

However, the availability of better quality hotels alone will not solve the industry's problems. Developments of this sort are contingent upon the provision of more basic infrastructure, and this has not been forthcoming. As a consequence, both domestic and international tourism has been affected by infrastructure bottlenecks and the resulting adverse comments of tourists are beginning to filter through to the international media. It is becoming clear that a new marketing strategy must be formulated to maintain the level of tourist arrivals, and that should be to attract precisely those tourists who are most able to cope with infrastructure problems or who desire an economy-class experience. In addition, there must be a significant expenditure of resources on training of tourism and hospitality staff. Only with these changes will the tourist perception of inadequate service be rectified and a positive tourist image be regained for the country.

References

Anonymous, 'Vietnam', *International Tourism Report* 2, 1997, pp. 79–99.

Arshall, S., 'Vietnam's ambivalence results in few tourists', *Wall Street Journal* 9 July 1997.

Cooper, M.J., 'Ecotourism development in Vietnam: the experience of the minorities', paper presented to the *Second International Conference on Tourism in Indochina*, Ho Chi Minh City, Vietnam, April 1996.

Din, K., 'Towards an integrated approach to tourism development: observations from Malaysia', in T. Singh, H. Theuns and F. Go (eds), *Towards Alternative Tourism: The Case of Developing Countries*, Peter Lang, Frankfurt, 1989, pp. 181–204.

Economic and Social Commission for Asia and the Pacific, *Possibilities for Sustainable Tourism. Development in Selected Least Developed ESCAP Countries and Viet Nam*, Report to ESCAP by H. Theuns, ESCAP, Bangkok, 1992.

Fforde, A. and de Vydler, S., *From Plan to Market: The Economic Transition in Vietnam*, Westview Press, Boulder, CA, 1996.

Gilbert, A., Hoa, N. and Binh, V., 'A strategic model for using information technology in developing sustainable tourism', *Journal of Vietnam Studies* 1(1), 1998, pp. 1–17.

Gill, T., *Indochina Tourism: Asian Tigers with gleams in*

their eyes, Inter Press Service English News Wire, 4 January 1996.

King, B. and Fahey, S., 'Indochina – Cambodia, Laos and Vietnam', *International Tourism Report*, 2, 1993, pp. 59–75.

Lamb, D., 'Vietnam hotels put out the 'Vacancy' sign', *Los Angeles Times* 6 September 1997.

Logan, W.S., 'Sustainable cultural heritage tourism in Vietnamese cities: the case of Hanoi', *Journal of Vietnam Studies* 1, 1998, pp. 32–40.

Lonely Planet, *Lonely Planet Travellers Reports*, http://www.lonelyplanet.com.au/dest/sea/vietnam.htm, 1998.

Mercer, D., 'Native peoples and tourism: conflict and compromise', in W. Theobald (ed.), *Global Tourism*, Butterworth-Heinemann, London, 1994.

Nguyen Thu Huong and King, B., 'Migrant homecomings: Viet Kieu attitudes towards travelling back to Vietnam', *Pacific Tourism Review* 1(4), 1998, pp. 349–361.

Oppermann, M., 'Intranational tourism flows in Malaysia', *Annals of Tourism Research* 19, 1992, pp. 482–500.

Richter, L., 'Tourism policy making in Southeast Asia', in M. Hitchcock, V. King and M. Parnwell (eds), *Tourism in Southeast Asia*, Routledge, London, 1993, pp. 179–199.

Theuns, H., 'Vietnam: tourism in an economy in transition', in F. Go and C.L. Jenkins (eds), *Tourism and Economic Development in Asia and Australasia*, Pinter, London, 1997, pp. 304–320.

Tisdell, C. and Wen, J., 'Foreign tourism as an element in PR China's economic development strategy', *Tourism Management* 12, 1991, pp. 55–67.

Truong Van Khoi, 'HCMC attempts to tackle tourism slump', *Vietnam Investment Review* 240, 20 May 1996.

Vietnamese National Administration of Tourism, *Summary Report of the Tourism Development Master Plan to the Year 2010*, VNAT, Hanoi, 1995.

Vietnamese National Administration of Tourism, *Vietnam Tourism*, VNAT, Hanoi, 1997.

Vietnam News, 'Socio-economic plan for 1996', *Vietnam News* 2 (January/February) 1996.

Vietnam Today, 'The hotel and tourism industry – distress alert', *Vietnam Today* 6(2), March/April 1997, pp. 15–24.

13

Tourism in Cambodia, Laos and Myanmar: from terrorism to tourism?

C. Michael Hall and Greg Ringer

Introduction

The emerging Southeast Asian nations of Cambodia, Laos, and Myanmar (Burma) are undergoing substantial change. Desperately seeking economic growth, these impoverished nations have been ravaged by decades of civil war from which they are now only beginning to recover. Tourism is a significant component of economic development which also has important political overtones in terms of the degree to which tourism is seen to give legitimacy to government, particularly with respect to Myanmar, where people are reported to have been forcibly used as labour for tourism-related developments (Hall, 1997). This chapter will briefly outline some of the key development issues associated with each country and the role that tourism plays in economic and political life.

Cambodia

To provide some sense of the dynamics of tourism and the challenges presented to the

people and institutions of Southeast Asia, this section examines recent efforts to promote tourism to Cambodia in the aftermath of the coup in July 1997 (see Berger, 1994 and Lam, 1998 for more detail on the situation pre-1997). The goal is to increase awareness of Cambodia's place and geography, both human and physical, in the region and to suggest that tourism may constructively assist Kampucheans in the reconstruction of their cultural landscape from 'killing fields' to tourist destination (see Anonymous, 1994).

Extraction

One of the smallest countries in Southeast Asia in total land area (181 035 km^2), Cambodia is, nonetheless, 'big' in terms of danger and difficulty in travel. Whilst the intense fighting between the Khmer Rouge and the government in the forested mountains of northern Cambodia has now formally ceased, illegal logging, the strip mining of gems and increasing urbanization and poverty constitute even greater threats to Cambodia's rehabilitation. Of equal concern is the indiscriminate use of land mines which continue to pose a serious threat to the population of Cambodia. Although demographic and economic data on Cambodia are notable for their absence in many global sources of statistical data, Dixon and Smith (1997) observed that the country's population of 7 million had very high mortality and low quality of life indicators, with among the highest crude death rates in Asia (15 per 1000 in 1993) and an infant mortality rate in 1993 of 117 per 1000 births.

Along the western border with Thailand, Cambodia's forests disappear to support the trade in guns-for-logs between rogue military commanders and former guerrilla soldiers, while Malaysian, Indonesian and Vietnamese loggers clear-cut in the northeast. Indeed, though the data is admittedly incomplete, so widespread and indiscriminate is the logging – legal and illegal – that some government officials and many international aid groups identify deforestation as Indochina's greatest environmental problem and lament that 'virtually all of Cambodia's primary resources [are now] under some kind of unaccountable foreign control' (Taylor et al., 1996: p. 24; see also Gray, 1994).

On the coast, the proliferation of commercial shrimp farms threatens natural fisheries through the loss of mangrove swamps and pollution from chemical fertilizers, while the clearing of forests along the banks of Tonle Sap, the largest freshwater lake in Southeast Asia and one of the world's richest fishing grounds as well as a vital source of protein for Cambodians, has caused increased flooding and reduced catches. Moreover, a series of twenty-six massive hydroelectric dams already under construction or proposed for the Mekong and its tributaries upstream of Cambodia will affect the hydrological regime of the region in ways still little understood (Kaplan, 1996; Johnston, 1997).

In a country where 90 per cent of the population of 10.4 million is rural, poverty, disease, crime and illiteracy present formidable challenges as well. While Cambodia's per capita income exceeds that of Laos and Vietnam, most Cambodians remain economically disadvantaged by the country's excessive war debt and notorious corruption, and the lack of even the most basic medical care or infrastructure in the countryside hinders reconstruction efforts and contributes to the growing imbalance between rural and urban areas (World Bank Report, 1997).

Acknowledging the seriousness of the threats confronting it, the Royal government designated twenty-three protected areas in 1993 and instituted several conservation management programs. The Ministries of Tourism and Environment, assisted by the United Nations and Worldwide Fund for Nature, also chose tourism as a major component of the country's redevelopment strategies for conservation and rural communities (Ministry of Tourism, 1996; Ringer, 1997). Efforts to encourage sustainable communities, tourism and the environment remain impeded, though, by a shortage of funds, equipment and trained staff outside the urban centres of Phnom Penh, Sihanoukville, and Siem Reap.

Attraction

Cambodia need not be a poor country, however, for it has the potential to be agriculturally self-supporting if political and social conditions stabilize, and the population growth rate (currently averaging 3–4 per cent per year) can be slowed. In addition, international tourism to Cambodia has natural appeal for both the national government, seeking additional sources of revenue, and for the tourism industry looking for new opportunities and destinations. Indeed, in the 1960s Cambodia was one of the most popular tourist destinations in Southeast Asia with annual visitor numbers of approximately 50 000–70 000 people (Lam, 1996). Tourism has slowly begun to rebound with growth occurring in a number of markets (Table 13.1), with the country reporting an 18 per cent increase in foreign visitors in 1996 over the previous year and a gain of more than 120 per cent since 1993 (Ministry of Tourism, 1996; Bangkok Post, 1997a)

Table 13.1 *Kingdom of Cambodia visitor arrivals by nationality, 1994–1995*

Arrivals	1995	1994	% change
North Americas			
USA	17 846	14 660	21.7
Canada	3 692	3 825	–3.5
Sub total	21 538	18 485	16.5
Europe			
France	19 437	19 165	1.4
Germany	3 499	2 730	28.2
Italy	1 810	1 244	45.5
Switzerland	1 832	2 004	–8.6
UK	5 809	5 643	2.9
Sub total	32 387	30 786	5.2
Northeast Asia			
China (PRC)	22 886	20 782	10.1
Japan	21 629	12 829	68.6
Sub total	44 515	33 611	32.4
Southeast Asia			
Malaysia	11 553	8 390	37.7
Singapore	9 155	6 844	33.8
Thailand	13 595	15 198	–10.5
Vietnam	1 834	1 336	37.3
Sub total	36 137	31 768	13.8
Australia/New Zealand			
Australia	6 634	6 963	–4.7
Sub total	6 634	6 963	–4.7
Other geographic areas			
Miscellaneous	78 469	55 004	42.7
Sub total	78 469	55 004	42.7
Total	219 680	176 617	24.4

Source: Ministry of Interior and Civil Aviation Authority, cited in Hall, 1997.

(Table 13.2). According to Leiper (1998), the largest group of arrivals is Cambodian nationals revisiting: over a million Cambodians emigrated during the war, settling in North America, Europe and Australasia. The problems for visitor statistics is that a large proportion of the former nationals now travel using their new country of nationality. Leiper (1998) observes that Cambodia has a low concentration ratio: that means that the country is not over-dependent upon a small number of source areas as main tourist markets. In terms of purpose of visit, Leiper (1998) argues that although a large proportion of visitors state they are visiting for vacation purposes, this masks a large business travel market, although business travellers also participate in recreational activities such as sightseeing. Using interviews with tour operators, Leiper (1998) noted that while business

visitors may form the largest category, cultural tourists (visiting Cambodia on packages structured around cultural experiences) are the next major category followed by people visiting friends and relatives. The fourth group, identified as sex tourists, which are euphemistically referred to in the Phnom Penh tourism business

Table 13.2 *Kingdom of Cambodia international visitor arrivals 1994–1998*

Year	Number of international visitor arrivals
1994	176 617
1995	219 680
1996	260 489
1997	218 843
1998	177 500*

Source: Hall, 1997; Reuters, 1998.
*Estimate only.

as massage tourists who largely originate from China and Taiwan. This business is seen as a lucrative sector to work in, given estimates that with a government official earning US$20 per month, a female child could earn three times that in a week (Hanson, 1998). The last category comprises independent travellers, many of whom are backpackers.

Tourist arrivals in Cambodia to the end of November 1998 were more than 17 per cent lower than the same period the previous year, largely owing to political uncertainty (Reuters, 1998). Inbound tourism witnessed steady growth in the first half of 1997 but arrivals plummeted after factional fighting in the streets of Phnom Penh in early July 1997 when then-Second Prime Minister Hun Sen ousted his coalition partner and co-premier Prince Norodom Ranariddh. A total of 167 418 visitors arrived in Cambodia up to the end of November 1998, compared with 203 220 during the same period in 1997, a 17.62 per cent drop. Cambodian tourism officials were expecting a total of 177 500 visitors for 1998, compared with 218 843 in 1997 and 260 489 during the peak year of 1996 (Table 13.2).

The economic benefits are equally significant, with Cambodia's earnings from tourism estimated at US$80 million in 1995 or US$200 per day per tourist (Ministry of Planning, 1995; Ministry of Tourism, 1996). Tourism accounted for one-third of all capital inflows in 1996. The industry earned some US$143 million in 1997, which was 16 per cent lower than in 1996 (Reuters, 1998). Yet as Leiper (1998) observed, it is the case that foreign investors are able to derive large profits with state regulation of labour costs (i.e. 10–12 hours work per day with rates of US$1–2 per day). This compares with room rates of US$50–150 for the country's 4462 rooms in 135 hotels (Leiper, 1998), with over 66 per cent concentrated in the capital (Phnom Penh) followed by Sihanoukville, Siem Reap and other regions. Siem Reap district is the main destination for cultural tourists, with the focal point Angor Wat, an archaeological site which is among the top nine World Heritage sites in Southeast Asia. The main constraint on arrivals, however, is the absence of direct international flights. Most visitors arrive at another destination and reach Cambodia on the state airline, Royal Air Cambodge, sold to Malaysian interests in 1994. The pressure on the government is to allow direct flights from neighbouring countries into Cambodia to Angor Wat by upgrading Siem Reap as an international airport. However, political pressures are important in this context, given the existing tourism investment and development in and around Phnom Penh which is designed to service the gateway and then allow onward trips to Angor Wat.

Not surprisingly, therefore, for both domestic and international visitors, the primary attraction is the monumental Angkor temple complex in northwestern Cambodia, recently designated a World Heritage site. Controlled by the Khmer Rouge during the Pol Pot years (1975–1979), tourists are now returning to Angkor Wat in significant numbers, and the Minister of Tourism suggests the site may attract 400 000 visitors by the year 2000 and more than 1 million by 2010 (*Cambodia Times*, 1997).

Hoping to capitalize on this interest, the international investors also announced plans for a sound-and-light show at the ruins that will 'be better than the Great Pyramids' (Lee, 1995: p. 4, Kaufman, 1997) in its depiction of Khmer history. Investors from YTL and Malaysia's Ariston Sdn Bhd also announced several high-profile tourism projects in Phnom Penh and Sihanoukville, including a US$1.3 billion casino resort and a second international airport (Huy, 1997; Robinson, 1997).

At the other end of the tourism spectrum, the Phnom Penh-based Society for Ecology and Wildlife Preservation has proposed that the entire country be designated a 'World National Park'. Intended to take advantage of the country's lack of infrastructure and the existing level of environmental degradation by stressing cultural identity, the protection of the environment and the history of Cambodia over industrial development and, in effect, turning its back on modernization, the enormously expensive project would require the international community to pay Cambodia US$5 billion over a five-year transition period to create a 'stable working environment, while encouraging foreign investment for ecotourism' (*Bangkok Post*, 1995a: p. A6).

Meanwhile, the Ministry of Environment, working through the Cambodia Environmental Management Program and assisted by UNTEP and other international aid organizations, has taken steps to promote nature- and culture-based tourism in Preah Sihanouk (Ream) and Preah Suramarit Kossomak (Kirirom) National Parks that directly benefit displaced soldiers and indigenous residents. Among the activities supported by local communities are home-stays among ethnic hilltribes, trekking opportunities into the Elephant Mountains and guided boat rides through the coastal mangrove forests (Ministry of Planning, 1995).

Challenge

There is no doubt that Cambodia possesses many significant attractions for both cultural tourism and nature tourism. There is certainly little question that tourism can play a constructive role in helping the Khmer people achieve some sense of normalcy after thirty years of ethnic conflict and the killing of nearly 2 million people in the genocide of the Khmer Rouge. Already, anecdotal evidence makes clear the return of tourists has resurrected some modicum of stability in Siem Reap and Sihanoukville and, perhaps most importantly, Cambodia is again experiencing a resurgence of traditional arts and a re-awakening of cultural identity among a people whose history of barbarity and successive 'one-reign dynasties' (Chandler, 1991: p. 101) in this century once left many feeling their culture had been irrevocably lost.

Cambodia's quest to generate greater tourism is fraught with difficulties, however. For one, it is competing for visitors in a region of the world where neighbouring countries not only promote

their own scenic and historic attractions, but also possess better-developed infrastructure, access and, perhaps most importantly, the perception – indeed, a reality until recently – that they are safer and more secure (Dohrs, 1991; Thami, 1996; *Bangkok Post*, 1997b; *Cambodia Times*, 1997). Leiper's (1998) argument that the real challenge for the future of Cambodia's tourism industry is that it cannot afford to be tarnished by the image of a thriving sex tourism industry, given the existing image problems related to the former civil war. Unresolved issues of land tenure and ownership throughout the country, conflicting jurisdictional questions and a lack of coordination between governmental agencies and institutions and problems with military-supported logging in protected areas, also make tourism problematic.

Nonetheless, Cambodia's natural environment and historic sites do offer the Khmer people and tourists the opportunity to engage in a unique experience in a country that remains undervisited and little appreciated. Furthermore, recent polls of tour operators and investors in Cambodia indicate that they remain optimistic concerning their long-term plans for the destination (*TravelAsia*, 1997). Consequently, the challenge for both operators and investors, and local residents is to develop and promote tourism that encourages visitation while, in time, helping Cambodians themselves reconnect to a history and geography from which they have been effectively disenfranchised for nearly three decades.

Laos

We want everything to go step by step. For other people, it may be too slow. For us, it is appropriate (Sannya Abhay, deputy director general of NTAL, in *TravelAsia*, 1996: n.p.).

Laos, a country of 4.5 million people comprising some sixty-eight different ethnic groups and with a per capita income of less than US$300, is one of the world's poorest nations. It has no railways, only limited electricity and telecommunications and a rudimentary road system. The country has 13 330 km of roads, of which only 20 per cent are paved. A country slightly larger than the UK, Laos is nevertheless rich in cultural and natural tourist resources. The greatest natural resource of Laos is its large forest cover: 70 per cent of Laos is covered with mountains and high plateaus, with only about 15 per cent being suitable for intensive agriculture. The physical geography of Laos is a major constraint on improving the country's infrastructure, which is seen as one of the government's major priorities (Rigg, 1997). With 80 per cent of Laos classified as mountainous, and a population density of 17 people per km², it does not have a critical mass of people to justify extensive investment. The problem is also compounded by damage caused during the Vietnam War, with the unenviable image of the most heavily bombed country on Earth per capita, as the American armed forces undertook clandestine missions to stem the flow of arms along the Ho Chi Minh trail from North Vietnam through Laos. Continued problems related to unexploded ordinance remain. A state socialist republic like its eastern neighbour Vietnam, it has been open to foreigners only since 1989. As in many other countries in South and Southeast Asia, the economic liberalization and deregulation of recent years has led to the Laotian government seeking to encourage foreign investment in tourism, particularly in the niche areas of ecotourism and heritage tourism (Hall, 1997).

Probably the most interesting insight into life and conditions in Laos are provided by Rigg (1997) citing evidence from the United Nations Development Programme-sponsored expenditure and consumption survey undertaken between March 1992 and February 1993. From a sample of 2937 households (19 574 people) spread throughout 147 villages, every province of the country was surveyed. The results of the Laos Expenditure and Consumption Survey, released in July 1995, show that 62 per cent of consumption is allocated to food, 13 per cent to housing and 5 per cent to personal care and recreation. For 1992–1993, average annual household consumption was less than US$100.

Although tourism to Laos has been affected by the overall image of instability that plagues the region in many Western eyes, Laos is fortunate not to have been racked by the political instability of either Cambodia or Myanmar, although attacks by bandits still occur in some rural areas. Arrival numbers have been rising steadily since 1990 (Table 13.3). In 1990, 14 400 visitors were recorded to have visited Laos. In 1994, 146 155 visitors were reported to have arrived in Laos. In 1995, this figure grew even further to over 346 000 arrivals, making average growth from 1990 to 1994 about 57 per cent per annum. Visitor arrivals for Laos had reached 403 000 in 1996 and 463 200 in 1997, according to recent statistics supplied by the National Tourism Authority of Laos to ASEAN (http://www.asean.org). In 1994 tourist expenditure was valued at US$18 million, with overall receipts from tourism valued at US$43 million.

Table 13.3 *Tourism in Laos 1990–1995*

Year	Arrivals (000s)	Average length of stay	Expenditure (US$m)	Receipts (US$m)	Earnings (US$m)
1990	14 400[a]	n.a.	1	3	–
1991	37 613	n.a.	6	8	2.25
1992	87 571	n.a.	10	18	4.51
1993	102 946	3.5	11	34	6.28
1994	146 155	5.07	18	43	7.56
1995	346 460	4.25	–	–	24.74

Note
[a]Estimate only.
Source: Hall, 1997; Kangwaan, 1997.

Tourism earnings rose from a mere US$2.25 million in 1991 to more than US$24.73 million in 1995, however, when compared with income from tourism the level of actual earnings indicates the extent to which tourist expenditures are leaking out of the economy (Hall, 1997).

Given the poor air connections to Laos, the majority of the visitors to the country arrive by road. Not surprisingly, the major sources of visitors are Thailand, which accounts for approximately 75 per cent of all visitors, and Vietnam (approximately 15 per cent). The next most significant sources of visitors in 1995 were France (2.9 per cent), the USA (2.5 per cent), Japan (1.8 per cent) and Germany (1.1 per cent) (Hall, 1997). The situation for 1996 and 1997 is shown in Table 13.4 which demonstrates a slight increase in intraregional tourists from within ASEAN countries.

Tourism investment in Laos has grown steadily from US$2.47 million in 1990 to US$280.21 million in 1994. *Asia Travel Trade* (1994) reported that investors have come from France, Singapore, Thailand, Taiwan and Korea, as well as Australia. The number of rooms in guest houses, hotels and resorts also grew from 1989 rooms in 1992 to 3345 rooms in 1995, although provision of accommodation is an important development priority. The National

Tourism Authority of Laos (NTAL) is aiming its marketing drive at the ASEAN countries, Japan, Australia, Europe and the USA (Kangwaan, 1997). NTAL is aiming to receive more than 843 000 international visitors in the year 2000, with the primary focus being on the ecotourism and heritage tourism markets. The 1995 Development and Promotion Plan sought to achieve these target figures by focusing on ensuring tourism is a major revenue-earner for the country through the promotion of its natural and cultural assets (Hall, 1997).

Problems of tourism development

Laos has numerous difficulties related to tourism development and these cannot easily be separated from the wider problems of economic development facing the country in the 1990s (Than and Tan, 1997). The lack of qualified and trained staff is gradually being dealt with through overseas assistance programmes, particularly from Thailand, which is positioning itself as a major access point into Laos. Indeed, Thailand and Laos signed an agreement on tourism cooperation in 1992 which has provided for exchange visits, destination management plans, personnel training, investment promotion and marketing (Tourism Authority of Thailand,

Table 13.4   *Visitor arrivals in Laos 1996–1997*

Country/region	1996		1997	
	Number	%	Number	%
ASEAN	301 450	74.8	353 266	76.3
India	17 238	4.3	5 866	1.3
China	16 707	4.1	17 661	3.8
France	11 608	2.9	13 745	3.0
USA	11 181	2.8	14 442	3.1
Japan	6 672	1.7	9 194	2.0
Australia	6 121	1.5	7 876	1.7
Germany	4 269	1.1	5 524	1.2
UK	4 162	1.0	6 054	1.3
Taiwan	2 638	0.7	(Included under others)	
Others	23 592	5.9	29 572	6.4
Total		100		100

Source: Kangwaan, 1997.

1998). Laos has a general lack of tourist accommodation as well as a lack of hotels of international standard. The NTAL estimated that nationwide demand will rise from the 1994 total of about 2560 rooms to 3260 rooms in 1996 and 6760 rooms by the year 2000 (*Asia Travel Trade*, 1995). However, the most significant problem facing tourism in Laos is the poor quality of the domestic and international transport networks.

Laos's admittance to full membership of ASEAN in 1997 provided for a considerable liberalization of its immigration procedures as well as other tourism-related procedures. The Laotian government has opened up more international entry points, apart from the capital Vientiane, including: Botene, Bokeo, Savannakhet, Chong Mek, Moungern, all bordering Thailand; Dansavanh and Keoneu, bordering Vietnam; and Luang Namtha, bordering China. Tourists can obtain visas on arrival at these entry points. Laos has also opened consulates in Thailand's northeastern Khon Khaen province and northern Nan province, which borders Laos's Moungern-Hongsa and where a road is being cut between the two provinces. When completed, visitors from Thailand will be able to drive from Nan, crossing into Moungern-Hongsa to Pakbaeng and on to Luang Phrabang, the former capital of Laos which has been designated a World Heritage site on the basis of its cultural and natural values (Kangwaan, 1997).

The Australian government-funded 'Friendship' bridge, linking Laos with Thailand across the Mekong River, has a pivotal role in the development of the Asian Highway, which will eventually allow for road travel from Singapore through to the southern Chinese city of Shanghai, via Laos. Laos is therefore becoming an increasingly important part of the tourism and transport chain in Southeast Asia. Laos is also working with China, Cambodia, Vietnam and Thailand in the construction of road projects which will form a regional network linking every country in the region, including Myanmar and other ASEAN members (Hall, 1997). The Mekong River, long the trade and communication link of the region, has also become increasingly important in tourism terms with ferry and rafting operations becoming available to tourists.

Airport development is also underway. A new terminal has been developed at Luang Prabang airport with an estimated investment of US$3 million from Thailand, while Japan is providing economic assistance for the improvement of runways at Vientiane and Luang Phrabang airports (*Asia Travel Trade*, 1995). The Luang Phrabang airport is expected to be able to take international carriers when it is fully upgraded, while the Laotian government has also provided for an increase in the number of international connections into Vientiane.

The Laotian government has attached great importance to tourism since introducing elements of a market economy in 1989. Learning from some of the perceived mistakes of its Asian neighbours, the Laotian government has come to favour 'ecotourism' in ecologically vulnerable areas and 'high value' tourism over relatively cheap day-trip visits (Hall, 1997). In focusing on this market, Laos faces the difficult task of maintaining the balance between preservation and development. However, the NTAL's approach appears to have reaped solid results as Laos attempts to maintain its culture and environment while seeking economic development and the benefits of modernity. As Sannya Abhay, Deputy Director General of NTAL, commented in the mid-1990s, the strategy of the NTAL is aimed at 'not killing the bird that lays the golden egg. We prefer day-by-day to have the egg and preserve the hen' (*Asia Travel Trade*, 1994).

Myanmar

Myanmar, more commonly known as Burma, is a country of some 43 million people (although Bailey (1998) argues the population could be between 46 and 60 million) with a land area of 677 000 km^2 (an area a little under the size of Texas), has received an extremely high media profile in the West in the 1990s (Hall, 1997). This former outpost of the British Empire, cut off from the West for many years, has been under the authoritarian rule of the State Law and Order Council (SLORC) since 18 September 1988 when SLORC assumed power in a coup and suspended the national constitution. Described as the 'Land of 1000 Pagodas', Burma has only recently begun to open up to large-scale international tourism. Tourism is an extremely significant component of SLORC's economic development strategy, particularly because of its ability to bring in large amounts of foreign exchange, plus tourism also has the capacity to convey political legitimacy on the unelected regime. As Hall (1997: p. 163) noted:

Any discussion of tourism in Burma cannot ignore the political issues that surround it. The army wields absolute political power. It also controls all businesses including tourism. Tourists are forced to stay in government owned hotels and change a minimum of US$300 foreign currency when they enter at the airport. The visitor deciding to visit Burma must consider the ramifications of supporting this military regime who are ruling Burma illegitimately. Only 10 per cent of households in Burma have electricity and heroin is the number one export.

Tourist growth

Tourism was gradually reintroduced in the 1980s with just over 41 000 visitor arrivals in 1987 (Campbell, 1996) (Table 13.5). However, following the 1988 pro-democracy demonstrations, tourism in Burma collapsed to just over 5000 visitors in 1989 and less than 9000 per annum in the early 1990s as a result of bans on independent travel and international media attention. However, the country received a major boost to tourism in July 1997 when it was admitted to ASEAN, a positive step since it has been the focus of trade embargoes owing to disallowing the results of the 1990s elections.

According to the official statistics of the Ministry of Hotels and Tourism (1996) Myanmar received 62 547 visitors in 1993–1994, increasing

Table 13.5 *Myanmar tourism arrivals and earnings, 1983–1995*

Year	Arrivals	Tourism earnings (US$000)
1983	29 963	13 820
1987	41 904	14 650
1988	22 252	9 050
1989	5 044	4 980
1990	8 968	4 980
1991	8 061	9 430
1992	8 944	–
1994	26 000	–
1995	100 000	32 000

Source: Directorate of Hotels and Tourism, Burma Centre, in Campbell, 1996.

by 50 per cent in 1994–1995 and again in 1995–1996 to 137 320 (Table 13.6). Visitors from Asia account for over 50 per cent of all arrivals. Japan is the most significant market, accounting for 13.6 per cent of arrivals in 1995–1996, while improved road access with Thailand has also led to a substantial increase in numbers. The main non-Asian tourist generating areas are Western Europe, in particular Germany, Italy and the UK, and the USA. Tourism earnings in 1995 were estimated at US$32 million, slightly double what they were eight years previously (see Table 13.5) (Hall, 1997).

In order to improve its profile overseas, attract much-needed foreign exchange and boost tourism numbers, SLORC declared 1996 Visit Myanmar Year (VMY) and set a target of 500 000 arrivals (Hall, 1997). However, the success of the year is highly debatable. According to Hospitality Net (1997: n.p.) 'Official figures on tourist arrivals vary. One official report put the total at 287 506 between April and December, 1996, and said that they spent nearly 400 million kyat ($1.6 million). Another official estimate for the same period put the total number of visitors at 219 319, of which only 180 254 were tourists'. This immediate problem is reflected where there is significant variation between the authors statistics, supplied from an official government agency and those supplied to Bailey (1998) from

Table 13.6 *Myanmar – tourist arrivals by nationality 1993–1996*

Nationality/region	1993–1994	%	1994–1995	%	1995–1996	%
North America	5 520	9.0	7 957	8	9 938	7.2
Canada	613	1.0	884	1	1 292	0.9
USA	4 723	7.7	6 985	6.9	8 224	6.0
Latin America	184	0.3	88	0.1	422	0.3
West Europe	14 720	23.0	26 524	29	38 770	28.2
Austria	613	1.0	884	1	1 518	1.8
Belgium	491	0.8	884	1	1 865	1.4
France	3 067	5.0	5 305	5.8	9 188	6.7
Germany	613	1.0	5 305	5.8	6 185	4.5
Italy	3 680	5.5	4 421	4.8	6 044	4.4
Switzerland	1 227	2.0	1 768	2	2 889	2.1
Sweden	–	–	–	–	437	0.3
UK	3 680	5.5	5 305	5.8	7 201	5.2
Other	1 349	2.2	2 652	2.8	3 443	2.5
East Europe	4 293	7.0	1 768	2	368	0.3
Russia	3 680	6.0	884	1	117	0.1
Other	613	1.0	884	1	251	0.2
Africa	1 227	2.0	2 652	3.0	2 865	2.1
Asia	35 560	57.0	51 190	56.0	82 590	60.1
Hong Kong	1 227	2.0	1 768	2.0	1 128	0.8
Japan	6 134	10.0	7 957	9.0	18 806	13.7
Malaysia	1 227	2.0	1 768	2.0	2 720	2.0
Singapore	1 227	2.0	3 536	4.0	5 621	4.1
Thailand	6 134	10.0	11 494	12.0	11 718	8.5
China	14 091	22.0	6 099	6.0	1 676	1.2
Other	5 520	9.0	18 568	21.0	40 921	29.8
Oceania	1 227	2.0	1 768	2.0	2 652	2.0
Australia	1 043	1.7	1 415	1.6	2 012	1.5
New Zealand	184	0.3	353	0.4	640	0.5

Source: Ministry of Hotels and Tourism, 1996.

the Immigration and Population Department. As Bailey (1998: p. 66) confirmed:

visitor arrivals are unclear. There are at least two major official sets – from the Directorate of Hotels and Tourism and from the Immigration and Population Department – and they often show different results. Moreover, current figures often re-state totals from previous years without explanation. The primary difference between the two sets of data, however, appears to be related to land-border crossings.

This, of course, makes it impossible to offer any definitive statement on tourism flows, patterns and the scale of change. However, what is clear is the failure of VMY, which led the Myanmar authorities to cut the target for

tourists expected in 1997 by half from the initial projection of 500 000 to 250 000 (Hospitality Net, 1997). In addition, there tends to be a lack of repeat visitation owing to the quality of tourism infrastructure, the two-tiered pricing system for hotels, high admission fees for historic and religious sites and the excessive paperwork for visiting areas outside the tourist-designated region, the Yangon–Mandalay–Bagan–Inle Lake quadrangle (Hall and O'Sullivan, 1996; Hall, 1997; Hospitality Net, 1997).

The failure of VMY has been blamed by SLORC on a number of factors, including bomb explosions and student demonstrations, while Lt. Gen. Kyaw Ba, Minister for Hotels and Tourism claimed: 'The smooth functioning of the hotel and tourist industry has been damaged by destructive elements within the country with the help of the Central Intelligence Agency' (Hospitality Net, 1997: n.p.). Nevertheless, while some industry commentators argued that the campaign carried out by pro-democracy groups around the world to encourage a boycott of Burma was more significant than domestic protest (Hospitality Net, 1997), other commentators argued that the human rights boycott had failed as tourist numbers still grew in record amounts (Gray, 1996).

Tourism planning and development

In terms of tourism planning, the rich archaeological heritage of the country, dating back to the first century, focused on the city of Bagan (a former capital from the eleventh century); it is a region surrounded by 2000 monuments (temples, stupas and indian-style pagodas) (Figures 13.1 and 13.2). The city of Mandalay, a former eighteenth-century capital, is also a focal point for tourist activity, along with a range of other sites (Putao in the north; Sittwe in the west; Myityina in the north and beaches west of Yangon, Dawei and Kawthaung where the Club Andaman resort is located). The provision of a cruise ship on the Ayeyarwady 9th Road to Mandalay, operated by the Orient Express Company, offers a range of cruises. Thus, government planning of tourism has ensured a strict control of tourist itineraries and activities, through the bureaucratic Ministry of Hotels and Tourism (established in 1992), with a hotel-operating division and a food and beverage division. Aviation is dealt with under a separate Ministry. The government involvement spans hotels, tourism, duty free and a tour operation division – Myanmar Travels and Tours. This was the only state-sanctioned tour operator under a socialist regime, although it now competes with overseas operators and locally owned operators, of whom there are now 600, 574 of which are locally based. Some fourteen of these are joint-ventures.

The Ministry of Transport controls aviation, of which the Department of Civil Aviation is

Figure 13.1 *Reclining Buddha, Chansk Htatt Kyee Pagoda, Myanmar (Copyright John Monin)*

Figure 13.2 *Shwerbya cultural attraction, Myanmar (Copyright John Monin)*

concerned with air transport and Myanmar Airways (which operates as a domestic and international airline). It was the only airline, but since 1993 it is a partner in Air Mandalay and Yangon Airways. Myanmar Airways International operates overseas flights, a joint venture with Singapore-based Hisonic and Myanmar Airways, with services to Bangkok, Hong Kong, Jakarta, Kuala Lumpur, Kunming and Singapore, with two Boeing 737s leased from Malaysian Airlines. In contrast, Air Mandalay, a joint venture with the Malaysian-based Kemayan Corporation and Myanmar Airways, operates tourist routes within Myanmar. It offers flights from Yangon to Mandalay, Bagan, Heho, Thandwe, Sittwe and Tachilek, using three ATR72 aircraft. Lastly, Yangon Airways, which operates tourist routes within Myanmar, is a joint venture with a Thailand-based company using three small aircraft. Each airline is reported to be facing economic problems with a downturn in business which could lead to mergers/take-

overs. The lack of international flight connections adversely affects the country, with Royal Brunei Airline's Abu Dhabi–London service and Condor's flight to Frankfurt withdrawn in 1997. These were the only direct long-haul flights and Bailey (1998) argues that with Myanmar Airways' weakness in marketing it is unlikely that there will be a flag carrier replacement. However, the country is now dependent upon other hubs such as Singapore, Bangkok, Kuala Lumpur, Dhaka, Calcutta and Kunming for non-direct flights (currently sixty-one per week). Thus, air travel is now a major constraint on the wider context of tourism development. It is also clear, as Bailey (1998) indicates, that marketing and promotional activity at all levels of tourism within Myanmar and overseas is weak, with the Directorate of Tourism wholly reliant upon the private sector to market the destination and products, which means it has little control or direction over the future image of Myanmar as a tourist destination (Bailey, 1998).

Problems of tourism development

Even if Myanmar did not have such an abhorrent human rights record, which Bailey (1998: p. 79) confirms, the country still has major tourism development problems. As well as insufficient airline capacity there is a dearth of airports, hotels and restaurants. Transportation infrastructure is far from adequate; the country's highways are in bad shape and trips in old buses over potholed roads can be a bone-jarring experience. Trains are unreliable and occasionally dangerous. Telephones and other modern communications technology on which the West has become so reliant simply do not exist (Hall and O'Sullivan, 1996; Hall, 1997).

Tourism is hindered by excessive bureaucratic red tape (Ross, 1998). Immigration and visa formalities, investment and tax procedures, exchange rates and the legal system all provide bottlenecks for tourists and investors in Burma. Nevertheless, tourism development has been rapid: in 1988 Burma had twenty state-owned hotels with 914 rooms, by 1997 the figure had reached 428 state-, private- and foreign-owned hotels with 9910 rooms (Hospitality Net, 1997). The government is actively seeking to encourage investment in order to further develop tourism infrastructure (Figure 13.3). Nearly US$1.63 billion has flowed into the tourism and hospitality sector in recent years, mainly from investors in Singapore and Thailand.

According to the Government of the Union of Myanmar (1998) 'foreign investment is an important component of the overall restructuring and development policy of the government. The main components of the policy are:

a. adoption of a market oriented system for the allocation of resources;
b. encouragement of private investment and entrepreneurial activity;
c. opening of the economy for foreign trade and investment.

Foreign investors are allowed to make investment either in the form of a 100 per cent wholly

Figure 13.3 *Hotel development in Yangon, Myanmar (Copyright John Monin)*

Table 13.7 *Foreign investment of permitted enterprises in Myanmar by country (as of 29 February 1996)*

Country	Total no. permitted enterprises	Approved amount (US$million)
Australia	6	30.00
Austria	1	71.50
Bangladesh	2	2.96
Canada	6	25.03
China	5	5.85
France	1	485.00
Hong Kong	17	64.44
Japan	6	118.21
The Republic of Korea	9	60.59
Macau	1	2.40
Malaysia	9	227.27
The Netherlands	2	83.00
Philippines	1	6.67
Singapore	38	683.88
Sri Lanka	1	1.00
Thailand	29	421.12
UK	18	666.22
USA	14	241.07
Total	166	3096.01

Source: http://www.myanmar.com/gov/trade/foreign.htm. Government of the Union of Myanmar, 1996.

Table 13.8 *Foreign investment of permitted enterprises in Myanmar by sector (as of 29 February 1996)*

Sector	Total no. permitted enterprises	Approved amount (US$million)
Agriculture	1	2.69
Fisheries	15	252.04
Hotels and tourism	34	647.63
Industrial estate	1	12.00
Mining	26	193.40
Manufacturing	52	180.16
Oil and gas	24	1435.42
Real estate development	6	251.45
Transport	7	121.22
Total	166	3096.01

Source: http://www.myanmar.com/gov/trade/foreign.htm. Government of the Union of Myanmar, 1996.

foreign-owned enterprise, partly owned, or in the form of a joint venture with a private or public local entity. If it is a partly owned concern or a joint venture, the minimum foreign capital is 35 per cent of the total equity capital (Government of the Union of Myanmar, 1998).

Despite debate about the ethics of investing in Myanmar, the level of foreign investment is substantial. Table 13.7 illustrates the major sources of foreign investment (Government of the Union of Myanmar, 1996). US$647.63 million or 20.9 per cent of all foreign investment is going into hotels and tourism, second only to oil and gas investment which accounts for almost half of all foreign investment (Government of the Union of Myanmar, 1996) (Table 13.8). With US$453 million invested in hotel development, Singapore is the largest investor in hotels and tourism in Myanmar (see Singapore Trade Development Board, 1995). Tourism-specific investments from Singapore firms include:

- Strait Steamship Land which has invested $US50 million in a five-star hotel in Yangon;
- Singapore Technologies Industrial Corporation and Liang Court which invested US$32 million in a business-class hotel in Yangon; and
- the Kuok group which has invested US$150 million in two hotels (Hall, 1997).

Although Myanmar received substantial foreign investment for tourism in the mid-1990s, the downturn in the East Asian economies and the less than expected number of tourist arrivals has led to a number of development projects being put on hold. Nevertheless, in 1998 the Japanese government agreed to assist with the repair of the runway at Rangoon's international airport with low-interest development loans of 2.5 billion yen (*South China Morning Post*, 1998). Locally funded tourism development is also often being undertaken with forced labour and/or with the forced removal of people from areas where they live in order to develop attractions for tourists (Holt, 1998). If this were not sufficient to act as a barrier to either tourism investment or tourist visitation, the Myanmar bureaucracy acts as a further deterrence. Although Myanmar is seeking to piggyback on Thailand's renewed tourism popularity by encouraging tourists to extend their holidays with a visit to Burma, a number of obstacles face the prospective tourist: visa procedures have been tightened, while individual travellers as opposed to group tourists must pay US$300 in foreign exchange certificates on arrival at Rangoon (Ross, 1998).

In a cultural context, there is also concern about the commodification of the Buddhist culture for tourism (Philip and Mercer, 1999).

While groups of tourists are easier to control for a government for whom control of the flow of people and ideas is an essential part of its survival, it is unrealisitic to expect tourism to flourish without greater ease of access. When Laos joined ASEAN, visa requirements became easier for nationals of other ASEAN countries; this has not yet happened in Burma. In the longer term tourism growth requires political stability, a perceived safe environment for tourists and ease of access. In the case of Myanmar none of these factors substantially exist.

Conclusion

The emerging countries of Southeast Asia have undoubtedly withstood substantial suffering in recent years as a result of civil war and foreign intervention. In the case of Myanmar and, to a lesser extent, Cambodia, such factors of political instability and the denial of human rights are still significant factors in the social, let alone the tourism, equation. The cultural and natural diversity of the area plus the awareness of the region in the media provides a climate in which appropriate tourism development is possible, without repeating the mistakes of other countries in Southeast Asia. However, such a scenario requires government regulatory action that is in the interests of the wider populace, not just of a small elite or junta. In the case of Myanmar this is definitely not occurring and, instead, tourism is being used as a tool for continued oppression rather than as tool for sustainable social and economic development.

If done imaginatively, sensitively, and sustainably, Cambodia and Laos may yet profit socially and economically from their redeveloping position in the Mekhong region. To succeed, however, tourism must be viewed as only one part of a holistic development process that links economic growth and job creation with community education and empowerment. This will require innovative ideas and alliances linking institutions, expertise and human resources in the three countries with those of global tourism and communities outside the region. Through such an integrative approach, the countries of the region may eventually be recognized once again as a destination for visitors and an inhabited place and source of cultural pride in their difficult transition from terrorism to tourism.

Acknowledgements

Greg Ringer would like to thank Alan and Karen Robinson, Yem Sokhan and Paulin Im, as well as the Cambodia Environmental Management Program and the Worldwide Fund for Nature, for their collaborative assistance and insightful comments. Travel costs were partially funded through a research grant from the Center for Asian and Pacific Studies, University of Oregon (USA). Michael Hall would like to thank Vanessa O'Sullivan for assisting with research on the region.

References

Anonymous, 'Networking in countries vulnerable to tourism: Cambodia and Burma', *Contours* 6(5), 1994, pp. 11–13.

Asia Travel Trade, 'Laos: juggling act between preservation and growth', *Asia Travel Trade* April 1994, pp. 19–20.

Asia Travel Trade, 'Guidance on guidelines', *Asia Travel Trade* October 1995, pp. 28–29.

Bangkok Post, 'Cambodia considers becoming a theme park', *Bangkok Post* 7 August 1995a, p. A6.

Bangkok Post, 'Environmental aspect of tourism given emphasis', *Bangkok Post* 28 July 1995b, p. B32.

Bangkok Post, 'Cambodia buoyant', *Bangkok Post* 23 January 1997a, p. 5.

Bangkok Post, 'Violent attacks rise after relative peace in Phnom Penh', *Bangkok Post* 30 January 1997b, p. 6.

Bailey, M., 'Myanmar', *International Tourism Report* 2, 1998, pp. 61–80.

Berger, M., 'Tourismus in Kambodscha – zuruck in die Zukunft (Tourism in Cambodia – back to the future)', *Geographische Rundschau* 46(4), 1994, pp. 240–244.

Cambodia Times, 'Focus on eco-tourism', *Cambodia Times* 17–23 February 1997, p. 1.

Campbell, D., 'Myanmar tourism under fire', *Timesnet*, Far East Trade Press and Times Information System (http://web3.asia1.com.sg/timesnet/data/tna/docs/tna2949.html). 1996.

Chandler, D., *Tragedy of Cambodian History: Politics, War and Revolution Since 1945*, Yale University Press, New Haven, CT, 1991.

Dixon, C. and Smith, D. (eds), *Uneven Development in South East Asia*, Ashgate, Aldershot, 1997.

Dohrs, L., 'Cambodian tourism: problems and potentials', *Journal of Southeast Asia Business* 7, 1991, pp. 14–21.

Government of the Union of Myanmar, *Foreign Investment*, Government of the Union of Myanmar (http://www.myanmar.com/gov/trade/foreign.htm), 1996.

Government of the Union of Myanmar *Foreign Investment Policy and Procedures*, Government of the Union of Myanmar (http://www.myanmar.com/gov/trade/for.htm), 1998.

Gray, D., 'Indochina faces a new onslaught', *Register-Guard* (Eugene, OR), 2 May 1994, p. A1.

Gray, D., 'Human rights boycott fails to stem Burma tourism surge', *Associated Press* release, 19 April 1996.

Hall, C.M., *Tourism in the Pacific Rim*, Addison Wesley Longman, South Melbourne, 1997.

Hall, C.M. and O'Sullivan, V., 'Tourism, politics and political stability in the Pacific Rim: image, ethics and reality', paper presented at *Pacific Rim Tourism 200: Issues, Interrelationships, Inhibitors*, Wairiki Polytechnic, Rotorua, 1996.

Hanson, J., 'Child prostitution in South East Asia: White slavery revisited?', in M. Oppermann (ed.), *Sex Tourism, Prostitution: Aspects of Leisure, Recreation and Work*, Cognizant, New York, 1998, pp. 51–59.

Holt, C., 'Lives wrecked by ruins', *South China Morning Post* 14 May 1998.

Hospitality Net, 'Burma – tourism: Too many hotel rooms, not enough tourists', *Hospitalty Net Inter Press Service* 2 October 1997 (http://www.hospital-itynet.nl/news/article/275921.htm).

Huy, T., Director of Tourism, Sihanoukville. Personal contact, 15 February 1997.

Johnston, P., Chief Technical Adviser, UN Development Programme, Environmental Technical Advisory Programme (ETAP), Phnom Penh. Personal correspondence, 19 March 1997.

Kangwaan, C., 'Laos sets its sights on eco-tourism focus', Timesnet (http://web3.asia1.com.sg/timesnet/data/tna/docs/tna4708.html, accessed 13 November 1998) 1997.

Kaplan, R., *The Ends of the Earth: A Journey to the Frontiers of Anarchy*, Random House, New York, 1996.

Kaufman, M., 'Barbarians at the gate: development at Angkor', *Conde Nast* January, pp. 82ff, 1997.

Lam, T., 'The revival of today's Cambodian international tourism', in M. Oppermann (ed.), *Pacific Rim Tourism 2000: Issues, Interrelations, Inhibitors, Conference Proceedings*, Waiariki Polytechnic, Rotorua, 1996, pp. 210–216.

Lam, T., 'Tourism in Cambodia: An overview of Cambodian international tourism and development potential', *Pacific Tourism Review* 1(3), 1998, pp. 235–241.

Lee, M., 'Sound-and-light show possible threat to Angkor Wat', *Bangkok Post* 1 August 1995, p. 4.

Leiper, N., 'Cambodian tourism: Potential problems and illusions', *Pacific Tourism Review* 1(4), 1998, pp. 285–298.

Ministry of Hotels and Tourism, *Tourist Arrivals by Nationality*, Ministry of Hotels and Tourism, Yangon, 1996.

Ministry of Planning, *First Socioeconomic Development Plan 1996–2000*, Royal Government of Cambodia, Phnom Penh, 1995.

Ministry of Tourism, *Program of the Congress to Recapitulate Tourism Work in 1994–95 and Tourism Working Goals for 1996*, Ministry of Tourism, Kingdom of Cambodia, Phnom Penh, 1996.

Philip, J. and Mercer, D., 'Commodification of Buddhism in contemporary Burma', *Annals of Tourism Research* 26(1), 1999, pp. 21–54.

Reuters, 'Cambodia tourism down but recovery expected soon', 16 December 1998.

Rigg, J., *Southeast Asia: The Human Landscape of Modernization and Development*, Routledge, London, 1997.

Ringer, G., *Recommendations for Recreational Development at Kirirom and Ream National Parks, South Central Cambodia*, Ministry of Environment, Phnom Penh, 1997.

Robinson, K., 'Developers bide time on Cambodian coast', *Bangkok Post* (Business Section), 10 February 1997, p. 11.

Ross, D., 'Road to Burma still potholed by bureacracy', *Bangkok Post* 5 November 1998.

Singapore Trade Development Board, 'Myanmar's tourism ministry officials to lure investment as Singapore becomes Myanmar's second largest investor', *Press Release* PR No.112/95, 10 October 1995.

South China Morning Post, 'Airport repair project marks resumption of Japanese help', *South China Morning Post* 27 February 1998.

Taylor, C., Wheeler, T. and Robinson, D., *Cambodia: A Lonely Planet Travel Survival Kit*, Lonely Planet Travel Publications, Hawthorn, Australia, 1996.

Thami, R., 'The business of tourism', *Phnom Penh Post* 13–26 December 1996, p. 13.

Than, M. and Tan, J. (eds), *Laos' Dilemmas and Options: The Challenge of Economic Transition in the 1990s*, St Martins, New York, 1997.

Tourism Authority of Thailand, *TAT Helps National Tourist Authority of Laos* (Press Release), Tourism Authority of Thailand, Bangkok, 12 February 1998.

TravelAsia, 'Sannya: what Laos wants', *TravelAsia* 12 April 1996.

TravelAsia, 'Operators stick to Cambodia', *TravelAsia* 18 July 1997.

Watling, D., *Review of the August 1996 Preah Sihanouk National Park (Cambodia) Management Plan*, UN Office for Project Services and UN Development Programme, Phnom Penh, 1996.

World Bank Report, *Economic Indicators: Cambodia*, World Bank, Washington, DC, 1997.

Part Three

Tourism in South Asia

14

Developing tourism in South Asia: India, Pakistan and Bangladesh – SAARC and beyond

C. Michael Hall and Stephen Page

One of the darker sides of us, the South Asians seems to be our habit of thinking that we know what is right and no body should bother to teach us. We are very good teachers but not necessarily good students. Now we should be learning from what others feel about us. We have to accept the fact that for long, we have been deceived by our own thought of greatness. For [sic] tourism industry to flourish and contribute to our national development we should learn to cater to the demands of the incoming tourists. The mere existence of almighty Himalayas, beautiful blue seas with their magnificent beaches, the grand palaces and forts left as heritage by our forefathers, the varied wild life, birth places of saints and lords or the archaeological heritage of 5000 years civilisation is not going to make foreigners with cash in their purse beg to be allowed to enter our countries (Vaidya, 1996).

Introduction

Travel and tourism have long been associated with South Asia. For example, in the seminal study of the geography of India and Pakistan, Spate and Learmonth (1954) identified the growing significance of tourism. They also indicated that the existing pattern of colonial transport infrastructure had been utilized and developed for domestic travel including the fledgling air transport network and intensive network of railways and roads. Religious pilgrimage has been, and is still, an important factor in the domestic travel patterns in South Asia and, increasingly, international visitation with the pilgrimage centres and routes which have developed over the past 3000 years remaining important to the present day (e.g. Kaur, 1985). Despite the relatively early development of resort tourism under the British, international tourism received relatively little consideration as an economic development mechanism by the governments of the region until the late 1970s in the cases of the Maldives, Nepal and Sri Lanka and, in the case of India, not until the early 1990s. However, although having one-fifth of the world's population and a number of world-renowned tourism attractions such as the Taj

Figure 14.1 *Countries of South Asia*

Mahal, the Himalayas and spectacular beaches and coastal scenery, the countries of South Asia (Figure 14.1) receive less than 1 per cent of the world's international tourist arrivals and tourism receipts. As Table 14.1 shows, the pattern of arrivals for 1990–1994 shows considerable variation and fluctuation with political conflict and other tensions causing significant variations. Indeed, one major reason for this may be the conflicting images and stereotypes of the exotic and the 'begging bowl' which are all wrapped together in the Western media portrayals of South Asia (Richter, 1989). Images of the sub-continent have become even more complicated in recent years by the hostage-taking of tourists in Kashmir, the ongoing political conflict between India and Pakistan and civil war in Sri Lanka. Even so, Mumtaz and Mitha (1996), in relation to Pakistan, highlight the cultural variety which creates cultural landscapes for tourism, rich in the ethnic diversity of localities and their people and traditions. For example, Pakistan alone has a range of languages and dialects including urdu, punjabi, sindhi, pashto and balochi; this adds to the attraction and experience of differentness observed in Chapter 1 which characterizes both Southeast and South Asia (Robinson, 1989).

Despite such difficulties, economic development has been steady in the region to the point where South Asia is now one of the world's fastest growing tourist regions, albeit from a low base (Hall, 1997; Ragaraman, 1998). International arrivals to South Asia grew by 4.8 per cent to

Table 14.1 *Visitor arrivals (000s) in South Asia 1990–1994 based on the World Tourism Organization regionalization*

	1990	1991	1992	1993	1994
Afghanistan (est.)	8	8	6	6	5
Bangladesh	115	113	110	127	140
Bhutan	2	2	3	3	4
India	1707	1678	1868	1765	1886
Iran	154	212	279	304	362
Maldives	195	196	236	241	362
Myanmar	21	22	27	48	80
Nepal	255	293	334	294	327
Pakistan	424	438	352	379	327
Sri Lanka	298	318	394	392	408
Total	3179	3280	3609	3559	3946

Source: World Tourism Organization (WTO).

Table 14.2 *World tourist arrivals in South Asia 1996–1997*

	Tourist arrivals (000s)		% change		Tourism receipts (US$million)		% change	
	1996	1997	97/96	96/95	1996	1997	97/96	96/95
Total South Asia	4332	4546	4.9	3.1	3914	4151	6.1	11.1
Bangladesh	166	184	10.8	6.4	34	42	23.5	47.8
India	2288	2376	3.8	7.7	2963	3155	6.5	13.6
Iran	465	476	2.4	2.9	165	168	1.8	3.1
Maldives	339	366	8.0	7.6	266	287	7.9	26.7
Nepal	394	418	6.1	8.5	161	164	1.9	−9.0
Pakistan	369	351	−4.9	−2.4	146	117	−19.9	28.1
Sri Lanka	302	366	21.2	−25.1	173	212	22.5	−23.1
Other[a]	9	9	0.0	0.0	6	6	0.0	0.0

Note
[a]Other: Afghanistan, Bhutan.
Source: World Tourism Organization (WTO) based on Chapter 15.

reach 4.6 million in 1997, while receipts climbed by 5.9 per cent to US$4.2 billion (World Tourism Organization, 1998b). India, which accounts for half of all arrivals in the region, showed an increase of 3.9 per cent in visitor arrivals in 1997 (see Table 14.2). Sri Lanka showed a spectacular turn-around in visitor numbers, with a 23.5 per cent increase in arrivals and 35.7 per cent growth in earnings. In contrast, tourist arrivals in Pakistan declined for the third consecutive year (World Tourism Organization, 1998a).

In terms of social and economic development, Table 14.3 provides a breakdown of the key indicators for the principal countries in the South Asian region. The reality of the respective development status of these countries cannot be separated from tourism: in some cases it is a vital ingredient in the experience and images with which visitors leave the region. The reality of rapid population growth, images of rural poverty and urbanization are also being inter-weaved with the essential cultural, environmental and historical attractions which visitors find juxtaposed with a background of less developed countries. Whilst existing regional surveys of the region and the respective countries, such as India (Singh, 1976), Pakistan (Saeed, 1995) and Bangladesh (Rashid, 1991), highlight the range of development problems facing the region's governments and the policies adopted to deal

Table 14.3   Selected indicators of socio-economic development for four South Asian countries

South Asia	Population 'millions' mid-1993	Total area '000s' miles²	Population density per mile²	GNP per capita US$ 1994	Average inflation rate (%) 1984–1994	Share of GDP (%) 1994			
						Agriculture	Industry	Manufacturing	Services
Bangladesh	117.9	144	819	220	6.6	30	18	10	52
India	913.6	3288	278	320	9.7	30	28	18	42
Pakistan	126.3	796	158	430	8.8	25	25	18	50
Sri Lanka	17.9	66	271	640	11.0	24	25	16	51

Source: modified from Alauddin and Tisdell, 1998.

Table 14.4 *Urbanization in South Asia*

	Urban population as % of total		Average annual urban population change (%) 1965–1995
	1965	1995	
Bangladesh	6.2	19.5	6.7
India	18.8	26.8	3.3
Pakistan	23.5	34.7	4.2
Sri Lanka	19.9	22.4	2.1
Asia	22.2	34.0	3.5
Europe	63.8	75.0	1.0
World	35.5	45.2	2.7

Source: modified from Alauddin and Tisdell, 1998.

with them, urbanization is emerging as a dominant process in time and space. For example, in 1995 the region had five of the world's top twenty-five largest cities: Bombay (15.1 million population); Calcutta (11.7 million population); Delhi (9.9 million population); Karachi (9.9 million population) and Dhaka (7.8 million population). Rapid urbanization is adding a new series of development problems for South Asia that also impact upon tourism (Table 14.4). These are epitomized by Alauddin and Tisdell (1998: p. 192) as

A feature of South Asian cities is that air pollution is well in excess of health standards and domestic and industrial effluents are released to [sic] waterways with little or no treatment. Water quality is therefore very poor and a threat to human health and aquatic life. In most cases there are vast squatter settlements and these are often located in areas experiencing the most environmental problems. Therefore, the poor in cities not only have very low incomes, but also live in the worst environmental conditions, often on land that no one wants because of the environmental hazards associated with it.

As noted in Chapter 15 by Singh and Singh, destination planning becomes extremely difficult when the choice is between homes for the homeless and hotels for tourists. Indeed, no tourist can fail to observe these problems, particularly as Battacharya (1995, cited in Alauddin and Tisdell, 1998) observed in the case of

Calcutta where the Hindu Survey of the Environment report found that

The city of Calcutta is suffering from serious environmental disorder. Collapsing sewer lines, stagnant canals, obsolete pumping stations, water-logging, heaps of garbage, increasing noise, air and water pollution, a rise in malaria and gastro-enteric diseases and shrinking wetlands are just a few of the problems plaguing the city (Battacharya, 1995: p. 146 cited in Alauddin and Tisdell, 1998).

In the case of Pakistan, Mumtaz and Mitha (1996) note the link between poverty and environmental destruction. The National Conservation Strategy highlighted many of the existing problems, such as loss of biodiversity and the need to involve local people in any measures designed to encourage sustainable development which can reduce the degradation impacts of human activity on a fragile environment. Aside from the environmental problems, it is evident that urbanization and economic development have also polarized the societies of the South Asian countries, as the example of Dhaka in Bangladesh shows. Alauddin and Tisdell (1998: p. 195) argue that 'while average incomes in cities such as Dhaka are higher than for the remainder for the country, income is very unevenly distributed'. In fact Islam (1996) found that 50 per cent of the population of Dhaka is living below the poverty line, of whom 30 per cent are in extreme poverty. The majority live in

Table 14.5   *Access of urban population to safe drinking water and sanitation in South Asia, 1980 and 1990*

	Percentage of urban population			
	Safe drinking water		Sanitation	
	1980	1990	1980	1990
Bangladesh	26	39	21	40
India	73	77	27	44
Pakistan	72	82	42	53
Sri Lanka	65	80	68	80

Source: modified from Alauddin and Tisdell, 1998.

slum dwellings which house approximately 3 million people and where many of the basic services (e.g. water and sanitation) do not exist. This situation remains in many developing countries, as Table 14.5 shows, despite the improvements in basic service provision.

In recent years economic development, particularly in India, has meant the development of a middle class which is seeking to travel. Outbound travel from the region to Southeast Asia, Europe and North America has therefore been strong, while domestic tourism has also gathered pace, especially in India (see Chapter 15). For example, since the early 1980s, outbound travel from the countries of the region has been increasing at approximately 8 per cent per year (Vaidya, 1996). However, in stark contrast to outbound travel growth, intraregional travel and inbound tourism has been relatively weak. Therefore, in order to try and improve on this situation and earn much required foreign exchange, a number of national and international initiatives have been developed.

This chapter examines some of the developments which have taken place in South Asian tourism in recent years, particularly with respect to the efforts of governments to attract investment and encourage tourism development. The chapter begins with an examination of the role of the South Asian Association for Regional Cooperation (SAARC) and then goes on to review some of the measures undertaken by various countries to open up their economies for tourism and reduce the role of government in the market.

The South Asian Association for Regional Cooperation (SAARC)

One of the most important political and economic initiatives in the South Asia region is the South Asian Association for Regional Cooperation (SAARC). Although it may surprise many readers, given the common colonial heritage of the countries in the region, the idea of regional cooperation in order to deal with common development problems did not take hold until the late 1970s when the late President Ziaur Rehman of Bangladesh promoted the concept. Indeed, even now intraregional trade within South Asia accounts for only approximately 3 per cent of all international trade in the region (Vaidya, 1996).

Following a series of meetings of Foreign Secretaries in the early 1980s which identified areas of cooperation, the first summit of South Asian countries (the People's Republic of Bangladesh, the Kingdom of Bhutan, the Republic of India, Republic of Maldives, The Kingdom of Nepal, The Islamic Republic of Pakistan and the Democratic Socialist Republic of Sri Lanka) was held in Dhaka in December 1985 and SAARC was formally launched. SAARC is significant because it not only provides a basis for economic cooperation and development between the various countries in the region but also provides opportunities for trust-building between several nations, and India and Pakistan in particular, which have gone through periods of substantial conflict. Traditionally focused on issues of agriculture and rural development, and the development of Preferential Trading Arrangements, tourism was a latecomer to the areas of interest for SAARC. Although, thanks to the assistance of the World Tourism Organization, 1975 was promoted as Visit South Asia Year by the South Asia Regional Travel Commission, it was not until the late 1980s that intraregional cooperation on tourism began to develop in earnest.

In August 1988 representatives of designated banks and agencies met to formulate recommendations regarding financial aspects of tourism (settlement of accounts and limited convertibility of national currencies for tourists from SAARC countries) under a scheme for the promotion of organized tourism in the region. A Technical Committee on Tourism within the framework of SAARC was established in 1991. However, the establishment of a Tourism Council by SAARC Chamber of Commerce and Industry (SCCI), the apex organization of business and industry representing the private sectors of all the countries of the region, had the objective of raising the level of regional cooperation and contributing to the development of the economy. This has probably been the most significant tourism initiative.

The overall mission of the Tourism Council is to 'contribute to the development of tourism sector and through it to the economic development of the region and promote regional cooperation at private sector level'. Its objectives are

1. to contribute to the development of the tourism sector of the SAARC countries by way of promotion of flow of tourists within the region and from outside the region;

2. to provide recommendations to the governments for the policy changes for promotion of tourism business in the region;
3. to act in a catalytic role for increasing cooperation on tourism related activities at the private sector level;
4. to work for easier travel procedures for citizens of the SAARC countries to travel inside the region;
5. to find out investment opportunities and promote investment in tourism-related business;
6. to contribute to the development networking of tourism related institutions of the region;
7. to promote direct air and other transport linkages among members of SAARC;
8. to facilitate in setting up a Tourism Information Network in the SAARC region;
9. to promote South Asian Tourism among clients outside the region;
10. to organize regional events like seminars, training, fairs, workshops on tourism;
11. to conduct and facilitate research on tourism-related issues in the region; and
12. to promote development of human resource related to tourism in the region (SAARC Chamber of Commerce and Industry Tourism Council, 1997).

Earlier attempts to promote regional cooperation in tourism in South Asia, such as the formation of the South Asia Tourism Association in 1984, were short-lived. However, the private–public partnerships involved in SAARC and SCCI would appear to hold more promise for tourism development. Nevertheless, the region faces substantial problems and issues. Vaidya (1996), in an excellent report to the SCCI Tourism Council Seminar in Colombo, Sri Lanka, identified four major issues which the Council and the region as a whole needed to face:

Political and economic stability and political commitment – in terms not only of a reduction in political conflict in the region but also in relation to issues such as passport and visa control, and concrete government commitment to regional cooperation.

Turning the potential into reality – through cooperation at the regional level in order to compete more effectively with other destinations at the international level, through such mechanisms as common tour packages.

Making common sense prevail on pseudo nationalism – Vaidya (1996) argued that one of the greatest threats to the promotion of tourism in the region was the dominance of perceived national interests over the interests of the region as a whole, and noted that the countries of the region 'have to accept the fact, a single country may not be saleable as a full destination but, if we could combine more than one country, it may be readily saleable as a full package. For promotion of tourism in the region, we should get away from pseudo nationalism and be able to project that the co-operation benefits all of us'. This is undoubtedly one of the great marketing opportunities for both National Tourism Organizations and the private sector within the South Asian region.

Getting away from the negative image of South Asia in the leading world tourism markets – finally, Vaidya (1996) observed that the common image of South Asia in the international media 'more often than not attracts negative type of coverage' and was often referred to 'as a place with beggars and fakirs, of people with little care for health and hygiene, with motorists, shopkeepers, kids and animals competing for the space in the streets. The news headlines on South Asia will be about their ethnic or sectarian conflicts or floods killing people or drought'. Instead, Vaidya (1996) argued, one of the aims of the Tourism Council and the region's tourism industry should be to project a positive image of South Asia as 'an interesting place with very friendly people'.

One of the major issues for tourism arising out of the problems faced by the region is the development of policy initiatives which adequately meet regional goals and objectives. Vaidya (1996), in his report to the Tourism Council, identified a number of intraregional and inter-regional initiatives, several of which have been influenced by tourism policy developments in

the ASEAN countries and the Pacific. Five policy initiatives were identified in relation to intraregional tourism:

Air connections: for intraregional tourism to develop, better airline connections are essential. Policy issues identified include the need for national airlines to choose to fly routes with high traffic rather than just prestige routes. The route development in South Asia is poor with it being easier 'to get to Europe or the USA from Kathmandu than to get to Colombo'.

Land transport: all SAARC countries, except Sri Lanka and Maldives, have land borders. There is therefore a need to improve road and rail transport linkages in order to reduce the cost of travel and provide opportunities for more sightseeing.

Frontier formalities: Vaidya (1996) argues that in the long term SAARC should look at allowing the free flow of citizens of one SAARC country to another. But, in the shorter term, the visa procedures for group tours organized by registered tour operators could be eased. In addition, governments could reduce visa fees for citizens of SAARC countries and speed up the time taken for the processing of visa applications by business travellers.

Preferential treatment of tourists from the SAARC region: in order to promote intraregional tourism and a better understanding among the people of the region, travellers from SAARC countries could get special treatment for travelling inside SAARC. For example, Nepal offers special ticket and hotel rates for Indian tourists. As Vaidya (1996) notes, 'if trade can be carried out in [sic] preferential basis why not allow travel also in [sic] preferential basis?'.

Infrastructure development: in order to encourage infrastructure development, regional investment could be encouraged through multilateral agreements to make investment easier by businesses of one SAARC member in another.

With respect to developing inbound arrivals from outside of the region two substantive policy areas were identified:

Marketing/promotion: marketing is essential in promoting South Asia as a destination and improving its image. Joint marketing efforts between the various national tourism organizations and key private-sector players can be used to promote SAARC countries as one destination. In order to do this measures such as collective participation in international tourism events and exhibitions may well be appropriate. In developing this concept the ASEAN village model, adopted by ASEAN countries at a number of trade fairs, is seen as being appropriate.

Combining the strength of national airlines: As in other parts of Asia and the Pacific Rim, some of the airline requirements of the various countries may be better served by replacing national airlines with a regional airline. However, in the short term, joint marketing campaigns may be useful. According to Vaidya (1996), 'combining the countries with stronger airlines (e.g. Pakistan) [*sic*] base with countries with stronger tourism base (e.g. Nepal) makes business sense as it generates business to both the countries'.

Finally, two policy areas were regarded as pertinent to both intra- and interregional tourism:

Human resource development and product standardization: as in other parts of Asia (American Express (AMEX) and PATA, 1994), one of the critical difficulties in tourism is the development of a human resource base. Therefore, substantial attention is being given to tourism training and education, in some cases with the assistance of foreign aid. Similarly, with respect to the provision of quality services, a degree of regional standards for products and services may be appropriate. According to Vaidya (1996), the adoption of such common standards would 'greatly facilitate the marketing of the region as a single tourism market'.

Exchange of information: one final policy initiative is the exchange of information among tourism business regarding the region. For example, SAARC has held a number of meetings in order to create tourism business networks, to exchange information and to create publicity for the regional tourism concept.

The various SAARC initiatives have had mixed success, with the main reason for the slow development of the regional tourism concept being the animosity between India and Pakistan over issues such as Kashmir and nuclear testing which has affected many other areas of potential cooperation, including tourism. Indeed, the very warnings of negative images arising from regional conflict suggested by Vaidya (1996) were borne out in 1998 through the nuclear testing programmes of India and Pakistan which received extensive coverage in the Western media. Indeed, 1998 was a very bad year in terms of regional publicity through such events as the serious floods in Bangladesh, renewed fighting in Sri Lanka between the Tamil guerrillas seeking an independent homeland and government forces, and further hostage taking of foreign visitors in Kashmir.

Undoubtedly, the economic and political linchpin of South Asia, and one of the keys in understanding its potential development, is India. As Richter (1989, p.107) noted, 'the central position of India within the context of intraregional tourism has potential for exacerbating the often considerable resentment that may exist among India's neighbours concerning the country's dominant political and military role on the subcontinent'. Nevertheless, it is noticeable that India is setting an important precedent in the region with respect to its efforts to open up the economy to market forces.

India

India is by far the largest country in the region in terms of population, wealth and influence. Spate and Learmonth (1954) provided an interesting observation on the growing significance of tourism in the 1950s in the Himachal Pradesh region of India which contains the central Himalayas. This theme was subsequently explored by Singh (1989) some thirty-nine years later in the context of mountain environments where the pressure of tourism on the hill stations of the former Raj days was reaching saturation point. A number of useful studies exist which also document the historical development of tourism in India in the post-war period (e.g. Ahuja and Sarna, 1977). However, tourism development in India has been influenced substantially`by its federal structure. Under the Indian constitution responsibility for tourism exists at both the state and national level, thereby leading to the possibility of substantial problems in policy coordination. Yet India saw the Sargent Report commissioned in 1945, which reported in 1946, on ways of developing domestic and international tourist traffic and, following independence, the Tourist Traffic Branch of the Ministry of Transport was established in 1949. This innovation under state control also saw funding set aside in the second Five Year Plan (1956–1961) to market India as a destination. In 1952, the first overseas tourist office was set up in New York and, in 1967, the Department of Aviation and Tourism was established.

Thus, government at all levels has historically played a major role in the supply of tourism facilities and infrastructure, with the majority of the higher quality accommodation being state owned. The organization of tourism in India is coordinated by a number of bodies which are based within the Ministry of Civil Aviation and Tourism. The Department of Tourism and Department of Civil Aviation are the lead bodies to deal with issues in a development, promotional and regulatory context in both the tourism and aviation fields. The Department of Tourism also has twenty offices throughout India and eighteen overseas, which support the head office function in New Dehli.

Nevertheless, in recent years substantial shifts have occurred in the nature of government involvement in tourism in India which have substantially influenced other countries in the region. First, direct government intervention in the economy has been reduced, with the privatization of a number of functions previously controlled by government. For example, the domestic aviation market in India has been substantially deregulated with the monopoly of Indian Airlines, Air India and Vayudoot (since merged with Indian Airlines) being ended in 1994. The results of deregulation were remarkable. By 1996 six private corporations had been granted scheduled airline status with nineteen air taxi operators being permitted to operate charter and non-scheduled services.

Second, new corporate tourism development bodies have been established at both the federal and the state level in order to encourage foreign and domestic investment in tourism infrastructure, often through public–private partnerships. For example, at the national level the India Tourism Development Corporation, which is a limited company under the auspices of the Department of Tourism of the Ministry of Civil Tourism and Aviation, has been created. This body operates a chain of hotels, duty-free shops and a travel agency. At the state level several states have created tourism development corporations. The Tourism Corporation of Gujarat, for example, developed a tourism plan which included several tax concessions for investors, such as exemption from luxury tax, sales tax, electricity duty, turnover tax and entertainment tax, and long-term loans from state institutions. This, in part, has helped to address the very negative image of India overseas as a tourist destination and the limitations on foreign direct investment for tourism prior to the government's economic liberalization measures in the 1990s (Chaudhary, 1996).

Third, and closely tied to the creation of new development bodies, has been the creation of incentives to encourage foreign investment in the tourism sector. For example, concessions at the state level have also been matched by central government fiscal incentives for tourism projects, including income tax exemptions on 50 per cent of the profits from foreign exchange earnings, exemption on the remaining 50 per cent if the amount is reinvested in new tourism projects and exemption on import duty on imports for hotel projects. In an effort to use tourism as a tool for regional development, the Indian federal government has explicitly sought to encourage such development by providing interest subsidies on term loans from eligible financial institutions for hotels in cities other than main centres, such as Mumbai (Bombay), Delhi, Calcutta and Chennai (Madras). Higher rates of subsidy are available for hotel development in designated tourist areas and for heritage hotels. The provision of financial incentives for tourism by the central government in the 1990s is indicative not only of increased attention by government to tourism's potential for generating employment and foreign exchange, but also the wider deregulation of the Indian economy to competition and foreign investment. In the accommodation sector the federal government now allows foreign management and up to 51 per cent foreign ownership of hotels.

Richter (1989, p.102) observed that 'India is arguably the most successful of the developing nations in its gradual, often clumsy, use of tourism for national development'. Several reasons were offered:

1. an extensive colonial transport infrastructure, particularly the railway system;
2. a federal system which allows innovation and differences between the states;
3. a domestic tourism tradition;
4. a tourism public policy process that is slow but usually self-correcting; and
5. policy decisions which reflect broader concerns than the growth and needs of the tourism industry.

Nevertheless, since Richter made her observations, the Indian government and many of the states have increased the emphasis they give to tourism, particularly given the growth of leisure-oriented domestic tourism in India. In the longer term, it therefore appears that India will have to face many of the same issues as other developing countries with respect to managing the downside of tourism in terms of environmental and social pressures. Kashyap (1990) outlined the ambitious plans of Indian government for a five-year plan to diversify from culture-oriented tourism to holidaymaking based on adventure activities, as well as wildlife and traditional beach-resort-based tourism.

There are also plans afoot to restore national heritage sites, while seeking new markets (Government of India, Ministry of Information and Broadcasting, 1994). Inskeep (1994) examines the tourism planning necessary for Goa to achieve its goals of beach/resort tourism and the development of the golf tourism market.

The tourism economy in India: recent trends and patterns of change

In 1993, travel receipts from tourism were US$2001.2 million and these increased to US$2265.2 million in 1994 (13.2 per cent). This is a reflection of the increase in international arrivals from 1.76 million in 1993 to 1.89 million in 1994, as well as an increased per capita spend by international tourists. Some 18.3 per cent of international arrivals were from Pakistan and Bangladesh in 1993 and this rose to 17.2 per cent in 1994. The tourism industry in India directly employed 6.4 million people in 1991/1992 and this is estimated to have increased to 7.8 million by 1994/1995. Indirectly, the tourism economy is estimated to have employed 18.4 million people in 1994/1995, with a further 1 million growth in jobs over the period 1993/1994–1994/1995. This means that a tourism multiplier of 2.36 exists for direct:indirect employment generated by tourism, which is very high (Bull, 1991) given the range of employment multiplier values from almost zero to over 2.0. This, however, may reflect the high labour–capital ratio for tourism, which implies that tourism creates more jobs compared with other sectors of the Indian economy. By the year 2000, the Ministry of Tourism optimistically forecasts that tourism will generate 30 million jobs within India. Ragaraman (1998) also reports that while domestic tourism is the major sector of the tourism business within India, the income multiplier for international visitors suggests that the impact is twenty-six times that of the domestic tourist sector, with a value of 0.93. This multiplier is large, indicating the major impact which tourist spending has on gross local values, with much of the international visitor expenditure retained as net foreign exchange earnings. Thus, tourism adds significant value to the Indian economy (see Ragaraman, 1998, for more detail on the Indian tourism economy).

Visitor arrivals: development and change in the 1980s and 1990s

Chapter 15, by Singh and Singh, provides a detailed discussion of the current trends and patterns of tourism, and the focus here is on the previous changes and developments in visitor arrivals, thereby setting a context for the discussion by Singh and Singh. In global terms, Ragaraman (1998) reports a worrying trend in visitor arrivals: India's share of world arrivals has dropped from 0.42 per cent in 1980 to 0.38 per cent in 1995. A similar trend is reported for receipts from tourism which dropped from 1.09

per cent to 0.69 per cent over the same period. These figures are somewhat removed from the Department of Tourism's ambitious target in 1992 to achieve 1 per cent of world arrivals by the year 2000. Thus, India's performance in attracting visitors is below the world average (Kumar, 1992). International visitor arrivals have grown from the first recorded count in 1951 when 16 829 visitors entered India, rising to almost half a million in 1976 and 1 million in 1986. In 1990, the figure rose to 1.71 million but the 1990s have seen the previous growth of arrivals impeded by a number of factors: political disturbances such as the Gulf war; political unrest in Kashmir and riots from time to time. It was not until 1995, that the 2 million mark was reached in visitor arrivals, although arrivals from neighbouring Pakistan and Bangladesh are worsening owing to the difficulties in bilateral agreements with Pakistan affecting visas.

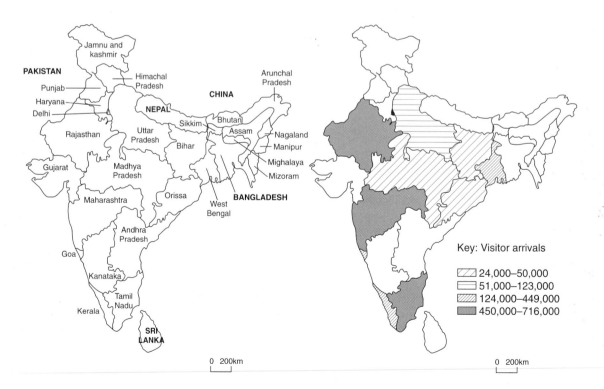

Figure 14.2 *Distribution of international arrivals in excess of 24 000 by Indian states, 1993*

The principal tourist generating regions for international arrivals for 1994 were: Asia (44.6 per cent), North America (12.3 per cent) and Western Europe (34.7 per cent). Within this, the UK was the main market (15.9 per cent market share) followed by the USA (9.4 per cent), Germany (4.5 per cent), Sri Lanka (4.7 per cent) and France (3.9 per cent). The geographical distribution of arrivals in 1993 reflects an interesting pattern. India received 1.8 million arrivals in 1993, and the arrivals by state total 3.2 million. This illustrates the pattern of visitation to different states within India (Figure 14.2) with the greatest growth in 1991–1993 occurring in Goa (118 per cent), Tamil Nadu (47 per cent) and Kerala (28 per cent). At the same time, Dehli recorded a decline of 32 per cent in international tourist arrivals. Thus, it is the southern states of India which have recorded the greatest increases in international tourism. Since India is a multi-destination country, it has amongst the longest length of stay for international visitors. In 1993, the average length of stay was 28.8 days for international visitors, although as many as 33 per cent are estimated to stay for more than 60 days. While visitors from Pakistan and Bangladesh tend to be visiting friends and relatives, 86.4 per cent of arrivals in 1994 stated they were on holiday and on sightseeing tours. A further 10.8 per cent were on business. The most popular month to visit was December, followed by January, March and February. However, the seasonal distribution in 1994 showed a slight decline for October and November owing to the outbreak of plague in Surat, Western India (Clift and Page, 1996; Grabowski and Chatterjee, 1997).

In terms of outbound tourism (Indians travelling overseas), Suri (1996) reports that the Department of Tourism, which is the principal source of information, and the Indian Association of Tour Operators estimate that 4 million outbound Indian tourists resulted from a growing liberalization towards foreign travel in 1995, with foreign exchange regulations eased and higher disposable incomes among some social groups. Approximately 60 per cent of the traffic is estimated to be for the Haj pilgrimage, 25 per cent

for business and the balance for pleasure. In contrast, domestic tourism has been fuelled by the growth in India's middle class (estimated at 250 million) and changing attitudes to travel. In 1991, domestic tourism movements were estimated at 86.7 million trips, 86.3 million in 1993 and around 100 million in 1994. In 1995, this is estimated to have grown to around 120 million trips; this does not include pilgrimage tourism which is estimated to account for a further 100 million trips within India. The geographical distribution of destinations by state for domestic tourism shows Andhara Pradesh dominates the pattern of visits followed by Tamil Nadu. In the case of domestic tourism, the patterns are influenced by the location of religious shrines, cultural icons and friends and relatives. The growth in domestic tourism has also been fuelled by the deregulation of the domestic airline industry since 1994, allowing a number of private airlines to operate (e.g. Modiluft, Jet Airways, East and West Airlines, NEPC Airlines, Damania Airways and Sahara Airlines). These are complemented by a number of regional airlines (e.g. Gujarat Air, UP Airways and Archana Airways). Of the 10 million domestic tourists who flew within India in 1994–1995, 66 per cent were carried by the state-owned airline – Indian Airlines.

In terms of international tourism, 98.4 per cent of arrivals are by air (excluding the Pakistan and Bangladesh nationals who cross the local borders). The main gateways through which international tourists arrive are Dehli and Bombay (78.2 per cent), followed by Madras (11.1 per cent), Calcutta (3.2 per cent) and Goa (3.5 per cent). In 1993, some 4.1 million passengers arrived at India's main international airports, of whom 1.4 million were international tourists and 2.7 million were returning Indian nationals. While Ragaraman (1998) discussed the problems of air capacity to India to facilitate a further growth in inbound tourism, in 1994/1995 the main capacity for air travel was provided by:

- Air India (3.06 million seats)
- Indian Airlines (1.13 million seats)

- sixty foreign carriers (8.45 million seats) who controlled 67 per cent of the market.

To offset some of the capacity problems reported by Ragaraman (1998), there has been greater use of charter flights to India, increasing from 205 in 1992 to 605 in 1993 to 982 in 1994, with 84 877 passengers. One of the main advantages of charters is that they can avoid the main gateways and locate the tourists nearer to their final destinations without much additional use of domestic airlines. To accommodate this growth in both scheduled and charter traffic, India's airports have undergone upgrading. The pattern of arrivals is largely concentrated among the main international gateways (Bombay, Calcutta, Dehli, Madras and Trivandrum) which handled 8.7 million international passengers in 1993/1994 and 9.1 million in 1994/1995. In contrast, the same airports handled 12.3 million and 13.8 million domestic tourists over the same period. The Indian government has also upgraded a further twenty-six airports to international standards to accommodate the growing charter business. This is likely to assist in the geographical spread of tourists from the main urban centres which act as gateways, with secondary cities recording a growth in accommodation to meet the demand. The number of hotel rooms in India is forecast to rise from 55 000 in 1994 to 90 000 by the year 2000.

India's path to tourism growth and development is seeing the emergence of multi-destination products, such as the South Pacific multi-destination model where tourists visit both Australia and New Zealand. In the case of India, the combination of India with the Maldives, Nepal or Bhutan reflects a growing sophistication and attempt to develop higher-yield markets such as golf tourism in Goa. However, this is not without its critics as Suri (1996) observes:

Another area which needs further attention is the need to target high-spending traffic rather than going for sheer numbers. Also, the government seems to have no sound sustainable
tourism development policy which can ensure a harmonious relationship between tourism and the environment on the one hand, and tourism and local communities on the other (Suri, 1996: p. 43).

While it may be likely that India's visitor numbers exceed 3 million after the year 2000, India is likely to face growing international competition from more demanding, adventurous and travelled tourists who are price conscious at a time when other South Asian destinations are seeking to expand their share of the global tourism market.

Pakistan

Alham-do-Lillah, Today we are, with Allah's Blessings, the proud citizens of a Nuclear power. No one can deny this established fact. Pakistan is fully capable of defeating any design on its sovereignty and integrity. We are grateful to God Almighty for giving us the strength to prove once again to the world that a determined nation can not be subjected to any kind of blackmail, be it political pressures or threats of physical harm. The credit for what we have achieved goes to every citizen of Pakistan. Now we must devote all our energies to meet another equally important challenge. That is the challenge of economic independence and self reliance (Dar, 1998).

Pakistan is a country with a population of over 130 million and a land area of 796 095 km which borders Iran, India, Afghanistan and China. It has an annual economic growth rate of 2.8 per cent and enormous trade deficit, foreign exchange reserves and balance of payments problems. It also has a nuclear capability. Thus, Pakistan presents an image to the West which would not usually involve tourism. Yet, Pakistan is a country which has substantial cultural tourism attractions, particularly in relation to its Islamic heritage, and tourism is growing fast as a significant foreign exchange

Table 14.6 *Tourism receipts and GNP in Pakistan, 1987–1988 to 1996–1997*

Year	GNP (million rupees)	Tourism receipts (million rupees)	Tourism receipts as a percentage of GNP
1987–1988	449 519	2684.8	0.60
1988–1989	468 799	2755.4	0.59
1989–1990	491 265	3356.1	0.68
1990–1991	509 417	3489.7	0.68
1991–1992	544 080	3744.2	0.69
1992–1993	553 189	2946.8	0.51
1993–1994	572 178	3218.2	0.56
1994–1995	604 117	3899.1	0.65
1995–1996	626 321	3914.3	0.62
1996–1997	621 838	5661.9	0.91

Source: modified from Ministry of Culture, Sports, Tourism and Youth Affairs, 1998.

earner, though most of its foreign exchange earnings during the 1990s have come from its overseas workers in the Middle East. This is aptly summarized by Hussein (1996):

> Tourism in Pakistan has been a slow growth industry. Although the country has tremendous tourism potential, there is much which has yet to be successfully exploited. Most of this potential is in the northern region of the country where the world's three greatest mountain ranges meet: the Hindu Kush, the Himalayas and the Karakorams. The opening of the Karakoram highway in the mid-1980s gave a major impetus to tourism. By contrast, the southern coast offers unspoilt beaches along the Arabian Sea and a great opportunity for the development of water sports. However, the lack of tourism infrastructure has inhibited growth (Hussein, 1996: p. 43).

A number of other factors have also inhibited the development of international tourism in Pakistan, notably the uncertain security situation in Karachi and the decline of the Pakistan rupee against the US dollar. However, major growth has occurred in domestic tourism. Much of this growth is a result of moderately increasing disposable incomes, the income of Pakistani return migrants and the role of the Karakoram highway in allowing the movement of tourists through Pakistan into China. Two growth areas which have been actively promoted by the

Pakistan Tourism Development Corporation are adventure travel and religious tourism (e.g. pilgrimages). Nevertheless, the limited impact of international tourism means that tourist expenditure contributes less than 1 per cent to GNP (Table 14.6). There is, however, a significant likelihood that this figure will increase, provided that the country can remain politically stable (Ministry of Culture, Sports, Tourism and Youth Affairs, 1998), although such growth will be nowhere near as great as the enthusiastic predictions of the 1993 National Tourism Policy (Ministry of Tourism, 1993). However, before discussing tourism, it is pertinent to examine changes in the economy of Pakistan and the role of the government which provides an important context for a changing business environment for tourism.

Pakistan's economy: state involvement and the privatization ethos for greater competition

In order to try and improve its economic situation, Pakistan, like India, has begun to substantially shift its economic policies to reduce the role of government in the economy and develop a deregulated business environment (see Saeed, 1995, for a detailed analysis of Pakistan's economy). In terms of international trade the Sharif government is seeking to eliminate the country's trade deficit by 1999, two years earlier than the original target of 2001. In order to do so Pakistan has launched a Self Reliance Programme as part of a National Agenda to achieve economic independence. As part of the programme a Medium-Term Export Development Strategy has been formulated which aims to improve export incentives, implement an export incentives modernization plan and strengthen institutional support mechanisms. The trade deficit at the close of the 1997–1998 financial year was expected to be US$1.53 billion. The Trade Policy initiatives planned for 1998–1999 aimed to bring down the trade deficit to about zero by 30 June 1999 (Dar, 1998).

Alongside changes in trade, investment and fiscal policy, which influence the range of encouragements that are provided for tourism development in Pakistan, the Pakistani government has also sought to corporatize or privatize many government assets in order to encourage foreign investment and the development of the private sector while reducing debt levels. A Privatization Commission is actively seeking to divest state assets while efforts to reduce government ownership is concentrated in such tourism-relevant areas as transport. For example, a number of airlines (Shaheen Airlines, Bhoja Air and Aero Asia) have commenced operation since the government sought to encourage private-sector involvement in the early 1990s. Nevertheless, though Pakistan International Airlines serves Pakistan well on the international front, Pakistan's efforts to open up its economy are also shared by the former East Pakistan, Bangladesh, which became an independent state in 1971.

Like India, the tourism industry in Pakistan is labour intensive in an economy where estimates of up to 25 per cent of the working population are underemployed. According to Atta (n.d.), in 1989 tourism was estimated to employ 1.5 per cent of the population and generate 430 000 jobs. The government estimates for employment generation in tourism by the National Tourism Policy, Sport and Tourism Division in 1990 forecast a growth in employment from 478 000 jobs in 1990 to 943 000 in 1998 and 1.16 million

in the year 2000. According to Hussein (1996) these optimistic estimates are based on a number of assumptions in relation to state privatization policy, improved levels of investment and a greater liberalization of the economy.

The organization and management of tourism in Pakistan

The government of Pakistan has had a long-standing interest in tourism since the establishment of a Master Plan for Tourism in 1965; in 1972, a Ministry for Culture, Sports and Tourism was created to promote and direct the development of the industry. An early study by Shaikh (1976) outlined the development of tourism in Pakistan since the 1960s and the structure which evolved to manage and develop it. The Ministry's role is to formulate policy and development plans. In a highly critical paper, Richter (1984) documented the catalytic effect that President Zia's coup in 1977 and subsequent rule had on the tourism industry. In 1990, a National Policy was launched to try and revitalize an ailing industry with incentives in line with the growing deregulation of the Pakistan economy. A range of investment incentives have been offered, with the result that tourism is now officially accorded 'industry' status, implying that it receives the same treatment as other industrial projects. The government has also waived work permit restrictions on employing foreign workers as managers and in the technical area. Foreign exchange controls have been lifted for inward investment in tourism. A Regional Development Finance Corporation has been established by the government to extend loan facilities for tourism projects in priority destinations. A number of tourist transport measures have also been undertaken, including: official granting of licences to operate charter flights to Islamabad, Lahore and Karachi on a point-to-point basis; a helicopter charter service from Lahore to any destination in Pakistan; private tour operators are able to charter special excursion trains; and steam locomotive services are offered at concessional rates to tourists. A number of the visa formalities have also been relaxed (Hussein, 1996), with 30-day visas issued at the airport for tourists with a return ticket and adequate foreign exchange.

The main tourism development agency, run by the state, is the Pakistan Tourism Development Corporation (PTDC) with the government as the main shareholder (United Nations Development Programme (UNDP), 1975). It seeks to promote domestic and international tourism and to attract overseas investors. Although financial restrictions mean that the PTDC does not have overseas marketing offices, it uses agents in the UK, Italy, Denmark, Japan, New York and Vancouver (Hussein, 1996). Within Pakistan, the PTDC operates seventeen information centres, while a subsidiary company – Pakistan Tours Limited – which offers package tours for domestic and international tourists. Attracting overseas investment remains one of the key challenges for the PTDC to enable the industry to reach its real potential.

Domestic and international tourism patterns

The scale of domestic tourism is reflected in the 45.14 million tourists who travelled in Pakistan in 1994, an increase of over 10 million domestic tourists in ten years (Table 14.7). Domestic

Table 14.7 *Domestic tourists in Pakistan 1988–1989 to 1997–1998*

Year	Domestic tourists (000s)	% annual change
1988–1989	33 859	–
1989–1990	35 044	3.5
1990–1991	36 270	3.5
1991–1992	37 540	3.5
1992–1993	38 854	3.5
1993–1994	40 214	3.5
1994–1995	41 621	3.5
1995–1996	42 795	2.9
1996–1997	43 993	2.8
1997–1998	45 141	2.6

Source: modified from Ministry of Culture, Sports, Tourism and Youth Affairs, 1998.

Table 14.8 *Foreign tourist arrivals in Pakistan 1988–1997*

Year	Foreign tourist arrivals (000s)	% annual change
1988	460.1	–
1989	494.6	7.5
1990	423.8	–14.3
1991	438.0	3.5
1992	352.1	–19.6
1993	379.2	7.7
1994	454.3	19.8
1995	378.4	–17.7
1996	368.7	–2.6
1997	374.8	1.2

Source: modified from Ministry of Culture, Sports, Tourism and Youth Affairs, 1998.

tourism in Pakistan is spatially concentrated in the northern valleys in the winter season, owing to the attractive climatic conditions and the scenery. Yet a striking feature of these patterns are the gender imbalance: the majority of domestic tourists are male and under forty years of age, of whom the majority travel by road and rail, with less than 5 per cent travelling by air (Hussein, 1996). The primary motivation for domestic travel is visiting friends, as well as business, sightseeing and religious reasons (Ministry of Culture, Sports, Tourism and Youth Affairs, 1998).

There has been considerable fluctuation in foreign tourist arrivals in recent years (Table 14.8), while a significant change has also occurred in the visitor mix. In the late 1980s, almost 50 per cent of arrivals were from India to visit friends and relatives and to pursue religious tourism. Yet since the early 1990s the proportion of South Asian tourists has declined substantially. These have been replaced by European tourists, primarily from the UK. In 1997 there were 84 100 arrivals from the UK (a dramatic fall from the 156 000 arrivals in 1994), with a market share of 22.4 per cent compared with 36 per cent in 1993 and 48 per cent in 1994. India is the second most important with 54 500 arrivals (14.5 per cent), USA (12.2 per cent), Afghanistan (6 per cent), Japan (3 per cent) and Germany (3 per cent). A significant proportion of the visitor population is of Pakistani origin who visit friends and relatives, therefore a significant component is based upon ethnic tourism (see Kang, 1998, for a more detailed discussion). This concept of ethnic tourism – returning to visit friends and relatives – has attracted comparatively little attention in the tourism literature despite its relationship with return migration and patterns of immigration, although its significance has been observed in patterns of tourist travel within the Pacific Islands (Hall and Page, 1996; Page, 1996). Hussein (1996) estimated that less than 100 000 visitors per year are of non-Pakistani origin.

International tourists largely arrive by air despite the land entry points into Pakistan. For example, the Khyber Pass, which is the main point of entry from Afghanistan, has been closed to tourist traffic because of civil war in Afghanistan, although a few tourists enter from Iran via the Nokundi entry point. The most important land crossing is at Wagah, near to Lahore for tourists entering from India. Yet political disturbances in the Indian state of Punjab have meant a sharp decline in crossings. The most scenic entry point is the Khunejrab Pass which is the land crossing point with China, open on a seasonal basis and is weather contingent. One of the greatest problems for developing international tourism in Pakistan, particularly with respect to intraregional travel in South Asia, is the poor border access that exists. Wagha is the only land border open between Pakistan and India (on the Lahore–Amritsar route), along with a limited train service between Lahore, Amritsar and New Delhi, while the border access to China, the Khunjerab Pass, is only open from 1 May to 31 October for groups and to 15 November for individual tourists (Government of Pakistan, 1998). As a result, land crossings declined from 43 per cent of arrivals in 1975 to 11 per cent in 1994, with air arrivals accounting for 88.5 per cent (Hussein, 1996), although this figure has since dropped slightly to 83.5 per cent in 1997 (Ministry of Culture, Sports, Tourism and Youth Affairs, 1998). The main gateway – Karachi – has

Figure 14.3 *Distribution of international visitors in 1985*

Figure 14.4 *Distribution of international visitors in 1994*

also seen a decline in terms of its importance as an entry point: 76.8 per cent of arrivals here in 1985 compared with 60.1 per cent in 1994. This is because the airports at Islamabad, Lahore, Peshawar and Quetta have led to a greater geographical dispersal of arrivals.

Of the international visitors to Pakistan in 1997, 78 per cent were male and over 50 per cent were less than forty years of age (Ministry of Culture, Sports, Tourism and Youth Affairs, 1998). The profile of international visitors has also changed significantly since 1985: in 1985, businessmen were the most important source of arrivals (18.8 per cent); in 1994, this had changed to professional (23.7 per cent) followed by housewives, students and businessmen (Hussein, 1996). Karachi is the dominant visitor destination and Figures 14.3 and 14.4 indicate the spatial pattern of visitation by international visitors during the period 1985–1994. What is apparent from the distribution of places visited is the dominance of urban tourism (Page, 1995), largely explained in terms of the dominance of visiting friends and relatives and for business and religious trips. Karachi, Lahore, Islamabad/Rawalpindi and Peshawar attracted 78 per cent of visitors, a function of the urban centres as primary and secondary gateway cities. These cities are also the country's main population centres. Mumtaz and Mitha (1996) observe that 32 per cent of Pakistan's population is urbanized and located in: Karachi (9 million); Lahore (6 million); Rawalpindi (2.9 million); Quetta (687 000) and Islamabad (613 000). Thus, the tourist pattern of visiting friends and relatives closely follows the urban pattern. These highly visited places also reflect the prevailing pattern of land-based transportation by road and rail and the existing patterns of air travel. The length of stay for overseas visitors is only 1.2 nights in serviced accommodation, a drop from 1.8 nights in 1987.

Tourist travel in Pakistan

Transportation for tourism is based on a well-connected international air service, with sixty airlines serving the country. The state airline, Pakistan International Airlines (PIA), is the main carrier, although a number of new domestic airlines have been licensed to operate on domestic routes using wet-lease arrangements (see Page, 1999, for more detail on these arrangements) with Central Asian republics. Since few of the airline staff speak urdu, Hussein (1996) reports major teething problems with the operations of domestic services which leaves PIA the main carrier. PIA is a long-established international and domestic carrier: it was launched in 1954 and an early Karachi–London service was begun in 1955. In 1959, the carrier was the first Asian airline to operate a jet service (a Boeing 707-320) on the London route through a leasing arrangement with PanAm. In 1998, PIA served forty-six countries and ninety cities, comprising a diverse range of markets for international tourist travel to and from Pakistan. In 1995–1996, PIA also introduced helicopter services from Islamabad, Abbottabad, Lahore and Sialkot to promote tourism, particularly scenic flights which are a lucrative market segment (Page, 1999). PIA also launched its website in the same year (http://www.piac.com). In terms of domestic airline services, PIA connects thirty-six places within Pakistan and investment in new airports has facilitated the growth of domestic and international air travel (Hussein, 1996). Domestic flights are among the cheapest in the world, estimated at PRs6 per km (Hussein, 1996), and are cheaper than rail or bus travel in some cases. While trunk routes in Pakistan (e.g. Karachi to Lahore) are profit making for PIA, cross-subsidization of feeder routes is costly, particularly as operating costs are high in Northern Pakistan owing to the unpredictable weather conditions, diversions and cancellations. Despite these costs, the government continues to subsidize PIA and air travel in Pakistan. In contrast, rail travel provides more direct access to many of the key tourist attractions with many railway lines routed alongside riverways which are low-cost and which have nostalgic appeal for some travellers with steam locomotives still operating on some sections. Special interest rail tours are also proving popular for European and Australian visitors.

Future prospects for tourism in Pakistan

The development of special interest tourism in Pakistan (e.g. trekking and mountaineering) has been an area of growth although, with limited resources from the government, tourism seems set to remain focused on the existing urban destinations. This is reflected in the growing presence of international hotel chains in the principal tourist cities, although the greatest need according to Hussein (1996) is for additional mid-range hotels in the northern and southern areas to tap the full tourism potential. While the government has focused on the private sector, seizing the opportunities through the provision of incentives (domestic and overseas investors), the state is playing a complementary role in providing infrastructure to assist in the natural development of the country's tourism industry. However, Richter's (1984: p. 12) comments still hold true in 1999:

> If Pakistan has done few things very well in terms of tourism development, it at least has not done much damage. Social costs have been minimal. The tourist who comes to Pakistan comes on Pakistan's terms. If tourist arrivals have not kept pace with projections it may be just as well. Rapid tourism influx could threaten the security of cultural treasures and incur severe social and environmental costs. Pakistan today lacks the political and administrative organization to monitor tourism development successfully.

Bangladesh

Bangladesh is a country of over 125 million people with a land area of 143 988 km². Of that land area, 1.4 million ha are inland water bodies: 10 per cent of the country is water. Two-thirds of the country is cultivated as arable land and

10 per cent of the land area is still forested while 90 per cent comprises alluvial plains less than 10 m above sea level. Bangladesh, formerly Bengal and East Pakistan (Spate and Learmonth, 1954; Stamp, 1957) prior to independence in 1971, is situated on the Bay of Bengal. It is one of the world's poorest, most densely populated and least developed nations (UNDP, 1998). It has a range of major environmental problems related to global rises in sea level, the monsoon season which exacerbates many of the water-related problems such as flooding (Thompson and Parvin, 1996), as well as the loss of forest and natural vegetation cover through population pressure on a slender resource base. As Alauddin and Tisdell (1998) argue, many of the country's environmental problems are interdependent, meaning that they are closely related to problems with water resources (i.e. flooding and shortages in the dry season). Alauddin and Tisdell (1998: pp. 81–82) aptly summarize the nature of the delicate physical environmental–human balance and impact of natural disasters in that:

> A large number of natural environmental problems such as floods, droughts and cyclones befall Bangladesh with monotonous regularity. To a considerable extent economic growth has magnified the effect of such natural disasters and has exacerbated environmental problems in rural Bangladesh. This can in the main be attributed both to economic developments and population growth in Bangladesh. It is also due to externalities or spillovers from economic developments and change in neighbouring countries such as India and Nepal. These have resulted in intensification of land- and water-use. This phenomenon in turn has entailed adverse environmental effects (Alauddin and Tisdell, 1998: p. 192).

Annual GDP growth has averaged over 4 per cent per year in recent years, although this is starting from a very low base and with a 1996 official unemployment rate of over 35 per cent. The economy is primarily agricultural, with the cultivation of rice being the most important activity in the economy. In fact Alauddin and Tisdell (1998: p. 34) argue that:

> A guiding principle of Bangladesh in pursuing economic development has been to attain self-sufficiency in grain supplies. But the 'one-eyed' pursuit of this policy has been economically detrimental to Bangladesh because adequate account had not been taken of spillovers or opportunity costs from water management/development projects and from other methods to improve grain production.

However, Bangladesh is plagued by the images and reality of having suffered a series of natural disasters from floods and cyclones which have severely curtailed economic development and which have affected investor confidence in the country. This includes floods in 1998 which inundated two-thirds of Bangladesh and left some 1200 people dead and 30 million homeless. Such is the economic impact of the floods that the World Bank have estimated that GDP growth in the 1999 financial year could decline to 3.3 per cent from the estimated 5.6 per cent in the 1998 financial year (Ahmed, 1998).

Coupled with natural disasters has been various periods of political instability, from the gaining of independence from Pakistan in the early 1970s, military rule in the 1980s, an independence movement in the Chittagong Hill Tracts which has now been settled through the signing of a Peace Accord and strikes and political confrontation between the two major political parties in the mid-1990s (World Bank, 1996; Zafarullah, 1996). Nevertheless, the Awami League government, which assumed power in mid-1996, has made some ground in improving the economy and has been particularly active in trying to encourage foreign investment in oil and gas development and in manufacturing and heavy industries. For example, in the 1998/1999 budget, the government paid special attention to factors such as export prospects, national priorities, backward linkage and employment generation potential in the development of special fiscal incentives for computer software and data processing, agro-based industries, solar power,

plastic and plastic products, leather, textile and ready-made garment industries (Kibria, 1998).

Tourism issues in Bangladesh come under the auspices of the Ministry of Civil Aviation and Tourism which is a small department in terms of its range of responsibilities and revenues. In 1997/1998 the department had a budget of 68.83 million takka as opposed to 57.23 million takka in the previous financial year. This figure represents only a minute fraction of the total budget outlay for 1997/1998 of 27 434.42 million takka. In contrast, the Roads and Railway Division had a budget of 1670.99 crore of takka (Ministry of Finance, 1997).

Tourist arrivals in Bangladesh declined over the period 1985–1992, from 146 000 to 110 000. However, the situation improved in 1993 with 127 000 arrivals, rising to 140 000 in 1994. In 1994, Bangladesh received 3.55 per cent of South Asia's total tourist arrivals. In 1995 Bangladesh received 156 231 foreign tourists bringing in over Tk.95 million in foreign exchange. According to the World Tourism Organization, tourists receipts have also fluctuated in Bangladesh from US$11 million in 1990 to US$8 million in 1992 to US$19 million in 1994. The main source areas for overseas visitors in the 1990s were: Japan, India, Pakistan, Nepal, Hong Kong, South Korea, the UK, Canada, France, Singapore and Australia (Bangladesh Parjatan Corporation, 1992). The majority (45 per cent) were on business, 20 per cent were visiting for pleasure and occupancy rates in hotels/guest houses was 45 per cent. The majority of international visitors to the country are business travellers working with private companies, aid agencies and other international organizations such as the United Nations and World Bank. In fact Inskeep (1994) argues that arrivals fluctuate according to the occurrence and severity of natural disasters. Tisdell (1997) advances the bureaucracy/inadequate infrastructure argument to explain the limited development of tourism in Bangladesh. This posits that institutional factors (e.g. those associated with the tourism bureaucracy in the country) prefer to use the lack of adequate infrastructure as the main explanation of poor performance.

For example, Inskeep (1994) estimated that in 1990 Bangladesh had only 3000 hotel rooms. However, a number of significant factors also affect its image as a tourist destination. Among these are the poor public image of the country's health and disease risks for tourist travel (Clift and Page, 1996). This is compounded by the occurrence of humid monsoon conditions during the main northern hemisphere holiday season, meaning that operational costs for tourism rise owing to the effective use of infrastructure and facilities for only 6–8 months per year. A visit to the Bangladesh Parjatan Corporation tourism website (http://bangla.org/tour) provides a detailed insight into the types of tourism being promoted (nature-based tourism, cultural and archaeology-based tourism) and detailed itineraries can be pre-planned by visiting the website (or   theguide@bangla.net)   which   provides detailed information. The Bangladesh Parjatan Corporation are keen to emphasize the availability of luxury tourism facilities despite the negative media images of the region owing to the floods and perceived health risks.

Nevertheless, despite many negative images associated with the country in the Western media, Bangladesh does have a number of cultural features which are attracting interest from heritage tourists, including a wealth of Buddhist and Muslim historical sites. The Bangladeshi government has also invested in tourism resorts and facilities in order to attract both international visitors and the developing Bangladesh middle class. Cox's Bazar, 152 km south of Chittagong, has the world's longest unbroken sandy beach of some 120 km. The government has developed resorts at Sonadia Island, 7 km from Cox's Bazar, and Teknaf, at the southernmost tip of Bangladesh, 85 km away from Cox's Bazar. In the northeast of the country the hill area used for tea growing is also attracting domestic and international visitors (Prime Minister's Office, 1998).

Within Bangladesh, internal transport remains a constraint on the rapid development of tourism. The country is served by two international airports at Dhakka and Chittagong by the

national carrier – Biman – and a range of other international carriers. Biman serves ten regional airports with internal flights. But travel to the west of Dhakka by rail is limited by ferry crossings and differing railway gauges as well as circuitous routings. Road travel by local bus is a local attraction owing to overcrowding, although there is a marked absence of hire cars. Land-crossings, which facilitate intraregional travel from India, are at Benopol–Haridispur (the land route from Calcutta) and at Chilihari–Haldibari (on the Darjeeling land route) and Tamabil–Dawki (on the Shilong land route). A number of unofficial crossings have also been in existence at Hili–Balugarat, Godagari–Lalgola and several other border crossing points (http://www.lonelyplanet.com.au/dest/ind/ban.htm). In the case of Myanmar, overland routes have been closed since the 1950s.

Tourism development and planning

Bangladesh's tourism planning and development plan was prepared in 1988 by the World Tourism Organization (UNDP and WTO, 1988) for the government national tourism organization – The Bangladesh Parjatan Corporation – which is a semi-autonomous body responsible for the regulation, marketing and some commercial aspects of tourism operations in Bangladesh. The Master Plan evaluated the markets for tourism, services available and infrastructure. The plan established a visitor target of 300 000 international arrivals, largely from the coterminous neighbouring states (e.g. India), of whom two-thirds are expected to be business-related. The plan also envisaged a significant growth in international tourism. According to Inskeep (1994), the Master Plan envisaged the following benefits accruing from tourism development in Bangladesh: increased balance payments from foreign exchange earnings, increased income for employees in tourism, increased employment opportunities in tourism as a labour-intensive industry, increased interest in conservation and additional investment in airport infrastructure.

Inskeep (1994) outlined the following objectives in the Master Plan which were to pursue:

- the planned growth of international and domestic tourism;
- marketing of selected international markets;
- the establishment of zones of tourism development for the purposes of clustering investment and tourism development in areas of potential;
- the conservation of the natural wildlife and cultural heritage;
- the development of an attractive tourism environment with the lifting of travel restrictions for inbound tourists;
- the promotion of youth culture and sport;
- the strengthening of the domestic tourism sector to reduce leakage from the economy by greater import substitution;
- the strengthening and improvement of the transportation sector for tourism (after Inskeep, 1994: p. 111).

As a result of the Master Plan, six tourism zones were established based on the areas of potential for development where investment and activities could be clustered to maximize the economic benefits from development. Naturally, Dhaka acts as an urban tourism gateway to the country. The Master Plan devised the zones with a themed tourism development strategy. For example, river tourism is developed as a theme to capitalize on the nation's landscape, which is dominated by the major rivers of the Jamuna, the Padma and the Meghna. Village tourism complements this theme based on the marine environment, where local benefits accrue to villages near to Dhaka promoting day trips for international visitors. The country's abundant cultural heritage, dating back 2000 years and, in more recent times, with a Moghul influence and a colonial theme from British rule, is seen as having an educational value. The conservation of these sites are seen as paramount and achievable through tourism development. Lastly, forested areas and the wildlife (see Shackley, 1996, for a discussion of wildlife tourism) of the

country are also seen as having tourism value. Tourism is seen as the underlying justification for a preservation strategy for the country's main wildlife and forested areas, particularly the endangered Bengal Tigers.

A fundamental requirement for the country's tourism strategy is the upgrading of the tourism product, particularly in the accommodation sector. Other improvements are also required in the handicraft, speciality shopping, nightlife and urban environment as well as in relation to sports. In fact, a new area of tourism development is the hosting of major events. Despite some initial concerns over health problems arising from the major floods earlier in 1998, Bangladesh hosted a cricket mini-World Cup in Dhaka in late October which included teams from Australia, England, India, New Zealand, Pakistan, South Africa, Sri Lanka, the West Indies and Zimbabwe. A cricketing-mad nation, the tournament was being used to both encourage the game and to improve the image of Dhaka and Bangladesh overseas.

The Master Plan also outlined methods for strengthening the organizational framework for tourism, with the establishment of a tourism development corporation, similar to that in India. This was viewed as absorbing the investment arm of the Bangladesh Pajatan Corporation. For the implementation of the structure plan, illegal tourism developments need to be controlled and prevented while the natural environment is conserved, together with historical and cultural artefacts. This requires close coordination and plans to be formulated in each tourism development zone, with the provision of appropriate development sites for the private sector. To reduce the leakage of economic benefits, strengthening of links between the agricultural sector and the tourism industry is advocated, as has occurred in other countries such as Indonesia. In terms of marketing, domestic and South Asian promotion was advocated until further product improvements have been made to encourage the marketing of more lucrative international markets. Ultimately, Bangladesh could capitalize on its location and potential role as a stop-over location en route to other destinations in South Asia. However, this will require a greater degree of cooperation among South Asian destinations and ultimately 'the marketing strategy could also include the need to portray a favourable but realistic image of the country. Image building is especially important in Bangladesh because of the international publicity that has taken place about the natural disasters which periodically occur in the country' (Inskeep, 1994: p. 115).

As with other countries in the region, Bangladesh has been seeking to encourage foreign investment. In order to do this substantial changes have been made to import controls and tariff levels (Wahid and Weis, 1996). Export production has been encouraged through the development of Export Processing Zones (EPZs). Firms in an EPZ can import capital and raw materials free of duty, retain foreign currency earnings, employ non-unionized labour and enjoy exemption from income tax for ten years. Although major government interest lies in attracting investment in manufacturing, heavy industry and other labour-intensive fields, tourism is recognized as an area in which foreign investment would be welcome (see Bangladesh Board of Investment, 1998). Nevertheless, as with Pakistan, Bangladesh has considerable problems in terms of foreign debt, unemployment and political instability. To facilitate economic growth, Quibria (1997) examines the policy context and the policy reforms introduced by the government to encourage a greater degree of competition in the economy.

Case study: special interest tourism in Bangladesh – tourism in the Sunderbans National Park

A recent study by Tisdell (1997) examined tourism in the Sunderbans region. This is a national park which borders India and Bangladesh on the Brahmaputra–Ganges river system which covers a large area of southwest Bangladesh (Spate and Learmonth, 1954; Rashid, 1991) and, in India, the southeastern region of

the state of West Bengal. On the Bangladesh side of the Sunderbans, the area is low-lying, largely unsuitable for agriculture and comprising mangrove swamp and stretches 80 km inland from the coast. The essential character of the area is embodied in the following entry:

The Sunderbans is a cluster of islands with an approximate area of 38,500sq. km. forming the largest block of littoral forests. It's beauty lies in its unique natural surrounding. Thousands of meandering streams, creeks, rivers and fresh estuaries have enhanced its charm. Sunderbans meaning beautiful forest is the natural habitat of the world famous Royal Bengal tiger, spotted deer, crocodiles, jungle fowl, wild boar, lizards, rhesus monkey and an innumerable variety of beautiful birds. Migratory flock of Siberian ducks flying over thousands of sail boats loaded with timber, golpatta (round-leafed, fuel wood, honey, shell and fish) further add to the serene natural beauty of the Sunderbans (Bangladesh Parjatan Corporation, website entry, www.bangla.org).

Tisdell (1997) provides a comparative analysis of the Indian and Bangladesh Sunderbans region and argues that the facilities for tourism in the Sunderbans are poorly developed, with the state organization – Bangladesh Parajatan Corporation – operating tours. To visit the area, tourists (90 per cent of whom are from overseas) require a permit from the Forestry Department. In 1991, some 210 permits were issued to overseas tourists, this increased to 291 in 1992. In contrast, 4595 permits were issued to domestic tourists. One of the reasons for low levels of visitation, according to Tisdell (1997), is the prevalence of disease in the region, mentioned on Parjatan Corporation literature (malaria, cholera and other tropical disease), which is an indication of the inhospitable nature of the terrain. Tisdell (1997) outlines a number of the features of tourism in the Sunderbans including: seasonality, where the season operates from September through to mid-March, avoiding the monsoon season; the inaccessibility of the Sunderbans from Dhaka; the local economic benefits of tourism, which are extremely limited owing to poor commercialization; infrastructure development projects by the tourism authority to promote greater access and package tourism at a greater volume.

Tisdell (1997) observes that the tourism product in the Sunderbans is uneconomic compared with the product in the Indian sector which is cheaper to visit and more accessible. The basic problem for tourists is that the noise of their activity prevents wildlife viewing in tropical forested areas such as the Sunderbans. Also, conflicts between conservation and the local community continue to exist with people hunting tigers illegally. Tisdell (1997) also emphasizes the limited economic benefits which currently accrue to the local population, although the nearest major town – Khulna – does benefit from tourism. Therefore, this type of ecotourism development, which is in its infancy, poses numerous planning problems which need to be addressed for the local tourism economy and for sustainable development in an ecosystem that could be easily degraded through heavy tourist use of key sites, if future expansion is not carefully managed.

Prospects for tourism in South Asia

South Asia is facing increasing competition in tourism in a global context. The immediate competition between the nations in South Asia and the added range and choice of destinations in Southeast Asia for tourist travel, pose specific challenges for the industry and also for government which assumes control for marketing and management. It is somewhat ironic that the analysis of Pakistan's future market potential by Shaikh (1976) is still as relevant twelve years after it was written: that is that the nation (and many of the other South Asian countries) are not gaining their rightful share of international arrivals. Yet there are many obvious factors which account for the often erratic patterns of tourist arrivals in the region: the absence of

political stability and confidence among volatile markets to visit destinations which have faced political turmoil, civil war and armed insurrections. Tourism cannot thrive unless there is regional political stability. There is also a lack of political cooperation between the neighbouring governments to facilitate a free flow of visitors across international borders with the minimum of restrictions. Whilst there is not space within this review to examine the factors acting against a further growth in arrivals and a lack of economic benefits to local areas, Ragaraman (1998) highlighted a fundamental issue common to many of the South Asian destinations: improved infrastructure in the gateway cities will not only improve the carrying capacity, but also enhance the image of the cities as destinations, with an investment in facilities which are able to yield wider economic benefits for the region in which tourism is based. There is also a need to upgrade environmental conditions which are described in the case of Dhaka by Hasan and Mulamsottil (1994).

The enormous scale of domestic tourism in the South Asian region is a feature often neglected in many of the published studies, although it is evident that it remains poorly commercialized and generates only limited economic benefits for the host areas. One theme which is common to each country pursuing tourism development in South Asia is the great potential tourism has to create employment owing to its labour-intensive nature. However, research and greater attention by policy makers and investors needs to be placed on generating tangible economic benefits for local people, particularly through the indirect benefits which visitor spending can yield.

It is also evident that a growing fashion for travel is permeating the region, reflected in the discovery of domestic travel despite the gender-specific nature in Islamic countries of much of it. For governments, the ability to fully understand what tourism is and the needs and demands it places on the environment and population seem to be issues which cannot be fully understood without overseas knowledge. All too often, the emphasis is on developing the tourism capability of the region, destination or sector without a full appreciation of the wider manpower requirements and the expectations of high spending tourists. There is no doubt that South Asia has many jewels to be discovered and developed, but the current concerns with the state of the environment in each country does not auger well for tourism. After all, tourism is one further human activity that can damage the environment if it is not managed correctly and critical thresholds established. Although many countries have development plans for tourism, effective environmental assessment and management systems seem to be far from the objectives of sustainable development. As Karim (1999) shows, traffic pollution in urban centres like Dhaka violate national and international standards which also impinge upon the development of urban tourism in developing countries. Perhaps one of the saving graces for many of the destinations relying on international visitors may be the emphasis on ecotourism products and experiences and high-spending, low-volume/low-impact tourism. Yet even studies of fragile and sensitive mountain environments (Singh, 1989) highlight the development dilemmas now facing areas wishing to pursue tourism as a viable economic business: to reach viability, increased numbers have to be nurtured, even though the carrying capacity of the area and region may be exceeded at peak times.

References

Ahmed, I., 'Expenditures to soar, reveals WB study on 1998 flood impact', *The Daily Star*, 2, no. 96, 16 November 1998.

Ahuja, S. and Sarna, S. (eds), *Tourism in India: A Perspective to 1990*, The Institute of Economic and Market Research, New Dehli, 1977.

Alauddin, M. and Tisdell, C., *The Environment and Economic Development in South Asia: An Overview Concentrating on Bangladesh*, Macmillan. Basingstoke, 1998.

AMEX and PATA, *Gearing up for Growth II: A Study of Human Resources Issues in Small to Medium Sized Enterprises in Asia-Pacific Travel and Tourism*, AMEX–PATA, Honolulu, 1994.

Atta, F., *Environment and Tourism in Pakistan*, National Conservation Strategy, Karachi, n.d.

Bangladesh Board of Investment, *Bangladesh Board of Investment*, Bangladesh Board of Investment, Dhaka (http://services.toolnet.org/boi/, accessed 15 November 1998) 1998.

Bangladesh Parjatan Corporation, *General Introduction to Tourism in the Region*, Bangladesh Parjatan Corporation, Dhaka, 1992.

Bull, A., *The Economics of Travel and Tourism*, Longman, Harlow, 1991.

Chaudhary, M., India's tourism – a paradoxical product, *Tourism Management* 17(8), 1996, pp. 616–619.

Clift, S. and Page, S.J. (eds), *Health and the International Tourist*, Routledge, London, 1996.

Dar, M.I., *Speech on Trade Policy by Mr. Muhammad Ishaq Dar, Minister for Commerce*, 22 June 1998 (http://www.epb.gov.pk/sapta.htm, accessed 19 November 1998).

Government of India, Ministry of Information and Broadcasting, *India 1993: A Reference Annual*, Research and Reference Provision, 1994.

Government of Pakistan, *Travel Hints*, Government of Pakistan (http://pak.gov.pk/govt/tourism/trvl info.htm, accessed 19 November 1998) 1998.

Grabowski, P. and Chatterjee, S., 'The indian plague scare of 1994', in S. Clift and P. Grabowski (eds), *Tourism and Health: Risks, Research and Responses*, Cassell, London, 1997, pp. 80–96.

Hall, C.M., *Tourism in the Pacific Rim: Development, Impacts and Planning*, Addison Wesley Longman, Melbourne, 1997.

Hall, C.M. and Page, S.J. (eds), *Tourism in the Pacific: Issues and Cases*, International Thomson Business Publishing, London, 1996.

Hasan, S. and Mulamsottil, G., 'Environmental problems of Dhaka city', *Cities* 1(3), 1994, pp. 195–200.

Hussein, M., Pakistan, *International Tourism Report* 3, 1996, pp. 43–64.

Inskeep, E., *National and Regional Tourism Planning: Methodologies and Case Studies*, Routledge, London, 1994.

Islam, N., 'City study of Dhaka' in J. Stubbs and G. Clarke (eds), *Megacity Management in the Asia Pacific Region, Volume 1*, Asian Development Bank, Manila, 1996, pp. 39–94.

Kang, S., Tourism, Ethnicity and Migration, Research Report submitted in partial fulfilment of the Master of Business Studies, Massey University at Albany, Auckland, 1998.

Karim, M., 'Traffic pollution inventories and modelling in metropolitan Dhaka, Bangladesh', *Transportation Research D* **4**, 1999, pp. 291–312.

Kashyap, S. (ed.), *Tourism Policy of Government of India*, Tata McGraw Hill, New Dehli, 1990.

Kaur, J., *Himalayan Pilgrimage and the New Tourism*, Himalayan Books, New Delhi, 1985.

Kibria, A.M.S., *Annual Budget 1998–99 Budget Speech by Shah A.M.S. Kibria, Finance Minister, Second Part, Fiscal Measures*, Ministry of Finance, Dhaka (http://www.bangladeshonline.com/gob/bgt99sp.htm, accessed 15 November 1998) 1998.

Kumar, M., *Tourism Today – An Indian Perspective*, Kanishka, Dehli, 1992.

Ministry of Culture, Sports, Tourism and Youth Affairs, *Tourism Growth in Pakistan 1997*, Planning, Development & Research, Statistics Section, Ministry of Culture, Sports, Tourism and Youth Affairs, Government of Pakistan, Islamabad, 1998.

Ministry of Finance, *Annual Budget 1997–98*, Ministry of Finance, Finance Division, Government of the People's Republic of Bangladesh, Dhaka (http://www.bangladeshonline.com/gob/bgt98.htm, accessed 15 November 1998) 1997.

Ministry of Tourism, *National Tourism Policy*, Ministry of Tourism, Islamabad, 1993.

Mumtaz, K. and Mitha, Y., *Pakistan: Tradition and Change*, Oxfam, Oxford, 1996.

Page, S.J., *Urban Tourism*, Routledge, London, 1995.

Page, S.J., Pacific Islands, *International Tourism Report*, 1996.

Page, S.J., *Transport and Tourism*, Addison Wesley Longman, Harlow, 1999.

Prime Minister's Office, *Bangladesh Profile*, Prime Minister's Office Press Wing, Dhaka (http://www.bangladeshonline.com/gob/bang_int.htm, accessed 15 November 1998) 1998.

Quibria, M. (ed.), *The Bangladesh Economy in Transition*, Oxford University Press, Dehli, 1997.

Ragaraman, K., 'Troubled passage to India', *Tourism Management* 19(6), 1998, pp. 533–544.

Rashid, H., *Geography of Bangladesh*, 2nd edn, The University Press, Dhaka, 1991.

Richter, L., 'The potential and pitfalls of tourism planning in third world nations: The case of Pakistan', *Tourism Recreation Research* 1, 1984, pp. 9–13.

Richter, L., *The Politics of Tourism in Asia*, University of Hawai'i Press, Honolulu, 1989.

Robinson, F. (ed.), *The Cambridge Encyclopedia of India, Pakistan, Bangladesh, Sri Lanka, Nepal, Bhutan and the Maldives*, Cambridge University Press, Cambridge, 1989.

SAARC Chamber of Commerce and Industry Tourism Council, *SAARC Chamber of Commerce and Industry Tourism Council*, SAARC Chamber of Commerce and Industry Tourism Council, Kathmandu (http://south-asia.com/saarc-tourism/index.htm, accessed 3 October 1998) 1997.

Saeed, K., *Economy of Pakistan*, Salam Publications, Lahore, 1995.

Shackley, M., *Wildlife Tourism*, International Thomson Business Publishing, London, 1996.

Shaikh, P., The Development of International Tourism in Pakistan, Thesis presented for the Masters in Professional Studies, Cornell University, Ithaca, NY, 1976.

Singh, G., *A Geography of India*, Atma Ram, Dehli, 1976.

Singh, T., *The Kulu Valley: Impact of Tourism Development in the Mountain Areas*, Himalayan Books, New Dehli, 1989.

Spate, K. and Learmonth, A., *India and Pakistan: A General and Regional Geography*, Methuen, London, 1954.

Stamp, D., *India, Pakistan, Ceylon and Burma*, Methuen, London, 1957.

Suri, M., 'India', *International Tourism Report* 1, 1996, pp. 21–43.

Thompson, P. and Parvin, S., 'Distributional and social impacts of flood control in Bangladesh', *The Geographical Journal* 162, 1996, pp. 1–13.

Tisdell, C., 'Tourism development in India and Bangladesh: General issues, illustrated by ecotourism in the Sunderbans', *Tourism Recreation Research* 22(1), 1997, pp. 26–33.

United Nations Development Programme, *Tourism in Pakistan*, United Nations, New York, 1975.

United Nations Development Programme, *Human Development Report*, United Nations, New York, 1998.

United Nations Development Programme and World Tourism Organization, *Strategic Master Plan for Tourism in Bangladesh*, World Tourism Organization, Madrid, 1988.

Vaidya, S., *Tourism in SAARC Region: Common Policies for Progress*, Paper presented at SCCI Tourism Council Seminar at Colombo, Sri Lanka, 2–4 September, 1996, (http://south-asia.com/saarc-tourism/srilanka.htm, accessed 3 October 1998) 1996.

Wahid, A. and Weis, C. (eds), *The Economy of Bangladesh*, Praeger, New York, 1996.

World Bank, *Bangladesh: Government That Works – Reforming the Public Sector*, World Bank, Washington, DC, 1996.

World Tourism Organization, 'Tourism growth slows due to Asian financial crisis', *WTO News* March–April 1998a.

World Tourism Organization, 'India hosts South Asian meetings', *WTO News* May–June 1998b.

Zafarullah, H., 'Towards good governance in Bangladesh: External intervention, bureaucratic inertia and political inaction', in M. Alauddin and S. Hasan (eds), *Bangladesh: Economy, People and the Environment*, Economics Conference Monograph Series 1, Department of Economics, University of Queensland, Brisbane, 1996, pp. 145–162.

15

Tourism in India: development, performance and prospects

Tej Vir Singh and Shalini Singh

Introduction

India is a giant on the South Asian scene. Few countries, with the possible exception of China, in this entire region of South and Southeast Asia can match India's rich natural and cultural diversity, history, economy and heritage. One of the core regions of the ancient world civilization, it presents a most fascinating cultural mosaic of Dravadians, Aryans, Greeks, Moguls, Persians, Turkish, Portuguese, French and British that makes for an extraordinarily diverse tourism destination.

While modern tourism in India may be only a half-century old, it has a classic tradition of domestic travel embedded in the Hindu pilgrimages, called *Yatras* (holy travel). This is a unique art of travel evolved by the Hindu missionaries which is regarded as highly organized, systems-based, self-sustained, environment-oriented and community-led (Singh, 1985). Marked with geopiety and reverence for the environment, *Yatra* bears a resemblance to the present-day so-called green tourism or ecotourism. To a Hindu, *Yatra* is a sacrament and a religious compulsion (Kaur, 1985). Hindus are ordained to visit the four

supreme pilgrimage resorts[1] (dhama), situated amidst dramatic scenery in the far-flung corners of this vast country for the good of their souls. National bathing festivals are organized periodically along the shores of holy rivers, especially the Ganga. *Rajas* and *Maharajas* took care to organize travel facilities for all visitors. Indeed, travel accounts of the Chinese travellers of sixth and seventh centuries are full of praise for the country's attractions and visitor facilities. However, with the inroads of mass tourism, particularly after the Second World War, this art of travel is gradually dying out. Modern tourism, unfortunately, has arrived unplanned or poorly planned, resulting in resource degradation and environmental loss.

Development: plans and policies

While hospitality in India is considered close to godliness, the new concept of commercial

---

[1] Badrinath in the higher Himalaya, Dwarika on the western coast of the Arabian Sea, Ramashwarm in the deep south and Puri to the east looking towards the Bay of Bengal.

hospitality was not introduced adequately, despite India's Five Year Plan promises and performances. It was only in the third Five Year Plan (FYP) that the India Tourism Development Corporation (ITDC) was established in 1966 to promote selected destinations and to develop quality infrastructure, particularly in the accommodation sector. During the sixth FYP (1982) an effort was made to frame a tourism policy which aimed to be viable, well defined and capable of being implemented. In 1986, a blueprint – an Action Plan for Tourism was conceived, with well designed travel circuits for an intensive and integrated development of recreation resources using a regional framework. The main objectives of the plan were to

- generate employment opportunities;
- develop domestic tourism with the budget tourist as a focus;
- encourage the conservation of national heritage;
- encourage the diversification of tourist products;
- develop international tourism and increase India's share in world tourism (Department of Tourism (DoT), 1992).

Real headway was made in the seventh FYP (1985–1990) when tourism was accorded the status of an industry which afforded many packages of incentives besides loan facilities from the newly set-up Tourism Finance Corporation of India. Another important event towards the development of tourism was the formation of the National Committee on Tourism (1986) to assess the resource development and its impacts on various environments (ecological and socio-cultural), as well as the drawing up of a long-term tourism development plan. The committee submitted its comprehensive report in 1988 which gave substance to the ambitious eighth FYP (1992–1997); this aimed to quicken the pace of implementation of the National Action Plan. Much emphasis was placed on the need for tourism infrastructure, effective marketing

strategies and training manpower for meeting the plan's targets. Better coordination between states and the Centre (the Indian name for the central or federal government) was envisaged as a key mechanism in achieving tangible results for the Action Plan, particularly given that tourism circuits extended over more than one state. It was also argued that tourism, considered as a national product, should not just be tied to administrative boundaries in attempting to achieve effective and regional socio-economic benefits. In June 1997, state tourism ministers met in Delhi and discussed with the Centre the issue of including tourism on the current list to facilitate legislation to make tourism an effective tool of socio-economic change (*Hindustan Times*, 1997). Indeed, these issues were being discussed in 1998 in terms of the framing of a more meaningful national tourism policy (*Times of India*, 1998).

Planners have also begun to realize that tourism as a multi-dimensional, multi-agency and multi-sectoral activity can hardly be handled by one single development agency, let alone the government. Its sound development is possible on a cooperative basis, involving government (Centre, state, district and local), other public-sector agencies and the private sector, as well as the proactive participation of local people, which necessarily demands a synergistic approach to policy development. Furthermore, in order to achieve sustainable development of tourism and recreation resources, many of which are highly fragile and constitute an important part of the national heritage, there is an urgent need to adopt a sustainable tourism policy which should be economically viable, socially responsible and ecologically sound, respecting the integrity of ecosystems. Unfortunately, India has realized too late to include these objectives in its eighth and ninth FYPs. However, it is encouraging to see that policy-makers at all levels are now discussing ecotourism policy for various types of tourist development. Indeed, many states have drawn up their master plans with a focus on aspects of resource sustainability.

Table 15.1 *International tourist arrivals (000s) and receipts (US$million) 1988–1997*

Years	1988	1989	1990	1991	1992	1993	1994	1995	1996	1997
Arrivals	1591	1736	1707	1678	1868	1765	1886	2124	2288	2374
Annual change (%)	7.21	9.11	–1.67	–1.70	11.32	–5.51	6.86	12.62	7.72	3.76
Receipts	1500	1535	1513	1757	2120	2001	2265	2609	2963	3152
Annual change (%)	4.90	2.33	–1.43	16.13	20.66	–5.61	13.19	15.19	13.57	6.38

Tourism performance

It has been argued that India performs better than her tourism industry (e.g. Singh and Singh, 1996). Given the size and splendour, mosaic of culture, wondrous mountains, bizarre monuments and men, India attracts less than 0.4 per cent of world tourist arrivals and earns only 0.7 per cent of world receipts. Such a situation is not encouraging when compared with the tourism industries of her smaller neighbours – Thailand, Indonesia, Malaysia and Singapore. The majority of India's international tourists are long-haul travellers, e.g. USA, UK, Germany and France, and those on extended stays (longer than 28 days).

Although India has a long history of tourism, product development and marketing has been sluggish and ineffective in a highly competitive market. One significant factor has been that most of the tourism business has been the responsibility of the public sector, which is characterized by unwieldy bureaucracy and red tape. Furthermore, the planning process has not only been piecemeal and ad hoc but the whole process is top-down and bereft of community participation, a feature observed by critics of regional tourism plans for quality tourism in Goa. In addition, there has been insufficient attention given to training and human resource management (Andrews, 1993). All these factors have contributed considerably to the slow growth. Only one out of two tourists travelling to South Asia visit India, but this small traffic has generated a revenue of US$3.1 million, almost 75 per cent of the region's earnings in 1997 (World Tourism Organization (WTO), 1998). Thus, India is the key tourism destination in South Asia attracting 52 per cent of total arrivals in the region. Tourist arrivals grew faster during the second half of the 1990s (Table 15.1), following a series of setbacks in the first half of the decade (1990–1993) owing to depressed economic conditions in major European source markets and the impact of the Gulf War. After 1994 the process of growth resumed, despite the plague epidemic in Surat (Gujrat) which is discussed in Chapter 14.

Europe is the most important long-haul tourist generating region to India (Table 15.2). Over 41 per cent of European tourists are from the UK, many of whom are visiting friends and relatives. The second most important country in continental Europe is Germany followed by France and Italy. The American market is largely dominated by the USA, accounting for three-quarters of total tourist arrivals from America. Canada is the second most important North American market with less than one-third of the total North American arrivals. In Asia, Japan was the most important single generating market with over one-quarter of total tourists to India from East Asia and the Pacific. However, arrivals from Japan in 1997 increased by only 1 per cent over 1996. Within the South Asia Region, Bangladesh dominates, with more than half of tourist flows to India, most being visits to relatives and friends. The main urban tourism destinations are the principal gateways: Delhi (54 per cent), Bombay (46 per cent), Chennai (18 per cent), Agra (17 per cent) and Jaipur (around 14 per cent) (DoT, 1998). According to Bala (1990), about 82 per cent of overseas tourist travel to India is undertaken independently. These independent tourists spend 54 per cent of their total expenditure on accommodation and restaurants and about 25 per cent on shopping.

Table 15.2   *World tourist arrivals in India by main markets 1995–1997*

Origin markets	Number of arrivals			% change	
	1995	1996	1997	1996/1995	1997/1996
UK	334 827	360 686	370 567	7.7	2.7
Bangladesh	318 474	322 355	355 371	1.2	10.2
USA	203 343	228 829	244 239	12.5	6.7
Sri Lanka	114 157	107 351	122 080	−6.0	13.7
Germany	89 040	99 853	104 953	12.1	5.1
Japan	76 042	99 018	99 729	30.2	0.7
France	82 349	93 325	92 449	13.3	−0.9
Canada	63 821	74 031	78 570	16.0	6.1
Malaysia	50 039	53 370	60 401	6.7	13.2
Italy	53 015	49 910	53 854	−5.9	7.9
Singapore	48 632	47 136	52 004	−3.1	10.3
Australia	36 150	48 755	50 647	34.9	3.9
Pakistan	42 981	41 810	45 076	−2.7	7.8
The Netherlands	40 147	40 246	44 843	0.2	11.4
Nepal	34 562	–	43 155	–	–
Switzerland	29 388	34 989	31 717	19.1	−9.4
Spain	24 411	24 419	22 903	0.0	−6.2
South Africa	18 750	19 328	22 218	3.1	15.0
Belgium	18 732	22 160	21 532	18.3	−2.8
Israel	14 806	18 387	20 162	24.2	9.7
United Arab Emirates	19 749	21 401	19 828	8.4	−7.4
Sweden	19 013	21 192	19 772	11.5	−6.7
Kenya	17 389	19 248	18 993	10.7	−1.3
Russian Federation	–	–	18 243	–	–
Thailand	14 462	16 188	16 494	11.9	1.9
Austria	13 114	17 084	16 369	30.3	−4.2
Oman	17 060	17 020	16 185	−0.2	−4.9
Sub-total	1 794 453	1 898 091	2 062 354	5.8	8.7
Total arrivals India	2 123 683	2 287 860	2 374 094	7.7	3.8

Positive factors favouring international tourism to India in 1997 were the continuation of liberalization policies; the development of new products (e.g. Ayurveda health resorts in Kerala and adventure tourism); a more liberal aviation policy on charters and private operators; introduction of fast, air-conditioned trains to tourist centres; research-based, focused marketing strategies; use of information technology and creation of a web site on Indian tourism on the internet; and, finally, the celebration of India's 50 years of independence (WTO, 1998). Despite these initiatives, outbound travel from India of 3.5 million people is still greater than inbound. Nevertheless, India could have improved its performance in inbound tourism, had there been no slowing of industrial growth,

no general elections and more hotel room capacity to meet the demand. India, at present, has approximately 63 000 hotel rooms, although it is estimated that there is demand for 130 000 (DoT, 1998).

Tourism is a major factor in economic development in India: it is the third largest export industry after ready-made garments, gems and jewellery. Hosting 2.37 million foreign tourists in 1997, India earned around US$3 billion, generating an estimated employment of 20 million people, directly and indirectly. Direct employment in tourism was estimated to be 9.1 million in 1996–1997 (Pradhan, 1998). The share of tourism in total employment generation is approximately 2.4 per cent. One of the most significant features was that tourism provided employment opportunities to young people and women, with the latter out-numbering men in tourism and hospitality employment, particularly in the hotel business, travel agencies, handicrafts, cultural activities and airlines (DoT, 1997a).

Domestic tourism

The mainstay of tourism in India is the domestic sector. In 1996 about 141 million domestic tourists were registered in various accommodation establishments (Table 15.3). In 1997 this number reached 160 million, of which 150 million were pilgrim-tourists. This market has, for the most part, remained relatively undeveloped. There is an urgent need to understand the importance of this almost neglected sector. A domestic tourist may not bring foreign currency to the country but, undoubtedly, is responsible for generating employment opportunities, construction activity and new development opportunities in the peripheral regions, besides sustaining the tourism industry during lean periods and fostering national integration. Resorts in the Himalayas, southern plateau, coastal areas and desert regions are burgeoning with tourism activity and so are the many pilgrimage resorts that host thousands of visitors every year. Domestic travel serves to redistribute wealth from one region to the other, as well as provide many socio-cultural benefits. With the emergence of a new urban middle class in India, this market has great potential for domestic tourism development and has been identified as such in the eighth and ninth Five Year Plans. Indeed, India's ageing population, and the growth of the 'organized sector' (civil servants and employees of public- and private-sector companies), consisting of all those who are entitled to paid holidays, illustrates the potential for the future development of domestic tourism.

Domestic tourism constantly poses challenges to decision makers and the industry managers who work with inadequate and often unreliable data on tourist measurement, resource appraisals, environmental impact assessments and environmental audits. Sometimes political compulsions override the planning process, resulting in resource misuse or abuse. For example, negative tourism impacts on the vulnerable Himalayan ecosystems have been reported by Singh and Kaur (1980, 1982), T.V. Singh (1989), S. Singh (1992) and Groetzbach (1996), while community protests and cultural shocks of coastal tourism in peninsular India have been noted in a number of studies (e.g. Albuquerque, 1988; WTO, 1989; Alvares, 1993; Tourism Concern, 1993; Singh and Singh, 1999). No tourism development can ever be sustainable without basic information on the resource base, its degree of tolerance to tourism activities and the state of development, yet, a comprehensive study on India's tourism/recreation resources is still to be undertaken.

Table 15.3 *Domestic tourists in India 1987–1996*

Year	Tourist visits	% change
1987	34 216 649	–
1988	38 337 474	10.1
1989	50 588 850	32.0
1990	63 970 024	26.4
1991	66 670 303	4.2
1992	81 293 841	21.9
1993	86 312 554	6.2
1994	123 371 730	42.9
1995	139 129 130	12.8
1996	141 170 657	1.5

Source: Market Research Division, Government of India, Department of Tourism, 1998.

Research: the key to success

No industry can flourish without the strong back-up of meaningful research. Unfortunately, Indian tourism has paid meagre attention to such matters. The documents and reports submitted from time to time by various tourism committees, including the National Strategy for

Development of Tourism, 1996 (DoT, 1997b), are quite impressive and their content is laudable, but these cannot be considered a substitute for research at macro-, meso- and micro-levels. Marketing and University tourism research has, unfortunately, not been incorporated into the mainstream governmental policy work and decision making for tourism planning, development and marketing. The former, for the most part, lays emphasis upon consumerism, whereas the latter are monodisciplinary and descriptive (S. Singh, 1992). The Indian Institute of Tourism and Travel Management (IITTM) was established by the Indian Ministry of Tourism in 1983 to address this problem but it seems to be in disarray and devotes itself only to middle-level job training (S. Singh, 1997).

India has not been able to build a tourism image that sells: the traditional images of the Maharaja or the Snake no longer charm visitors. Therefore, substantial research is required on destination image at both the national and regional level. Given its continental dimensions, India clearly has a number of diverse and distinct regions that need to be studied for their potential to attract different tourist markets. For example, in the Himalayan region, the sub-regions of Kashmir, Himachal, Uttarakhand and Darjeeling each have their own personality that should be reflected in the composite image of the country. Thus, the Himalayan tourist product would be different from the products processed from the old Deccan Plateau, the Rajasthan desert or the coastal lands of the eastern and western seaboards of the Indian peninsula.

Marketing and promotion

Marketing of tourism products is a major challenge, especially when it requires continuous updating and modernization in a fiercely competitive international market. India has not done well in this field. A major change in strategy is therefore required to one which concentrates on specified tourist circuits/destinations.

Trade fairs, conventions and conferences have helped encourage tourism growth in India. The National Action Plan for Tourism aptly advised the developing agencies to organize trade fairs every three years, where the local industry and foreign travel agents and tour operators could meet. In addition, the government of India has introduced tourist information services (Tournet) which should accelerate promotional activities.

Infrastructure

Among other basic infrastructure needs, tourist accommodation demands serious attention. A country that struggles with the idea whether to build houses for the homeless or hotels for tourists clearly finds it difficult to undertake cohesive visitor destination planning. India is estimated to be short of approximately 67 000 hotel rooms in order to meet current demand. However, the biggest hurdle for hotel development is the lack of suitable sites in large cities of India. Even if suitable sites are available, the cost is prohibitive, comprising as much as 25–40 per cent of the total (Chib, 1989). Despite many incentives and subsidies provided for this sector, the future situation does not appear to be promising.

A recent proposal examined the development of a landbank for creating more hotel rooms in places of tourist interest (Goswami, 1998). Recently, the Indian railways have developed user-friendly tourist packages of heritage trains, a 'palace on wheels': Shatabdi and Rajdhani trains that would link popular tourist centres and also provide a suitable accommodation facility (Malik, 1998). The concept of heritage hotels has been of considerable advantage in converting old places, *havelis* (residences of Indian lords), castles and forts, built before 1950, into accommodation units, as these traditional structures represent the lifestyle of the Raj which still has considerable impact in the Western imagination. For the domestic budget tourists, moderately priced tourist bungalows, youth hostels, *Yatrikas, Yatri Niwas* (pilgrim accommodation) and *Dharamshalas* (religious inns) have gone a long way in assisting the visitor. Much has to be done by way of popularizing the paying guest system. Similarly, tented accommodation, especially in the more remote regions, can also mitigate the accommodation supply problem, provided adequate camping sites are developed.

The Indian Tourism Development Corporation (ITDC) has also developed an elaborate infrastructure in terms of hotels, beach resorts, travel agencies, car rental services and convention/conference facilities across the length and breadth of the country, along with duty-free shops at all the airports of India. The Ashoka Group is the largest private owner, having thirty-three hotels at twenty-six destinations offering accommodation ranging from luxury suites to modestly furnished rooms. Because of Non-Resident Indian (NRI) involvement in the Indian economy, the up-market hotel sector has also received a big boost in recent years. Should political stability be reassured, the hotel industry is bound to flourish with increased participation of the private sector and foreign direct investment.

Conclusion

Despite global recession and recent economic difficulties in Southeast Asia, political upheaval in the country, India's recent Pokhran test blast in the Rajasthan desert and the subsequent political fallout, Indian tourism can still achieve a better growth rate, provided it takes note of the quality research input and the environment in which the tourism industry operates which will finally shape future strategies for marketing tourism products. India should also strive for better regional and sub-regional cooperation for promoting interregional and intraregional tourism (see Chapter 14). This sort of cooperation will be helpful in joint promotion for the princi-

pal market, outside the region and to further the growth of tourist traffic within the region. India has a rich culture and heritage tourism product complemented by a fascinating and attractive natural environment. It has many of the essential ingredients for successful tourism development, together with a structured planning framework in which future growth can be assessed systematically. Whilst investment may be a constraint upon development, and a degree of modernization is required in relation to infrastructure, one of the principal concerns is the impact of existing and future development on the environment, people and community structure. Future development needs to be particularly concerned with the cost:benefit ratio of tourism: it may yield important economic benefits, but there are also major opportunity costs which are frequently overlooked by policy-makers and planners. India's tourism future needs to recognize the important trade-offs that are being made if investment in tourism is at the expense of improvements to the wider well-being and quality of life of the population.

References

Albuquerque, T., *Anjuna: Profile of a Village in Goa*, Promilla and Co., New Delhi, 1988.

Alvares, C., *Fish Curry and Rice, Citizen's report on Goa*, The other India Press, Goa, 1993.

Andrews, S., 'India', in T. Baum (ed.), *Human Resource Issues in International Tourism*, Butterworth-Heinemann, Oxford, 1993, pp. 177–191.

Bala, U., *Tourism in India: Policy and Perspectives*, Arushi Prakashan, New Delhi, 1990.

Chib, S.N., *Essay on Tourism*, Cross Section Publications, New Delhi, 1989.

Department of Tourism, *Tourism Action Plan*, Department of Tourism, New Delhi, 1992.

Department of Tourism, *Annual Tourism Plan*, Department of Tourism, New Delhi, 1997a.

Department of Tourism, *National Strategy for Development of Tourism, 1996*, Department of Tourism, New Delhi, 1997b.

Department of Tourism, *Tourism Statistics*, Department of Tourism, New Delhi, 1998.

Goswami, B.K., 'Need to develop basic infrastructure', *Hindustan Times*, 27 September 1998.

Groetzbach, E., 'Tourism in the Indian Himalaya and problems of further development', in S. Singh (ed.), *Profiles of Indian Tourism*, APH Corporation, New Delhi, 1996.

Hindustan Times, New Delhi, 28 June 1997.

Kaur, J., *Himalayan Pilgrimages and the New Tourism*, Himalayan Books, New Delhi, 1985.

Malik, S.K., 'Railways linking diversity of India', *Hindustan Times* (New Delhi), 27 September 1998.

Pradhan, A., 'Indian tourism: glorious legacy', *The Pioneer* (Lucknow), 27 September 1998.

Singh, S., 'Geographers on tourism geography', *Tourism Recreation Research* 17(1), 1992, pp. 60–67.

Singh, S., 'Development of human resources for the tourism industry with reference to India', *Tourism Management* 18(5), 1997, pp. 299–306.

Singh, S. and Singh, T.V., 'Preface', in S. Singh (ed.), *Profiles of Indian Tourism*, APH Corporation, New Delhi, 1996.

Singh, T.V. (ed.), *Integrated Mountain Development*, Himalayan Books, New Delhi, 1985.

Singh, T.V., *The Kulu Valley: Impact of Tourism Development on the Mountain Areas*, Himalayan Books, New Delhi, 1989.

Singh, T.V. and Kaur, J. (eds), *Studies in Himalayan Ecology and Development Strategies*, Himalayan Books, New Delhi, 1980.

Singh, T.V. and Kaur, J. (eds), *Himalayas Mountains and Men: Studies in Eco-development*, Print House, Lucknow, 1982.

Singh, T.V. and Singh, S., 'Coastal tourism, conservation and the community: case of Goa', in T.V. Singh and S. Singh (eds), *Tourism Development in the Critical Environments*, Cognizant Communication Corporation, New York, 1999.

Times of India, (Lucknow), 9 August 1998.

Tourism Concern, *Sweet Poison*, Press release, 26 January 1993.

World Tourism Organization, *Tourism Carrying Capacity Goa*, World Tourism Organization, Madrid, 1989.

World Tourism Organization, *South Asia: Tourism Market Trends*, World Tourism Organization, Madrid, 1998.

Sri Lanka and the Maldives: Overview

Ross Dowling

Sri Lanka and the Maldives are two Indian Ocean island nations comprising extreme contrasts in tourism development. Sri Lanka is a large island which, as well as offering a beach environment, also has a rich and exotic variety of wildlife, verdant vegetation and ancient monuments. By contrast, the Republic of the Maldives comprises nearly 1200 islands in 26 atolls and its key attractions are the beach and marine environments.

Tourism ostensibly began in Sri Lanka before the Maldives. However, examples of tourism in the Maldives date as far back as 1152 A.D., with the visitation of Arab travellers and the subsequent conversion of the population to Islam (http://www.visitmaldives/history.html). Between 1948 and 1966, international tourism in Sri Lanka was small and only a limited amount of promotion was carried out by the central government tourism bureau. In the early 1960s, a hotel school was established where tourists could stay in the training hotel, which was one of the few hotels in Colombo at that time (Richter, 1989). In 1966 Sri Lanka established the Ceylon Tourist Board to act as the promotion, development, control and regulatory authority for all aspects of tourism. In contrast, tourism in the Maldives began in 1972, but until the 1980s it was very dependent upon Sri Lanka with

tourists coming via that country. Visitors were mainly from India and Europe, predominantly German and Italian, and this is still the case in the late 1990s. However, it was not until an airport was built at Gan that the Maldives established greater autonomy and control over its international arrivals. The country's first tourism law (which outlined the basic regulations for the industry) was enacted in November 1989.

Growth and development

In the 1970s tourist arrivals to Sri Lanka increased at 21 per cent annually. The 19 000 visitors in 1967 had grown to 407 230 by 1982 and tourism had become the fifth largest source of foreign exchange in the country (World Tourism Organization, 1997). Unfortunately, a series of riots in 1983 resulted in a large drop in the number of visitors when 75 per cent of all tours were cancelled, all charters suspended and the average occupancy rate in the hotels plummeted to 15 per cent (Richter, 1989). A similar pattern of growth occurred over the same period in the Maldives. In 1972 the total number of tourists was 1100 but by 1980 the number had reached 42 000 (World Tourism Organization, 1997). As the 1990s draw to a close, the number of international tourists visiting Sri Lanka appears to have levelled off, with figures during the 1990s similar to those of the 1980s (http://www.lanka.net/ctb/profile.html).

Impacts

Tourism in Sri Lanka has caused a number of positive and negative economic, social and environmental impacts. In the past the government had provided tax breaks for hotels, with the result that there were fewer funds available for local housing; this has now been rescinded (Richter, 1989). However, there are also positive impacts. Some locals achieve an independence and security that they have never known before, from selling handicrafts, renting out rooms or cooking for tourists. Sri Lanka developed what Richter (1989) calls 'enclave tourism'. Over 93 per cent of the tourists arriving in 1977 indicated sun, sand and sea as their primary motivation for visiting the country and the government has since attempted to develop beach-front areas on the more sparsely populated eastern coast of the island. In this context, tourism in the Maldives is not dramatically different, given the environmental resources which have been promoted for international tourism to generate hard currency. In addition, in order to strive to achieve sustainable tourism development, Sri Lanka has enacted substantial laws and regulations concerning environmental conservation, wildlife and forest protection, anti-pollution laws and cultural heritage conservation. They have implemented an environmental impact assessment (EIA) system. EIA ensures that any environmental consequences are recognized early and taken into account in project designs. Initial

environmental examination reports or EIA reports are required for any hotel tourism resort or project which provides recreational facilities exceeding ninety-nine rooms or 40 ha (World Tourism Organization, 1997).

The future

One of the major questions facing the Maldives is whether its tourism product will continue to attract a growing numbers of holidaymakers. There has been a feeling since the beginning of the decade among tour operators from Europe and other parts of the world that even the most ardent beach- and SCUBA diving-lovers are starting to tire of the attractions of a Maldives-type holiday (World tourism Organization, 1997). This partly explains why the combination of Sri Lanka and the Maldives for a twin destination package was so appealing in the heyday of Sri Lankan tourism. It could, of course, be revived or the Maldives as a destination could be combined with another country in the region such as India (Ritcher, 1989). However, it does highlight the importance of cooperative marketing and promotion in South Asia as other destinations compete for the same tourists.

References

Richter, L.K., *The Politics of Tourism in Asia*, University of Hawai'i Press, Honolulu, Hawai'i, 1989.

World Tourism Organization, 'Tourism 2000: building a sustainable future for Asia–Pacific', Final Report of the Asia Pacific Ministers' Conference on Tourism and the Environment, Maldives, 16–17 February 1997, World Tourism Organization, Madrid, 1997.

16

Tourism in Sri Lanka: 'Paradise on Earth'?

Anne de Bruin and
V. Nithiyanandam

Introduction

The development of international tourism has clearly been a function of global economic growth. Rising standards of living, increased value of leisure time and developments in transportation (Page, 1999) have been directly responsible for the steady growth of the tourism industry world-wide. The average annual growth of receipts from international tourism has exceeded exports of commercial services and merchandise exports in the decade to 1995 (Youell, 1998: p. 2). Tourism is a key contributor to global economic activity and a major generator of wealth and employment. In the case of the contribution of tourism to less developed countries (LDCs), however, both the nature of the industry and its role in relation to a country's economic development is not only different but, in many ways, also more complex (Sinclair and Vokes, 1993; Sinclair and Stabler, 1997).

An aspect of this complexity is that tourism, like many other developments in the developing world, may be viewed as subject to a 'dependency syndrome' (see Britton, 1991; Harrison, 1992; Oppermann and Chon, 1997). As per capita incomes in the developed world grew, so did the demand for tourism. The role of developing countries is often conceptualized in terms of the provision of the necessary supply to meet this demand. The popularity of coastal resorts in LDCs has, to a certain extent, been replaced in developed countries by the rise of island tourism and resort tourism, owing to the development of charter flights and package holidays controlled by tour operators. The comparatively cheap cost of overseas travel to LDCs has not only made such trips fashionable from developed countries, but reductions in the price of travel have widened the market for such holidays in the late 1980s and 1990s.

An important outcome of the dependency element has been the lop-sided nature of tourism growth in LDCs. Although, according to the World Tourism Organization classification, tourism takes three basic forms, namely domestic, inbound and outbound, this categorization has little meaning for most LDCs. Tourism development in these countries focuses almost exclusively on the receipt of inbound tourists, almost to the gross neglect of domestic tourism, although the exceptions in South Asia are India, Pakistan and Bangladesh where the market is significant but not nurtured officially.

One interesting argument in Britton's (1991) research is that in tourism, dependency and post-colonialism have ironically meant that many developing nations are now heavily dependent upon the revenue earned by the tourism sector. Several countries have reached a stage where a decline in tourism could have an immediate impact on current development prospects and the contribution to GDP. Even when sensitive socio-economic or political decisions are made, prudent governments in LDCs always keep an eye on possible repercussions on the tourism industry, given their naïve assumption that tourism may be a panacea for the economic development problems facing the country. This chapter highlights some features of this aspect of tourism development and traces the evolution of the industry, examining key issues and commenting on long-term growth and development prospects.

The image of tourism

Sri Lanka has manifold advantages which make it a desirable island tourist destination among LDCs. It is a country with lavish endowments to meet tourist demands, as the following description shows:

> The physical environment with its warm sunshine, azure skies, golden palm-fringed beaches, emerald sea, varied natural scenery, tropical fauna and flora; the rich cultural heritage with its ancient historic buildings, temples, frescoes, religious pageants, forms of music and dancing, arts and crafts; the people described as intelligent, warm, friendly, hospitable, fun-loving and artistic – all these provide the ingredients which make Sri Lanka a fascinating country for visitors (Mendis, 1981: p. 1).

These benefits apart, the international image of Sri Lanka in recent times has undergone a transformation. From being a 'model ... colony that made the transition from dependence to sovereign status without rancour or violence' (Wilson, 1974: p. 1) in the middle of the twentieth century, it could today be dubbed a country with a persistent civil war. The country's yet unresolved ethnic problem cast a long shadow and it is difficult to single out an activity in any area – economic, political, social or cultural – that has been spared its impact. Tourism has, in fact, been an area that has been largely affected by the ongoing ethnic crisis. No account of the tourism industry can, therefore, escape comment of the ill effects the crisis has had, and is still having, on the fortunes of the industry. In fact, the chapter illustrates many of the political issues associated with tourism in the Southeast and South Asia region which are discussed in Chapter 5 and also dealt with in more detail in Hall (1994).

Tourism planning and development: historical issues

Despite inherent advantages, tourism as an economic sector in Sri Lanka did not begin early. Although in past times pilgrims and other travellers came to Sri Lanka, it was during the British colonial days that a constant flow of travellers developed, linked to the colonial trading relationship. In particular, this was given an added boost by the fact that Colombo served as an important staging post between Europe and the Orient. Nevertheless, these flows were not developed or tapped as an economic resource. In fact, this is a classic feature of early tourism development in Southeast and South Asia, epitomized in the reviews by the regional geographers of the post-war period who reviewed the regions' historical legacy and patterns of economic development (e.g. Fisher, 1964). In Sri Lanka, even after independence from colonial rule in 1948, the situation did not undergo much change until the mid-1960s. While the Ceylon Tourist Bureau, a government department within the Ministry of Commerce, undertook tourism promotion on a very small scale, the necessary infrastructure for a tourist industry was altogether absent. The country was lacking in 'high quality hotel facilities, technical know-how of the travel trade, and a well planned marketing and promotion programme' (Mendis, 1981: p. 1).

The real impetus to tourism development came in 1966 with the establishment, by an Act of Parliament, of the Ceylon Tourist Board within the Ministry of State, replacing the Ceylon Tourist Bureau. The role of the Ceylon Tourist Board was to encourage, promote and develop the travel trade. In addition, it was also expected to provide adequate, efficient and attractive tourist services. Another notable development in 1966 was the creation of the Ceylon Hotels Corporation. The Corporation was a mixed venture with investments from both the government and private entrepreneurs. The Ceylon Hotels Corporation Act of 1966 also empowered the Corporation to acquire land for tourist-related developments and to establish other essential facilities such as transport and entertainment. Two years later a further Act of Parliament, the 1968 Tourist Development Act, enhanced the role of the Tourist Board. The Act enabled the Board to regulate the provision of tourism services. It provided for the setting up of the necessary infrastructure to promote investment in the tourist industry. One possible area of development, for example, was the establishment of resort areas. The Act also facilitated the introduction of regulations for the supervision, classification, inspection, and control of tourist services.

The series of state legislation and the areas on which focus was placed, clearly indicate the positive approach of the government to tourism. This was reinforced in 1967, when an American firm drew up the Ceylon Tourism Plan, a ten-year plan of development for the tourism industry in Sri Lanka, with financing from the US Agency for International Development. In many respects, this plan could be described as a comprehensive document although, in hindsight, its projections regarding tourism revenue and visitor arrivals were grossly over-estimated (Mendis, 1981: pp. 2–3). It provided some useful background information on the country's history, geography, economy and culture; it also furnished data on world, as well as domestic, travel; analysed facilities available for accommodation, food and beverages and entertainment; enumerated tourist attractions; and proposed a facilities development plan and a public works programme. The role of the government was delineated and a marketing and a community-relations programme was also outlined.

Apart from its gross over-estimation of projected foreign exchange earnings from tourism, several other elements of the tourism plan attracted the attention of critics. While a detailed discussion of these criticisms is beyond the scope of this chapter, what is important to emphasize in line with this chapter's theme, is that the fundamental approach of the document was a reflection of the dependency syndrome. As Crick asserts, the plan was 'very much an overseas travel industry view' (1994: p. 28). The industry was considered to be an 'export industry' and its entire analysis, estimates, proposals and recommendations were based on this premise. This is a similar problem to that observed by Fagence (1996) in the context of the Pacific Islands where inappropriate tourism plans based on a Western view of growth and development have failed to incorporate realistic assessments of the future development scenarios for tourism.

Despite harsh comments at an academic level, the Ceylon Tourism Plan formed the basis of future tourism-sector growth in Sri Lanka. A decade after its publication, for example, the Chairman of the Ceylon Tourist Board saw 'no reason for a new plan' (de Zoysa, 1978: p. 12). This statement also signalled the manner in which the tourism sector was growing in Sri Lanka. The objective had always been to promote the image of Sri Lanka as an attractive tourist destination to *foreigners*. Even the ideological differences in terms of Western *vis-à-vis* national influences between the two major political parties, the United National Party (UNP) and the Sri Lanka Freedom Party (SLFP), which had been in power successively, did not alter this approach. This becomes more evident when, even after the name of the country was changed from *Ceylon* to *Sri Lanka* under the newly promulgated 1972 Constitution of the SLFP, in almost all tourism-related activities, the former name was retained. This remains true to this day. A continuity that is more than rare at policy-making levels in other sectors of the political economy, ensured smooth growth of the tourism industry until the ethnic conflict intervened in 1983.

The development of the tourism industry during the period 1966–1982 has been described as 'a story of growth' (Crick, 1994:p. 37), with the possible exception of 1971 when the insurrection against the SLFP government of that time discouraged tourist arrivals. Between 1966 and 1979, it is estimated that tourist arrivals grew at an average of 21.9 per cent per annum, outstripping the world growth rate in international tourism and the growth rates of other South Asian countries (Crick, 1994: p. 37). Yet, there were no strong links between the tourism industry and the rest of the economy, making a mockery of the multiplier of between three and four that the ten-year tourism plan had envisaged. Tourism remained a typical enclave development.

Sri Lanka also took measures to establish a viable airline of its own, during this period. Although Air Ceylon had been operating under the Department of Civil Aviation since independence, its record was unimpressive. It had for many years 'created sizeable losses and achieved little success in bringing an increasing proportion of tourists to Sri Lanka' (Crick, 1994: p. 40). With a view to overcoming these shortcomings, Air Lanka was floated in 1979 as a state-owned enterprise (SOE). Operating losses of the airline nevertheless not only continued, but very often also surpassed the losses incurred by its predecessor, Air Ceylon. These losses exceeded the aggregate annual losses of Sri Lanka's other industrial SOEs, with annual government transfers of around 1 million rupees to Air Lanka (Kelegama, 1997: p. 493). The airline's contribution as a tourist carrier also left much to be desired. In 1982, for example, when

tourism was at its peak, Air Lanka accounted for only a little over 30 per cent of tourist arrivals (Crick, 1994: p. 40).

The Tourism Master Plan (United Nations Development Programme/World Tourism Organization (UNDP/WTO), 1992) is a more recent attempt by government at planned growth of the tourism sector. This plan focuses on economic objectives and endorses a strategy to move toward more up-market tourism, chiefly through support for upgrading existing, and large-scale new investment in, hotels. A doubling of hotel rooms from a base of less than 10 000 by the year 2001 is suggested. The government has a target of 1.5 million international tourist arrivals by 2001 (Anonymous, 1993: p. 67). As with the ten-year tourism plan, these targets appear overly optimistic, especially in the light of the continuing ethnic disturbances. Market diversification and promotion of natural and cultural attractions so as to move away from the beach-oriented tourism that Sri Lanka has relied on in the past, are steps in the right direction (World Tourism Organization, 1994: p. 204). According to Saleem (1996), in the absence of any ethnic unrest, the pattern of tourism resources which are evident from Figure 16.1 illustrate that the pattern of tourism development would be based upon a diverse range of natural, cultural and coastal resources. The issue of tourism sustainability also needs to be given serious consideration. It is suggested that with appropriate socio-cultural and environmental policies, Sri Lanka could sustain 'over 100 per cent growth in visitor numbers during the next five years' (Saleem, 1996: p. 56). Coastal management remains a high priority. Some beach resorts, such as Hikkaduwa and Negombo, have already exceeded their carrying capacity (Saleem, 1996: p. 57), hence, diversification into other tourist areas such as heritage and cultural tourism becomes all the more pressing. Market diversification, however, remains constrained. In particular, increased in-roads into the East Asian market are unlikely to be achieved owing to the economic crisis that has beset these economies since late 1997.

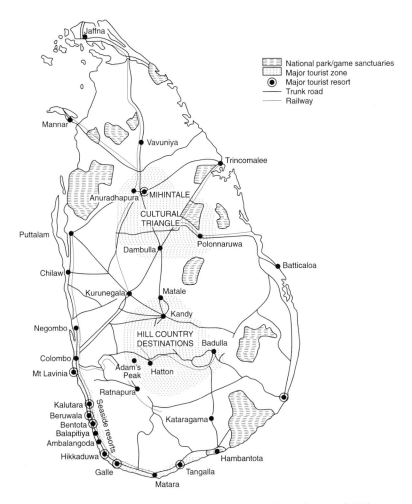

Figure 16.1 *Tourism resources in Sri Lanka according to Saleem (1996)*

The promotion of tourism within the South Asia region is a further element of recent strategy to diversify into newer markets. At a meeting in Colombo in 1997, the tourism ministers of the seven South Asian countries (Bangladesh, Bhutan, India, Maldives, Nepal, Pakistan and Sri Lanka) which comprise the South Asian Association for Regional Co-operation (SAARC), met to discuss tourism within the region. Focusing on the removal of barriers to development and measures to promote intraregional tourism, it was agreed that the SAARC Scheme for Promotion of Organized Tourism (SPOT) be launched (Ministry of Foreign Affairs,

Sri Lanka, 1997). So far, however, the extent of cooperation achieved by the SAARC has been more rhetorical than real. Nevertheless, with global strengthening of regionalism, the SAARC could well represent a region that will 'take-off' in the future. This will augur well for the growth of inter-SAARC tourism. In 1998 the Ceylon Tourist Board continued with its efforts to promote Sri Lanka to international visitors, marketing the country under the slogan *Paradise on Earth*. It has adapted to the demands of the new information and communications era, for example maintaining a comprehensive and up-to-date web site. Similarly the tourist industry has not been slow to tap into new tastes such as the preference for natural medicine and health.

A preoccupation with healthy living is now a feature of modern life in the developed world. Travel choices and spending patterns of travellers are increasingly being influenced by their preference for natural health 'alternatives' and 'Eastern' spiritual values as a form of health tourism. Sri Lanka's long tradition of Ayurveda is being used as a basis for catering to these preferences. Ayurveda, from the Sanskrit words *Ayus* (life) and *Veda* (knowledge or science) adopts a holistic view of health, with the use of traditional herbal remedies together with dietary, massage and exercise regimes. It is being marketed by the tourism industry chiefly through Ayurveda centres or herbal healthcare centres which are often part of the facilities provided by luxury hotels (Wijesekera, 1998). The internet is one of the modes being used to promote holidays offering ayurvedic treatments. For instance, the Sri Budhasa Ayurveda Health Resort, a beach resort on the south coast, has a web site advertising itself with the slogan 'Ayurveda: More Years to Your Life, More Life to Your Years'. Ayurveda has given a boost to tourism in Sri Lanka (Brady, 1998).

An important feature of tourism in Sri Lanka is its link with religion. Thus, for instance, a major event on the tourism calendar is the Kandy *Perahera*, associated with the procession to honour the sacred tooth relic of Lord Buddha. Religious rituals and symbols have also been commodified to cater to the international tourist trade (Simpson, 1993, 1997). In fact, apart from the coastal beach resorts and wildlife sanctuaries, most of the tourist sites have a religious significance. Places like Anuradhapura, Kandy, Kataragama and Adam's Peak, have become prominent mainly owing to their religious connotation. Despite the multi-religious character of Sri Lanka, Buddhism has been accorded the status of a state religion and, consequently, places of Buddhist interest have received government patronage. This has meant that these places have always been properly maintained with necessary improvements and facilities for visitors. It is such

care and protection that elevated most of these to the status of tourist attractions. When religious significance combines with other factors such as scenic beauty and close proximity to Colombo, an ideal formula for tourism development emerges. Kandy provides the best example of such a development. Another interesting phenomenon relating to places of religious significance is their contribution to pilgrimage and domestic tourism (Sievers, 1987). It has an area of spontaneous development, however, without much effort from any tourism-related institutions, state or otherwise. Here, a close identity prevails between the 'tourist' and the 'pilgrim'. Locals choose to visit these sites as part of their religious obligations and, in this sense, they become 'pilgrims' rather than 'tourists'. Here it is pertinent to mention that annual pilgrimages (in Sinhalese terminology *vandanava*) form a part of the life of most Sinhalese villagers. These pilgrims tend to 'rough-it-out', bring their own food and are the recipients of community generosity. No significant employment spin-offs result.

The tourism economy: earnings and employment

Research on Sri Lanka's tourism economy is limited and much of the existing knowledge dates back to an influential but now dated study by Attanayake *et al.* (1983). While this study is a useful starting point to gauge the development, economic consequences and impact of tourism in the period 1960–1980, it has not been followed by any major study which has updated the situation. Within Sri Lanka, tourism earnings, especially foreign exchange receipts, constitute a major economic contribution from the industry. Although from the early 1960s enhancement of earnings from tourism was seen as a solution to Sri Lanka's foreign exchange problems and a means of diversifying the economy and reducing dependence on the uncertainty of traditional primary product export earnings, it was only during the late 1970s, that tourism became a

Table 16.1   *Earnings from tourism 1970–1979 (millions)*

Year	Rupees	US$	SDRs
1970	21.5	3.6	3.6
1971	20.3	3.4	3.4
1972	43.8	7.3	6.5
1973	79.5	12.8	10.4
1974	107.1	16.4	13.3
1975	157.1	22.4	18.6
1976	237.8	28.2	24.5
1977	363.1	40.0	34.8
1978	870.0	55.8	44.4
1979	1188.0	76.3	59.0
Average annual rate of growth (%)	56.2	40.4	36.4

Source: Mendis, 1981, p. 7.

significant source of earnings. A change of government, economic liberalization policies and greater integration of the economy into the global market, saw a corresponding boost to tourism. As Table 16.1 shows, foreign exchange earnings from tourism by 1979 had climbed sharply to US$76.3 million and 59 million units of International Monetary Fund (IMF) Special Drawing Rights (SDRs). Although earnings expressed in rupees also increased substantially, devaluation of the rupee makes these nominal figures less meaningful. The end of the decade saw tourism rank fourth, after tea, rubber and petroleum products, as a foreign exchange earner.

The growth in tourism earnings continued into the 1980s, but since 1983 has been hit by waves of civil disturbances, leading to sharply fluctuating numbers of tourist arrivals, as seen in Table 16.2. Earnings were, consequently, adversely affected. Although by 1995, rupee earnings picked up to Rs11 569 million, recording a growth of 2 per cent over the previous year, in SDR terms there was a drop of 7 per cent (Central Bank of Sri Lanka, 1995: p. 114).

It should be noted that the earnings statistics presented in Tables 16.1 and 16.2 are gross earnings. What is more meaningful is to gauge the net contribution to foreign exchange earnings from the tourism sector. There is substantial leakage of foreign exchange because tourist facilities are partly owned by foreigners, there is a high import content of food consumed by tourists in hotels, there is a necessity for capital imports for infrastructure and the operation of duty-free shopping complexes (this issue is discussed in more detail in the context of Kenya by Sinclair, 1992). While there are no

Table 16.2   *Key indicators for Sri Lanka's tourism industry 1980–1995*

Year	Number of tourist arrivals	Direct employment	Indirect employment	Total employment	Annual occupancy rate	Earnings (rupees, million)
1980	321 780	22 261	30 357	52 618	57.8	1 830
1981	370 742	23 023	32 457	55 480	54.5	2 546
1982	407 230	26 776	37 486	64 262	47.8	3 050
1983	306 824	22 374	31 234	53 608	35.9	2 896
1984	317 734	24 541	34 357	58 898	35.6	2 669
1985	257 456	22 723	31 810	54 533	32.7	2 233
1986	230 106	22 285	31 199	53 484	32.9	2 300
1987	182 260	20 338	28 473	48 811	31.5	2 415
1988	182 662	19 960	27 944	47 904	32.1	2 438
1989	184 732	21 958	30 741	52 132	31.0	2 740
1990	297 888	24 964	34 950	59 914	47.2	5 303
1991	317 703	26 878	37 629	64 507	48.4	6 485
1992	393 669	28 790	40 306	69 069	55.3	8 825
1993	392 250	30 710	42 994	73 704	57.0	10 036
1994	407 511	35 064	49 090	84 154	56.6	11 375
1995	403 000	36 260	51 100	87 360	52.6	11 569

Source : Central Bank of Sri Lanka, *Annual Reports* (various dates).

definitive calculations of overall leakage, i.e. the difference between gross and net foreign exchange earnings, it is estimated to be between 25 and 35 per cent. With a change in equity rules allowing 70 per cent foreign ownership of new hotel plant from 1982, however, this estimate could be as high as 40 per cent (Crick, 1994: p. 53).

The development of tourism, a labour-intensive industry, is a common recommendation for mitigation of the severe unemployment problem faced by developing countries such as Sri Lanka. This is true for many other South Asian countries and illustrates the appeal of this economic activity for addressing unemployment and, more significantly, underemployment as highlighted in Chapter 14. Table 16.2 indicates that the tourism sector provides employment, both direct and indirect, for significant numbers of people. Direct employment includes those employed in the service sectors such as hotels, restaurants, travel agencies and retail outlets for tourists. Indirect employment arises from involvement in sectors supplying the tourism industry with commodities such as arts and handicrafts, food and beverages. The 1992 Tourism Master Plan estimates an overall tourism multiplier of 1.82 and suggested that for every 250 000 rupees earned in the tourism sector, one extra direct job is created (Anonymous, 1993: pp. 47, 49). This multiplier, compared with the estimate of between 3 and 4 in the ten-year tourism plan, looks modest. It nevertheless remains the case that a structural weakness of the tourism sector in Sri Lanka has been the absence of strong links with the rest of the economy, so only time will tell whether this new multiplier estimate is a realistic one. This also highlights the need for local areas and government agencies to develop links with the local economy to assist in import substitution and to reduce income leakage.

While the job creation potential of tourism is undeniable, it should be mentioned that owing to the seasonality of the industry, around one-fifth of hotel employees are hired on a temporary/casual basis. Furthermore, as Table 16.2

suggests, tourist numbers have fluctuated, which has a direct impact on employment. The regional distribution of employment has also been skewed. 'Colombo City, along with the west and south coasts and the "ancient cities" region (i.e. bounded by the "cultural triangle" of Kandy, Anuradhapura and Polonnaruwa) account for over 95 per cent of direct employment in the sector' (Anonymous, 1993: p. 49). Moreover, since involvement in the tourism industry has been the monopoly of the Sinhalese, the majority ethnic group in the country (Richter, 1992: p. 42), this has meant that economic gains from tourism have largely by-passed the Tamils, who comprise around 18 per cent of the population. This ethnic inequality is also highlighted in the recent synthesis of tourism and ethnicity in Southeast Asia by Picard and Wood (1997) and is certainly an area worthy of further research to assess the significance of such an issue throughout Southeast and South Asia.

The impact of political instability

Politics in LDCs, instead of guiding the economy, can also become a major hindrance to growth and development. This is particularly true when it threatens the peace of the country. Although Sri Lanka, unlike many other developing nations, can boast of a continuous parliamentary democracy since the end of colonial rule, that has not in any way curbed or reduced its stock of political problems or their violent manifestations. On the contrary, political violence has resulted in a large-scale destruction of both physical and human resources, from about the 1980s. International tourism has, in fact, been one sector that took the full brunt of its consequences.

Political instability in Sri Lanka is evidenced in two largely unrelated conflicts. Firstly, the conflict between the majority and the minority communities, commonly referred to as the 'ethnic conflict' and secondly, youth unrest, resulting mainly from socio-economic reasons.

The latter is usually identified as the 'JVP problem', where 'JVP' refers to the *Janatha Vimukti Peramuna*, a political organization of the youth. Both, though not initially, ultimately recognized violence as the primary mode of protest. Both have had the youth in the forefront, fighting the government in power. The main difference, however, has been that while the ethnic conflict led to Tamil youth militancy, JVP membership has been predominantly Sinhalese and resulted in Sinhala youth militancy. The difference is also reflected in the regions where each is active. Whereas Tamil militancy was confined to the north and east of the country, JVP operated in the southern regions. Yet, what is more crucial is that both groups at some stage of their struggle were determined to make their presence felt in Colombo, the capital city, so as to bring more pressure on the government. Judging by events, there is no doubt that their efforts were largely successful. The impact these events had in Colombo dealt a severe blow to the tourism industry. Again, it is the dependent nature of the industry, in the form of its heavy reliance on an international clientele, which magnified the proportion of the troubles. Before turning to consider these, it is pertinent to mention that the 'JVP problem' hit its peak during the late 1980s, when the government of the day succeeded in curtailing it after resorting to some stern but, from a human rights point of view, highly debatable measures. This success, however, could not be repeated in the case of the ethnic conflict. While the ethnic problem is still unresolved, its violent repercussions have mushroomed into a full-scale war between the government security forces and the Tamil militants, rallied around the *Liberation Tigers of Tamil Eelam* (LTTE). With no end in sight in the foreseeable future, the war has become a sustained 'drain' on the entire economy, let alone tourism. It has also had a detrimental impact on sport tourism events where the issue of tourist safety (World Tourism Organization, 1996) has tarnished the image of the country as an international sporting venue.

Thus, an instant casualty of political instability and its violent ramifications has been the image of the country as a whole. Beginning in 1983, violence against the Tamils not only caught the international eye but also came in for close scrutiny at different levels (see, for example, *Race and Class*, 26(1), 1984). The more it was probed, the more the Sri Lankan image suffered. Since then, militant activities in various forms, either by the LTTE or the JVP, have only made the problem worse. Nevertheless, so long as the government was able to convince foreign visitors that violent militancy was regionally contained (either north and east or south), there was a small respite. This, however, quickly evaporated when Colombo came to be targeted by both militant groups. With the kind of advancement seen in modern communication systems, this was an inevitable outcome. Although the government took various countermeasures, ranging from full-scale propaganda to media censorship, they all could not but end up in failure. Bandara (1997: p. 277) clearly shows that separate incidents of violence in Colombo in 1995/1996, which were given extensive coverage in the international media, had a drastic impact on tourist arrivals. Such a decline in tourist arrivals quickly extends to other areas and affects the entire tourism industry. Thus, excess accommodation capacity has been a feature of the tourism industry, largely owing to the adverse impact of political instability on Sri Lanka's image as a safe tourist destination. Occupancy rates in Table 16.2 show an average annual occupancy rate of a low 39.2 per cent in the 1980s, with the high of 57.8 per cent in 1980 plummeting to 31 per cent in 1989. This latter figure, the lowest recorded in the period 1978–1996, reflects the movement of the focus of conflict to the south, the heart of the beaches and coastal tourist developments. The JVP insurrection in 1989 was a sharp blow to the tourism industry of the southern region. To this point it was believed that the southern coastal region was a safe haven, with the fallout of ethnic tumult felt elsewhere in the island.

From an economic standpoint, the chief purposes of the tourism industry may be described as the earning of foreign exchange, employment stimulation and regional diversification. Whenever there is a drop in tourist arrivals there is no denying that all three generally suffer. Yet, while the effect on the first two may be captured by available data (see Table 16.2), it is difficult to capture the total regional impact through available statistics, especially since the image-building exercise undertaken by the government has had a bearing on the regional dimension. The government, to this day, continues with a policy of barring overseas tourists from visiting any of the troubled areas of conflict, on the pretext of their safety. The more obvious reason for this action is concern over any 'wrong' impression the visitors could carry away about the country and its government. This may be construed as an attempt to raise tourist numbers at the expense of balanced regional development. The success of this attempt, nevertheless, is difficult to gauge.

Amidst an altogether grim picture, the continuing political instability has, ironically, led to a rather favourable development in the tourism industry. This chapter has maintained that the tourism industry has been subject to a dependency syndrome, searching for overseas patronage to the neglect of domestic customers. Yet, falling foreign visitor arrivals and the consequent unused capacity, especially hotel accommodation, have diverted industry attention towards the domestic market. Despite the fact that sunk (fixed) costs in the industry are high, so long as total revenue earned covers variable costs it is always more profitable to keep the industry running. It is in this respect that the role of internal visitors proved vital. Facilities such as hotels and transport offered concessionary packages to local customers. It should, however, be emphasized that these represent neither any remarkable change in the inherent nature of the tourism industry nor genuine steps towards promotion of local tourism; they were simply measures to keep heads above water. Even here, the industry was not without constraint. Economic implications of the political problems made local customers reluctant to use tourist facilities. The industry could not,

therefore, hope for more than very minimal relief.

Social and cultural impacts of tourism

There is a well established literature on the social and cultural impacts of tourism (Smith, 1989; Picard and Wood, 1997) and the issues related to the effect of tourism on host communities is well documented. Sex tourism is an inescapable aspect of the industry around the world and accounts for a significant proportion of all tourism (Oppermann, 1998). The child prostitution aspect of sex tourism, however, is a contentious issue that has received increased attention in the 1990s. Widespread prevalence of child prostitution associated with the informal sector of the tourist trade in Sri Lanka, as well as the use of child labour in the industry, is now well documented (Bond, 1980; Mendis, 1981; Seneviratne, 1994; Black, 1995; U.S. Department of State, 1997; Beddoe, 1998). The extent of the problem was highlighted in 1980 when a report asserted that Sri Lanka was one of the chief centres for international paedophile activities (Bond, 1980). As with all illegal activities in the informal sector, statistics on the extent of child prostitution, however, vary. Government figures estimate that there are over 2000 active child prostitutes, most of whom are boys catering to tourists chiefly in coastal resort areas (U.S. Department of State, 1997). Non-governmental sources, for example ECPAT (End Child Prostitution Pornography and Trafficking),[1] a global network of agencies and individuals dedicated to ending the commercial sexual exploitation of children, nevertheless quote higher figures. Anecdotal evidence also suggests that especially with recent law changes in developed countries

---

[1]Initially the ECPAT campaign addressed the burgeoning phenomenon of child sex tourism in Asia, but now has been extended to include prostitution of children, child pornography and trafficking of children for sexual purposes.

which allow prosecution of paedophiles in their home country, paedophile rings have shifted their activities from the more closely monitored Asian countries such as Thailand, to relatively less scrutinized places such as Sri Lanka.

The government of Sri Lanka is committed to protecting the welfare and rights of children and ratified the United Nations Charter on the Rights of the Child in 1991. Criminalization of child sex tourism began in 1995 with an amendment to the Penal Code which imposed tougher penalties for trafficking of persons. Although a Task Force was also appointed by the Ministry of Media, Tourism and Aviation to look into sex tourism and related offences, no new steps have been taken to deal with the problem. While the legal framework is adequate, law enforcement resources are inadequate, especially as the war with the LTTE is a severe drain on these resources. Sex tourism in Sri Lanka is also intertwined with the 'beach boy' and tour guide culture (Crick, 1992; Beddoe, 1998) that has developed for over two decades. The lure of material gain and the ever-present hope that it would provide a ticket out of the country and the coveted Western lifestyle, is largely the motivation behind the activities of the guides and beach boys involved. Parental poverty and ignorance are also contributory factors. Unfortunately, as long as the twin forces of the demonstration effect leading to imitation and even romanticization of the lifestyle and 'culture' of the tourist; and inequalities of wealth and power continue to be coupled with limited law enforcement, social ills such as the sexual exploitation of children will continue to be a part of Sri Lanka's tourism industry.

Conclusion

As Sri Lanka's tourism industry enters the new millennium, it is evident that it has now reached the crossroads. As an industry nurtured and developed as an 'export industry' giving priority to an affluent 'Western market', it has done little to lessen dependence on fickle, fluctuating demand patterns dictated by the developed world. Domestic customers have been turned away or been treated differently or indifferently and, until very recently, the neighbouring South Asian market was all but ignored. The tourism sector has been the gateway for several social evils incurring high social costs. The sector has not been without outright condemnation, even accusations that tourism in Sri Lanka had created 'a new kind of colonialism' (Mendis, 1981: p. 22).

The partisan approach to tourism has been unable to stand above the difficulties emanating from the socio-economic framework of the country. The entire tourism industry has become bogged down in the country's political instability and the ethnic conflict in particular. Current indications are that the ever prolonging nature of the conflict and its various consequences have brought the industry to ruin. In order to make it a viable sector of the economy, a rebuilding exercise is necessary. This need to rebuild can also provoke rethinking on how this should be accomplished. It will take more than the re-branding, repositioning or a new marketing campaign to remove the damage caused by the recent ethnic conflict.

First and foremost, there is a need to resolve the dilemma of whether the tourism sector should be developed for its own sake or, on a narrower perspective, purely as a foreign exchange earning enterprise. The strategy has, up to now, been dominated by the latter. What is urgently required in Sri Lanka is a more unifying character to its entire socio-economic fabric. If tourism, as a sector, is to make a worthwhile contribution in this respect, a much broader outlook is essential. There has to be some conscious effort to promote the domestic market as well as the market originating from neighbouring countries. It is in this context that the regional dimension of tourism development and the involvement of the SAARC should be viewed as an important area to nurture. While this would enable the industry to lessen the range of criticisms at the socio-cultural level, it would also remove the hitherto embedded dependency syndrome. It could further strengthen cultural ties with countries such as India.

A prerequisite for either this 'closer to home' approach, or any other alternative approach, however, is to create a conducive socio-political environment. Experience has proved beyond doubt that as long as the environment is subject to instability, growth can only be hindered. Even steps in the right direction can soon be foiled. The latest example in this regard is a Ceylon Tourist Board project to attract Indian tourists, which has run into trouble. The project involves building temples for Rama, Sita and Hanuman in Sita Eliya (near Nuwara Eliya in the Central hills of Sri Lanka), where Ravana, the demon king, was supposed to have kept Sita captive. The Ceylon Tourist Board teamed up with a Calcutta-based heritage tour operator and even sought, through the Sri Lanka Ministry of Tourism, the assistance of the Indian Ministry of Tourism. Yet objections to the project have been raised by certain factions of the Sinhala–Buddhist community, mainly on political grounds. It is alleged that the project would turn the area into one of Hindu–Tamil domination and could form the nucleus for a '*Malai Nadu*', a separate state for Indian Tamils (*Hindustan Times*, 23 November 1998). Whither Sri Lankan tourism and 'Paradise on Earth'?

References

Anonymous, 'Sri Lanka', *International Tourism Report No. 1, Economist* Intelligence Unit, London, 1993.

Attanayake, A., Samaranayake, H. and Ratnapala, N., 'Sri Lanka', in E. Pye and T. Lin (eds), *Tourism in Asia: The Economic Impact*, Singapore University Press, Singapore, 1983, pp. 241–337.

Bandara, J.S., 'The impact of the Civil War on tourism and the regional economy', *South Asia* 20 (Special Issue), 1997, pp. 269–280.

Beddoe, C., 'Beachboys and tourists: Child prostitution in Sri Lanka' in M. Oppermann (ed.), *Sex Tourism and Prostitution: Aspects of Leisure, Recreation, and Work*, Cognizant Communication Corporation, New York, 1998, pp. 42–50.

Black, M., *In the Twilight Zone: Child Workers in the Hotel, Tourism and Catering Industry*, International Labour Office, Child Labour Collection, Geneva, 1995.

Bond, T., *Boy Prostitution in Sri Lanka: The Problems, Effects and Suggested Remedies*, Terres des Hommes, Colombo, 1980.

Brady, S., 'Spiritual journeying: Om away from Om', *Time* (Asia edition) 6 July 1998, 151(26).

Britton, S., 'Tourism, capital and place: Towards a critical geography', *Environment and Planning D: Society and Space* 9 1991, pp. 451–478.

Central Bank of Sri Lanka, *Annual Report*, Central Bank Printing Press, Rajagiriya, 1995.

Crick, M., 'Life in the informal sector: Street guides in Kandy, Sri Lanka' in D. Harrison (ed.), *Tourism and the Less Developed Countries*, Belhaven Press, London, 1992, pp. 135–147.

Crick, M., *Resplendent Sites, Discordant Voices: Sri Lankans and International Tourism*, Harwood Academic Publishers, Melbourne, 1994.

de Zoysa, C.N., 'Development of tourism in Sri Lanka', in *Tourism in Sri Lanka. The First Decade*, Department of Information, Colombo, 1978.

Fagence, M., 'Planning issues in Pacific tourism', in C.M. Hall and S.J. Page (eds), *Tourism in the Pacific: Issues and Cases*, International Thomson Business Publishing, London, 1996, pp. 91–108.

Fisher, W., *South East Asia*, Methuen, London, 1964.

Hall, C.M., *Tourism and Politics: Policy, Power and Place*, Belhaven, London, 1994.

Harrison, D. (ed.), *Tourism and Less Developed Countries*, Belhaven Press, London, 1992.

Hindustan Times, 23 November 1998.

Kelegama, S., 'Privatisation: An overview of the process and issues', in W.D. Lakshman (ed.), *Dilemmas of Development: Fifty Years of Economic Change in Sri Lanka*, Sri Lanka Association of Economists, Colombo, 1997.

Mendis, E.D.L., *The Economic, Social and Cultural Impact of Tourism on Sri Lanka*, Christian Workers' Fellowship, Colombo, 1981.

Ministry of Foreign Affairs, Sri Lanka, 'Sri Lanka News Update', 25 September 1997. Ministry of Foreign

Affairs, Colombo, 1997. http://www.lanka.net/Directory/lankaupdate/25_sep_97.html lkupdate1.

Oppermann, M., 'Who exploits whom and who benefits?' in M. Oppermann (ed.), *Sex Tourism and Prostitution: Aspects of Leisure, Recreation, and Work*, Cognizant Communication Corporation, New York, 1998, pp. 153–160.

Oppermann, M. and Chon, K., *Tourism and Developing Countries*, International Thomson Business Publishing, London, 1997.

Page, S.J., *Transport and Tourism*, Addison Wesley Longman, Harlow, 1999.

Picard, M. and Wood, R. (eds), *Tourism, Ethnicity and the State in Asian and Pacific Island Societies*, University of Hawaii Press, Honolulu, 1997.

Richter, L., 'Political instability and tourism in the Less Developed Countries', in D. Harrison (ed.), *Tourism and the Less Developed Countries*, Belhaven Press, London, 1992, pp. 35–46.

Saleem, N., 'A strategy for sustainable tourism in Sri Lanka', in L. Briguglio, R. Butler, D. Harrison and W. Filho (eds), *Sustainable Tourism in Islands and Small States: Case Studies*, Pinter, New York, 1996.

Seneviratne, M., *Evil under the Sun – Child Prostitution in Sri Lanka*, Swastika Publications, Colombo, 1994.

Sievers, A., 'The significance of pilgrimage tourism in Sri Lanka', *National Geographical Journal of India* 33(4), 1987, pp. 430–447.

Simpson, B., 'Tourism and tradition: from healing to heritage', *Annals of Tourism Research* 20(1), 1993, pp. 164–181.

Simpson, B., 'Possession, dispossession and the social distribution of knowledge among Sri Lankan ritual specialists', *Royal Anthropological Institute Journal* 3, March 1997, pp. 43–59.

Sinclair, M.T., 'The tourism industry and foreign exchange leakage in a developing country: The distribution of earnings from safari and beach tourism and Kenya', in M.T. Sinclair and M. Stabler (eds), *The Tourism Industry: An International Analysis*, CAB International, Wallingford, 1992, pp. 185–204.

Sinclair, M.T. and Stabler, M., *The Economics of Tourism*, Routledge, London, 1997.

Sinclair, M.T and Vokes, R., 'The economics of tourism in Asia and the Pacific', in M. Hitchcock, V. King and M. Parnwell (eds), *Tourism in South-East Asia*, Routledge, London, 1993, pp. 200–213.

Smith, V. (ed.), *Hosts and Guests*, 2nd edn, University of Pennsylvania Press, Philadelphia, PA, 1989.

United Nations Development Programme/World Tourism Organization, *Sri Lanka Tourism Master Plan*, Draft Summary, UNDP/WTO, New York, 1992.

U.S. Department of State, *Sri Lanka Country Report on Human Rights Practices for 1997*, released by the Bureau of Democracy, Human Rights, and Labor, 30 January 1998. Available http://www.state.gov/www/global/human_rights/1997_hrp_report/sri lanka.html, 1997.

Wijesekera, M., 'Going herbal', *Explore Sri Lanka* 12(5), 1998, pp. 17–22.

Wilson, J., *Politics in Sri Lanka 1947–1973*, Macmillan, London, 1974.

World Tourism Organization, *National and Regional Tourism Planning*, Routledge, London, 1994.

World Tourism Organization, *Tourist Safety and Security: Practical Measures for Destinations*, World Tourism Organization, Madrid, 1996.

Youell, R., *Tourism: An Introduction*, Addison Wesley Longman, Harlow, 1998.

17

The Maldives

Ross Dowling

Introduction

The Republic of Maldives is a scattered group of islands with an estimated land area of 298 km^2 that stretches over an area of 90 000 km^2 of the Indian Ocean. The islands extend across the equator in a north–south strip that is some 754 km long and 118 km wide. The archipelago consists of 1190 low-lying islands, comprising twenty-six natural atolls and no island is more than 1.8 m above sea level. The country's economy is based upon two main industries: fisheries and tourism (Sarwar, 1980). These account for approximately 30 per cent of the Gross Domestic Product (GDP) and are major sources of foreign exchange earnings and government revenue. Tourism is estimated to be responsible for 20 per cent of GDP. The coral reefs and their dependence on the ocean has been the major source of livelihood of the country's population. The atolls are low-lying, surrounded by shallow, crystal-clear water and are enclosed by coral reefs. The climate is tropical with two pronounced monsoon seasons. Daily temperatures vary little throughout the year. The annual mean temperature is 28°C with a maximum of 32°C and a minimum of 25°C.

The population of the Maldives in 1997 was 263 189 with an annual growth rate of 2.9 per cent. The population is spread over 200 islands with the most populous island, and the centre of commerce being the capital Male (65 000 people;

26 per cent of the population). The remainder of the islands are largely uninhabited except for seventy-four islands which have been developed as tourist resorts. More islands will also be developed as resorts in the near future, in accordance with the Tourism Master Plan (Commission of the European Community, 1996). In many ways, the Maldives (in contrast to Sri Lanka) displays many of the characteristics of small island tourism (Conlin and Baum, 1996), with a development history as a former British protectorate dating back to 1887 which received independence in 1965 (Phadnis and Luithui, 1985). However, in an environmental context, the major challenge for the islands, as recent United Nations studies have shown, lies in the possible disastrous consequences of a rise in sea level as a result of global warming and climate change (United Nations Environment Programme, 1986; United Nations Development Programme, 1991). For this reason, the current rate of population growth, the impact of tourism and environmental pressures highlight the importance of sustainable management of the natural environment (Pren and Englebrecht, 1994).

The development of inbound tourism

The early development of tourism in the Maldives was in essence an unplanned activity

Table 17.1   *Tourism growth in the Maldives 1993–1997*

	1993	1994	1995	1996	1997
Number of arrivals	241 020	279 982	314 869	338 733	365 563
Percentage growth	2.2	16.2	12.5	7.6	7.9
Tourist bed nights	2 092 298	2 350 830	2 725 064	3 038 698	3 275 249
Percentage change	6.0	12.4	15.9	11.5	7.8
Bed occupancy (%)	64.8	67.9	70.5	72.8	77.5
Percentage change	–1.1	3.1	2.6	2.3	4.7

Source: adapted from statistics of the Ministry of Tourism, Statistics and Research Section, 1997.

Table 17.2   *Bed capacity by type of units 1993–1997*

	1993	1994	1995	1996	1997
Resorts (73)	9 061	10 160	10 688	11 472	11 962
Hotels	158	216	312	312	276
Guest houses	467	472	400	409	407
Vessels	665	790	912	1 278	1 484
Total beds	10 351	11 638	12 312	13 471	14 129
% increase		12.4	5.8	9.4	4.9

Source: adapted from statistics of the Ministry of Tourism, Statistics and Research Section, 1997.

which was largely driven by the private sector. In 1972 there were around 280 hotel beds and this increased to 2400 by the end of the decade. In 1978 the government established the Department of Tourism and Foreign Investment (later known as the Ministry of Tourism). Its aim was to promote and guide the development of the industry and to set the policy direction. In the early 1980s the Sri Lankan riots, which had adversely affected tourism in that country, also caused a drop in the number of tourists to the Maldives. However, by the end of the decade the country witnessed a resurgence in visitor numbers and the emergence of two new markets, Japan and Australia. This growth has continued with tourism in 1990 contributing 18 per cent to the GDP and accounting for 11 per cent of total employment (World Tourism Organization, 1997). Tourist arrivals have increased from 83 814 in 1984 to 338 733 in 1996. In the late 1990s international tourism is growing with 338 733 visitors in 1996 and 365 563 visitors in 1997 (Table 17.1). Similarly the number of hotel beds has risen in the same years from 13 471 to 14 129 (Table 17.2).

The huge demand for tourism from the merging economies in Asia has complemented arrivals from Europe (Table 17.3). This has decreased the earlier dependence on European tourists. WTO has been actively assisting the Maldives with the development and promotion of tourism over the past ten years. A school for hotel and catering was set up, more than 5000 resort personnel were trained in various aspects of hotel management and assistance was provided for effective tourism marketing. Notwithstanding these impressive developments, there are several constraints to further

Table 17.3   *Tourist arrivals by nationality 1997*

Country	Jan.–Dec. 1997	% share 1997 (Jan.–Dec.)
Europe	272 918	74.7
Asia	72 739	19.9
Africa	8 075	2.2
Americas	6 101	1.7
Oceania	5 730	1.6
Total arrivals	365 563	100.0

Source: Statistics Section Ministry of Tourism.

expansion and sustainable development of the sector. Reflecting the weak system of land ownership, over the years resort operators have continued to encounter difficulties in obtaining financing for investment, either from domestic or overseas banks. In particular, the fixed-term lease period, together with uncertainty over lease renewal, has tended to discourage developers from investing in upgrading of resorts, particularly near the end of the lease period from an initial term of 5 years to 35 years for investments exceeding US$10 million and 21 years for investments less than this amount. More than one-third of the total expatriate work force in the country is engaged in the tourism sector, reflecting the high dependence of the sector on foreign labour. Tourism is the largest foreign exchange earning sector. The outflow of foreign exchange earnings as expatriate workers remittances has been increasing over the years.

Tourism development

In the Maldives Islands, opportunities for land-based ecotourism are almost non-existent, owing to the small land area (298 km^2) and low diversity of terrestrial flora and fauna. However, approximately 90 000 km^2 of shallow water, with some of the world's most extensive and unspoiled coral reefs, supports a thriving diving sector, which serves as an important adjunct to the well-established sun, sea and sand tourism industry located on isolated 'resort islands' (Inskeep, 1991, 1994). The physical configuration of tourism in the Maldives is highly unusual. The resorts each occupy a separate island and are totally self-contained, accessible only by boat from the international airport. Most of the resorts have been located on uninhabited islands in order to reduce any possible social and cultural impacts. For example, Inskeep (1994) highlights the strict maintenance of Islamic codes and dress standards; nude bathing is prohibited. Infringement of the nude bathing code could result in bathers and the resort being

fined. Tourists are only allowed to visit atolls approved by the government to minimize socio-cultural impacts and, where visits to villages are permitted, they are strictly managed. The Ministry of Tourism has also embarked on an education programme to explain the economic importance of tourism to the Maldivian economy and the fragile nature of the environment. The public education programme about tourism is conducted in the public school system and on the radio. A hotel and catering training school, assisted by the United Nations Development Programme, World Tourism Organization and European Community was opened in Male in 1987.

Each resort must provide its own infrastructure and other services, and also housing and community services for its employees. The families of the employees remain on their home islands, often some distance away. Most of the resorts are developed in Kaafu (Male) Atoll, where the capital city and international airport are situated, with a lesser number located on nearby Alifu (Ari) Atoll. The Ministry of Tourism was established in 1978 and, during the 1980s, was very active in guiding the growth of tourism and applying strict development and operating standards to new and existing resorts. One of its important functions is to formulate and implement environmental protection policies and regulations. Inskeep (1994) highlights the strict enforcement powers which the Ministry of Tourism possesses. If resorts do not meet satisfactory standards, they can be closed. The government recognizes that tourism is dependent upon preservation of the environment. The present government policy is to continue expanding tourism for its economic benefits, but in a systematic manner, with strict environmental controls applied. The government has established carrying capacity standards based on several factors:

- control of tree cutting so that the natural appearance and facade of the island is maintained, with no building allowed to be higher than the tree tops;

- the maximum island area to be utilized by buildings is 20 per cent, with two-storey buildings allowed to conserve land area if there is sufficient vegetation to conceal these buildings from view, and with equal space left free on the island for every building developed on the lagoon; and
- in order to preserve the tourists' perception or image of the beach orientation of tourism in the Maldives: all guest rooms should face the beach; there should be a minimum of 5 m of linear beach available in front of each room; 68 per cent of the total length of beach on the island should be utilized for guest room frontage, 20 per cent for general resort facility frontage and the remaining 12 per cent left as open space (Inskeep, 1994).

Inskeep (1994: p. 165) also lists the criteria used by the government to maintain high standards of environmental protection and these include:

- architectural control of resort buildings;
- limiting the height of buildings and their proximity to the shore line;
- the adequate provision of water through reverse osmosis and collection from roofs to avoid affecting ground water systems;
- provision of solid waste and sewerage systems;
- controls on the marine ecology such as prohibiting tourists from collecting coral, seashells and rocks from the reefs and marine environment (see Allison, 1996, for a discussion of snorkeller damage to reef corals); and
- controls on the vulnerable turtle colonies.

The problem of waste management is addressed through the compulsory installation of incinerators, bottle crushers and compactors in all resorts. The installation of desalination plants and provision of desalinated water in tourist resorts have substantially reduced the stress on the aquifer.

The Ministry of Tourism has also implemented a Tourism Master Plan where top priority areas for tourism development have been identified (Commission of the European Community, 1996). In the latter part of the 1990s the government is making considerable efforts to diversify the tourism product. This is being carried out by enhancing the cultural attractions of the Maldives as well as through the development and expansion of activities such as surfing, cruising and big game fishing. In this regard, the cruise product has expanded steadily over the past few years: the number of floating beds has increased dramatically, more than doubling since 1993. The government is also concentrating on providing the necessary infrastructure for tourism development. In order to expand the tourism industry through systematic selection of new regions, the government in 1983 selected Ari Atoll (south of Male Atoll) as the new zone. An assessment is currently being made of the services that have developed in an ad hoc manner over the past years to cater to the Ari Atoll resorts to determine areas where improvements are needed and what additional facilities are required. In addition, a 700-bed resort is still under construction in the tourism zone.

Currently, there are sixty-one upgrading and re-development projects being undertaken by the private sector in existing tourist resorts (Maldives Ministry of Tourism, 1998). These projects were scheduled for completion in 1998 and resulted in an additional 314 beds. Development of a tourism service centre is taking place in Ari Atoll, Dhangethi tourism zone. From the fourteen islands selected for resort development under Phase 1 of the second Tourism Master Plan, nine islands were leased out in August 1997. Construction work is in progress on these projects and four of the resorts opened in 1998. A new luxury hotel is currently being developed in Male and it is estimated to have a minimum bed capacity of 300. In the Addu Atoll at Villiingili a hotel has been proposed with a bed capacity of about 1500. Another major project is the South Asia Integrated Tourism Human Resource Development Program. This is a joint initiative of seven South Asian countries, with assistance from the

European Commission. The project commenced in 1995 with the establishment of national- and regional-level committees for coordinating project activities. The major technical components are the training of trainers in various disciplines of the hotel and tourism industry, and the preparation of training manuals and establishment of regional skills standards for human resource development for the tourism industry. On the Male Atoll at Villingilli, the development of a Hotel and Catering Training Institute has been proposed by the Indian government.

The above developments have boosted tourism in the Maldives, resulting in an increased contribution to GDP from 11.5 per cent in 1980 to 18 per cent in 1990, close to one-third of total government earnings and more than 60 per cent of foreign exchange receipts. Moreover, tourism now directly accounts for about 11 per cent of total employment and one-third of the total expatriate work force. As such, tourism today has become the major vehicle for the country's impressive socio-economic development over the past two decades. The Maldives attracted over 365 000 high-spending tourists in 1997, paying US$150 per night to enjoy the sun, sand and reefs with their spectacular marine life. The Maldivian government had started a master plan aimed at increasing the number of resorts and bed capacity.

Marketing

Maldives tourism is healthy and market growth has been relatively steady during the last five years. In 1994 and 1995 there was a dramatic increase in tourist arrivals with an increase of 16.2 per cent and 12.5 per cent, respectively. In 1996 and 1997 growth was steady, although not as dramatic as the previous two years, with an increase of 7.6 per cent in 1996 and 7.9 per cent in 1997. Europe has been the major generator of tourism to the Maldives since the start of its tourism industry in 1972. The main countries are Germany, Italy, UK, Switzerland and France.

The other main market for the Maldives is Japan. Some 91 per cent of tourists in 1991 were on package tours, and overseas tour operators dealt with all but 0.6 per cent of tourists whose arrangements were made through domestic Maldives tour operators. A market that has grown during the past three years is The Netherlands: 9547 arrivals in 1997 compared with 5239 in 1996. The most significant potential markets for the Maldives are India, Eastern Europe and the USA. Eastern Europe also has good potential owing to the economic prosperity and political stability in some Eastern European countries. Flight connections to and from Europe to the Maldives are already established enabling relatively easy access for Eastern Europeans to the Maldives.

The US has the greatest number of scuba divers and, since one of the major attractions in the Maldives is the unique diving possibilities, it is a great attraction for the diving segment of the American market. However, there are problems relating to the lack of direct flights and distance involved.

Impacts

Tourism development within the Maldives has focused on 'enclave tourism'. All but one of the resorts, which vary in size from as few as six to more than 150 rooms, occupy separate islands and are totally self-contained. Hence, each resort is an autonomous unit that provides its own power, sewage, garbage disposal arrangements and water supply (Economist Intelligence Unit, 1995). The inhabitants of the resort islands also comprise only staff and guests which has helped to minimize the negative aspects of tourism, allowing for local cultures, traditions and lifestyles to be sustained without undue alien pressure on society. At the same time, it has also become apparent that in allocating islands for tourism development a careful balance is required between both the geographical spread and population densities (World Tourism

Organization, 1997). The environment began to receive attention in 1984 when a National Council for the Environment Protection was established. To limit environment degradation and to help sustain the natural integrity of the environment as far as possible the government has taken a number of measures. These include the introduction of comprehensive regulations and guidelines for resort development and operations. Carrying capacities for tourist resorts to limit the number of users below environment thresholds have been defined. Only 68 per cent of beach length can be utilized for guest rooms, 20 per cent has to be reserved for public use and 12 per cent must be left as open space.

Issues

With the expansion of Male International Airport and the development of air links, the tourism industry has been able to achieve some degree of market diversification. Nevertheless, the major generating market still continues to be Western Europe. However, as tourism is increasingly competitive internationally, the Maldives needs to have an effective marketing strategy. Many of the environmental problems faced by the Maldives are common to other island economies and are threatening the sustainability of the industry. Issues include those of water quality, sanitation, pollution of land and water, deforestation, solid waste collection and disposal, environment-related health problems owing to urban congestion and loss of biological diversity. In addition there is a high degree of economic dependence on the natural environment.

The environmental impact of tourism is disproportionate when tourist numbers are compared with the number of local inhabitants. The production of solid waste by resorts is considerable and in per capita terms, much higher than the Maldivian average, with resorts producing up to 16.5 kg of solid waste per visitor per week. At present the majority of resort waste is either dumped at sea or incinerated, while the resort survey indicates that operators are currently spending US$300–500 per month on beach cleaning. However, the problem does not seem sufficient to prevent loss of amenity and deterioration of local environment. However, the Maldives policy currently addresses only one aspect of carrying capacity and refers only to land space. To maintain the natural beauty of the island environment, regulations state that the built environment should utilize no more than 20 per cent of the total land area. As the Maldives markets beach tourism, the regulations require there to be 5 m of beach for every room, every room should face the beach and 68 per cent of the beach length should be utilized for guest rooms in this way. According to the tourism authority, the capacity of each island has to be determined individually, given the land area and the layout and design of the resort.

Discussion

According to Brown *et al.* (1997) the strategy to try to overcome some of the local problems of environmental degradation has been that of dispersal. In the Maldives, this has meant developing new atolls for tourism. Evidence suggests that environmental degradation continues and looks unlikely to be halted despite the regulations which have been enforced in both Nepal and the Maldives. In the Maldives, the economic impact of such degradation will show almost immediately in reductions in visitor rates amongst repeat visitors. Although regulations are now in place which restrict the nature of tourist development in the Maldives, further expansion of the tourist industry is planned, though this will only occur through developing new areas and exploiting new atolls. The indicators which Brown *et al.* (1997) have examined suggest that the carrying capacity of the islands may have been reached and that the environmental impacts of expansion of the industry may soon take their toll. One issue is whether policy can be implemented which enables revenue from tourism to continue to increase, whilst visitor numbers are restricted, a stated aim of the Maldives government.

The Maldives ambitious tourism growth programme of doubling the number of 12 000 beds in its seventy-four holiday resorts may be adversely affected by environmental problems. However, this growth is scheduled to occur at the same time as most of the country's 1200 low-lying coral islands could disappear as the ocean level rises owing to global warming. The plan to increase the tourist bed capacity to 22 500 by the year 2005 is therefore now being reconsidered by the Maldivian Tourism Minister, Ibrahim Hussain Zaki, who stated that 'We do not want to spoil our environment at the cost of tourism'. However, fourteen islands with 3000 additional beds are being developed as new resorts and will be ready by 1999. Holiday resorts in the Maldives are separate islands that import everything from drinking water to manpower and guests are requested to take their plastic bottles and other non-biodegradable items back to their own countries instead of polluting the Maldivian environment.

Future prospects

Within the Maldives there is probably still room for further diversification of the islands' attractions. Considerable progress has already been made in this area – resort islands now have a much wider range of sporting facilities such as tennis, as well as discotheques, speciality restaurants and film evenings. Excursions are also organized for tourists to visit the inhabited islands although, as indicated, these are made in moderation so as to avoid culture shock for local populations. However, more could perhaps be done to revive some of the local arts and crafts, for example, or to provide information on and excursions to see the cultural and historic development of the Maldives (Economist Intelligence

Unit, 1995). Another area that is rapidly developing is cruise ships. The number of floating beds has increased dramatically, more than doubling since 1993 (Maldives Ministry of Tourism, 1998).

There are a number of both public- and private-sector projects currently in progress or about to be commenced within the Maldives. Currently, there are sixty-one resorts being upgraded and fourteen islands proposed for development. Within the public sector a major waste-management project is underway and also an integrated Tourism Human Resource Development programme. The latter is a joint initiative of seven South Asian countries, with assistance from the European Commission (Maldives Ministry of Tourism, 1998). According to the World Tourism Organization, over the period 1995–2000, tourist arrivals to South Asia are projected to increase to around 7 per cent annually. While the Maldives has been able to experience rapid and impressive growth in visitor arrivals in the past, to capture its share of tourist arrivals to Asia during the rest of the decade will require investment to increase resort bed capacity, policies to attract foreign investment in resort development and a larger pool of skilled labour. In 1997, in the light of these facts, the Maldives embarked on a second ten-year Master Plan. The Plan envisages the following:

(a) to create 10 000 beds in phases of development;
(b) to bring into use the first 3000 beds in the next two years;
(c) to harmonize tourism with other economic activities; and
(d) to achieve a better geographic spread of the benefits of tourism.

Tourism is regarded by many countries, particularly resource-poor countries, as a potential stimulus to the economy. In reference to the Maldives and Nepal, Brown et al. (1997) state that both countries are currently employing 'dispersal' techniques to overcome the adverse impacts of tourism, but such strategies do not address the fundamental problem of maintaining tourism revenues whilst minimizing environmental damage (Brown *et al.*, 1997). Tourism development in the Maldives may have occurred in a systematic manner, but this chapter has shown that it is far from the overtly positive and uncritical image painted by Inskeep (1994: p. 167):

The Maldives have developed a very suitable form of tourism – it is appropriate for their small island environment; does not generate any serious environmental or socio-cultural impacts; creates substantial economic benefits; and meets tourists expectations and satisfaction levels. Success has been based on government policy when it is widely acknowledged that many of the products and goods consumed by tourists have to be imported given the limited opportunities for import substitution.

Nevertheless, since 1985, tourism has consistently been the largest sector in the economy, with a sectoral contribution of about 18 per cent. There has been a direct employment benefit of roughly 81 per cent of the labour force and indirect benefits in the form of increased building construction activity and, to a lesser degree, a revival of local handicrafts (Hameed, 1997).

References

Allison, W., 'Snorkeller damage to reef corals in the Maldive Islands', *Coral Reefs* 15(4), 1996, pp. 215–218.

Brown, K., Turner, R.K., Hameed, H. and Bateman, I., 'Environmental carrying capacity and tourism development in the Maldives and Nepal', *Environmental Conservation* 24(4), 1997, pp. 316–325.

Commission of the European Community, *Maldives Tourism Master Plan 1996–2005: Volume 1 Main Report*, Commission of the European Community, Brussels, 1996.

Conlin, M. and Baum, T. (eds), *Island Tourism: Management Principles and Practice*, Wiley, Chichester, 1996,

Economist Intelligence Unit, 'Maldives', *International Tourism Reports* 2, 1995, pp. 26–43.

Hameed, M., 'Presentation by Maldives', in *Tourism 2000: Building a Sustainable Future for Asia–Pacific*, World Tourism Organization, Madrid, 1997, pp. 155–160.

Inskeep, E., *Tourism Planning: An Integrated and Sustainable Development Approach*, Van Nostrand Reinhold, New York, 1991.

Inskeep, E., *National and Regional Tourism Planning*, Routledge, London, 1994.

Maldives Ministry of Tourism, 'Marketing of the Maldives Tourism Product', Unpublished Report, Ministry of Tourism, Maldives, 1998.

Phadnis, U. and Luithui, E., *Maldives: Winds of Change in an Atoll State*, South Asian Pubishers, New Dehli, 1985.

Pren, C. and Englebrecht, C., 'Background, conceptual structure and organizational-administrative establishment of a sustainable development strategy for coral islands: The example of the Maldivian Archipelago', *GeoJournal* 22(4), 1994, pp. 433–442.

Sarwar, L., *The Maldives: An Introductory Economic Report*, World Bank, Washington, DC, 1980.

United Nations Development Programme, *Towards Sustainable Development for Atolls and other Small Islands*, United Nations Development Programme, Washington, DC, 1991.

United Nations Environment Programme, *Environmental Problems of the Marine and Coastal Area of the Maldives*, United Nations Environment Programme, Nairobi, 1986.

World Tourism Organization, 'Tourism 2000: building a sustainable future for Asia–Pacific', Final Report of the Asia Pacific Ministers' Conference on Tourism and the Environment, Maldives, 16–17 February 1997, World Tourism Organization, Madrid, 1997.

18

Tourism in Nepal, Bhutan and Tibet: contrasts in the facilitation, constraining and control of tourism in the Himalayas

Nepal

David G. Simmons and
Shankar Koirala

Introduction

This chapter reviews the history of tourism growth and development in Nepal, with a further section examining the contrast with Bhutan and Tibet. In many respects the issues addressed mirror the myriad of issues implicit in tourism development in less developed countries (English, 1986). Key tourism resources are unique mountain systems, in this case the world's highest mountain chain, the Himalayas; and the unique cultures that have evolved in these places. Like her near neighbours Tibet and Bhutan, access into Nepal was almost impossible until borders were opened to international traffic in the early 1950s. The lure of the high mountains and the particular challenge and history of climbing on Sagamatha (Mt Everest), and a more liberal policy to tourism has meant that for Nepal the rate of change has been more rapid than that of many neighbours. Cockerell (1997) cites the Asian Development Bank report in 1995 which stated that Nepal needs to spend at least US$90 million to restore its environment to maintain its 'Shangri-La' image. Democracy as a new form of governance has required the development of new agencies and responsibilities at the same time as Western influences, of which tourism is but one, have challenged traditional cultural relationships, systems and resource use. Yet, as Cockerell (1997: p. 41) argued 'until recently tourism development was not considered a priority by the Nepalese authorities, who never really committed public-sector investment to the industry. This attitude now seems to have changed, however, with the recognition of tourism's potential to Nepal's economic growth and employment growth'. While much has been achieved and new models of tourism management are being developed, tourism remains but one among many pressing problems.

Tourism products and resources

Nepal was traditionally known as a remote and inaccessible Himalayan mountain frontier, isolated from the outside world. The twin images of high mountains and previously inaccessible areas and cultures gave Nepal a mystic aura that remains to the present. Writing of Pokhara, now Nepal's second major tourism hub, Hagen, a Swiss geologist and early explorer, commented the 'Pokhara area shows the greatest contrast in landscape. Nowhere in the world can the highest mountains reaching an 8,000 metre level be admired from such a small distance and from the tropical lowland without any intermediate mountain ranges. Pokhara is certainly one of the most extraordinary and beautiful places in the world' (Hagen, 1961; cited in Raj, 1993: p. 1).

Major tourist attractions and activities

Nepal is known throughout the world as a 'mountain destination'. Its primary attraction is the southeastern zone of the Himalayan chain which includes the world's highest mountain peaks. As a tourist attraction the Himalayas are today well augmented by opportunities for wildlife watching and, for Nepal alone, the presence of over fifty recognized ethnic groups. For less adventurous visitor groups, especially for other Asian visitors, major religious sites (including shrines to the

Hindu Lord Pasupatinath in Kathmandu, Muktinath; and Lumbini, the birth place of Lord Buddha) are a primary attractions.

In spite of the diverse geographic spread of tourism sites, the overwhelming number of tourists remain in the Kathmandu Valley where there is now a concentrated development of sight-seeing and cultural attractions (see Shackley, 1994). The flow of tourists from outside Kathmandu has been concentrated in a few areas and increasing the regional spread of visitation has been a constant focus of policy action. Today more than 40 per cent of visitors are attracted to Nepal's sixteen protected natural areas which encompass more than 15 per cent of the total area of the country (Department of National Parks and Wildlife Conservation (DNPWC), 1996). However, among the sixteen protected areas, four (Chitwan, Annapurna, Sagamatha (Everest) and Langtang) receive 98 per cent of the tourism volume (DNPWC, 1996; King Mahendra Trust for Nature Conservation (KMTNC), 1996). This means that some of the parks are heavily visited and have suffered to some extent from various problems including deforestation, litter and cultural modification (Bhattarai, 1985; Gurung, 1990; Zurick, 1992; Wells, 1994; Baskota and Sharma, 1995). Thus, tourism in Nepal presents a useful case study of many of the tensions inherent in third-world tourism development: an urgent need for foreign exchange and investment, fragile mountain environments, diversity of cultures, set against pressing domestic challenges in population growth and associated infrastructure, health and education services.

Tourist arrivals

The coming of democracy in 1951 when the country was first opened to foreign visitors marked a new era in Nepal (Belk, 1993). After the climbing success of Tenzing and Hillary on Mt Everest (Sagamatha) in 1953, Nepal became a highly sought-after destination for climbers (Thakali, 1994). During the first decade following the opening of borders to foreigners (1950–1960), over 100 large and small mountaineering expeditions visited Nepal, in addition to scientists, geographers, anthropologists and other tourists (Engma Consultants, 1989).

Tourism development in Nepal was also cultivated by foreign diplomats. In the 1950s, several embassies and missions were opened and there was an increasing inflow of diplomats and their families. They found Nepal a wonderful country, rich in diverse attractions of natural beauty and cultural heritage. In their writings, and among their peers, they encouraged others to visit this unspoilt mountainous land. Hence, this period can be classified as a period of 'diplomat sponsored tourism' (Koirala, 1997).

Following the era of 'diplomatic tourism', Nepal became better known in the 1960s for its easy access to drugs, cooperative and easy natured people (Adams, 1992), and cheap living. At this time, many 'hippies' were attracted to visit Kathmandu by Hindu cults (Sill, 1991). However, in the early 1970s, at the time of the coronation of His Majesty King Birendra, the Nepalese government enforced new visa and foreign currency regulations and also banned the cultivation and

selling of drugs (Belk, 1993). Consequently, the flow of hippies to Nepal has gradually declined, and from the mid-1970s 'mountain tourism' or 'adventure tourism' became more popular and acceptable images (Koirala, 1997).

Until 1965, the total number of tourists arriving in the country was less than 10 000 annually. During the 1970s, the figure increased five-fold, with an average annual growth rate of 13.9 per cent, before levelling off in the 1980s (average annual growth 5.7 per cent) (Department of Tourism (DOT), 1995). In the early 1980s, tourist numbers stagnated because of rapidly rising oil prices and airfares and subsequent economic recession in the West, and unrest in Northern India (Sill, 1991). Recent growth in visitor arrivals since this time has fluctuated, but has shown an overall annual increase in excess of 10 per cent per annum (Table 18.1).

In 1988, the government requested an increase in the number of tourists visiting Nepal to 1 million by the year 2000. The private sector criticized the government for projecting an over-ambitious and unreliable plan in contrast with the little support it had generated to provide the necessary infrastructure to achieve it (Sharma, 1995). An independent

Table 18.1 *Tourist arrivals and gross foreign exchange earnings 1984–1996*

Year	Tourist arrivals			Gross foreign exchange earnings in convertible currencies		
	Number	Growth rate (%)	Average length of stay (days)	Total earnings (US$ 000)	% change in US$	Average spending per visitor per day (US$)
1984	176 634	−1.5	10.6	41 273	15.7	33.0
1985	180 989	2.5	11.3	39 185	−5.1	27.0
1986	223 331	23.4	11.2	50 841	29.8	27.0
1987	248 080	11.1	12.0	60 229	18.5	27.0
1988	265 943	7.2	12.0	63 502	5.4	27.0
1989	239 945	−9.8	12.0	68 343	7.6	29.0
1990	254 885	6.2	12.0	63 701	−6.8	27.2
1991	292 995	15.0	9.3	58 589	−8	31.0
1992	334 353	14.1	10.1	61 090	4.3	26.4
1993	293 567	−12.2	11.9	66 337	8.6	26.4
1994	326 531	11.2	10.0	88 195	32.9	39.4
1995	363 395	11.3	11.3	116 784	32.4	42.0
1996[a]	393 613	8.5	13.5	117 000	–	–

Note
[a]World Tourism Organization, 1998.
Source: Nepal Rastra Bank 1994, cited in DOT 1995; DOT (unpublished data) 1996.

study of tourism development programmes, funded by the Asian Development Bank (ADB) for the Ministry of Tourism, Nepal, more conservatively projected a total of around 950 000 tourists per year by the year 2010 (Touche Ross and New Era, 1990). The current estimates of the impact of tourism on the economy suggest that between 12 000 and 15 000 people are employed in tourism activities.

In 1998 Nepal launched a 'Visit Nepal year'. Key promotional themes were 'Nepal '98 – A world on its own' and 'a sustainable habitat through sustainable tourism'. Their promotional material indicates current policy direction: 'The theme highlights the needs to make tourism work better for Nepal and ensure the development of environmentally sound products, improvement of our service standards and distributions of the benefits of tourism to our people in the cities and the remotest regions alike' (Ministry of Tourism and Civil Aviation, Nepal, 1998). Implicit in this statement is recognition of fundamental tensions surrounding the deployment of natural and cultural resources for (third world) tourism development, although these may be argued to be particularly acute for Nepal given the poverty of the local people, rate of population growth, constant and at times rapid growth in visitor arrivals and poor infrastructure. As Cockerell (1997: p. 42) observes 'The campaign has two dimensions. For national consumption, tourism is positioned as a socio-economic activity that touches the lives of all Nepalese. For the outside world the campaign highlights the natural resources of the country, the friendliness of the people and stresses Nepal's 'huge variety of plant, bird and animal life within its sharply tilted terrain and its wealth of natural scenic wonders, in addition to its cultural and historic attractions'.

tourist inflow to Nepal until the late 1970s. Since the 1980s Asia has been the major source, with a total of 180 377 Asian visitors (49.6 per cent of tourist arrivals) to Nepal in 1995 (DOT, 1996).

The major reason for an increasing inflow of Asian tourists to Nepal is the greater number of Indian tourists. For 1995 a total of 117 260 visitors (65 per cent of the Asian market) originated from India. Indian tourists are attracted to Nepal for a variety of reasons, including: Kathmandu's easy accessibility without the need for passports and visas; Nepal is an adjacent Hindu country with significant religious monuments, such as the temple of Lord Pasupatinath and Lumbini, the birthplace of Lord Buddha; it is a market-place for foreign goods (Folsom, 1988); and it offers an alternative mountain destination for Indians because of the political instability in Kashmir (Sill, 1991). Importantly, the cooler altitudes of Nepal also offer respite from the heat of the monsoon and so extend the tourist season into thee months when Western visitor numbers are low.

Today Western Europe remains in second place as a source of visitor arrivals (133 803 in 1995) with North America third (29 702 arrivals in 1995) (DOT, 1996). Within the Western European market, significant increases occurred in arrivals from the UK, Austria, Belgium and Switzerland, while declining numbers were recorded from Germany in 1995. The remainder of tourist arrivals are from Australia and the Pacific (11 499 visitors in 1995 (3.1 per cent)) with a very small flow from Africa making up the total (DOT, 1996). The majority of arrivals are by air (88 per cent in 1995) and seasonality in arrivals poses particular problems for the tourism industry and occupancy rates (Cockerell, 1997).

Tourist arrivals by nationality

Tourists from nearly forty-five different countries visit Nepal. By continent, Western European tourists were the major source of

Purpose

Most tourists visit Nepal for holiday/pleasure (50.5 per cent) and trekking (23.8 per cent). The number of trekking tourists has increased steadily as Nepal has become widely known as a trekking destination. The longer length of stay of trekkers and their regional spread gives them a greater importance in tourism in Nepal than their numbers suggest. Businessmen, government officials and convention attendees constituted about 14 per cent of arrivals (DOT, 1996).

Trekking

The opening of the Nepalese Himalayas for sightseeing created a new demand for trekking (see Zurick, 1992; Shackley, 1994). The intensive use of the Himalayas is the main focus, with the local culture and way of life being a secondary attraction. The Tourism Master Plan of 1972 recognized the importance of trekking and also emphasized the development of Pokhara (the nearest city to the Annapurna Conservation Area (ACA) Treks) as its base (Ministry of Commerce and Industry, 1972). Because historical trails linking villages are used, trekking can be comparatively easy for the inexperienced traveller.

Commercial trekking, both from Pokhara and Sagamatha, started in the mid-1960s for wealthy tourists (Adams, 1992; Pagdin, 1995). By 1994, there were 76 865 tourists who visited Nepal for trekking. The majority of these (58.2 per cent) visited the ACA, while Everest and Langtang were used by 17.5 per cent and 10.6 per cent of all trekkers, respectively. During this period there has also been a progression from fully escorted, multi-porter groups to the independent trekker who makes greater use of local accommodation and resources. The process of opening new areas to tourism continues as a primary means to regional development. Recently two new trekking areas, Kanchanjunga in the Eastern Himalayas and Dolpa to the west of the Annapurna range, have been opened to trekkers in 1989, and the Resort Area Development Projects at Dhanakuta in the Eastern Hill were also established (Sill, 1991).

More recently, as a reaction to the problems of tourists in concentrated areas, specialized ecotourism projects have been established in

Nepal to minimize negative impacts and to maximize the economic benefits to the local people (Curry and Morvardi, 1992; Thakali, 1995). The first of such an approach was started in 1992 in the Ghalekharka–Sikles area in the ACA as a model eco-trek (Gurung and De Coursey, 1994). Since then, various projects, the Langtang Ecotourism Project in 1995 (The Mountain Institute 1998) and recently the Manaslu Ecotourism Project have been established.

Major issues and problems of tourism development

Tourism in Nepal is in very many respects a microcosm of tourism issues in the developing world (English, 1986; Belk, 1993), whereby tensions inevitably exist between domestic development pressures, the pressing needs for foreign exchange and employment (Britton, 1982), and the dual and often conflicting needs of government to both stimulate and foster tourism as a new industry while at the same time protecting the essential environments and cultures that provide the core of the tourism product (De Kadt, 1979; O'Grady, 1982; Crick, 1989). The research by Wanhill (1992) which examined tourism manpower issues, specifically the challenge for human resource management and training to meet the needs of expanding numbers of visitors, provided a model of likely needs by the year 2000. But this has to be set against constraints on the development of the tourism industry. As Cockerell (1997: p. 50) observes:

Probably the biggest practical problem that Nepal's tourism industry faces is a lack of airline seats for visitors to reach the destination. International air traffic has increased significantly over the past ten years, but this has nevertheless been inadequate to meet demand. The potential for profitability on tourist routes to Nepal is not considered sufficiently good by many carriers to justify starting a service. Others, like Thai Airways International, have had their request to increase frequencies and capacity turned down by the Nepalese authorities for fear of jeopardising the national carrier's, Royal Nepalese Airlines, (RNAC), market position.

As a result, arrivals on RNAC in 1995 at Tribhuvan International Airport were 48 per cent, twice that of its nearest rival – Indian Airlines. This is quite impressive for an international airline which operates two Boeing 757s and a number of Boeing 727s while serving thirteen destinations in ten countries. Thus, in 1995 RNAC carried 432 265 to/from Nepal on scheduled flights, while Indian Airlines carried 204 958, followed by Tahi Airways (93 595), Biman Bangladesh (38 466), Lufthansa (34 981), Pakistan International Airlines (23 440), Singapore Airlines (21 845), Aeroflot (8784) and Druk Air (5657) which serves Bhutan. A further 33 190 passengers arrived/departed on charter flights in 1995. However, in May 1997, Lufthansa announced its decision to cease flights after inaugurating the service in 1987. Losses of DM4 million in 1994 and DM10 million in 1995 have forced it to withdraw services, with high operational costs owing to high-altitude flying, a short runway (reducing the load factor for safety reasons) and the negative image of flying into Kathmandu which is in a valley hemmed in with hills.

In Nepal, while early growth was led by private-sector interests, government tourism policy has been focused primarily on increasing tourist numbers in order to acquire economic benefits. As a result, the negative consequences of tourism development have tended to be overlooked or ignored. Consequently, leakage of tourist expenditure, environmental and cultural impacts, over-exploitation of resources and inadequate infrastructure facilities and services are cumulative problems, to the extent that they now challenge overall tourism development in Nepal. For instance, by 1983, 70 per cent of tourist revenues in Nepal had been spent on imports (Richter, 1989). Similarly, the industry's own estimates show a 45–75 per cent leakage from tourism receipts (Richter, 1989).

In the environmental arena deforestation is the key problem debated in the literature. Over the last two decades, there have been a number of reports of large areas of virgin forest being cut down to meet the needs of trekkers (Richter, 1989; Touche Ross and New Era, 1990; Belk, 1993; Nepal Watch UK, 1993). For example, in the Sagarmatha National Park, tourism was estimated to have increased the local demand for wood by 85 per cent (Sharma, 1992). Other commentaries point to high levels of indigenous population growth, larger houses (as incomes rise) and large-scale movements of government and military personnel as additional or overriding factors contributing to the problems of deforestation (Ives and Messerli, 1989). However, there are indications that the government is seeking to address decades of tourism impacts on the environment, such as the removal of rubbish from the Himalayas. For example, in 1996, the Nepal Mountain Association and the government organized the fifth expedition to remove rubbish from the mountain. On Mount Everest, up to 16 m^3 of rubbish were removed since the first expeditions took place in 1952. This is certainly very good for international media publicity and for overseas promotion, together with the high-profile visits by international dignitaries associated with sustainable development projects.

Cultural impacts are a similar problem in certain contexts. Some argue that tourism undermines traditional cultures and values, while drug abuse, prostitution and smuggling are reported to be on the increase (Belk, 1993; Nepal Watch UK, 1993; Sharma, 1995). Other writers (e.g. Thakali, 1994) argue that many Nepali groups have been traders over many generations, that tourism merely represents a new form of trade and that cultures can and do adapt to such changing circumstances. Notwithstanding these arguments, the particular effects of rapid tourism growth are of concern to the government, religious authorities and the overall population in Nepal (Hansen-Sturm, 1983, cited in Richter, 1989: p. 173). There are a number of factors commonly associated with the above problems:

- tourism development in Nepal has always been viewed in terms of how to increase foreign earnings through growth in tourist numbers, with little or no attention paid to local needs and interests (Baskota and Sharma, 1995);
- there is a lack of both control over tourism expansion (Belk, 1993) and local participation in planning and implementation of tourist activities (Koirala, 1997);
- tourism planning has often been enacted in isolation from conservation, natural resource and parks management, horticulture and livestock concerns (Sharma, 1992; Baskota and Sharma, 1995);
- government regulations are not effectively implemented or monitored (Sharma, 1992; Koirala, 1997) and government is ill-equipped to deal with problems such as deforestation (Richter, 1989; and
- there is a lack of strong and effective coordination between the various sectors (public and private) for tourism development. For example, government agencies often narrowly define their area of jurisdiction and take care of only those problems that directly affect their sectoral interest (Baskota and Sharma, 1995; Koirala, 1997).

A lack of institutional capacity to monitor and regulate the environmental impacts of tourism is seen as the key structural factor limiting balanced tourism policy, planning and implementation. Similarly, the Eighth Five Year Plan (1992–1997) also noted that a lack of appropriate policy, administration, rules and regulations, and their effective implementation, is the major issue of tourism development in Nepal (National Planning Commission (NPC), 1992). As an initial move the government has aimed to reshape its key tourism agencies and gain greater private-sector input into tourism policy through a new Tourism Board.

For all its trials and tribulations tourism has grown to be a major industry in Nepal and a source of much needed cash. There are also some emerging areas of success that are gaining international recognition. Among these is the Annapurna Conservation Area project administered by a non-governmental organization, the King Mahendra Trust for Nature Conservation. The work of this organization in administering the ACA project area includes managing two major trekking areas – the Jomson–Annapurna circuit and Annapurna Sanctuary (Annapurna Base camp) – which accommodate up to 60 000 trekkers per year. Here the goals of conservation and development are integrated within a village-based protected area framework. Key implementation processes are based on high levels of local participation in decision making, alongside high local ownership of key tourism plant (Parker, 1997).The overarching aim is to ensure that tourism fulfils its development tasks by contributing both to community needs and projects (via entry fees) as well as individual entrepreneurship. This model has much to recommend it and could well serve as a basis for community-based tourism development elsewhere (Gurung and De Coursey, 1994).

Tourism planning in Nepal

Although Nepal is located on traditional Asian trading routes, and there had been some early explorers prior to the opening of borders in 1951, modern tourism development in Nepal was initiated by early explorers, such as Colonel Jimmy Edwards of Tiger Tops (an exclusive resort at Royal Chitwan National Park) fame. These individuals had the connections to both outside markets and business skills to ensure early market development and success. Thus, it is probably fair to say that tourism discovered Nepal, rather than the other way around and, as such, the government has been a late arrival at the policy table. In Nepal's case this is especially so given its relatively recent (and ongoing) evolution of democracy and associated bureaucratic governance. Notwithstanding these comments, tourism has always had support from the Monarchy and has had a Department of Tourism since 1956.

At the national level, the first recognition of the importance of tourism planning was given in 1956 when the First Five Year National Development Plan indicated tourism as a means for economic development and made an attempt to increase tourist numbers and to improve tourist facilities such as hotel accommodation and travel agencies (NPC, 1956).

In 1972, a ten-year 'Tourism Master Plan' was prepared. The main objectives of the plan were to increase foreign exchange earnings and to use tourism as an economic force in regional development. To achieve the above objectives, the plan provided for: developing tourist services (i.e. roads, air-services, accommodation and resorts); publicity and advertising; developing tourist centres outside the Kathmandu Valley; training; and providing reasonable entertainment for tourists (Ministry of Commerce and Industry, 1972). The market segments considered in the 1972 plan were: organized sightseeing tourism; independent 'Nepal-style' tourism; trekking; and pilgrimage.

The original Nepal Tourism Master Plan 1972 was reviewed in 1984. This review considered that the private sector had responded well to the Tourism Master Plan 1972, but that public-sector efforts fell short of what had been envisaged (Steigenberger Consulting and Speerplan GmbH, 1984). Tourism has been a feature of each Five-Year National Development Plan, and the Eighth Plan (1992–1997) is no exception. The Eighth Plan was prepared after the 1991 restoration of democracy (after a brief period of communist party rule) which has led to the adoption of more open policies. A task force of public- and private-sector interests in tourism has been formed to guide implementation. The major planning objectives of this plan are: to encourage tourism, especially high-spending visitors; to encourage employment opportunities; to decentralize tourism away from Kathmandu; and to reduce foreign exchange

'leakage' by reducing both the export of tourism-generated income and tourism-related imports (NPC, 1992).

As is the case elsewhere, effective tourism development requires a high level of public-sector coordination. Nepal is no exception, with a National Planning Commission (NPC) which is responsible for inter-sectoral coordination in plan formulation and periodic monitoring and evaluation of plans and progress. Meanwhile, two lead agencies exist for tourism: a ministry with policy responsibilities and a department which provides oversight of marketing and promotion and some local infrastructure development initiatives. Physical infrastructure planning is normally designed by various sectoral ministries, such as Public Works and Transport, Local Development, and Housing and Physical Planning and implemented by their local line agencies. Immigration, border control, police and civil aviation are also other key agencies. At the local level, municipalities and village development councils (VDCs) have a key integrating and planning role.

Recent reviews, for example a UNDP-funded 'Quality Tourism Project', indicate some overlap and confusion between the roles of the Ministry and Department of Tourism and advocate a national Tourism Board as a public–private sector partnership to advance and coordinate ongoing tourism policy. With the emergence of three main tourism hubs (Kathmandu, Pokhara, and Sagamatha/Everest) tourism policies and processes are now required to be developed and integrated at the local level (Koirala, 1997).

Conclusion

Nepal has a relatively recent, but at times intense, involvement with tourism development. Early beginnings with explorers and climbers have given way to a steady stream of both holidaymakers and trekkers. This latter group has also evolved away from fully escorted tours to an increasing reliance on free independent travel, which is argued to have supported greater regional and local entrepreneurship and development. In terms of tourism policy, the opening of new areas and trekking routes to tourists remains a major policy vehicle, as the economic successes of early tourism areas, such as the Sagarmatha/Everest region, have become apparent.

Tourism development has not been without its cost and detractors. Important among these is ongoing debate about the significance and role of tourism as one of many agents of environmental and socio-cultural change. In this sense, tourism development needs to be seen as just one set of challenges in a wider development context. In the recent past, Nepal has responded to ongoing concerns for sustainable development. While tourism is today a significant source of overseas funds and remains a sought-after means of wider economic and social development, Nepal has achieved some considerable success in its participatory approaches to tourism development. These models are receiving international appreciation and have much to offer other countries who are also struggling with participatory approaches to nature- and culture-based tourism development.

Tibet and Bhutan

C. Michael Hall and Stephen Page

Tibet and Bhutan both offer similar products and experiences to Nepal. Data on Bhutan remain scant. As indicated in the Introduction to this chapter, they differ primarily in their forms of governance and the freedoms accorded to tourists. Tibet is located to the northwest of Nepal and has only relatively recently been opened to 'controlled' levels of tourist visitation. Travel is possible within Tibet, but it has to be carefully negotiated via Chinese agencies to which Tibet is politically annexed. An early paper by Sessa (1989) examines some of the rudimentary aspects of tourism development in Tibet since, like Bhutan, it has attracted comparatively little tourism research. Various media indicate the problems of travelling within Tibet, although an increasing number of excursions and some independent travel are made from both Nepal and overland from China. There are current inter-government policy initiatives to improve tourism provision in the area by joint cooperation on larger circuit treks. International media interest in the political ramifications of the Chinese policy of resettlement of Chinese nationals to maintain a legitimacy over annexation and its effect on a historic and fragile culture are certainly of concern to Western observers. Much of Tibet's unique heritage (Bentor, 1993) has been ideologically removed since Chinese annexation but the remnants of Tibet culture and lifestyle (Crossett, 1996) still offer a major attraction to Western tourists, despite the fact that the religious leader, the Dalai Lama, and the government are still in exile.

Bhutan is in a similar situation in that it is an autonomous state with its own Monarchy. In many respects these two regions present interesting alternative methods for dealing with the reported difficulties of modern mass tourism (Inskeep, 1992). Both presumably want the foreign exchange income, but neither enjoys the challenge of articulate Westerners ranging freely within their relatively highly controlled communities. Key mechanisms are the requirement that visitors are 'guided' on well-known and approved circuits and that visa fees are used as a direct means of controlling demand. Visitation is low, although the above policy context suggests that there are overriding concerns about possible negative (especially social, cultural and political) impacts. Only scant official data are available for visitation to Bhutan. In WTO (1998) statistics, 5000 overnight visitors were reported for 1996, up from 3000 in 1992. All visitors are reported in the 'holiday /leisure' segment, with 1000 originating from the Americas, 2000 from Europe and 2000 from Asia–Pacific. US$6 million is the reported tourist expenditure. Bhutan offers a direct contrast to Nepal, since arrivals are strictly controlled. In these terms Bhutan (and Tibet) are both in the very early stages of a tightly controlled tourism development.

Klieger (1992) argued that Tibet has long excited the Western imagination and explained how the easing of Chinese restrictions on both inbound foreign travel and outbound indigenous travel has played a role in bringing about a convergence of both Tibetan and Western attitudes to sacred Tibet. More recently, Shackley (1994) also undertook fieldwork in the area and reported on the first six months of international arrivals following the Chinese relaxation of travel restrictions. Klieger's (1992) research is also of interest since it examined the 'contemporary rise of Tibetan nationalism and its apparent support by various groups in the west, where a general reform movement, beginning in 1979 under Hu Yaobang, re-established the practice of religion and traditional pilgrimage activity in Tibet, suppressed since 1959' (Klieger, 1992: p. 122). Klieger (1992) and Shackley (1994) observe that political reforms have led to a growth in inbound tourism. However, the interesting political dimension discussed by Klieger (1992) is the trend among overseas visitors prepared to live and travel among Tibetans,

instead of using official tourist infrastructure constructed at great cost by the occupying power. As Klieger (1992: p. 122) suggests, 'distorted representations of Tibet crafted by Chinese agencies appear increasingly incredulous to many westerners, the apparent beneficiary of increased interaction brought about by tourist travel appears to be awareness of Tibetan self-determination'.

Here politics and tourism are inseparable. Tourism is desired as a means of development, but the ideology and behaviour of tourists are presumably seen as something less than desirable. A reading of tourist guides and web pages indicates that the notion of a locked up, inaccessible and somewhat untouched culture and environment adds further challenge to the modern explorer who seeks every opportunity to circumvent rules and regulations. While tourism in these two adjacent areas will likely remain under strong political scrutiny, the history of tourism development in Nepal could well offer a most useful template for both Tibet and Bhutan should they ever be open to higher intensities of visitation. For this reason, both Tibet and Bhutan provide an interesting contrast with Nepal, where the impact of tourism as Cockerell (1997: p. 41) points out does highlight the impact of development:

only 40 years after the landlocked Hindu kingdom was first opened to the rest of the world, its exotic attraction as a living museum of culture, art and ancient civilisations has been severely eroded as a result of uncontrolled urban pollution in the Kathmandu valley and irreparable damage to the country's natural Himalayan environment. These problems are compounded by poor access and inadequate tourism infrastructure throughout the country – not to mention crippling power and water shortages.

Thus, in these fragile mountain environments of the Himalayas, Nepal offers a good example of the fragile nature of the natural and cultural environment to both development and tourism. If Bhutan and Tibet observe these constraints and problems, it is a good model of how to plan tourism from a highly controlled and managed perspective, given the snowball effect which tourism has: once the development begins to take hold, development and dependence on foreign exchange earnings become self-reinforcing so that impacts become virtually impossible to mitigate in the name of progress in the wider national interest.

References

Adams, V., 'Tourism and sherpas, Nepal: Reconstructing reciprocity', *Annals of Tourism Research* 19(3), 1992, pp. 534–554.

Baskota, K. and Sharma, B., *Royal Chitwan National Park: An Assessment of Values Threats and Opportunities*, King Mahendra Trust for Nature Conservation, Kathmandu, 1995.

Belk, R.W., 'Third World tourism: panacea or poison? The case of Nepal', *Journal of International Consumer Marketing* 5(1), 1993, pp. 27–68.

Bentor, Y., 'Tibetan tourist thangkas in the Kathmandu valley', *Annals of Tourism Research* 21(1), 1993, pp. 10–37.

Bhattarai, S., 'Environmental impact of tourism on mountain ecosystem', in *Proceedings of the International Workshop on the Management of National Parks and Protected Areas in the Hindu Kush-Himalaya, Kathmandu, May 1985*, The King Mahendra Trust for Nature Conservation (KMTNC) and International Centre for Integrated Mountain Development (ICIMOD), Kathmandu, 1985.

Britton, G.S., 'The political economy of tourism in the Third World', *Annals of Tourism Research* 9(3), 1982, pp. 331–358.

Cockerell., N., 'Nepal', *International Tourism Report* 1, 1997, pp. 41–57.

Crick, M., 'Representation of international tourism in the social sciences: sun, sex, sights, saving and servility', *Annual Review of Anthropology* 18, 1989, pp. 307–344.

Crossett, B., *So Close to Heaven: The Vanishing Buddhist Kingdoms of the Himalayas*, Vintage Books, 1996.

Curry, S. and Morvardi, B., 'Sustainable tourism:

Illustrations from Kenya, Nepal and Japan', in C. Cooper and A. Lockwood (eds), *Progress in Tourism, Recreation and Hospitality Management, Volume 4*, Belhaven, London, 1992, pp. 131–139.

De Kadt, E., 'Social planning for tourism in developing countries', *Annals of Tourism Research* 6(1), 1979, pp. 36–48.

Department of National Parks and Wildlife Conservation, *Annual Report, 1995/1996*, DNPWC, Kathmandu, 1996.

Department of Tourism, *Nepal Tourism Statistics, 1994*, DOT, Kathmandu, 1995.

Department of Tourism, *Nepal Tourism Statistics, 1995* (Unpublished statistics), DOT, Kathmandu, 1996.

English, E.P., *The Great Escape? An Examination of North–South Tourism*, The North–South Institute, Ottawa, 1986.

Engma Consultants, *Study on Recreational Tourism Development in Nepal: A Report for the Ministry of Tourism*, Engma Consultants, Kathmandu, 1989.

Folsom, D., 'Nepalese tourism: a pause or a problem?', *Tourism Recreation Research*, 13(1), 1988, pp. 41–46.

Gurung, C.P. and De Coursey, M.D., 'The Annapurna Conservation Area Project: a pioneering example of sustainable tourism?', in E. Cater and G. Lowman (eds), *Ecotourism: A Sustainable Option?*, John Wiley & Sons, New York, 1994, pp. 177–194.

Gurung, H., *Environmental Aspects of Mountain Tourism in Nepal*, International Trade and Tourism Division of Economic and Social Commission for Asia and Pacific, Bangkok, 1990.

Inskeep, E., 'Sustainable tourism development in the Maldives and Bhutan', *Industry and Environment* 15(3/4), 1992, pp. 31–36.

Ives J.D. and Messerli, B., *The Himalayan Dilemma: Reconciling Development and Conservation*, United Nations University/Routledge, London, 1989.

King Mahendra Trust for Nature Conservation, *Annual Report, 1995/1996*, KMTNC, Kathmandu, 1996.

Klieger, P., 'Shangri-La and the politicisation of tourism in Tibet', *Annals of Tourism Research* 19(1), 1992, pp. 122–125.

Koirala S.P., 'Towards an institutional framework for tourism development: a case study of Pokhara, Nepal', Unpublished MPRTM Thesis, Lincoln University, New Zealand, 1977.

Ministry of Commerce and Industry, *Nepal Tourism Master Plan 1972*, Ministry of Commerce and Industry, Kathmandu, 1972.

Ministry of Tourism and Civil Aviation, Nepal, *Visit Nepal Year – 1998*, http://www.south-asia.com/dotn/visit.htm, 1998.

National Planning Commission, *First Five-Year Plan: 1956–1961*, NPC, Kathmandu, 1956.

National Planning Commission, *Eighth Five-Year Plan: 1992–1997*, NPC, Kathmandu, 1992.

Nepal Watch UK, *Focus on Nepal*, No. 2, October 1993.

O'Grady, R., *Tourism in the Third World*, Cordin Books, New York, 1982.

Pagdin, C., 'Assessing tourism impacts in the Third World: a Nepal case study', *Progress in Planning* 44(3), 1995, pp. 191–266.

Parker S., 'Annapurna Conservation Area Project ; in search of sustainable development?', in K. Brown (ed.), *Approaches to Sustainable Development*, Pinter, London, 1997, pp. 144–168.

Raj, P.A., *Pokhara: a valley in the Himalayas*, Nabeen Publications, Kathmandu, 1993.

Richter, L., *The Politics of Tourism in Asia*, University of Hawaii Press, Honolulu, 1989.

Sessa, A., 'Tourism development in Tibet', *Rassegna di Studi Turistica* 24(1/2), 1989, pp. 15–25.

Shackley, M., 'Tourism in the land of Lo, Nepal/Tibet: The first eight months of tourism', *Tourism Management* 15(1), 1994, pp. 17–26.

Sharma, P., 'Tourism and sustainable development', in *Nepal Economic Policies for Sustainable Development*, Asian Development Bank and International Centre for Integrate Mountain Development, Kathmandu, 1992, pp. 112–119.

Sharma, P.R., *Culture and Tourism: Defining Roles and relationship*, Discussion Paper Series No. MRE 95/2, International Centre for integrated Mountain Development, Kathmandu, 1995.

Sill, M., 'On the development trail', *The Geographical Magazine* 63, 1991, pp. 4–7.

Steigenberger Consulting and Speerplan GmbH, *Nepal Tourism Master Plan Review: A Report for Ministry of Tourism*, Steigenberger Consulting and Speerplan GmbH, Frankfurt-Main, 1984.

Thakali, S., 'Renegotiating tradition: tourism and cultural invention in Nepal', Unpublished Masters Thesis, Roehampton Institute, University of Surrey, 1994.

Thakali, S., 'Mountain tourism perspectives from NGOs and the private sector, Nepal', in P. Sharma (ed.), *Proceedings of the Hindu Kush–Himalayan Regional Workshop on Mountain Tourism for Local Community Development*, Kathmandu, June 1995, International Centre for Integrated Mountain Development, Kathmandu, 1995.

The Mountain Institute, *Langtang Conservation and Enterprise Project*, http://www.mountain.org/langtang.html (accessed 20 September 1998) 1998.

Touche Ross and New Era, *Nepal Tourism Development Programmes: A Report for the Asian Development Bank and Ministry of Tourism*, Touche Ross and New Era, Kathmandu, 1990.

Wanhill, S., 'Tourism manpower planning: The case of Nepal', in P. Johnson and B. Thomas (eds), *Perspectives on Tourism Policy*, Mansell, London, 1992, pp. 87–104.

Wells, M.P., 'Parks tourism in Nepal: reconciling the social and economic opportunities with the ecological threats', in M. Munasinghe and J.A. McNeely (eds), *Protected Area Economics and Policy: Linking Conservation and Sustainable Development)*, The World Bank/IUCN, Washington, DC, 1994, pp. 319–331.

World Tourism Organization, *Compendium of Tourism Statistics (1992–1996)*, WTO, Madrid, 1998.

Zurick, D.N., 'Adventure travel and sustainable tourism in the peripheral economy of Nepal', *Annals of the Association of American Geographers* 82, 1992, pp. 608–628.

19

China: a growth engine for Asian tourism

Alan A. Lew

Introduction

This chapter describes the development of tourism in China, with particular focus on how China's tourism development affects South and Southeast Asia. The discussion begins with an overview of modern tourism in China, how it has developed in recent decades and how it is projected to grow in the future. This is followed by an examination of the tourism relationship between China and its neighbours to the south, in terms of: travel between China and South and Southeast Asia, tourism investments between China and South and Southeast Asia, and border tourism between China and South and Southeast Asian countries

Modern tourism to China

China was essentially closed to foreign visitors following the victory of the Chinese Communist Party (CCP) in 1949. The few foreigners who did succeed in visiting China in the 1950s and 1960s were mostly from the communist bloc countries of the Soviet Union, Eastern Europe, North Korea and North Vietnam. Some early efforts at resurrecting a tourism industry were made in the mid-1950s, but these were set back by the

political instability of the Great Leap Forward in the late 1950s (Lew, 1987). Following this period of disarray and starvation in rural China, a revived interest in tourism resulted in the establishment of the Bureau of Travel and Tourism in 1964. A minimal number of tourists from Western countries (4500 in 1966) were allowed to visit China during this period just before the start of the Cultural Revolution (late 1960s to early 1970s) when tourism was almost non-existent.

Travel to China prior to 1971 was limited to political, trade and professional purposes – although cultural experiences were typically a major part of any visitor's experience (Zhang, 1995). The only category of visitors who were not limited to these narrow objectives were Chinese 'compatriots' from Hong Kong and Macao, who were given relatively free entry to visit relatives in China. This situation was a two-way street since, until 1971, it was illegal for citizens of the USA, as well as of many other countries, to visit communist China. In that year the USA lifted this ban and the US national table tennis team made its historic 'ping-pong diplomacy' tour of China. This was followed in June 1971 by Secretary of State Henry Kissinger making the first official visit to China by a US government diplomat. In January 1972, US President Richard Nixon visited China and established formal ties between the world's most populated country and the world's wealthiest. This event marked the first true beginnings of the era of modern tourism to China.

Tourism in the early 1970s, however, remained tightly controlled by China's central government. Between 1971 and 1977 China granted only 15 000 visa applications from over 200 000 that were made by Americans alone to visit China. The fortunate few who went to China typically travelled in groups of fifteen to twenty-five people with some shared institutional or professional background. The high cost of travel to China during this period was another major factor in keeping numbers low. The remnants of the Cultural Revolution still fostered anti-foreign sentiments and caution in dealing with foreign visitors continued to be the norm throughout Chinese society. Tourism, as a 'bourgeois' endeavour, continued to be considered as suspect by Maoist elements in the Chinese bureaucracy (Tan, 1986). Thus, the form of tourism was very similar to what had gone on before, except that the new visitors came in greater numbers and from non-communist countries than in the past. In the mid-1970s, foreign tourists (not including compatriot Chinese) averaged around 30 000 per year (Lew, 1987).

Mao Dzedong died in September 1976 and, within a month, moderate supporters of Deng Xiaoping took control of the Chinese Communist Party and China's central government. By the end of 1977, with the moderates in firm control, the Chinese government announced the beginning of a concerted effort to make tourism a major sector of the Chinese economy. The official goals of this policy shift were (1) to 'promote friendship' and (2) to 'accumulate funds for the speeding up of China's socialist modernization' (*Beijing Review*, 1978a). In 1978 the Bureau of Travel and Tourism was upgraded to the 'State General Administration of Travel and Tourism' and foreign airlines and travel agents were, for the first time, given authority to develop their own tours to China (instead of relying solely on tours packaged by the Chinese government). Major cities and

provinces also established their own tourism agencies, independent of the central government (Xue, 1982: p. 681). Within a few months of the 1977 official 'opening-up' of China, 100 sites had been designated as 'open' to foreign tourist and thirty new hotels were under construction (*Beijing Review*, 1979a). The country's first tourism training school was also opened in 1978 in Jiangsu province (*Beijing Review*, 1978b). By the end of that year 229 646 foreign tourists had come to China, an increase from only 30 000 in 1977 (*Beijing Review*, 1979b). That number shot up another 50 per cent in 1979 and again in 1980 as the industry began to explode (Table 19.1).

In 1985, China received 1.37 million foreign tourists, generating US$1.3 billion in foreign currency (CNTA, 1998). By this time, China had started marketing efforts to bring international conventions to the country to develop the fledgling business travel market (Wright and Wright, 1984; Goldsmith, 1985), while Club Med opened a resort in the Shezhen Special Economic Zone (adjacent to Hong Kong) in 1984 and another near Beijing in 1986 – both of which were largely oriented at the Japanese market.

The opening-up of China to tourism was an integral part of Deng Xiaoping's 'Four Modernizations' policy, designed to rapidly bring China's economy into the global marketplace. Since this policy was instituted, China has undergone nothing short of an economic miracle. Buoyed by economic growth rates of 10 per cent and more per year for the past decade, China (excluding Hong Kong) had become the world's seventh largest economy by 1996 (GDP of US$906 billion) and a major force for economic growth and stability in the Asia–Pacific region (World Bank Group, 1998).

China's tourism sector was targeted by central planners for major investment and development from the start of the 'Four Modernizations' reforms (Zhang, 1995). Despite considerable expansion, during the first few years of the reforms (up to 1982) education and diplomacy remained the primary objectives of tourism in China. However, a significant shift in government policy occurred in

Table 19.1   *China's international tourist arrivals 1978–1997 (000s)*

Year	Arrivals	% Change	Foreigners	Compatriots		Overseas Chinese Nationals
				Hong Kong	Taiwan	
1978	1 809.2	–	229.6	1 561.5	–	18.1
1979	4 203.9	132.4	362.4	3 820.6	–	20.9
1980	5 702.5	35.6	529.1	5 139.0	–	34.4
1981	7 767.1	36.2	675.2	7 053.1	–	38.9
1982	7 924.3	2.0	764.5	7 117.0	–	42.7
1983	9 477.0	19.6	872.5	8 564.1	–	40.4
1984	12 852.2	35.6	1134.3	11 670.4	–	47.5
1985	17 833.1	38.8	1370.5	16 377.8	–	84.8
1986	22 819.5	28.0	1482.3	21 269.0	–	68.1
1987	26 902.3	17.9	1727.8	25 087.4	<2.5	87.0
1988	31 694.8	17.8	1842.2	29 773.3	437.7	79.3
1989	24 501.4	–22.7	1461.0	22 971.9	541.0	68.6
1990	27 461.8	12.1	1747.3	25 623.4	948.0	91.1
1991	33 349.8	21.4	2710.1	30 506.2	946.6	133.4
1992	38 114.9	14.3	4006.4	33 943.4	1317.8	165.1
1993	41 526.9	9.0	4655.9	36 704.9	1527.0	166.2
1994	43 684.5	5.2	5182.1	38 387.2	1390.2	115.2
1995	46 386.5	6.2	5886.7	40 384.0	1532.3	115.8
1996	51 127.5	10.2	6744.3	44 228.6	1733.9	154.6
1997	57 587.9	12.6	7428.0	50 060.9	2117.6	99.0

Note
Figures prior to 1978 are unreliable. In general, foreign visitors numbered between 25 000 and 35 000 per year from 1974 to 1978, and about 2000 or less per year prior to that. Compatriot Chinese numbered between 1 million and 2 million per year prior to 1979, and the same or less prior to the 1970s. Overseas Chinese nationals hold a Chinese passport but live in a country outside of China.
Source: China National Tourism Administration (CNTA), 1998.

1982 when the tourism industry was officially transformed from a political service to an economic activity (Zou, 1993: p. 2). International tourism has since become one of China's major sources of foreign currency earnings, with receipts from international tourism contributing US$10.2 billion (1.1 per cent of GDP) to China's economy in 1996 (CNTA, 1998). Many, although clearly not all, of the country's enormous population of 1.22 billion people (July 1997 estimate) have moved from poverty to varying levels of prosperity as a result of the country's economic growth. Although China ranked about 100th in per capita GNP (US$860 and PPP$3570; World Bank Group, 1998), its middle class is estimated to number between 50 million and 100 million. Tourism has played a major part in increasing the country's level of prosperity, especially in the densely populated coastal provinces.

China's tourism boom continued throughout the 1980s as it became the newest destination in the world – big, exotic and unknown. Infrastructure problems were constant, despite the many new hotels that dotted the post-Second World War skyline in all of China's major cities. The whole country was in the throws of change in the late 1980s when, in June of 1989, the Chinese military attacked pro-democracy demonstrators in Beijing's Tiananmen Square. International arrivals to China immediately plummeted and it took two years for their numbers to return to pre-1989 levels. Roehl (1995) has shown that the make up of China's visitors had actually started to change prior to the Tiananmen Square incident, with a proportional decline in purely recreational visitors and a rise in business travellers. This trend has become more prominent in recent years, with China's continued economic growth being the main engine driving up the international visitation numbers.

Even taking into account the Tiananmen Square incident, China's average annual growth in tourist arrivals and receipts since 1980 has been 19.2 per cent, far surpassing the world-wide average of 5.5 per cent growth (cf. Table 19.1). The World Tourism Organization (WTO) ranked China as the sixth most visited international destination in 1997 (*Chicago Tribune*, 1998). However, this ranking was based on a total count of 23 770 000 international visitors to China, excluding family visits from Hong Kong and Macao (*South China Morning Post* (SCMP), 1996). Had China's official number of 57 million visitors for 1997 been used, China would have ranked second, behind France (67 million), and ahead of the USA (49 million). Despite these oddities in counting, the WTO has projected that China will be the most visited country in the world by the year 2020, with 137.1 million international visitors (Newsweek, 1998). China's international travel and tourism industry employed an estimated 13.5 million people in direct-industry jobs (1.9 per cent of all jobs in China), and an additional 33.5 million in indirect jobs in 1997 (*Straits Times*, 1998a). The WTO projects these numbers to increase by 2010 to 19 million (2.4 per cent of employment) direct jobs, plus 50 million indirect jobs.

Travel to China

The vast majority (91 per cent in 1997) of China's international visitors come from Hong Kong, Macao and Taiwan, referred to either as 'compatriot Chinese' or as 'HMT' visitors (Table

19.1). Most of these visitors travel to visit friends and relatives (VFR) and their travel patterns differ considerably from those of other international travellers (Lew, 1995). For example, HMT visitors are almost twice as likely to visit either Guangdong Province (adjacent to Hong Kong) or Fujian Province (across from Taiwan) than is the average foreign visitor. Business travel is also often associated with family ties for this group, although China does not publish statistics indicating travel motivation. Removing the HMT influence (along with Chinese citizens who visit China while residing abroad – 99 000 in 1997), China's 'foreign' visitors numbered almost 7.5 million in 1997, comparable with Asia's other leading destinations including Malaysia, Thailand and Singapore (6.5 million to 7.5 million in 1997), but well below Hong Kong (10.4 million in 1997, 22 per cent of whom were from China) (Loh, 1998). However, if only because of its size, China's growth potential is far greater in the long term than these other Asian destinations.

Excluding the HMT compatriots, well over half of China's 'foreign' visitors in 1997 came from Asian countries (Table 19.2). This has also been the fastest growing segment of China's visitors, while Europe and North America have slowed considerably in their growth rates. Again, this points to the major shift in travel to China in the 1990s.

Since the 1980s, Japan has consistently ranked as the leading source of visitors to China, while the USA has fallen from second to fourth place

Table 19.2 *China's inbound foreign visitor markets: world regions, 1992 and 1997 (000s)*

Regions	1992	1997	% of 1997 total	% Change 1992–1997	% Change 1996–1997
Asia (excluding compatriots)	1848.0	4411.1	59.4	138.7	8.5
Europe (including Russia)	1519.9	1888.8	25.4	24.3	15.7
Americas	495.4	867.2	11.7	75.1	7.2
Oceania	105.5	193.4	2.6	83.3	11.5
Africa	26.7	49.1	0.7	83.9	4.1

Sources: CNTA, 1998; Liu, 1995: pp. 36–37.

Table 19.3 *China's inbound markets: leading countries, 1994 and 1997 (000s)*

Country	1994	1997	% of 1997 total	One year % change 1994–1996
1. Japan	1141.2	1581.7	21.3	38.6
2. Russia	399.8	813.7	11.0	103.5
3. South Korea	340.3	781.1	10.5	129.5
4. USA	469.8	616.4	8.3	31.2
5. Malaysia	208.7	361.3	4.9	73.1
6. Mongolia	301.2	342.9	4.6	13.8
7. Singapore	231.9	316.8	4.3	36.6
8. Philippines	184.9	276.7	3.7	49.6
9. UK	167.0	227.9	3.1	36.5
10. Germany	148.8	184.7	2.5	24.1
11. Canada	113.2	174.1	2.3	53.8
12. Thailand	163.7	168.5	2.3	2.9
13. Australia	109.5	156.8	2.1	43.2
14. Indonesia	120.4	147.3	2.0	22.3
15. France	111.8	131.3	1.5	17.4
16. Kazakhstan	106.3	94.9	1.3	−10.7
17. North Korea	57.0	71.4	1.0	25.3
18. Italy	55.5	65.1	0.9	17.3
19. India	35.6	60.5	0.8	69.9
23. Burma/Myanmar	<20.0	31.6	0.4	
24. Vietnam	<20.0	31.2	0.4	
26. Kyrgyzstan	31.6	30.2	0.4	−4.4

Sources: CNTA, 1998; Liu, 1995: pp. 36–37.

(Table 19.3). Australia and the UK were regularly ranked third and fourth in visitor arrivals to China until 1989 when major global changes shifted China's predominant arrival patterns toward Asia and its immediate neighbours (Yu, 1992). Tense political relations between China and the USSR softened in 1989 as the Berlin Wall fell and Mikhail Gorbachev, the leader of the USSR, paid a major visit to China. China and the USSR (now the Russian Federation) share one of the longest land borders in the world (3645 km) and border crossings and trade developed rapidly after the Gorbachev visit, propelling Russia to the second largest source of visitors to China by 1997 (Zhang and Lew, 1997). In addition, over 100 000 arrivals to China in 1997 were from the former Soviet states of Kazakhstan and Kyrgyzstan. South Korea and Mongolia are two other north- and inner-Asian countries for which geographic proximity combined with economic interests and cross-border cultural ties have resulted in large numbers of visitors to China. South

Korea's rise is dramatic since it was only in 1994 that the South Korean government lifted its ban on travel to China.

Taiwanese visits to the mainland have increased dramatically since the Taiwan government relaxed its restrictions on such visits in November 1987 (Andrews, 1992). Illegal visits had been taking place through Hong Kong since the mid-1980s, when China began admitting Taiwanese without stamping their passports. If treated as a separate country, Taiwan would have been the single largest source of international visitors to China throughout most of the 1990s, which is somewhat ironic given the tense political situation between the mainland and island. The most popular destination for Taiwan visitors is nearby Fujian Province, where many Taiwanese have relatives and have invested in business ventures (Lew, 1995).

Southeast Asia comprises the next largest Asian grouping that has come to displace the formerly dominant English-speaking group in international travel to China. A major reason for the increase in Southeast Asian visitors in the 1990s was the new laws adopted by Southeast Asian countries in the late 1980s making travel to China more accessible to their citizens (Zhang, 1990). This was also occurring in Taiwan at the same time and mainland China quickly become the new place to go for the more wealthy citizens of Taiwan and Southeast Asia. In Southeast Asia this trend began in the Philippines which, at 104 791 visitors in 1991, was China's fourth largest market, followed by Singapore and Thailand (Sun, 1992). Rapid growth in visitors from Russia, Southeast Asia, and Taiwan helped China recover from the decline in western (North America, Europe and Australasia) visitors following the 1989 Tiananmen Square incident (Zhang, 1990; He, 1991; Chang, 1992). The growth in arrivals from Southeast Asia continued in the 1990s reflecting improving political and economic relationships between China most Southeast Asian countries, as well as the growing middle and upper economic classes in these countries. The major ASEAN countries had come to play a dominant role in visitation to China by the time the Asian economic crisis first hit Thailand in July 1997.

The Asian economic crisis dramatically reduced the number of Thai arrivals (–12.8 per cent from 1996) and kept Japanese visitations the same in 1997 (2.1 per cent) over 1996. By early 1998, Japanese visitor rates were down by 25 per cent and South Korean and Thai visitation rates were down by 50 per cent from the same period in 1997 (SCMP, 1998a). Singapore and the Philippines, which have weathered the economic turmoil better than their neighbours, were expected to continue to show growth in travel to China in 1998, as were countries that border China and those in Europe and North America – although the rates of growth were expected to slow considerably. As a result, overall tourism revenues were expected to increase by 8 per cent of 1997 (SCMP, 1998b). To encourage Southeast Asian tourism, China's National Tourism Administration (CNTA) developed lower-cost short package trips to coastal areas in southern China, and has focused more on expanding the Indian and

Russian markets which China sees as currently underdeveloped (Kwang, 1998). The economic situation in Russia, however, is at least as bad as in Asia, and its spillover has caused economic problems in most of China's northern and western border towns, as well as in the marketplaces of Beijing itself (*The Economist*, 1998: p. 10).

China's travel ties with South Asian countries are far less than those with Southeast Asia. Political tensions between China and India over disputed border territories and China's military assistance to Pakistan have kept them modest, although India was still a larger source of travellers to China than neighbouring Burma and Vietnam in 1997. None of the other Asian nations rank within the top twenty-six source countries for visitors to China. In general, despite its size, India has not been a major source of outbound travellers to the rest of the world (estimated at only 4 million in 1995 – about 20 per cent less than from China in the same year) (Suri, 1996: p. 33). If and when the subcontinent awakens to tourism, it is likely to have a major impact on destinations throughout Asia, including China.

A major difference between India and Southeast Asia as sources of visitors to China is the large number of ethnic Chinese in Southeast Asia. Elsewhere I have estimated that some 15 per cent of the foreign visitors to China in the early 1990s were ethnic overseas Chinese (Lew, 1995). Although this percentage appeared to be declining over time, it still amounted to over 400 000 foreign visitors in 1991, and possibly as many as 1 million visitors in 1997. Some of these visitors have maintained ties to their relatives in China since migrating overseas earlier this century, as have many compatriots from Hong Kong, Macao and Taiwan. Many more, however, have long lost these ties, but still feel a strong sense of attachment and nostalgia for their ancestral homeland. Pan (1990) has described the experience of the overseas Chinese tourist succinctly:

Each time they visit they ask themselves, 'Why are we here? Why do we keep coming back?' Why

must they return to this cruel, tormented, corrupt, hopeless place as though they still needed it? Could they never achieve immunity? And yet had China meant nothing to them, any other place thereafter would have meant less, and they would carry no pole within themselves, and they would not even guess what they had missed ... yet they realize that they could never live there. Deep in their hearts they know that they love China best when they live well away from the place (Pan, 1990: p. 379).

It is estimated that 80 per cent of the 29 million ethnic Chinese residing outside of China, Hong Kong, Macao and Taiwan, are found in Southeast Asia (Table 19.4). Thus, the potential cultural basis for tourism and economic ties between China and Southeast Asia is considerable. This translates directly into leisure and business travel and investment. In

Table 19.4   *1990 compatriot and overseas Chinese estimated populations*

	Number of ethnic Chinese (000 000s)
Indonesia	7.2
Thailand	5.8
Malaysia	5.2
Singapore	2.0
Burma	1.5
Philippines	0.8
Vietnam	0.8
Southeast Asia total	23.3
USA	1.8
Canada	0.6
Latin America	1.0
Americas total	3.4
Rest of Asia and the Pacific	1.8
Europe	0.6
Africa	0.1
Overseas Chinese total	**29.2**
Hong Kong	5.9
Macao	0.5
Taiwan	20.7
Compatriot Chinese total	**27.1**
World total	**56.3**

Sources: The Economist, 1992; Kao, 1993.

1990, the liquid assets of the 56 million overseas and compatriot Chinese world-wide are estimated at between $1.5 billion and $2 billion (*The Economist*, 1992). On a per capita basis, this amount is higher than the approximately $3 billion in liquid assets held by Japan's 124 million people (in 1990), and is far higher per person than that found in any other country. This personal wealth was built on the same traditions of family ties and economic mobility which drives overseas Chinese tourism to China today. Combined with social and business networks built through family associations, overseas ethnic Chinese communities have become dominant economic forces in many Southeast Asian countries (Sender, 1991; Kao, 1993).

The per capita tourist expenditures of Hong Kong Chinese, Taiwanese, and Southeast Asian Chinese are much lower than those of other international visitors to China, including American Chinese and overseas Chinese from elsewhere in the world (Lew, 1995). Compatriots and Southeast Asian Chinese are more likely to stay with relatives or in inexpensive Chinese hotels than in international hotels. In addition, Taiwanese tourists have received special incentive prices that have cut into profits. At the same time, the rise in tourists from among these groups has provided a new market for the older Chinese hotels in the PRC (Zhang, 1990). It has also resulted in an increase in the production of rosewood furniture, artistic room screens and calligraphic art, which are popular among these groups. These groups also played a big role in China's recovery from the tourism decline following the Tienanmen Square incident in 1989.

For travel agents and tour operators in Southeast Asia, China has been seen as the destination that will help bring them through their gradual recovery from the Asian economic crisis (*New Straits Times*, 1998c). It is closer and less expensive than North America and Europe and is sufficiently different and diverse to make for an interesting cultural experience. Thai tour operators, for example, view China as the international destination that will experience the greatest growth for Thai travellers in the near future (Taemsamran, 1998). To encourage travel in both directions, Thailand's second designated carrier, Angel Airlines, has applied to Thailand, China, Myanmar, Laos and Cambodia to offer flights in the Mekong region using Chiang Rai in northern Thailand as a hub (Muqbil, 1998a). From a more distant location, Singapore has been working to develop air package tours that include itself and destinations in southwest China that can be sold to long-haul visitors from North America and Europe (Lew and Ahmed, 1999).

Investment in China

The government of China has encouraged foreign investment since initiating the 'Four Modernizations' policy to rapidly bring the country into the global economic system. Since 1979, huge amounts of capital have been invested in China's accommodation and transportation sectors to meet the ever-growing needs of travellers. Most of this money has come from compatriot HTM Chinese, followed by investments from Western industrial countries and overseas ethnic Chinese, primarily citizens of Southeast Asian countries. In 1996, overseas interests invested US$42.1 billion in direct foreign investment in China, a nine-fold increase in five years (US$4.7 billion in 1991) (State Statistical Bureau, 1997: p. 605). Well over half (59.2 per cent) of this money came from Hong Kong, Macao and Taiwan, while almost equal amounts came from the USA (8.2 per cent), Southeast Asia (7.6 per cent) and Europe (7.0 per cent).

In 1995, foreign investments accounted for 69 per cent of the funds to construct forty-seven new joint-venture hotels (*Travel Trade Gazette*, 1998a). The international hotel industry has been a particularly attractive area for foreign investment as it often requires special knowledge of international markets, technological expertise and management skills that have been lacking in the local population. In 1994, of the 2995 international hotels in China, 529 were owned either by foreign companies or by entrepreneurs from Hong Kong, Macao and Taiwan (Liu, 1995). Most of these hotels are better equipped, star-rated facilities and are used primarily by international visitors and wealthy Chinese entrepreneurs. The income from these foreign-managed hotels accounted for about half of the national total from the accommodations sector in 1994.

Guangdong Province, next to Hong Kong, is home to 60 per cent of China's joint-venture hotels. Some of this amount is in wholly foreign-owned enterprises. However, the vast majority (about 95 per cent of all investments) are as 'equity joint ventures' (*hezi jingying*) and 'cooperative or contractual agreements' (*hezou jingying*) (Leung, 1990: p. 406; Thoburn *et al.*, 1990: pp. 16–17). For both of these arrangements, foreign investors and local Chinese government entities or state companies share the cost, management and profits of a factory or hotel. Foreign direct investment has also occurred in the transportation and catering industries to serve the tourism industry.

Despite these large foreign investments, China has experienced ongoing capacity problems in many of its tourist destinations (Zhang and Lew, 1997). Hotels were often too full or too empty, roads were often in disrepair and clogged with traffic and service personnel were often poorly trained. Airports continue to be too small and the country's airline industry probably grew too fast in the 1990s, resulting in major problems and several fatal air accidents (Yu and Lew, 1997). Environmental impacts have been serious as mountains, gardens and beaches have received far too many visitors (Gormsen, 1995a). A boom in the growth of domestic tourism since the mid-1980s (reaching 643 million leisure trips in 1997) has further exacerbated many of these difficulties (Gormsen, 1995b; CNTA, 1998).

Since its economy is more controlled (for example, foreign investments are strictly limited) China has been less affected than other Asian countries by the region's 1997 economic downturn. Because of the importance of Hong Kong and Southeast Asian investment, China had anticipated a 33 per cent decline in foreign investment in 1998 (Kwang, 1998; *Travel Trade Gazette*, 1998a). To further promote tourism, China's central government decided to allow foreign joint ownership of travel agencies in China for the first time in 1998 (*China News Digest*, 1998). At the same time, large Chinese firms actively sought investment funds from Southeast Asian entrepreneurs (*Bangkok Post*, 1998b; Choong, 1998), and countries such as Singapore have major tourism development projects in China (cf. Bangsberg, 1998).

Table 19.5 *China outbound travel, selected years 1985–1998*

Year	Trip
1985	529 900
1992	2 800 000
1993	4 082 504
1994	4 045 468
1995	4 864 340
1996	–
1997	5 300 000
1998	6 000 000[a]

Note
[a]Projected.
Source: WTO, 1997; Brady, 1998.

Chinese outbound tourism

For most of its recorded history, few Chinese left China proper. By the third century A.D. (the Three Kingdoms period), military expansion, followed by migration out of the north China cultural hearth had extended the area of Han Chinese settlement into what is today central and southern China. While China became a major sea-trading nation in the Indian Ocean during the Tang Dynasty (618–906), it was still both rare and illegal for Chinese to leave their homeland (Pan, 1990). Most of those who did leave were traders (actually pirates) from the southern coastal province of Fujian, plying the route through Southeast Asia to South Asia and beyond. This situation changed considerably in the late 1800s when European warships forced Ching Dynasty leaders to allow freedom of travel for its citizens, many of whom then migrated to become cooley workers on European plantations in Southeast Asia.

China's doors were closed within a few years following the communist victory and Mao Dzedong's rise to leadership in 1949. Prior to the 1980s it was very rare for Chinese nationals to travel abroad. Since the opening up of China in 1978, the central government has gradually eased its control over outbound travel. Each year larger numbers of Chinese have been granted permission to leave the country for short business or private trips, or to become a permanent resident in a foreign country (Table 19.5). This has been especially true since the late 1980s. Hong Kong and Macao were the first places that were opened to Chinese package tours, followed by countries in Southeast Asia. A 'Travel Abroad' campaign was initiated in the early 1990s to encourage overseas travel with the goal of advancing the knowledge and skills of China's professionals and government officials (Zhang and Lew, 1997). Attendance at conferences, trade fairs, art shows, music performances or sporting events outside of China were particularly encouraged as part of this campaign.

The emphasis on employment-related travel meant that most outbound travellers were Communist Party officials and employees of government-owned companies. In 1993, the number of trips made by these business travellers accounted for more than 61 per cent of total outbound travel (Liu, 1995). Because the money used to pay for these trips came from the country's foreign currency reserves, the Chinese central government became increasingly critical of individuals using public funds for unnecessary or unauthorized trips abroad. These criticisms seemed to have been effective, as 1994 experienced a decline in business travel abroad (to 55 per cent), along with an increase in private travel abroad (44 per cent).

Table 19.6 *China's outbound destinations to regions and selected non-Asian countries, 1995*

	1995	Average annual % change 1985–1995	Total 1995 % market share
Hong Kong and Macao[a]	2 915 411		59.9
East Asia/Pacific[a]	1 143 514	25.6[b]	23.5
Europe	577 584	41.5	11.9
Russia	(390 477)	n.a.	
Germany	(117 069)	n.a.	
UK	(32 000)	n.a.	
Spain	(14 477)	10.1	
Americas	190 046	8.7	3.9
USA	(166 520)	7.7	
Brazil	(7 749)	14.0	
South Asia[a]	23 651	11.2	0.5
Africa	7 185	11.0	0.1
Middle East	6 949	7.1	0.1
Egypt	(5 930)	7.1	
Total world-wide	4 864 340	24.8	100.0

Notes
[a]See Table 19.7 for Asian country details.
[b]Rate for East Asia includes Hong Kong and Macao.
Source: WTO, 1997.

Chinese outbound travel is primarily within Asia (Table 19.6). Two factors account for the high Chinese visitors that some Asian countries receive: business ties and leisure travel. Chinese wishing to travel for leisure purposes have the greatest freedom to do so when visiting places that have been designated a 'tourism liberalization country' (Zhang and Lew, 1997; Yatsko and Tasker, 1998). Tourism liberalizing countries are destinations which are officially approved by the Chinese government for visitation on organized leisure tours. Business travel accounts for much of the remaining outbound travel pattern to non-tourism liberalizing countries, although it is common for such business trips to be combined with considerable leisure activity.

Hong Kong and Macao became the first international destinations for Chinese tourists in the mid-1980s, when travel to these territories of China was opened up to Chinese citizens on an 'experimental' basis. This was first time that China had allowed residents to leave the country for non-official purposes since the early 1950s (Lew, 1995). In 1990 the status of Hong Kong and Macao became formalized at the same time that Thailand, Malaysia and Singapore became the first 'tourism liberalizing countries' (Yatsko and Tasker, 1998). These countries were selected because of their close proximity, growing trade relationships with China and large numbers of ethnic Chinese citizens (Table 19.4). It was expected that non-business travellers would primarily be visiting friends and relatives (VFR), in the same manner that many of the visitors from these four countries travel to China. To meet the growing demand for outbound travel, the Philippines was added to the 'tourism liberalizing countries' list in 1992, followed by Australia in 1997, South Korea and New Zealand in 1998.

When the first set of 'tourism liberalizing countries' was designated in 1990, potential travellers were required to certify that a relative in the destination country would pay for the trip before a passport or visa would be issued (Yatsko and Tasker, 1998). This greatly limited the number of people travelling to these countries. By 1994, most travel agents were ignoring this requirement and in 1997 it was dropped completely. Still, the process is not easy, requiring approvals from one's place of work first, followed by China's Public Security Bureau (an exit visa) and an entry visa from the destination country (Brady, 1998). Approximately 40 per cent of exit visa applications were approved in 1997 and 1998.

Just because a country is not on the 'tourism liberalizing countries' list does not mean that Chinese do not travel there. South Korea, for example, was not on this list in 1996, but still managed to receive more Chinese visitors than Malaysia which is on the list (Table 19.7).

Similarly, the Philippines (on the list) received far fewer Chinese visitors than do Indochinese countries that border China (not on the list). However, it is much more difficult for leisure travellers to visit non-listed countries and the large numbers that places such as South Korea and Laos receive are indicative of the developing business links that China has with those countries. The most dramatic indication that there are other factors involved in Chinese outbound travel can be seen in the case of Vietnam, which received twenty-five times as many Chinese visitors in 1996 than in 1994 following a major reduction in border tensions.

With almost half a million visitors in 1996, Thailand is the leading international destination for Chinese travellers, after Hong Kong and Macao (the World Tourism Organization has decided to continue to treat Hong Kong and Macao as 'international' destinations for China, despite their incorporation into China proper in 1997 and 1999, respectively. It appears that this

Table 19.7 *China's outbound destinations to selected Asian countries, 1994, 1995 and 1996*

	1994	1995	1996	% change 1994–1996
Hong Kong	1 943 678	2 243 245	2 311 184	18.9
Macao	245 320	543 240	604 227	146.3
Thailand[a]	257 455	375 564	456 912	77.5
Vietnam	14 381	62 640	377 555	2525.4
Japan	193 486	220 715	241 525	24.8
Singapore[a]	164 893	201 965	226 685	37.5
S. Korea[b]	140 985	178 359	199 604	41.6
Malaysia[a]	95 789	103 130	135 743	41.7
Australia[b]	29 700	42 600	58 800[c]	98.0
Indonesia	37 096	38 895	32 189	−13.2
Cambodia	20 782	22 886	22 029	6.0
Laos	2 473	4 076	16 707	575.6
Philippines[a]	9 259	8 606	15 757	70.2
New Zealand[b]	6 487	8 919	13 646	110.4
Pakistan	7 192	9 105	7 375	2.5
Nepal	4 587	5 109	5 673	23.7
India	5 833	5 111	5 551[c]	−4.8
Bangladesh	3 408	4 016	3 878	13.8

Notes
[a] Designated as 'tourism liberalizing countries' in 1990 and 1992.
[b] Designated as 'tourism liberalizing countries' in 1997 and 1998.
[c] Projected.
Source: WTO, 1997; Yatsko and Tasker, 1998.

status will continue so long as border formalities continue to exist between China and these special administrative territories). The number of Chinese arrivals in Thailand dropped to 440 000 in 1997, owing primarily to a major crackdown on illegal travel agencies in China, after which only eighty-six travel agencies remained that were legally allowed to organize tours from China to Thailand (Muqbil, 1998c; *Straits Times*, 1998c). Chinese travellers are attracted to Thailand because they find it affordable, somewhat modern and culturally exotic. Thailand's often raunchy sex shows, in particular, hold an initial fascination for visitors from the far more restrained Chinese society. Despite the 1997 downturn, Thailand's tourism industry sees China as its highest potential growth market (followed by Taiwan and India) for visitors and has initiated several marketing campaigns to attract Chinese visitors in 1998, including the dropping of pre-arrival entry visa requirements (Jariyasombat, 1998; Muqbil, 1998c).

Malaysia has also targeted China in its tourism promotional efforts (*New Straits Times*, 1998b), the relaxation of visa requirements from Chinese travellers entering Malaysia from Singapore (*Straits Times*, 1998b), and efforts to develop new destinations for direct flights from China (*New Straits Times*, 1998a). Indonesia also sees China as a major potential source of visitors, even though the number of arrivals dropped to only 12 000 in 1997 (a 45 per cent decline from 1996) owing to the internal strife in that country (*Jakarta Post*, 1998).

Achieving 'tourism liberalizing country' status has not been an easy task. South Korea, Australia and New Zealand, in particular, had been lobbying for this designation since the early 1990s (*Korea Herald*, 1998a, b). Achieving this status in 1997 and 1998 could not have come at a better time for Australia and New Zealand, respectively, which have experienced major declines in Japanese and Southeast Asian visitors because of Asian economic turmoil. Australia is anticipating a 30 per cent increase in Chinese arrivals in the short term, and far more

in the longer term as China sets its sights on 100 million outbound travellers per year by 2010 (Yatsko and Tasker, 1998).

The newly designated 'tourism liberalizing countries' are also good news for Chinese travellers, although travel to the more distant locations will cost more. In 1998, a quick weekend getaway to the Philippines from Guangzhou could be purchased for as little as 2679 renminbi (US$325), and a six-day package from Shanghai to Bangkok cost only $3800 renminbi (US$460) (Yatsko and Tasker, 1998). However, the most desirable destinations for Chinese travellers are the more developed Western nations. According to a survey conducted by Roper Starch of 600 people from Beijing, Shanghai, and Guangzhou who had travelled overseas since January 1991, most prefer more expensive destinations for future trips (Muqbil, 1996). For 34 per cent of the respondents, the USA was their most desired destination, while 11 per cent indicated Japan. Australia and Singapore were preferred by 8 per cent and 7 per cent, respectively, followed by France, Germany, Italy, Thailand and Taiwan. According to the survey, more than 80 per cent of the respondents had a college education and a considerable number of these leisure travellers actually worked at universities and research institutions, giving them more flexible work schedules and higher disposable incomes than most Chinese.

Border tourism

China has one of the longest land borders of any country in the world (22 143 km), which it shares with fourteen countries: North Korea, Russia (in two parts), Mongolia, Kazakhstan, Kyrgyzstan, Tajikistan, Afghanistan, Pakistan, India, Nepal, Bhutan, Myanmar, Laos and Vietnam. Historically, cross-border travel was common as ethnicity, cultural traditions and economic livelihood were often shared on both sides along all of China's boundaries. However, in the twentieth century, political and military conflicts between China and the USSR to the north, and with India and Vietnam to the south, had largely sealed China's borders or otherwise seriously limited the vibrant trading situation of the past. The opening of China to the world, however, has also resulted in the opening of its land borders to neighbouring countries. As with China's tourism in general, the process of opening up these borders has been gradual and did not occur in a major way until after 1989 – the year in which the 'Iron Curtain' came down in eastern Europe and the Tiananmen Square incident dramatically reduced visitations from Western industrialized countries (Yu, 1992). As noted above, it was at this same time that Asian travel to China in general began to catch up with and exceed European levels.

Both South Asia and Southeast Asia represent major Chinese border areas that have generated tourism development interests in the 1990s. In Southeast Asia, Vietnam, Laos and Thailand have been working with China to develop transportation, tourism and trade in their shared border region. In 1993 construction began on the 'Friendship Bridge' over the Mekong to allow lorry trucks and tourist buses to travel from Thailand through Laos and on to Kunming, the capital city of China's Yunnan Province (*The Economist*, 1993). This potential, however, has been slow to emerge. As of 1998, China was still reluctant to allow the transport of most goods and tourists by land into Thailand (*Straits Times*, 1998c). Instead, Chinese travellers to Thailand were only allowed to enter the country through selected Thai airports.

To demonstrate the feasibility of land transportation, the governor of the Tourism Authority of Thailand (TAT) led a journalist-filled motor caravan from Thailand to Kunming in January 1998 to petition the Chinese to loosen their border crossing formalities so that this 'last frontier still untouched' could be opened to tourists (*Straits Times*, 1998c: p. 13). To further push this goal, Thailand then announced that it would allow Yunnan residents to visit the nine northern provinces of Thailand with only an entry/exit pass, instead of a passport and visa (Muqbil, 1998b). Border entry formalities are also becoming easier in Laos and Vietnam as part of a regional tourism development plan adopted by ASEAN in 1997. Only Myanmar has been somewhat resistant to these changes, which also include development of the Asian Highway Network from Singapore to London.

Laos, which was initially cautious of being overrun by Thai and Chinese entrepreneurs when the Friendship Bridge was first announced in the early 1990s, is now playing a leading role in the region's tourism development (Marukatat, 1998). Through its Visit Laos Year 1999–2000, it hopes to develop its linchpin position as a transportation corridor between the surrounding large economies of China, Vietnam and Thailand. The large increase in Chinese travellers to Laos and Vietnam in 1996 (Table 19.7), as well as to Myanmar (Meyer, 1998) reflects considerable loosening of border restrictions in that year. In 1997, Laos received 17 661 visitors from China, making it the third source of the country's visitors after Thailand (261 826) and Vietnam (65 545) (Citrinot, 1998). However, only 32 per cent of the Chinese visitors stayed overnight, greatly limiting their economic impact on Laos.

Chinese border officials have been cautious of making crossings too easy as smuggling and illegal immigration have been major problems which may increase if regulations become too lax (*Bangkok Post*, 1998a). In addition to border formalities, this multinational border area faces numerous other obstacles, including roads that are in poor condition, varying transportation laws and regulations and, in some places, roadside crime (Muqbil, 1998b). There is often inadequate, if any, signage and police and medical assistance can take a long time to arrive at accident sites. The Asian economic crisis has largely put efforts to address some of the problems in the region on hold (*Bangkok Post*, 1998a). Land transportation, however, is seen as a way of both increasing intraregional travel and tourism without putting additional pressure on the region's overburdened airports. It also allows the countries bordering the infamous 'Golden Triangle' region to develop a marketing synergy that could make for a very attractive, multicultural tourist destination and bring much needed economic development to this remote area.

While there has been a lot of activity, even if much of it has been only talk, toward developing the China–Southeast border region, the same cannot be said of the China–South Asia border. The border between China and South Asia has been an area of high tension since the Communist victory in China in 1949. In 1951, China invaded Tibet, which had been largely autonomous since the Republic of China was established in 1911. Highly repressive measures by the Chinese military against Tibetans in the 1960s caused large numbers of them to flee into India and Nepal. India fought wars with Pakistan over Kashmir (a region in India along the China border) in 1965 and 1971, and with China over their shared border in 1962. China's military support of Pakistan, continuing into the 1990s, along with ongoing internal turmoil in Kashmir and international concerns over Tibet, have seriously limited travel to and across the China–South Asia border. This is not to say that border problems cannot erupt in Southeast Asia, as well. China announced plans to build an airport and start tours to the Paracel Islands in 1998, over the protestations of Vietnam which also claims the islands as their territory (*Washington Times*, 1998).

It is somewhat easier to cross the borders that Pakistan and Nepal share with China, although this normally only occurs with considerable pre-trip planning and as part of an organized tour. Tourism has been a major focus of China's efforts toward economic development in Tibet, where it is the primary source of income for much of the population (*Bangkok Post*, 1996). Travel to Tibet, which was only opened to visitors in 1980, is expensive and largely limited to package tours which are easier for the Chinese to control. In 1997, Tibet received 81 800 international visitors (89 per cent foreigners), the third lowest of any province or region in China

(CNTA, 1998). Some of these expensive package tours have been allowed to enter from Nepal, where religious pilgrimage trips have also been approved by Chinese officials. Pakistan is the staging point for 'Silk Road' tour groups, which often take 20 days passing over the Karakoram Highway into China (*Travel Trade Gazette*, 1998b). The 'Silk Road' was a major part of China's international tourism promotional efforts in 1998, which focused on bringing tourists to some of the more remote regions of China (Pringle, 1998). Civil unrest in nearby Afghanistan, however, resulted in some Silk Road tours being cancelled in mid-1998, reflecting the ongoing problems of travel in this region. Much of western China (including most of Tibet) is still off-limits to foreign travellers for military security reasons.

Conclusion

The history of contemporary international tourism in China began cautiously, coming after a period of considerable internal social turmoil. Along with the liberalization of economic and social policies in virtually every sector of Chinese society, both international and domestic tourism expanded rapidly in the 1980s and 1990s. Infrastructure problems have plagued China throughout this period of growth, although it has also drawn considerable foreign investment in the industry as well. Steady increases in tourist arrivals and revenues, even in times of global economic recession, indicates that the tourism policy decisions of the present government have been both sufficiently pragmatic and aggressive to compete on an international scale.

Despite continuing steps toward decentralizing and opening up China's tourism industry and its borders, there is no doubt that China remains a more highly centralized society than is found in most of the countries from which its visitors come. Large areas of China are closed to foreign travel, Chinese citizens face major challenges and limitations in selecting travel destinations and bureaucratic rules and regulations can hinder the competition and efficiency in tourism services. In addition to the general economic changes that have occurred in China and have also changed the tourism industry, there are several other major shifts that have occurred in China's tourism over the last couple of decades. These include the major shift after the death of Mao Dzedong from tourism for political purposes toward tourism for economic purposes, the development of the Asian tourism market in the 1990s and the expansion of domestic and outbound Chinese travel which will increasingly impact Asia and the world in the next century.

Tourism will continue to increase in China as facilities, access and services are improved, and as the economy expands. China is the largest country in the Asia–Pacific region and an active member of the Pacific Area Travel Association (PATA). Its potential as both an inbound and outbound destination, compared with the already thriving tourism industries in neighbouring countries, is enormous. After nearly two decades of tourism development and modernization in China, the country is still searching for better ways of developing and using travel and tourism to further the welfare of its citizens and the country as a whole. Domestic and outbound tourism is part of that process, as are the jobs generated by inbound visitations. As a unique and interesting destination, China will continue to be a major factor in the future development of tourism in Asia.

China's cautionary approach toward opening its economy has meant that at times its tourism industry has not been as effective as it could be in the international tourism marketplace. This has been due, in part, to inadequate facilities, transportation infrastructure limitations, antiquated business operations, ineffective promotional efforts and poor service. For tourism to continue to be successful in China, the country needs to continue to place the improvement of its transportation infrastructure as a top priority. Instead of the current policies which focus on increasing the numbers of international arrivals, greater effort should be made to improve the productivity of the industry and to meet the needs of domestic travellers. China also needs to pay greater attention to the management and protection of its tourism resources. The degradation and destruction of tourism resources by careless development or uncontrolled tourist use can destroy the drawing power that pulls the tourists to China in the first place.

The potential of China to dramatically transform the intra-Asian pattern of travel and tourism cannot be underestimated. Intra-Asian travel was just beginning on a trajectory of phenomenal expansion when the Asian economic crisis hit in mid-1997. Full economic recovery will probably take some time and will vary from one country to another. The large size and relative stability of China's economy make it one that every other country in the region needs to take into account in its economic development planning, especially when considering tourism and travel. Who China partners with in tourism development, where the 100 million Chinese outbound travellers go in the next century and how this vast country will continue to maintain its economic growth and social stability are all key questions that will make, break or at least shape the pattern of tourism development throughout Asia well into the foreseeable future.

References

Andrews, J., 'China fever', *The Economist*, 325, 1992, pp. 15–17.

Bangkok Post, '"Roof of the world" truly takes visitors' breath away', *Bangkok Post* 24 October 1996, Horizons section, p. 5.

Bangkok Post, 'Development of border areas: Experts say turnaround is possible despite woes', *Bangkok Post* 4 October 1998a.

Bangkok Post. 'Investment and trade: China delegation will look for opportunities in Thailand', *Bangkok Post* 25 April 1998b.

Bangsberg, P.T., 'Singapore terminal operator to expand its China venture', *Journal of Commerce* 20 October 1998, Maritime section, p. 2B.

Beijing Review, 'More tourists', *Beijing Review* 21(35), 1978a, p. 3.

Beijing Review, 'Tourist news', *Beijing Review* 21(38), 1978b, pp. 30–31.

Beijing Review, 'China's tourist service', *Beijing Review* 22(2), 1979a, p. 38.

Beijing Review, 'Expanding tourism', *Beijing Review* 22(11), 1979b, pp. 6–7.

Brady, S., 'China's outwardly mobile', *Time*, Asia edition, 21 September 1998, p. 10.

Chang, P.H., 'China's relations with Hong Kong and Taiwan', *The Annals of the American Academy of Political and Social Science* 519, January 1992, pp. 127–139.

Chicago Tribune, 'World favorites', *Chicago Tribune* 22 March 1998, Travel, p. 2.

China National Tourism Administration, *Tourist Statistic Data*, CNTA, accessed 11 December 1998.

China News Digest, 'China to open tourism to foreign investors', cited at China Vista website (http://www.chinavista.com/business/news/archive/feb98/feb18-01.html, accessed 11 December 1998), 16 February 1998.

Choong, A., 'China Everbright seeks business partners', *New Straits Times* (Malaysia) 22 January 1998, p. 17.

Citrinot, L., 'Laos', *International Tourism Report* 4, 1998, pp. 17–25.

Economist, The, 'The overseas Chinese: a driving force', *The Economist* 324, 18 July 1992, pp. 21–22, 24.

Economist, The, 'Bridge to the world', *The Economist* 329 (7834), 23 October 1993, pp. 43–44.

Economist, The, 'Breakdown on the new Silk Road', *The Economist* 349 (8089), 10 October 1998, p. 42.

Goldsmith, C., 'The business traveler', *The China Business Review* 12(3), 1985, pp. 46–47.

Gormsen, E., 'International tourism in China: its organization and socio-economic impacts', in A.A. Lew and L. Yu (eds), *Tourism in China: Geographical, Political, and Economic Perspectives*, Westview Press, Boulder, CO, 1995a, pp. 63–88.

Gormsen, E., 'Travel behavior and the impacts of domestic tourism', in A.A. Lew and L. Yu (eds), *Tourism in China: Geographical, Political, and Economic Perspectives*, Westview Press, Boulder, CO, 1995b, pp. 131–140.

He, G. (ed.), *The Yearbook of China Tourism Statistics 1991*, China Travel and Tourism Press, Beijing, 1991.

Jakarta Post, 'Government urged to attract more Chinese tourists', *Jakarta Post* 10 August 1998.

Jariyasombat, P., 'Sights set on visitors: Pitak also proposes roadshow to China, Taiwan and India', *Bangkok Post* 9 October 1998.

Kao, J., 'The worldwide web of Chinese business', *Harvard Business Review* 71(2), 1993, pp. 24–27, 30–35.

Korea Herald, The, 'Editorial: Tourism on Cheju Island', *The Korea Herald* 11 May 1998a.

Korea Herald, The, 'Tourism industry preparing for influx of Chinese tourists', *The Korea Herald* 14 May 1998b.

Kwang, M., 'China to woo S-E Asia visitors with cheap tours', *The Straits Times* (Singapore), 7 April 1998, p. 15.

Leung, C.K., 'Locational characteristics of foreign equity joint venture investment in China, 1979–1985', *Professional Geographer* 42(4), 1990, pp. 403–421.

Lew, A.A., 'The history, policies and social impact of international tourism in the Peoples Republic of China', *Asian Profile* 15(2), 1987, pp. 117–128.

Lew, A.A., 'Overseas Chinese and Compatriots in China's tourism development', in A.A. Lew and L. Yu (eds), *Tourism in China: Geographical, Political, and Economic Perspectives*, Westview Press, Boulder, CO, 1995, pp. 155–175.

Lew, A.A. and Ahmed, Z.U., 'Tourism 21: Keeping Singapore on top in the next century', in H.D. Huan and I.P. Polunin (eds), *Cases in Hospitality and Tourism Management in Singapore and ASEAN*, Prentice-Hall, Singapore, 1999 (Forthcoming).

Liu, Y. (ed.), *The Yearbook of China Tourism*, National Tourism Administration of the People's Republic of China, Beijing, 1995.

Loh, H.Y., 'HK woos China and Taiwan visitors to revive tourism sector', *Business Times* (Singapore), 30 May 1998, p. 5.

Marukatat, S., 'Survey will study road link to Laos', *Bangkok Post* 6 July 1998. (http://www.bkkpost.samart.co.th/news/BParchive/BP19980706/060798_News14.html) 1998.

Meyer, M., 'New year, old China: A Chinese new year in Yunnan, the remote province that's attracting travel insiders', *Los Angeles Times* 4 January 1998, Part L, p. 1.

Muqbil, I., 'China travelers seek clean and pleasant lands', *TravelNews Asia* 20 May 1996, http://web3.asia1.com.sg/timesnet/data/tna/docs/tna3249.html. 1996.

Muqbil, I., 'Travel monitor: Angel opens new era of travel in northern Thailand', *Bangkok Post* 20 November 1998a.

Muqbil, I., 'Travel monitor: Thailand set to become gateway to Mekong region', *Bangkok Post* 3 August 1998b.

Muqbil, I., 'Travel monitor: tourism drive targets China and India', *Bangkok Post* 21 September 1998c.

New Straits Times, The, 'Call to organise more chartered flights via Senai', *The New Straits Times* (Malaysia), 7 October 1998a.

New Straits Times, The, 'Johor goes on hard-sell to boost earnings from tourism', *The New Straits Times* (Malaysia), 1 February 1998b, p. 7.

New Straits Times, The, 'Tourism sector feeling the pinch due to slowdown', *The New Straits Times* (Malaysia), 25 June 1998c, p. 24.

Newsweek, 'Go east, young man', *Newsweek* 6 April 1998, p. 17.

Pan, L., *Sons of the Yellow Emperor: A History of the Chinese Diaspora*, Little, Brown and Co., Boston, MA, 1990.

Pringle, J., 'Paradise regained', *The Times* (London), 23 May 1998.

Roehl, W.S., 'The June 4, 1989, Tiananmen Square incident and Chinese tourism', in A. Lew and L. Yu (eds), *Tourism in China: Geographic, Political, and Economic Perspectives*, Westview Press, Boulder, CO, 1995, pp. 19–39.

Sender, H., 'Inside the overseas Chinese network', *Institutional Investor* 25 September 1991, pp. 37–42.

South China Morning Post, 'A snapshot of tourists to the Middle Kingdom', *South China Morning Post* 11 July 1996, China Business Review section, p. 7.

South China Morning Post, 'Asian tourists cancel holidays', *South China Morning Post* 20 February 1998a, Business Post section, p. 4.

South China Morning Post, 'Turmoil hits tourism revenue', *South China Morning Post* 22 May 1998b, Business Post section, p. 4.

State Statistical Bureau, *China Statistical Yearbook 1997*, China Statistical Publishing House, Beijing, 1997.

Straits Times, 'China's tourism to spawn 21 million jobs', *The Straits Times* (Singapore) 3 November 1998a, p. 16.

Straits Times, 'Johor plan to attract China tourists in S'pore', *The Straits Times* (Singapore) 30 July 1998b, p. 21.

Straits Times, 'Thailand plans overland route to southern China', *The Straits Times* (Singapore) 2 February 1998c, p. 13.

Sun, G. (ed.), *The Yearbook of China Tourism Statistics 1992*, China Travel and Tourism Press, Beijing, 1992.

Suri, M., 'India', *EIU International Tourism Reports* 1, 1996, pp. 21–43.

Taemsamran, J., 'Outbound travel – China due for more attention', *Bangkok Post* 10 December 1998.

Tan, M., 'China tourism: big growth, immediate problems', *China Reconstructs* 35(6), 1986, pp. 8–10.

Thoburn, J.T., Leung, H.M., Chau, E. and Tang, S.H., *Foreign Investment in China Under the Open Policy: The Experience of Hong Kong Companies*, Grower Publishing Co., Brookfield, Vermont, 1990.

Travel Trade Gazette, 'China eyes foreign cash', *Travel Trade Gazette* (UK and Ireland) 1 April 1998a, p. 33.

Travel Trade Gazette, 'Struggle to milk the Silk Road', *Travel Trade Gazette* (UK and Ireland) 7 October 1998b, p. 36.

Washington Times, 'Hainan plans tours to disputed Paracels', *Washington Times* 17 April 1998, Final edition, Part A, p. 14.

World Bank Group, *Development Data Website, Gross National Product Tables*, World Bank Group, http://www.cdinet.com/DEC/wdi98/new/databytopic/databytopic.html (accessed 16 December 1998), 1998.

World Tourism Organization, *Tourism Market Trends: East Asia and the Pacific, 1986–1996 and Tourism Market Trends: South Asia, 1986–1996*, WTO, Madrid, 1997.

Wright, R. and Wright, R., 'Conference facilities in China', *The China Business Review* 11(3), 1984, pp. 12–15.

Xue M. (ed.), 'Rapid development of tourism', in *Almanac of China's Economy 1981*, Modern Language Company, Hong Kong, 1982, pp. 677–683.

Yatsko, P. and Tasker, R., 'Outward bound: just in

time, ordinary Chinese catch the travel bug', *Far Eastern Economic Review* 26 March 1998, pp. 66–67.

Yu, L., 'Emerging markets for China's tourism industry', *Journal of Travel Research* 31(1), 1992, pp. 10–13.

Yu, L. and Lew, A.A., 'Airline liberalization and development in China', *Pacific Tourism Review* 1(2), 1997, pp. 129–136.

Zhang, G., 'China's tourism development since 1978: policies, experiences, and lessons learned', in A. Lew and L. Yu (eds), *Tourism in China: Geographic, Political, and Economic Perspectives*, Westview Press, Boulder, CO, 1995, pp. 3–17.

Zhang, J., 'Down but not out: Taiwan and Southeast Asia are Keeping China's wounded tourism industry alive', *The China Business Review* 17, Nov.–Dec. 1990, pp. 12–14, 16.

Zhang, Y. and Lew, A.A., 'The People's Republic of China: Two decades of tourism', *Pacific Tourism Review* 1(2), 1997, pp. 161–172.

Zou, T., *Tourism Development and Planning*, Tourism Education Press, Beijing, 1993.

20

Conclusion: prospects for tourism in Southeast and South Asia in the new Millennium

C.Michael Hall and Stephen Page

The chapters in this book by no means represent a complete assessment of tourism in Asia. Moreover, they present only a partial analysis of probably the most diverse and dynamic tourism region in the world, in spite of the impact of the Asian economic crisis. Whilst recent texts (e.g. Hitchcock *et al.*, 1993; Hall, 1994, 1997; Go and Jenkins, 1997) present a disparate range of themes and country studies of tourism with respect to Asia and the Pacific Rim, no other text to date has sought to examine the themes and issues facing both Southeast and South Asia in a systematic manner. The tendency in the Western tourism literature has been to focus on Southeast Asia and ASEAN member countries and to neglect South Asia. Yet, as the chapters within this book undeniably show, there are complex interrelationships which exist in terms of the tourism markets, regions and activities within Southeast and South Asia. International visitors to both Southeast and South Asia often visit a range of destinations. Furthermore, neighbouring Asian countries often provide

major tourism markets for each other. This is reflected in the complex web of airline routes that exist in Southeast and South Asia which are intraregional in nature, often short- or medium-haul cross-border trips. For example, the growth of the Indian and the Chinese middle class has substantial implications for intraregional travel. What is also consistently overlooked in the tourism literature is the growing domestic tourism market in Asian countries, despite most national tourism organizations emphasizing inbound tourism because of the economic benefits it brings. But in some cases (e.g. Sri Lanka and Malaysia), tourism authorities have also tried to use domestic tourism as a substitute for a decline in international visitor arrivals.

One of the immediate problems facing the researcher in reconstructing patterns of tourism visitation, activity and expenditure is the absence of up-to-date, reliable and consistent tourism statistics. Whilst the World Tourism Organization and the Pacific Area Tourism Association perform a valuable role in collating visitor statistics and in encouraging destinations to adapt appropriate methodologies to enumerate tourism arrivals, the authors in this book frequently faced problems in accessing reliable, up-to-date and meaningful tourism data. At a time when many destinations seek to encourage inward investment, governments need to acknowledge the necessity of accurate and authoritative tourism statistics to improve business confidence in major tourism investment decisions. Without easy access to such data, investors are likely to require additional inducements to make any contribution to inward investment, while assessment of the wider social and environmental impacts of tourism will also occur within a research vacuum. Furthermore, there are a number of tourism concerns in the region which are clearly under-researched. These include not only issues of tourism impacts raised throughout this book and applied concerns such as promotion and marketing and destination management, but also such issues as the role of multinational corporations in tourism in the region, the health of travellers and destination safety amidst political instability and the relationship of tourism with other forms of development.

The chapters in this book report a range of common themes affecting the governments of many countries that have influenced the organization and management of tourism. Probably the most widespread change affecting the region is the privatization of former state-owned tourism assets and the privatization of capital-intensive plant and infrastructure associated with hotels and airlines. Yet many tourism destinations in South Asia have retained state control of their flag-carrier to continue to retain an influence over arrivals. This is often a complex decision based on domestic and external economic and political factors, including the financial and political instability affecting the region which can easily affect tourist arrivals and the profitability of commercial airline activities. In contrast, more established destinations have encouraged privatization and greater competition in aviation to improve access and market penetration and to reduce levels of government borrowings and debt. The real difficulty which many governments in the region have faced is the complex change in ideology which privatization, competition and the new economic and political openness may bring. It often means a commitment to new 'rules-of-the-game' after years of authoritarian government, where the economic rationale, balance sheet, rule of law, and the ballot box was of less significance than power, elite interests and central planning and control; and, as has become apparent in some countries, gross corruption. Nowhere is this more evident than in tourism – for some governments it is too big a risk – to commit to an unknown, uncertain and uncontrollable tourism future where the state has less influence and where the flow of ideas can be hard to contain. This sometimes means that political posturing, rhetoric and ideology are not matched by action unless an immediate goal needs to be achieved (i.e. a rapid growth in direct foreign investment in tourism to upgrade and develop essential tourism infrastructure).

Numerous examples are provided in the book of governments relying on inward investment to fund tourism development. In fact, it can be argued that an over-reliance on foreign investment was one of the root causes of the current Asian crisis. As a result, many of the international aid agencies and financial authorities, such as the International Monetary Fund, World Bank and the Asian Development Bank, have had to play a major role in assisting Asian governments to deal with the effects of economic overheating, over-expansion and financial mismanagement to which they may, in fact, have contributed. It is therefore not surprising to suddenly find many of the affected countries emphasizing inbound tourism and, latterly, domestic tourism as vital providers of foreign currency to develop much-needed sources of revenue and contribute to improving the balance of trade payments.

At a strategic level, many governments throughout Southeast and South Asia view the economic development benefits from tourism as providing much needed sources of potential employment. In fact, many of the chapters are highly critical of the cyclops mentality of government management of tourism development: 'growth, growth, and more growth', because of the necessity of dealing with structural economic problems such as debt, unemployment and underemployment. Underemployment in Southeast and South Asia can be partly addressed through the development of labour-intensive industries such as tourism, but all too often such strategies are not accompanied by integrated manpower planning and human resource management plans for the tourism and hospitality sector, while linkages between tourism and other sectors, such as agriculture, are also given insufficient attention (Telfer and Wall, 1996). A consistent theme emphasized throughout the book is the inability of the tourism sector to reach growth targets for skilled indigenous staff. In many cases, governments have promoted growth in inbound tourism but failed to see the synergistic relationship with investing in people, their education and training needs to ensure the long-term viability of the tourism sector. Recognizing the human resource needs of the tourism businesses in the region is not new (see Baum, 1993) but all too often tourism planning fails to acknowledge the human dimension in what is, in essence, 'a people business' (Hall, 2000).

Rather belatedly, many Asian governments have recognized the benefits of regional cooperation in tourism, as the recent experiences of ASEAN and SAARC and the Mekong Basin imply. But evaluating the tangible benefits of regional marketing cooperation, multi-destination marketing and greater private-sector participation in overseas marketing has not necessarily led to immediate plans and activities which promote these objectives. For many countries sharing common borders and similar inbound markets, greater cooperation to persuade visitors to extend the length of stays through dual-destination marketing has yet to be realized. To date, many countries, even within ASEAN (e.g. Myanmar), have been overly protective and nervous about such cooperation. In some cases (e.g. India, China, Bangladesh and Pakistan) political problems and ideology differences are unlikely to be overcome in the short term to promote a South Asian tourism experience.

Returning to the issue of strategic planning, many destinations in Southeast and South Asia base their tourism industries on a growing urbanized experience related to the principal gateways in the region. It is ironic that, with the exception of Singapore, these increasingly urbanized countries continue to promote strongly images of rural and relatively natural areas in their tourism literature. The problem here is that with the emergence of highly urbanized regions with an array of environmental problems, the tourist's experience on entering each country may be tarnished by wider problems of economic and environmental degradation (e.g. overcrowding, pollution and severe congestion in the absence of appropriate transport infrastructure). One of the principal explanations is that the former colonial infrastructure needs significant investment, redevelopment and replacement to meet the demands now being placed upon it through tourist use.

In this context, tourism planning and management needs to be included in many of the centralized plans still in vogue in many countries in the region (e.g. India, Pakistan, Indonesia), so that tourist expenditure is used to reinvest in vital physical and social infrastructure. In certain instances, overseas investment has been secured to upgrade essential infrastructure such as airports, civil aviation facilities, as well as leasing agreements on new aircraft. Even in 1998, the colonial legacy in South Asian states is highly visible in terms of the routeways, modes of transport and travel patterns of domestic and some international tourist itineraries.

In a social and cultural context, the rapid growth of tourism in Southeast and South Asia has generated a complex, diverse and often controversial range of impacts. The impact on indigenous culture, the loss of cultural identity and commodification of culture to generate economic benefits has not been without its critics. However, the most controversial aspect of tourism and its impact on local people is sex tourism. Not only has this raised health concerns in the region in terms of the rising tide of HIV cases and the exploitation of women and children, but has also adversely affected the international image of many destinations and caused issues of gender, power and dependency to be fundamentally questioned (e.g. Kinnaird and Hall, 1994). In a similar vein, there is also a growing concern that rapid tourism development has not been accompanied by adequate planning to ameliorate short- and long-term environmental impacts. While general short-term impacts of visitors on the environment can often be ameliorated through the application of visitor management techniques and strategies, the effects of longer-term, indirect impacts, e.g. inadequate sewage disposal from resort developments, may have substantial implications for the quality of life of local residents, the health of residents and visitors alike and the continued attractiveness of destinations.

Ecotourism has also become an increasingly important part of the product mix for the region, along with marine and cultural tourism. Nearly all countries in the region are seeking to develop ecotourism attractions, usually national parks and reserves, in order to attract high-yield tourism although, in the search for the tourist dollar, the temptation to attract more and more tourists to environmentally sensitive sites seems to be unstoppable. The relationship between tourism and the environment is therefore problematic. Tourism has equally provided the justification for the conservation of cultural and natural heritage, and the conservation of biodiversity, throughout the region, e.g. through the creation of national parks and reserves, as it has led to its destruction. While appropriate environmental strategies for tourism are important, probably the most significant factor is the development of integrated planning and management strategies which seek to manage the synergistic and cumulative relationships within and between environmental uses. In this sense planning for tourism must be able to encompass more than just tourism. Indeed, one of the biggest drawbacks in tourism planning and development in the region is such a tunnel vision towards tourism.

One of the emerging issues in tourism development in the region is also the relative weight to be given to the national and regional development goals compared with the benefits sought at the local and individual level. While Western tourism planning models abound with the desire to allow for participation in the tourism development process (see Hall, 2000), such models may have little relevance to situations in which legislative and political structures put power in the hands of undemocratically elected elites and authoritarian regimes. Indeed, considerable debate exists as to what relevance Western notions of human rights, democracy and participation have in South and Southeast Asia at all, although much discussion of tourism planning in the region has ignored such basic issues.

In this age of globalization questions of power, rights, cultural representation, 'otherness' and identity have become part of the vernacular of at least some students of tourism. However, it would be true to say that they are not part of the industry lexicon or even a large part of tourism academia. Instead, most concerns surround such issues as infrastructure capacities (particularly transport and accommodation capacities), levels of repeat visitation, effective marketing and promotional campaigns, efficient use of resources and presenting the best possible image to the outside world of a place where the locals are friendly, interesting, and a little bit different (but not too different) and where the destination is safe, peaceful and attractive. Such uncritical perspectives have often been reinforced by some academics and researchers who have not wanted to rock the government and tourism industry boat, perhaps because they do not want to be seen to bite the hand that feeds them. Unfortunately, such attitudes can no longer hold true, particularly given the effects of the financial and political crises affecting much of the region and the tourism industry in particular. Indeed, more wide-ranging research and debate of tourism in the region has become more vital than ever before, particularly given that factors often regarded as on the periphery of tourism research, e.g. political and socio-cultural issues, have now become central to industry interests at a time of instability. This, though, requires a willingness of government, industry and academics to step outside the box and be willing to communicate and listen to alternative perspectives on tourism even if they may be regarded as critical of the received view.

It is therefore extremely appropriate that this book is being completed at a time when, in many countries throughout the region, the need for open political debate is being conveyed more than ever before. Political stability, one of the mainstays of destination attractiveness, emerges from the idea of civic and public interest, in which participation and debate is essential and ongoing, rather than from the dictates of an authoritarian or military regime. Academic commentators have their part to play in such a debate, and it is hoped that some of the perspectives and insights contained in this book will help lead to the development of more sustainable forms of tourism in a century in which Asian concerns will likely dominate, economically and politically.

References

Baum, T. (ed.), *Human Resource Issues in International Tourism*, Butterworth-Heinemann, Oxford, 1993.

Go, F.M. and Jenkins, C.L. (eds), *Tourism and Economic Development in Asia and Australasia*, Cassell, London, 1997.

Hall, C.M., *Tourism in the Pacific Rim: Development, Impacts and Markets*, 1st edn, Longman Australia, South Melbourne, 1994.

Hall, C.M., *Tourism in the Pacific Rim: Development, Impacts and Markets*, 2nd edn, Longman Australia, South Melbourne, 1997.

Hall, C.M., *Tourism Planning*, Prentice Hall, Harlow, 2000.

Hitchcock, M.J., King, V.T. and Parnell, M.J.G. (eds), *Tourism in South-East Asia*, Routledge, London, 1993.

Kinnaird, V.H. and Hall, D.R. (eds), *Tourism and Gender*, John Wiley & Sons, Chichester, 1994.

Telfer, D.J. and Wall, G., 'Linkages between tourism and food production', *Annals of Tourism Research* 23(3), 1996, pp. 635–654.

Index